Endorsements for *No Wastelands*

'What we are seeing in our own time from Pope Francis to people like Ash and Anji Barker is a new and broad emphasis on orthopraxy ("correct practice"), which is gratefully returning after centuries of fruitless arguing about correct words, thinking of mere verbal truth as "orthodoxy". This book will help you to both think with the universal mind of Christ--and to do what you must do with the endless compassion of God in local communities to see sustainable change happen. "What we received as a gift, we must give as a gift." (Matthew 10:8)' **Father Richard Rohr**, *Centre for Action and Contemplation, Albuquerque, New Mexico, USA.*

'In a time where good news can feel hard to come by, here's some good news. In a time when there is lots of deconstruction of things that need to be deconstructed, here is a book about constructing something beautiful and liberating. I've been honored to call Ash and Anji Barker friends, and partners in holy mischief, for two decades. They embody a version of Christianity that looks like Jesus, loves like Jesus... and their faith is a confrontation to the counterfeit Christianity that is so prevalent today. In *No Wastelands*, Ash reminds us that good stuff comes from the compost... even the compost of Christendom.' **Shane Claiborne**, *author, activist, co-founder of Red Letter Christians, Philadelphia, USA.*

'We've spent so many years focusing on God as an architect with measured plans, imposed buildings, exact formulas, and dead materials that we've forgotten the God of Genesis: an expert Gardener who creates a wild, living, breathing, expanding and re-creating world. To hear the lived wisdom of Ash is to fall in love with Creator God all over again. The Barkers' experience invites us to welcome dirt (often disguised as difficult places) and shit (experienced most often as rejection and pain) as necessary parts of the surprising, wonderful, living, creative PLAN for LIFE to bring beauty and flourishing to every part of this world. BE prepared for this holy seed to take root and grow in you!' **Danielle Strickland**, *author and advocate, Toronto, Canada.*

'I've often talked about living in community but I've never done it myself. Ash Barker and his family, on the other hand, have made a beautiful reality out of the idea of community. Where and how they have lived is a testimony to the integrity of his preaching and teaching. He and Anji have enabled people to live and grow together in ways that declare the Kingdom of God in the here and now more effectively than any sermon. In this book Ash takes us with him through the agonies and ecstasies of his journey, and shares his hard-won wisdom about joyfully making a difference in the name of Jesus.' **Tony Campolo**, *Phd. Professor Emeritus of Sociology, Eastern University, St. Davids PA, USA*

'We have been incredibly inspired by Ash, both in the way he lives and serves people, but also in his teaching and training. His innovative mindset, and deep compassion for humanity, is a unique combination and we're always keen to listen to anything he has to say.' **Tim and Rachel Hughes**, *Gas Street Church, Birmingham, UK.*

'*No Wastelands*, by Ash Barker, offers a powerful report from the frontlines and the messy middle of everyday community life. Spanning three continents and multiple disciplines, most particularly theology, he weaves hard-won practice-based insights into a soulful narrative that reveals the sacred presence and potential to be found in every community, when the scales of deficiency fall from our eyes. This book is a revelation in that it calls our attention to the abundance that lies hidden behind the cloak of scarcity narratives. Narratives that unintentionally put communities down in order to secure funding and top-down supports, with the promise such extrinsic interventions will lift them up. Such narratives are laced with a sickness idiom, that sees communities as wastelands. Ash Barker's book provides ample evidence that such an approach by churches will result in harm to the very communities they hope to heal. It is an important antidote to the lurking Messiah complex and the wounded/wounding healer within us all. A timely reminder that the Good Samaritan foreclosed on the impulse to be the rescuer and provide unsustainable undercutting charity; instead, he turned to the community, with the question: "Will you be his neighbour?". After many refusals. Eventually, the innkeeper said yes. The promised land is closer than we think, if we are prepared to fail at being God.' **Cormac Russell**, *author and Nurture Development, Dublin, Ireland.*

'I prepared these words on a crowded commuter train. The only free seat was by a young man. He was wearing his Jewish yarmulke and praying. I said: Shalom. He smiled, and with such warmth. I said: Shalom to Jewish folks. Shalom to Palestinian folks. Shalom to all humanity. He echoed back: "To all humanity." We were blessed. I journeyed on. I witnessed to it in a talk to 100 people in the divinity school at Edinburgh University. There is the power of Shalom. This is a book that resets the seeds of peace, that resets the seeds of Eden. Even as I write these words, I have watched them germinate.' **Professor Alastair McIntosh**, *author of Soil and Soul and Poacher's Pilgrimage, Glasgow, Scotland.*

'Ash Barker has launched Christian community development initiatives in diverse settings all around the world and here he shares the principles that have guided him in the hope that they might spark our imaginations for what might be possible in our contexts. Using the metaphor of a tree, he unpacks both the roots of community service (compassion, innovation, resilience) and its branches (connecting, learning, enterprise development). His insights, experiences and stories give tangible expression to his vision for a world made whole. This is an essential handbook for the planting of the tree of shalom in our own neighbourhoods.' **Michael Frost**, *author and Morling College, Sydney, Australia.*

'*No Wastelands*'; imaginative, perceptive, bathed in common sense born of experience and inspirational, all for one simple reason. Ash Barker is imaginative, perceptive, bathed in common sense born of experience and inspirational.' **Steve Chalke MBE**, *author and Founder Oasis Charitable Trust, London, UK.*

'Increasingly I want to be with people who are life-giving. Not just people who just make you feel better because they tell you everything is just fine – but people who bring the LIFE. And they are invariably characterised by joy, hope, challenge and humility. Ash is such a person. For a world, and a church, which can trip over itself in an understandable desire for results, Ash's book is a gift of paying attention to conditions, values, practices and hope in an entirely Christian way. The poet T. S. Eliot said, 'take no thought of the harvest, but only of proper sowing.' In Ash's company we can't fail to get our hands dirty in sowing the seeds of the gospel, as we faithfully and sacrificially join the call to partner with the God who is the giver of all life.' **The Rev. Canon Chris Russell**, Archbishop of Canterbury's Advisor for Evangelism & Witness, Lambeth Palace, London, UK.

'The world is in a mess. Poverty, injustice, suffering, exploitation, warfare, cruelty, bigotry are everywhere and we've probably all had moments when we've said that "someone" should be doing something about it. But what if that "someone" is meant to be us? Where could you possibly begin to get your head around it all, let alone manage to make some sort of difference? There will be many pathways to a lifegiving future, but the inspiration most of us need is likely to come through stories – stories of those who have made a difference, who aren't afraid to get out there on the edges and just see what's possible. While telling the story of his own family Ash Barker introduces us to some ordinary people fired by an extraordinary vision and who are making a remarkable difference. They are mostly people you've never heard of and are never going to meet but the thing they all have in common is a vision inspired by a story of divine love and translated into human action. Ash writes as a reflective practitioner so if you need a deeper understanding of the how and why of it all, you'll find some of that here as well – not to mention an introduction to some Celtic themes that speak into our concerns alongside practical suggestions for how you can make a start on bringing fresh hope to your own community. Read, enjoy, be inspired, but above all take up the challenge to action!' **John Drane and Olive Fleming Drane**, spiritual entrepreneurs, mission consultants, practical theology professors, but first and foremost followers of Jesus, Glasgow, Scotland.

'Ash Barker is a proven cultivator of hope. He digs in, gets his hands dirty, and the seeds he plants nurture growth and community. This book conveys the essence of what he's learnt and what he lives. Always listen to the practitioner who has road-tested his faith.' **Rev. Tim Costello AO**, author, advocate and Executive Director of Micah Australia, Melbourne, Australia.

'In *No Wastelands* Ash Barker writes of the protagonist in the Parable Of The Sower: 'The Sower is not ridiculed for trying to grow a harvest in ... diverse soils. The Sower is willing to give opportunity to all kinds of terrain and to see what can grow over time.' This book is the autobiography of the Sower in today's world.' **Dave Andrews**, author and activist, Brisbane, Australia.

'*No Wastelands* is a capacious invitation to discover afresh that you are somewhere! That where you are matters. And that God whispers to you through your place, wooing you to discover Shalom with your neighbours and neighbourhood. Ash Barker has invested his life listening for God's invitation through the places he's called home becoming a trustworthy guide unto fullness of life by joining God's mission in the Here and Now. If you are anything like me, as you read *No Wastelands* you will feel a profound YES deep within, expanding your imagination for "the good life" and arousing desire for community, goodness, and beauty. Ash is pointing us toward a spirituality that is far more than religion; it is loving neighbour and neighbourhood as a faithful expression of loving God and self. I recommend you pick up three copies; giving a couple to neighbours, reading it together and wondering as a collective, what God might be whispering to you through your place and all its inhabitants?' **Dwight J. Friesen**, *Professor of Practical Theology at The Seattle School of Theology & Psychology, author of numerous books, including: 2020s Foresight, The New Parish, and Thy Kingdom Connected, Seattle, USA.*

'This is a kaleidoscope from one of God's unique entrepreneurs. His journey takes us through pains and joys of earthing a bit of God's Shalom in some of the world's neediest places. Hectic, unique, it gives us glimpses of 'God in Benefits Street,' offers us tools, insights into how to release local talents, and even links us with the saints' uprisings.' **Rev. Ray Simpson**, *author and Founding Guardian, The international Community of Aidan and Hilda, Berwick-upon-Tweed, UK.*

'We are deeply moved by the powerful narrative and transformative message that this book carries. It beautifully captures the essence of community development, faith, and hope. The challenges and obstacles Ash and Anji faced, along with their family, are presented with raw vulnerability, never sugar-coated. This approach makes their triumphs all the more inspiring. Their unwavering commitment to nurturing seedbeds of shalom in Winson Green and beyond is truly commendable. The honest storytelling compels readers to see how their own well-being is intimately connected to that of their own local communities and, a powerful, heartfelt reminder that even in the most challenging circumstances, hope and the potential for growth and renewal is present, regardless of how dark things may seem. Yay God! We wholeheartedly recommend *No Wastelands* to anyone hungry for a renewed sense of purpose at a gut level. Be prepared to be moved, challenged, and inspired as you embark on this remarkable journey of faith, hope, and the pursuit of shalom.' **Arthur and Dani Cherrie**, *Winepress church, Melbourne, Australia.*

'I have taken groups to visit Ash in Winson Green over the last 7 years and they always come away challenged and inspired. The reason is simple – they are living out the gospel in their neighbourhood in ways that are bringing visible change and shalom. Ash has so much experience having done 4 cycles of living in urban neighbourhoods round the world facing multiple challenges. *No Wastelands* distils the wisdom of that experience, practice, and theology into one accessible volume. It's a mix of inspiring stories, gritty honesty, practical ideas, advice and frameworks, spiritual practices, theology and missiology, combining into an amazing handbook to guide anyone else wanting to follow in this direction, of which I hope there will be many. It is rich and deep. Ash's passion for enabling innovative leaders and changemakers from inside those neighbourhoods shines through – that's the thing that has grabbed me personally the most. I will be coming back to this again and again and passing it on to others.' **Jonny Baker**, *author and Britain Hub mission director at Church Mission Society, Oxford, UK.*

'Ash and Anji Barker inspired us when we met them 25 years ago in their early years of UNOH and they have been inspiring us ever since. Not many people hold the deep theological reflection right alongside the amazing neighbourhood engagement. The Barkers consistently have. So, we've always kept an eye on what they're thinking and how they're living it out (including a trip to Birmingham on our recent sabbatical where we came away once again declaring them to be faithful/faith filled legends of community transformation). In this latest book Ash once again puts out the prophetic challenge with actual guidance to those of us who want to make a positive difference with the one life we have. In *No Wastelands*, Ash addresses the big issues, challenges and angst of our moment in history. Rather than becoming overwhelmed or remaining disillusioned he brings us fresh wisdom and sustained passion, grounded as usual in real stories of struggle and hope . Empowering community leadership, not just in our solidarity and care but in supporting people to actually flourish, is Ash and Anji Barker's life calling. Using the metaphor of growing good seed, Ash's book is fresh, critical, honest, practical and hopeful. After 30 years of our own missional engagement, this is a book that leads us and our community forward.' **Bishop Justin and Jenny Duckworth**, *Urban Vision Aotearoa/New Zealand and Diocese of Wellington, NZ.*

'There are books about theory and then there are books like *No Wastelands* – a book written from the deep well of lived experience and practice. Ash Barker sheds light, shares insight and brings restorative wisdom that helps the rest of us discover how to join in with the revolution of hope - and not just momentarily - by inviting us to step right in with others, working together and being together as one to see, to be bringers of change, and grace and peace.' **Jill Rowe**, *Oasis Ethos & Formation Director, London, UK.*

'The opening chapter challenges with its inspiring account of Ash's "Jonah" journey. As an honest account of the transformational journey of the apostolic prophet it is in itself essential reading for all who sense that calling - from ideal through ordeal to the new deal! The rest of the book is also worth reading for its practical insights, but also for the testimony to the costly grace of God in Ash's life, thank you.' **Peter Neilson**, *author and Church of Scotland Minister, The Kingdom of Fife, Scotland.*

'Ash has been an insightful and inspiring voice for our work over the years as we've been reimagining what communities of Shalom in post-Christian Europe can look like. His life demonstrates the extraordinary impact community-driven initiatives can have in fostering peace and hope. His insightful strategies and real-life examples make him an invaluable resource for community leaders and activists.' **Eric Smith**, Church in Action, Frankfurt, Germany.

'There are few people who live with such integrity and meaning as Ash and Anji Barker and this book is a brilliant distillation of a rich life laced with stories, practical tips and biblical reflection. *No Wastelands* reminds us again that the redemption of people and place is at the heart of God's mission and for those seeking proximity in relationships and community this deeply practical and thoughtful work will be a valuable guide.'
Sarah Small, *Head of Eden Network UK, The Message Trust.*

No Wastelands

How to grow seedbeds of Shalom in your neighbourhood.

Ash Barker

First published in Great Britain in 2023.

Published by Seedbeds Communications
seedbeds.org

Copyright © Ash Barker 2023

All rights reserved. No part of this book may be reproduced or transmitted in any form or by any means, electronic or mechanical, including photocopying, recording, or by any information storage and retrieval system, without permission in writing from the publisher.

Unless otherwise noted, scripture quotations are taken from The Holy Bible, New Living Translation, Copyright© 1996. Used by permission of Tyndale House Publishers, Inc., Wheaton, Illinois 60189. All rights reserved.

Editors: Sally Mann and Stephen Parker
Proofreaders: Paul Ellis, Lizzie Ellis, Dave Mann and Jonah Bateson
Cover: Chris Grech
Interior: Amy Van Eymeren

Barker, Ash
No Wastelands: How to grow seedbeds of Shalom in your neighbourhood

ISBN 978-0-6484725-5-1 (Paperback)
ISBN 978-0-6484725-6-8 (eBook)

Printed by Ingram Spark

Dedicated to:

The Barker family whose love and support makes so much possible for me: Anji, Amy, Aiden, Mum and Dad,

The local communities where I belong and found home: Dingley, Springvale, Klong Toey and Winson Green.

Contents

Foreword	xv
Introduction: Not Buried, But Planted	1
PART A. BEATING THE WEEDS (AS BEST WE CAN)	35
Chapter 1: Weeds That Choke Potential	37
Chapter 2: Invasive Weeds That Choke The Harvest	47
Chapter 3: Weeds As Signs Of Life In Wastelands?	75
Chapter 4: Treating Weeds With Hope	83
Part A. Practices To Try	101
PART B. SOWING SEEDS OF SHALOM: WHAT CAN GOD'S VISION OF SHALOM MEAN LOCALLY?	107
Chapter 5: Place-making And The Seeds Of Shalom	109
Chapter 6: 'Fear Not!' - Seeds Of Shalom And Resisting Fear	125
Chapter 7: 'Great Joy' - Joy And The Seeds Of Shalom	135
Chapter 8: 'Shalom On Earth?'	145
Part B. Practices To Try	155
PART C. THE SOIL WE NEED	167
Chapter 9: Soils And Enchanted Worldviews	169
Chapter 10: Hard Paths - Lacking Awareness	185
Chapter 11: Stony Fields - Lacking Grit	191

Chapter 12: Thorny Grounds - Lacking Trust ... 201

Chapter 13: Good Soils - Praxis Understanding And Action ... 211

Part C. Practices to Try: Toward an incarnational spirituality - entering your C.A.V.E daily. ... 223

Part D. Sustainable Roots, Branches Ready For Fruit ... 239

Chapter 14: Not All Roots And Branches Can Grow The Fruit We Need ... 241

Chapter 15: Roots Systems For Sustainability ... 249

Chapter 16: Branches Prepared For Fruitfulness ... 271

Part D. Practices To Try ... 305

Part E. Grow In Seasons (Not Against Them) ... 317

Chapter 17: The Celtic Season of Samhain - Winters Of Our Discontent And Discovery ... 319

Chapter 18: The Celtic Season Of Imbolc - Spring's Gestations And Birthing. ... 335

Chapter 19: The Celtic Season of Bealtaine - Summertime's Flourishings And Rests ... 343

Chapter 20: The Celtic Season of Fomhar - Autumn's Harvests And Endings (Again) ... 355

Part E. Practices to Try: Eternal Seasons Labyrinth Walk ... 365

Conclusions: Possibilities for Seedbeds of Shalom ... 371

Endnotes ... 388

Foreword

When you stand with someone up to your knees in muck, working in a rice field in a poor rural community in Thailand, you forge a special bond.

The bond grows stronger as you bend in the sun for hours on end, side by side, planting little bundles of rice seedlings. The bond grows stronger still when you sleep outdoors under a tin roof with geckoes pooping on you, and when you eat meals prepared with love by a local mom whose life was changed forever by the kindness and creativity of a couple of Australians.

That's how Ash Barker and I became friends. Ash and his wife, Anji, organised the experience we shared planting rice. They wanted to help a couple dozen people from around the world better understand the lives of farmworkers … the labor, the sweat, the skill, the minimal pay, ten hours a day, fifty two weeks a year, as many decades as you can keep going. Ash wanted to help us understand how conditions among the rural poor are connected to the lives of the urban poor … how, for example, the low pay of Thai farm workers drives people to cities, and how that influx supports the sex tourism industry for which Thailand is (in)famous. I came home seeing connections I had never seen before, and more than just seeing them. I felt them.

I think I learned more in my few days with Ash than I have in any other few days in my life. And what I learned wasn't just theoretical 'head learning.' It was muck learning. Sunburn learning. Homecooked meal learning. Gecko poop learning. Heart learning.

No Wastelands

He taught us with words, but more, with experience. The ache in our backs, the muck splattered on our clothing, the good-natured laughter when local farm workers had to teach us outsiders again and again things that were so simple and obvious to them.

That story about planting rice seems especially important to share with you as you begin this beautiful new book from Ash. *No Wastelands* is a book about planting; planting not just seeds, but seedbeds. And not just seedbeds of rice, as important as that is ... but seedbeds of wholeness and wellbeing, community and peace, seedbeds of shalom.

Ash's journey took him from Australia to Thailand and then, from Thailand to Birmingham, England, to a part of the city known for its huge prison. The places changed, but Ash's vision was the same: how can places where it's difficult and dangerous to live become places of wellbeing and thriving? How can normal people invest their lives to make a difference for the world's poorest and most vulnerable people?

Many of us are oblivious to the needs around us. We're entirely occupied with our own problems. Others of us are deeply aware of the needs around us. We may feel overwhelmed by them, and guilty for not doing more. We may feel confident that we can end poverty and fix everything, so we plunge in and give our all, leaving us disillusioned when reality doesn't cooperate with our big dreams and good intentions.

Whoever you are, *No Wastelands* will help you learn what I have been learning from Ash over the years: that making a difference is neither as simple as we think nor as impossible as we think. Planting seedbeds of shalom begins with clearing away weeds, sowing seeds, enhancing soil, supporting healthy roots for abundant fruit, and working with the seasons. This book gives you just what you need to be a lifelong shalom farmer, wherever you live.

Brian D. McLaren

Introduction:
Not Buried, But Planted

This former wasteland is now like the Garden of Eden! The abandoned and ruined cities now have strong walls and are filled with people!
Ezekiel 36:35

Unless a grain of wheat falls into the ground and dies, it remains only a single seed. But if it dies, it produces many seeds.
John 12:24

The desert can bloom. Watch time-lapse footage of what seems like a desolate place in drought come back to life after a heavy rain. What seemed a dusty and dead moonscape was merely dormant and in fact teeming with life ready to be activated. As the refreshing rains flow, the plants, flowers and even streams burst into life and colour. What seemed a wasteland becomes a paradise.

Local communities can sometimes feel like 'wastelands.' Even after decades of intentional effort by well-intentioned governments, community activists and community developers, they can seem dry, arid and unresponsive. Fresh investment evaporates as fast as it's given. The few with helpful leadership qualities leave as quickly as they can. Those left behind are exasperated: 'Nothing ever changes around here.'

Neighbourhoods like these can also spread like a desert taking over fertile lands. The most vulnerable residents soon become transitory and spill over to the next neighbourhoods they can afford. Resented there for taking up precious resources, the fears of social unrest and instability grow. Another place, another wasteland.

Institutions often lack credibility, influence and legitimacy in this regard. Without functioning churches, politics, health care or education for generations, and with high-capacity organisational leaders unwilling to go there or stay for long, a kind of doom cycle emerges for the social infrastructure of a region. Major church denominations recognise that their steep decline is tied, at least partly, to their loss of meaningful engagement in inner cities and outer estates. Bishop Philip North, for example, notes that for the Church of England, "the proportion of people who attend an Anglican church in England is 1.7%. On the estates that figure is less than half at 0.8%. Moreover, the rate of decline on the estates is almost four times faster than the rest of the country."[1]

It doesn't have to be this way. There are outlier communities who have grown leadership from within and through relentless intentionality witnessed regenerative change happen. I have seen them and experienced this for myself. It takes time few have patience for, but what seems like wastelands can burst back into life before our very eyes.

This book explores art and practises any local community can use if they are to overcome complex challenges and flourish in God's love and Shalom together. Through stories, scriptures, hard won insights, and practical exercises I will seek to outline how 'seedbeds of Shalom' can help release the unique potential from within your local community.

I hope this book can be a sign of hope for those overwhelmed, stuck or weighed down in their experiences of local community life, but also a guide for those just starting out. It's for both emerging and established community leaders who love their neighbourhoods and know many of the current models of church, charity and community building are no longer sustainable or regenerative. May it encourage those who still hope ancient prophecies can come true: "This former wasteland is now like the Garden of Eden! The abandoned and ruined cities now have strong walls and are filled with people!" (Ezek. 36:35)

Introduction

Winson Green as a Seedbed of Shalom?

I was in a bustling, humid food court in Kuala Lumpur in 2014 when I first heard 'seedbeds' used as a metaphor for our ministry. Dr John Perkins, the famous civil rights leader, author, and founder of the Christian Community Development Association in the USA, met up with a few of us organisers between sessions of the International Society for Urban Mission Summit. He was so inspirational, sharing honestly about growing up in poverty in Mississippi and the tragic, preventable deaths of his mother and brother.

It was a time of huge transitions for me and while moved by Dr Perkins, I was also preoccupied with my own future. Not only had I just moved out of the Klong Toey slum in Bangkok, Thailand that had been our home for 12 years, but we were also leaving Urban Neighbours of Hope, the organisation I had founded and led since I was 22 years old. I was now 45 and preparing to start again with very little left in my hands. Dr Perkins suddenly turned, looked to me and asked,

'So, why will you move to Birmingham, England?'

I gulped and felt my face getting even redder. How could I explain this craziness, in a way that made sense quickly and without embarrassing myself in front of a living legend and peers? I took a deep breath and blurted out something like,

> 'In the second half of my life I want to invest my best energies in local leaders and their communities. We need to find out what is possible ourselves, in a particular place, but also see a new generation go further than we could. I want to live in a world where local communities decide their own futures and grow their own leaders. I think that if we can start that anew, planted in Winson Green, then we can be available and accessible to support long-term change in cities and nations around the world too.'

I then held my breath and shut up. It went quiet on our table as the buzz of the food court seemed to grow louder. Dr Perkins slowly looked up at me and then grew animated.

'I know what you're trying to do.... You wanna grow seedbeds! You want to offer fertile soil and nutrients and water and help new shoots grow up that wouldn't normally do that. You wanna see more fruit grow in unexpected places. Some seedlings may get replanted someplace else and they can grow there in new ways they couldn't before, but you wanna grow seedbeds!'

He was right. Four months after this encounter we moved as a family to Winson Green, an inner-city region of Birmingham, UK. We left with just a few bags and little money, but I had this deep sense of call to start a seedbed there. We needed this dream. Those first few years buried us alive. Dr Perkins' dream for us of planting seedbeds that could nurture local leaders into God's Shalom kept reoccurring. We, and our seedbed, were being planted.

As I write this, I'm conscious that Dr Perkins' metaphor was a kind of prophecy for me. Not only has Winson Green experienced deep change through local leaders from within, but we now support diverse community leadership programmes with participants from five cities in England, as well as in Scotland, Ukraine, Myanmar,[2] and Australia. Primarily we do this thorough an organisation we started, eventually named Seedbeds. Informally too, through our Seedbeds Communications, our books, speaking, and media work has inspired and informed many more in their attempts. This book is part of that fruit and all proceeds from the sale of this book will go back into the Seedbeds venture. We want to keep growing Seedbeds wherever we can. We want to see places some consider wastelands renewed to become like seedbeds of Shalom.

Will you join us? Prepare to be buried.

'Not buried, but planted'

Anji and I have had our fair share of feeling buried in wastelands over more than three decades of married life and ministry together. We have experienced some dark places together that had the smell of death. However, each time we found that we weren't so much buried in failure, as planted, ready for new seasons of Shalom in that place. In so many ways, three particular places on three different continents chose us, and our personal destiny was entangled with theirs. As we let go of previous places and focused on facing our fears, working with God's Shalom there, we found we experienced a deep joy together in fresh ways. These adventures are the making of us. As the exiles in Babylon were told: "Work for the shalom of the city where I sent you into exile. Pray to the LORD for it, for its shalom will determine your shalom" (Jer.29:7). You'll notice that themes like fear, shalom, and joy are weaved throughout this book, as I explore how we intentionally tied our wellbeing with that of our local community.

I was born and raised in Dingley, Melbourne, Australia. When I consider now all the places I have been and families I have seen, I know it was a blessed upbringing. At the time, to enjoy family, friends, schools, sports, church, and youth group all within a short walk or a bike ride away was all I knew. Of course, by the time I was a teenager I felt like we were too contained and hemmed into a 'village life' and dreamed of escaping. I played a lot of Bruce Springsteen music; I felt like I was *born to run* too! I especially hated school and often found it cruel and humiliating. I later found out I had dyslexia and probably Attention Deficit Disorder at a time when schools just thought I was 'thick.' I went to Keysborough Technical School, a 25 minute bike ride from home, but a world away, to prepare me for a trade or some other labouring work. I felt frustrated or bored in class most days, and in recess tried to survive our school's infamous gangs, drugs, and bullies. Unfortunately, I also had a competitive streak that expressed itself passionately in my football obsession outside of school. This led to me falling far behind in class, which in turn made me feel like a loser. My handwriting to this day is almost illegible. In those days there were no computers to clear it up and most marked assignments needed to be handwritten. Shame is a potent force. For all my blessedness in growing up in Dingley, I ran away from home at 16 with a mate from youth group. I quickly returned, but knew things couldn't stay the same.

Things changed for me when I found my passions. As an 18-year-old in 1988 I stood up at a huge Christian Conference, where American sociologist, author and preacher Tony Campolo spoke, and committed to 'go anywhere for the cause of Christ.' I soon met Anji too, who had been at the same meeting. It was this wider world, facing poverty and injustice, that God loved and that motivated us to go out to serve. Our blessed life growing up was not an accident or luck. It had come at the cost of others who suffered. Not just from Christ's sacrifices for us, but also through indigenous peoples, colonisation, and unjust structures that stripped bare a continent ready for white people like me. Campolo linked the lack of indigenous people at this huge Christian gathering with the needs of the poor around the world and with the work of Christ. This captivated me! The great redemption I needed called for great reversals if all would experience the promises of God. For some reason I thought I would go to China and Anji thought she was going to Haiti, but we were married as 20-year-olds and our first house was in Dingley. We started work with young people in Dingley, but also through Youth for Christ started visiting youth detention centres. I found I could relate and connect well with the guys there who were just like the kids I went to school with. In fact, I knew they could have been me.

In 1991 Anji and I sensed a call to relocate to Springvale, just down the road from Dingley. Could we prevent young people getting into the prison system by strengthening their families and communities? This relocation transformed our lives and set us on a path we continue to this day. Those 10 years shaped and formed us in a multi-cultural context, and we learnt how to start churches and groups with local leaders. This led naturally enough into our starting Urban Neighbours of Hope (UNOH), a missional order as part of the Churches of Christ in 1993. We would live out the gospel, immerse ourselves in the life of neighbourhoods facing urban poverty, and join the risen Jesus to seek transformation from the bottom up in Australia and beyond.

In 2002 we relocated from Springvale to the Klong Toey slum in Bangkok, Thailand as part of UNOH for another 12 years. These years too formed us, but nearly killed us as well as we found our callings in intense urban poverty living among 100,000 people in a square mile. All this happened before our move to Birmingham, UK in 2014. We had new dreams to invest in a new generation of local community leaders and see Winson Green become like a seedbed of shalom.

Each new re-planting brought unique, buried challenges. Perhaps being buried was an integral part of our calling?

Birmingham was different to our other burials. This time I especially felt connected to the biblical story of Jonah. Here this prophet is thrown overboard, nearly drowns and is swallowed whole by a giant fish. None of his plans survived impact. God knew his limitations, but used him anyway. Certainly, that has been our experience over the decades, but I thought it would be less brutal this time.

Knowing the right track to see a dream happen can be a challenge, especially when things start going wrong. Had we correctly discerned our focus and move? Had we not read the signs right? Were there other paths to greener pastures we should have taken? Should we have stayed where we were? When Jesus was asked for some kind of sign he simply answered, "A wicked and adulterous generation asks for a sign! But none will be given it except the sign of the prophet Jonah" (Matt. 12:39). As we arrived in Birmingham in November 2014, we gradually began to know about what this sign of Jonah means for us, in a way we hadn't before.

There is often the ideal.
Jonah had a call as a prophet of God. He may well have understood this as a position of power and privilege, speaking for God against injustice and corruption as so many previous prophets had done. Having some idealism and vision can be a good start but holding too tightly to expectations of certain results quickly creates resentment. Finding self-worth in our own measurements of impact creates emotional roller coasters and undermines our unique, God-given call and gifting. In Jonah's case, God called him beyond his own shores to help a city made up of those outside his own ethnicity and religion. Instead of going to the city of Nineveh as directed, Jonah tried to run away from 'God's presence' to Tarshish, a city far more in keeping with his ideal of himself and role. Tarshish was exotic and prosperous, a place where King Solomon had imported gold, silver, ivory, monkeys, and peacocks (1 Kings 10:22). Somewhere to make a name for yourself without the need for heartbreak, pain, or the presence of God. Eugene Peterson puts the temptation of Tarshish this way:

> Somehow we American pastors, without really noticing what was happening, got our vocations redefined in the terms of American careerism. We quit thinking of the parish as a location for pastoral spirituality and started thinking of it as an opportunity for advancement. Tarshish, not Nineveh, was the destination.[3]

God loved Jonah, knew him well, and got his attention in dramatic fashion to turn him around. Ideals and good intentions may be a beginning, but they will not last long enough to see real change grow in places considered wastelands.

God had given us a strong call to relocate to Winson Green and invest in a new generation of local community leaders. I felt a deep sense of God's authority in this. This seemed to be confirmed both from those who invited us and those who were sending us. The doors kept opening. The opportunities kept multiplying. However, like Jonah, this call and what we attached to it, was to be tested and transformed.

When people in the UK first hear my accent, they quickly know I'm not from Birmingham, but often can't quite pick where my accent is from, or where I fit on the class ladder.

> 'Where you from?'

> 'Well, I was born and raised in Melbourne, Australia to British parents, but lived in Bangkok for 12 years before Birmingham became home in 2014.'

> 'Australia! Why would you move here?' is the most common response. Like nothing else I talked about after living in Australia had any interest.

> 'Well…. I'm mainly here for the weather!' is my usual reply, so I don't have to talk about the soaps like *Neighbours* or *Home and Away*.

The truth is harder to explain. All I can say is that Winson Green in Birmingham was the neighbourhood that chose us. We fell in love with this unique place and its quirks and opportunities almost as soon as we heard about it! It had a community ecosystem we could join and were invited to come. This was not unlike what happened to us relocating to Springvale, Melbourne in 1991 or Klong Toey, Bangkok in 2002.

Like so much in our lives this transition started by paying attention to a niggle. For years I have risen early to prepare for my days. As I began in silence asking for where life had been found and resisted, I had an unexpected sense from Jesus that change was arriving. It's hard to describe, even now, but it seemed like our time in Bangkok was coming to an end and that new horizons called us. I tried to discuss this niggle with those impacted, but these were difficult conversations to start without sounding like betrayal. So much was at stake. I had hit a wall with my health with wave after wave of tropical illnesses and was ready for a new challenge spiritually. Local leadership was in place in most of the Thai organisations we worked with now and I felt I had taken UNOH as an organisation as far as I could. Emerging leaders wanted UNOH to go a different way and I didn't want to be the typical founder who stood in their way. We also had a window to move given the age of our children. Eventually, we began to dream again. If we had 20 years before retirement age in one more place, what could that look like? By mid-2013 we started to think about a possible transition out of Bangkok, but where in the world would we go?

I also had a niggle about Birmingham, UK. I'm not sure why, but since I was a boy I have held aspirations to return to the home of my family and ancestors in the UK. Dad was a carpenter and my mother's name is Mary, so was there any chance I wouldn't have a Messiah complex!? Dad was born and raised in Whaley Bridge in the Peak District, Derbyshire and left for Australia when he was twenty-seven as a '£10 Pom.' Mum was born in Tayport, Scotland and, with her extended family, left when she was eleven. I was born in Melbourne not long after Mum and Dad met there and were married. Mum thought Dad's accent sounded a bit like one of The Beatles, who had been touring at that time. If you see old black and white films of The Beatles in Melbourne's concert, look out for my Mum screaming her head off! At a basic level, if it wasn't for the Beatles I wouldn't be here! Mum and Dad settled in Dingley Village and Dad built many houses there.

I first visited the UK in 1977 with my family when I was eight years old. As we travelled the length and breadth of the UK I was fascinated by all the family connections as well as the ancient legends and history. From Loch Ness, in Scotland to Arthur's Tintagel Castle in Cornwall, these myths sparked my imagination for more. However, the next time I was in the UK was in 2012 with a Tearfund gathering.[4] A growing wonder about the UK unsettled me as we visited then. This unsettledness continued on a number of later ministry visits as part of UNOH, exploring an invitation for a new UNOH team to start there. I felt like I had come home but dismissed it as fantasy as we had planned to be in Bangkok until we died. Anji literally had her funeral planned there! However, I remember telling friends on a trip to Birmingham during that time that, 'If I had another life, this is where I'd love to spend it. There is just so much potential with so much access to so many people nearby too.'

By late 2013 we had decided to transition out of Bangkok and UNOH. But where would we go? I already had my connections with the Churches of Christ in Birmingham and an invitation to start a centre for urban mission and ministry as part of their Springdale College seemed the right next step to us. What would Anji do there? It needed to be something special if Anji was to move from her dream context. Unexpectedly, a few weeks after the decision to leave Bangkok, we hosted a group of international Christian speakers, leaders, and theologians in Bangkok called Mesa. The idea was that we host, bond, and ground this eminent group together so they could better explore the future of church, theology, and mission collectively. We took them out to the rice fields of Lot Buri and had heroes of the faith like Brian McLaren and Steve Chalke knee deep in shitty water working alongside Thai day labourers, picking chillies and planting rice, sleeping in shacks at night. Little did I know when Anji and I met Steve Chalke from Oasis in a rice paddy that he would point us to our new home and place to belong.[5] 'All the things that you do in Klong Toey you can do in Winson Green!' By the time the Mesa group had left, Steve had a job lined up for Anji as a 'community hub leader' in a local primary school that Oasis was resurrecting there. These roles and the place sounded just like they were made for what was next for us.

Introduction

If you ask people who have lived in Birmingham, 'what do you know of Winson Green?' the most common response would probably be 'The Prison.' Since Victorian times, Birmingham's prison has been located in Winson Green and the last hangings in the UK happened there too. Officially, it's called HMP Birmingham now, but it's still known as 'Winson Green' or 'The Green' to those both inside and outside the prison. And when your locality is most known as a prison, that's a hint that it may be seen as a wasteland.

Negative images of Winson Green were compounded when a controversial Channel Four documentary series, *Benefits Street*, was screened on British TV in 2014 and then syndicated around the world. What the local community thought was to be a documentary about how neighbours in one Winson Green street stick together and overcome hard times, ended up ridiculing them on a global scale. Certainly, the nation got to know these characters at their worst and the level of hate and bile toward them in social media was unprecedented. 'Waste of space' was a common insult.

It is true that on all kinds of indexes Winson Green struggles, not least with unemployment. The Birmingham Ladywood constituency, of which Winson Green is a part, often has, "the highest number of people claiming unemployment benefit in the entire country, as a proportion of the population. A House of Commons report shows that 11.9% of the 'economically active' population in Ladywood are claiming benefits. That's 7,120 people."[6] We will explore further in this book how this can happen to a local community, and the doom loop it can perpetuate to create wastelands, but Winson Green has certainly experienced that cycle of neglect and disempowerment.

However, we felt excited about Winson Green. It has far more just below the surface than any of those cheap stereotypes. It's a place with so many inspiring layers, it's hard to know where to start. The hyper-diverse and predominately young neighbourhood oozes potential now, but it also has a fascinating history. Not least is that Charlie Chaplin, the famous black-and-white movie star, was born in Black Patch Park here and helped spark the modern movie industry. James Watt first manufactured the steam engine at the Soho Foundry here and helped spark the industrial revolution. World class footballers for nearby West Bromwich Albion and Aston Villa came from our area and helped change the footballing globe too. However, it was another Winson Green character that most inspired me, and one we wanted to honour with our place-making efforts if we could.

Lesslie Newbigin (1909-1998) served as a Minister in Winson Green for seven years in the 1980s after he returned from 40 years of Christian service in India and after lecturing at nearby Selly Oaks Colleges. Mission historian Wilbert Shenk described Lesslie Newbigin as "one of the decisive influences on the theology of mission in the twentieth century."[7] Geoffrey Wainwright, Newbigin's authoritative biographer, considers him "comparable to the early church fathers by nature of his heart and mind, pastoral work, ecumenical endeavour, missionary strategy, social vision, the comprehensiveness of his ministry, and his sheer stature as a man of God."[8] While ministering in Winson Green, Newbigin wrote such influential books as *The Gospel in a Pluralist Society*, *The Open Secret* and *Foolishness to the Greeks*. A man before his time, he articulated the tough urban questions and dedicated his life to finding and living the answers in both Majority and Western World urban contexts. Lesslie Newbigin also influenced my own views of mission, like so many Ministers theologically formed in Australia in the 1990s. Newbigin's insights were so critical for us in Thailand and in shaping the ethos of UNOH as a confident, but not arrogant, missional community. My friend Mike Frost, the brilliant Sydney-based writer, speaker, and missiologist, even wore a wristband that had WWND? What Would Newbigin Do?

Newbigin was exactly who we wanted to honour and emulate in this place. Could Newbigin's life and insights inspire a new generation of Christian workers to respond to growing urban injustices in our day, and to help see abundant community cultivated from the ground up around the world?

Where we would make home in Winson Green became a point of prayer. In March 2014 we visited Winson Green as a kind of reconnaissance mission with the Cooking with Poo team who toured the UK with us. Thrive Together leader, Fred Rattley, had been helping Church of

England Parishes in Birmingham reimagine what was possible with their buildings for the sake of their local communities. When he heard about our initial visit and interest in Winson Green he quickly organised to show us the 1,000 seat Bishop Latimer church building and the eight-bedroom parsonage next door. The parsonage in Winson Green had not had a vicar living in it for many years and was rented out privately. The massive Victorian era, Grade II listed church building was left cold and empty with the small existing congregation, made of Newbigin's old URC church and the Parish one, moving to the hall next door for their services.

'Do you want them?' Fred joked.

'Well, I'm not sure about the church building, but the parsonage would be a wonderful base for us to live and share life, community, and ministry from. We could offer great live-in community placements from here too.' I replied.

What a place for a Seedbed!

Fred asked me to come up with a proposal for the Bishop of Birmingham. The basic idea flowed quickly as we thought about a residential community that could also be opened up as a local community house and base for our new training centre. In fact, within a month Bishop David agreed for us to launch what would be called 'Newbigin House' from the old parsonage if we could come up with the market rent. Steve Chalke had read to Lesslie in his older age when he was going blind and had kept in touch with the family. They also gave special permission for us to rename this parsonage in honour of Lesslie Newbigin himself. This just seemed to be another confirmation of the sense of call to this place for this next season of life. Before we had even left for England permanently, our plans were coming together in remarkable ways.

I can still remember being at Melbourne airport early in the morning on Thursday, November 20, 2014. I had said goodbye to my Mum and Dad at this airport many times before as we went back and forth from Bangkok. I cried again as I said goodbye, but this felt different. We were ready for a new adventure, but this seemed like our last relocation. We were leaving with all our possessions which were amassed to the few suitcases in our hands, but we had big dreams of what might be possible in Birmingham at the other end of the flight. We had roles with UK organisations lined up, our supporters had even given these groups seeding grants to help get us going. What could possibly go wrong this time?

We especially felt relieved that we wouldn't need to shoulder the responsibilities of organisational leadership and fundraising anymore. We had founded and led Urban Neighbours of Hope as a faith venture for over 20 years. Trusting God for provision was exhilarating at times, but it was also exhausting, nearly wringing the life out of us by the end. It wasn't an easy transition out of UNOH generally or Bangkok specifically, but we'd left everything we'd built up with the emerging leaders of UNOH and local Thai organisations. UNOH's new leadership had led for over a year without me in post and they really needed to hold onto all the existing financial resources and supporters they could. We were ready to focus on our new ministries directly and not have to lead or raise money for organisations anymore.

No plan, however well devised, survives first contact. Like Jonah we got buried and swallowed whole. Sometimes the ideal falls victim to the ordeal. Mostly, the ordeals are just as necessary as the ideals. Seeds of vision need to be buried before they can bear fruit, but without that seed it's just talk, analysis or conversations. The ideals get us out there, beyond our comfort zones. If we knew in advance what a calling takes, we probably would avoid it. Jonah comes to his senses in humility as he heads for Tarshish and offers to be thrown overboard to change course to Nineveh. Likewise, only humility connects and joins us to God's authentic dreams for us and our local communities. Without vision and humility, our sense of God can quickly turn egotistical and self-serving. We can think we can make things happen without God and without pain or suffering. Like Jonah we can, deep down, believe we should really be self-sufficient in Tarshish, not living by faith in a wasteland like Nineveh.

Introduction

There is the ordeal.
Jonah ended up buried deep inside the belly of a huge fish. There was a kind of death and grief that he had to face about himself and only in the dark and smelly spaces could burn off the false images he had of himself and his call. Change from within us can often only be incubated in humility. Jonah simply couldn't run away from himself and God's call on his life. Indeed, Jonah would not have had the capacity to be a change maker without this trauma and humiliation inside a huge fish. Richard Rohr writes of this sign:

> It seems to demand that we must release ourselves into a belly of darkness before we can know what is essential. It insists that the spiritual journey is more like giving up control than taking control. It might even be saying that others will often throw us overboard, as was the case with Jonah, and that will get us to the right shore—and even by God's grace more than any right action on our part … Jonah indeed is our Judeo-Christian symbol of transformation. Jesus had found the Jonah story inspiring, no doubt, because it described almost perfectly what was happening to him!⁹

We found that being 'buried' changed us… again. Jesus reminds that "unless a grain of wheat falls into the ground and dies, it remains only a single seed. But if it dies, it produces many seeds" (John 12:24). I expected that our transitions to the UK in 2014 would be a bit tricky, but not belly of the beast stuff.

It hardly started well! I had resigned from leading UNOH in October 2013 after the previous 18 months of handing over leadership and management responsibilities starting in January 2012. We had stayed in Bangkok during this transition, but by March 2014 we went to Birmingham together as a family and then back to Bangkok. Anji needed to stay in Bangkok with our 11-year-old son Aiden as he finished his schooling there. I went to Melbourne to be with Amy, our 18-year-old daughter, completing high school. The final year of high school is a tough year for anyone, but Amy had been quite vulnerable toward the end of her time in Bangkok and I really wanted to stand with her through this final year.

No Wastelands

In so many ways I can relate to Jonah. Almost as soon I landed in Melbourne from Bangkok in late March 2014 things started to go wrong. My accommodation that was lined up for me as part of a 'theologian in residence' role with a city-centre mission in the transition was delayed. We couldn't afford what would be nine months' rent and so I needed to couch surf with kind family and friends for four months until that promised flat eventually became possible in July. Amy's accommodation with her housemates started to unravel too and she also needed new accommodation. Then there was a military coup in Bangkok where Anji and Aiden still lived. When Anji and Aiden did arrive in Melbourne from Bangkok we faced more upheaval trying to get UK visas for them and failed at our first attempt. Even though I had UK citizenship (through my parents), the hot-button issue of UK immigration meant the laws (and prices!) kept changing. By the time Anji and Aiden would finally get permanent leave to remain years later, we had paid over £16,000, almost three times what we expected to pay.

A month before we were to leave for Birmingham, the parsonage in Winson Green we were due to live in fell through too. There were no guarantees we would live there at any time soon either. Internal politics in the Birmingham Diocese and the local Parish had closed the offer down. In the meantime, we found a place online to rent a private house nearby from a dodgy landlord who needed six months payment up front. And if the feelings of Jonah-like burial weren't real enough, I am sure it was no accident that this first home in Winson Green was literally on Nineveh Road! After six months we bought and moved into a local terrace house so that we could be fully invested in Winson Green. All the time I still felt that God had given us that parsonage to become Newbigin House and that the Diocese just didn't recognise it yet!

We had deeper problems than even these. Not only had what we thought was a certain place to live in fallen through, but the similarly certain roles, with certain goals in mind were quickly swallowed up too. Indeed, our initial ministry plans hardly survived the impact of landing in the UK. The college that had invited me to set up a new centre for equipping leaders in urban ministry based in Winson Green went through a restructuring and rebranding, and was no longer in a position to follow through on what we had agreed about Newbigin

Introduction

House, even if we could get it. New roles were being offered to me from the college that meant more time on the road and allowed little connection with Winson Green within that role. Pressure to move from Winson Green grew. Friends in Sydney talked with me about seeing our plans for Newbigin House happen in Western Sydney, and this was very tempting. By the end of 2015, only twelve months in the UK, we were personally deep in debt, despairing, and not even able to afford a ticket to return to Melbourne or run away to any other place we thought more suitable. Darkness closed in on us. Neither Tarshish nor prophetic ministry in Nineveh seemed possible. We were in the belly of the beast. We were buried alive.

Anji was going through her own buried darkness too. The grief of leaving Bangkok hit Anji hard. In her heart she never really wanted to leave Klong Toey and now this new dream, one she'd trusted and followed me to the other side of the world for, was falling apart. Not only did I need to work incredible hours all around England just to keep things going with the college, everything was far more expensive than we'd expected and our debt increased. Even worse, her own role based in a Primary School was far more restrictive than she was used to. Anji is a creative force of nature and not meant to be confined in the tight, restrictive environment required of life in an English Primary School!

However, there were glimmers of light to hold onto even then. In March 2015, I had the chance to take our son Aiden on pilgrimage to the Holy Island of Lindisfarne. It had been a dream to go to the place where his namesake St Aidan had founded a monastic and missional base that prepared leaders to change the world in the dark ages. It was an original seedbed for change and the Celtic monks re-evangelised Europe from there, over 1400 years ago. During prayer one morning at Lindisfarne, I had a renewed sense of call: to be planted locally in Winson Green to keep learning and demonstrate what local renewal is possible, but also to be connected globally to grow local community leaders around the world. We could still be a Seedbed in Winson Green. Come what may, we needed to keep pursuing this. Christian activists and leaders in Birmingham too looked to create ways we could stay. I remember my new friend Tim Evans, who lives in an estate in Firs and Bromford, meeting me at our local Black Eagle pub. He said some

Birmingham leaders felt embarrassed at what was happening to us and were desperately trying to find a way for us to stay. Could we still do this or was the dream beyond us now?

Out of the blue, those who had privately rented the Winson Green parsonage moved out, leaving only their son by himself. The Archdeacon called us into the Diocese head office and told us it could be available to us if we paid market rent, six months in advance and promised not to plant any churches. The planting of local churches was part of our story with UNOH and it seemed to have frightened the powers that be at that time. We raised the money through Australian supporters for the six months' rent and were more than happy not to be responsible for any church plants.

After many attempts, I knew I needed to leave the college I was working at if our Seedbeds dream was to be realised in Winson Green and if I was to honour the seed backing of our supporters. One of the most humbling trips of my life was at the end of 2015. UK friends gave me money for an airfare so I could return to Melbourne to make sure our daughter Amy was okay and I also needed to reassure supporters we still believed God had called us to Winson Green. While fulfilling our call needed to look different to what we had initially planned, we still felt it was right. Amy was in good spirits and transitioned from a photography degree to a community work course and never looked back. However, I had to keep looking into the eyes of supporters and churches who had trusted us and given the initial funds to help with our transition and try to explain what went wrong and what we wanted to do next. I felt ashamed but determined. Throw us overboard, if need be, but we had a dream and needed to start up new organisations that we could lead ourselves by faith. We couldn't run from that dream any longer. We would land on the right shore in the end.

In February 2016 I left the College and was able to be employed as a community prison chaplain with Yellow Ribbon and be partly based in Winson Green prison. I had literally been walking and praying around the prison and later met the Yellow Ribbon founder, Pauline Mack, at a Christian festival. The role started as salaried full time, my first for over 25 years, which enabled us to both get back on our feet financially, immersed us into the local scene, and orientated me to UK systems. However, it also had the flexibility to be gradually reduced to create time to set up organisational containers that would better suit our long-term leadership and vision.

We needed to let go and slowly pick up leadership responsibilities again. Perhaps our Tarshish was the temptation not to lead and found faith-based organisations again? Anji would eventually leave Oasis Foundry Primary School hub to lead Newbigin Community Trust, a community-based charity to renew Winson Green, and would also become a United Reformed Church Minister based here. I would eventually lead Seedbeds (initially set up as the Newbigin School for Urban Leadership) to release the unique potential of local people and places through community leadership programmes, as well as lead URC Lodge Road Community Church. It would take years in Winson Green to get to these roles, and have the needed organisations fully into place, but the way was reset for us in that formative second year in 2016. We could have freedom to pursue our call, or we could have security. We couldn't have both.

I am so grateful for the handful of supporters in Australia who stayed with us in those early UK days to help us keep the dream alive. Those who knew us, trusted us, and believed in us enough to financially back us had become few and far between. Part of this was intentional, so UNOH had its best chance of surviving with existing support, but many friends and former colleagues dropped us and no longer returned our messages. Eventually new supporters in the UK joined us too. It was Australian supporters who raised the money to rent Newbigin House from the Birmingham Diocese for the first two years and some friends moved in initially to keep this offer alive.

Through this time, we became different people as God worked in us to build our capacity for transformation through us in this unique time and place. We faced fears, found God's will, and experienced unexpected joys on the way. We were more than buried, we had been planted for such a time as this. Although our ideal had become an ordeal, we had a suspicion that there was more to the story. We desperately hoped that there would be. Like Jonah, we knew we were at least on the right shore now!

There can be a new deal.
Jonah was spat out by the great fish in the place that God had intended all along. He landed on Nineveh's shore smelling of fish guts and his skin bleached white, but this strange man was now ready to offer nothing but a deep and authentic sense of God's presence and message for change. God had changed the messenger and Jonah's Message would see a whole city transformed, far beyond his wildest imagining.

Nineveh was an unloved city in many ways. Though it was once a prestigious city, it was built on a faultline and had frequent earthquakes. It was often sacked by different powers who rebuilt the city roughly over ruins.[10] It was socially disordered, dangerous and chaotic. Nahum the prophet even writes:

> And all who look at you will shrink from you and say,
> 'Wasted is Nineveh; who will grieve for her?'
> Where shall I seek comforters for you?
> (Nah. 3:7 [English Standard Version]).

Nineveh was a wasteland. Often literally. Yet, God had called the reluctant Jonah to see it transformed.

I am convinced we can only make our unique change-making contributions in the providence and power of God. If we let go of our ego's fragility and become the unique, even strange, people God is preparing us to be, we can see transformations we couldn't even dream up if we tried. All change and growth is a living grace. A gift we cannot earn, but one we can recognise and nurture.

I know resurrections are possible for people and places. This is the 'Sign of Jonah' that Jesus talked about. Jesus' resurrection is a sign that we will see deadness burst into new life. We can have our own small and not-so-small resurrections too. In September 2015 we had a foretaste of the joy that was to come as we took up Newbigin House. It was a brilliant day when the local community saw the Bishop of Birmingham bless the launch of Newbigin House. The BBC covered the story, including the mobile petting zoo Anji had set up at the local Oasis school. John Newbigin, Lesslie's son, also came and he was a highlight for me. He said:

Introduction

'My Dad didn't really want to come to Winson Green. He had spent all those years in India and had just retired from his role as a lecturer in Birmingham. There had been talks about closing down the local church here. Dad said, 'The church can't withdraw from the inner-city. I'll go myself if I need to!' And so, he came. As I look around today and see this energy, diverse people and vision, I'm sure he'd feel vindicated.'

We moved into Newbigin House ourselves in April 2016 with the hope that it could be a kind of live incubator for change through sharing life and offering hospitality. Volunteers and students moved in with us. It felt like we had taken back a community asset and opened it up for the local community too. While our bedrooms were upstairs, the ground floor had large meeting rooms, kitchens, and a study that local people would come in with ideas and then leave with plans soon activated. Local initiatives like 'Flavours of Winson Green' cooking school, 'Animal Encounters' petting zoo, 'Soho Albion FC,' homework clubs, youth groups, blacksmith groups, as well as community meetings and training all had their genesis here. These connections were fun and inspiring. I think we had community barbecues in the backyard each night for the first two months, despite the weather, as people just didn't want to leave. Neighbours, nervous at first, soon felt like they belonged here and that Newbigin House belonged to them too. An expat friend visited Newbigin House from Bangkok and looking around at all the action said, 'This is just like Klong Toey. Only inside!'

To be grounded in a local reality was essential to our new vision. We needed to keep learning as well as sharing life with others. New kinds of urban engagement are mostly caught more than taught. That is why we needed to live and work from a residential community based in Newbigin House and quickly began Newbigin Community Trust as a local community-based organisation seeking the long-term renewal of Handsworth and Winson Green. This is why Seedbeds was formed, to help find ways to cultivate a community context for growing leaders and communities into fullness of life. But Seedbeds was also established to take up invitations and invest in local seedbeds beyond Winson Green too. A key hope was to raise up diverse streams of local community leaders around the world. We knew that it takes people to reach people, communities to reach communities. We had our place, and were on our way. We've learnt to be less afraid of feeling buried alive. That, like Jonah, we will get to the shore God wants us to get to in the end. Like Jonah, we too have been grumpy and ungrateful at times, but exhaustion, heartbreak, and finding limits are part of sharing life. Indeed, only by being planted deeply can growth and fruitfulness come. This is all the more true for places considered wastelands. If we can find what gifts and limitations we really have to offer and not simply what 'ought to be done,' we have found that deep change is possible. Becoming aware of our core virtues and vices helps us to begin to face them honestly and boldly in the stress of real life. Others may even think they buried us, but if we are seeds the evidence will follow. Parker Palmer put it this way:

> If we are to live our lives fully and well, we must learn to embrace the opposites, to live in a creative tension between our limits and our potentials. We must honor our limitations in ways that do not distort our nature, and we must trust and use our gifts in ways that fulfil the potentials God gave us. We must take the no of the way that closes and find the guidance it has to offer-and take the yes of the way that opens and respond with the yes of our lives.[11]

Nothing quite happened the way we'd anticipated. Our ideal had certainly become an ordeal, but now we had an opportunity to live out a new deal. Like Jonah, we would see transformations far beyond our imaginings. Abundant living in former wastelands was possible for us.

This transformation was especially seen in our Seedbeds 'Change Makers' emerging community leaders' programmes. In so many ways this book with its principles, insights, and stories is the fruit of their transformations. It started as a pilot with some local leaders in Winson Green in 2016 and then grew to have nine cohorts with local leaders from around England and Scotland at the time of writing. We started by discovering what was strong in these emerging leaders, and would incubate their gifts, lives, and ideas, ready to pitch an idea to a resource panel. Many community projects, social enterprises, and campaigns resulted. Local communities look different now because Change

Makers alumni found their passion and calling to share within their own community. Change Makers has also been inspirational in helping other Seedbeds programmes emerge too, like Seedbeds Learning (postgraduate units with Nazarene Theological College in Manchester and Ukrainian Evangelical Theological Seminary in Kyiv), Seedbeds Incubators (Enterprise Development in Myanmar), Seedbeds Pioneering (church planters and lay pioneers in Britain), and Seedbeds Pilgrims (St Cuthbert's Way and Camino pilgrimage experiences in Europe). I've come to believe that this flourishing is possible anywhere.

Is the pain worth the gain?

When I consider the cost of this vocation over the decades, personally and with my family, I have to ask myself, has this odyssey been worth it? Surely community change can happen in safer ways and with less costly involvement with local people and places? Most change leaders I know have needed to make similar kinds of calculations too. Jesus himself even encouraged it (Luke 14:26-33). Those of us who stay involved conclude that the liberation of local community leadership is worth far more than anything we can ever give up. As civil rights and urban activist Vincent Harding once wrote, "There is no way to save and be safe at the same time."[12] Local community building then, with all its associated 'dangers, toils and snares,' is costly. To share life is critical to faith and not something we can simply outsource to others.

I know this calculation of risk doesn't always add up the same way for everyone. When most government, education, church, health, and civic leaders consider their budgets and priorities, for example, very few conclude that building the capacities of local community leadership is something worth investing in. If this idea even made it onto a business agenda meeting, few would know what to do next. It's unclear to most institutions what local people and their places would do with any investment anyway, especially with those considered living in 'wastelands.'

If institutions and their investors can develop their own clear service provision plan that they think will meet needs with appropriate predicted outcomes, then the choice for them is obvious. If we invest in this service, then we'll get that. Simple and clean. Local community leaders, on the other hand, are unpredictable to institutions because their primary loyalty is to the wellbeing of their own local community, not the institution. What happens locally could easily be wasted if the narrow scheme of institutional objectives is considered. As we shall see, however, what seemed so safe and responsible for institutions has failed, creating more loneliness, inequality, and instability in neighbourhoods. Indeed, reliance on professional service provisions have, in part at least, disempowered and isolated individuals, creating the very wastelands we are talking about.

These themes have been taken up powerfully by the Asset-Based Community Development movement. Cormac Russell, for example, puts it this way:

> In general, there are four main modes of social change: to, for, with, and by. 'Doing to' involves imposed change that is coercive/directive and seeks to fix or cure; this approach can often be authoritarian and serving of the needs of distant agendas. 'Doing for' is less coercive, and is generally benevolent and well-intentioned, but still sees 'professionals' and outsiders in the driving seat. 'Doing with' seeks change via more equal and reciprocal relationships between communities and outside players. Finally, 'doing by' makes communities the architects and drivers of their own change.[13]

Doing 'to' or 'for' is still by far the most invoked approach to change in communities like ours. Local gifts have therefore laid dormant too long, while outside service professionals have taken over and drained the very sources of power from within and stripped any outside resources for local communities too. Community building has now become a lost art form. Using the same change models will not alter this, no matter how much more efficient their deliveries can be. A Tarshish fantasy, without the need for God's presence, is more alive than ever for the vast majority of organisations, even the explicitly religious ones. A kind of functional atheism dominates, and few institutions risk the required prophetic acts in places like Nineveh.

Why invest all we have in local community leadership and places? Why take the time to discover what communities can do by themselves, with all the capacity they have? This book unashamedly champions the importance of discovering the transformative power of local community leaders, but this is not based on wishful thinking. This focus provides an essential, sustainable, and strategic correction to the loss of connection ravaging our world. Isolation is killing us and making local neighbourhoods wastelands. This is no overstatement; the research is in. For example,

> In 2015, psychology professor Julianne Holt-Lunstad of Brigham Young University led a meta-analysis of 70 papers involving more than 3.4 million participants followed over an average of seven years. The study found that a lack of social connections was as great a risk factor for early death as smoking 15 cigarettes a day, and that it constitutes a greater risk than such lifestyle risk factors as obesity and lack of exercise. Other recent studies have connected loneliness and social isolation with a range of health problems, including heart attacks, strokes, drug abuse, alcoholism, anxiety and depression.[14]

Local community is by far the most important unit of change. It's in local proximity that connections can be made and isolation healed. As Wendell Berry wrote:

> I believe that the community - in the fullest sense: a place and all its creatures - is the smallest unit of health and that to speak of the health of an isolated individual is a contradiction in terms.[15]

We need to focus our best attention on local ecosystems and not try to separate individuals out, to treat them in isolation. This focus is what can change 'wastelands' to 'gardens of Eden.' In fact, the healing of our planet depends on this refocusing.

Here are five quick reasons then, why investment in local leadership is worth it, for any organisation interested in community growth and change, despite any cost.

1. Local community leaders are the key to sustainable neighbourhood change. They are the ones who understand the unique needs and assets of their community and are best equipped to identify and address the root causes of local issues.

2. By raising up local community leaders, we create a network of change agents who can work together to tackle complex issues and build a stronger, more resilient community.

3. Investing in local community leaders is a long-term strategy for neighbourhood transformation. By releasing local talent with the skills, knowledge, and resources they need to lead effectively, we can create a ripple effect of positive change that extends far beyond any single project or initiative.

4. Local community leaders are essential for creating a sense of ownership and belonging in the neighbourhood. When residents feel that they have a stake in the community's future, they are more likely to get involved and take action to make it a better place.

5. Investing in local community leaders is essential for creating a more just and equitable society. By giving voice to those who have been marginalised or excluded, we can work towards a future where everyone has access to the resources and opportunities they need to thrive.

Our organisations and local congregations should especially be investing in local people and places. I would argue this is true, even more so for Christians than for any other group in society. As Christians, we are called to love our neighbours and to serve others in our communities as Jesus would. This kind of love is both self-emptying and liberating (Phil. 2). How is such love possible if it is not personalised and localised? Jesus didn't try to just love us abstractly from afar. The apostle Paul describes three virtues that "remain" forever (1 Cor. 13), that investing in faith, hope, and love in the people and places around us is what lasts. Such love is never wasted.

Introduction

As Christians, we believe that God has a plan for our lives, and for the world around us, and is reconciling all things through Jesus (2 Cor. 5:18–20; Eph. 2:16; Col. 1:20–21). We live in anticipation of this hope. This includes harmony between people, places, and God. Lesslie Newbigin put it this way, writing in Winson Green, that:

> The church in each place is to be the sign, instrument and foretaste of the reign of God present in Christ for that place; a sign, planted in the midst of the present realities of the place but pointing beyond them to the future which God has promised; an instrument available for God's use in the doing of his will for that place; a foretaste—manifesting and enjoying already in the midst of the messianic tribulations a genuine foretaste of the peace and joy of God's reign.[16]

What a vision of Christian hope and local congregational life! How many of our local congregations ever set their agenda as being a sign, foretaste, and instrument in their local community they feel responsible for? By investing in local community leadership development, we are helping to shape the future of our communities in a positive way, helping fulfil the promises of God.

Ultimately, the vision of this book is to see God, people, and place living in harmony together – that's what Shalom means. By working together, raising up local leaders in seedbeds of Shalom in our neighbourhoods, we can create a better future for ourselves, our communities, and our planet.

Hopes for this book

Over the years I have met so many local church, charity, and community-building leaders who are buried, exhausted, and stuck in survival mode. The systems that used to help keep local life afloat seem now to be weighing us down, even drowning us, especially if we can't paddle any longer against the stream. I've been one of them.

No Wastelands

Yet, I still believe our best way forward is local and with what is in our own hands here to share. The Great Commission in John's Gospel is simply: "Yeshua said to them again, "Shalom aleichem! As the Father has sent Me, I also send you" (John 20:21 [Tree of Life Version]). This speaks of entering into the suffering of local people as Jesus did with particular humans and seeking wellbeing from the inside out. Lao Tzu in sixth century BC put it this way:

> Go to the people.
> Live with them,
> Learn from them,
> Love them.
> Start with what they know,
> Build with what they have.
> But with the best leaders,
> The work done, the task accomplished,
> The people will say,
> 'We've done it ourselves.'[17]

Why isn't our best thinking, energy and leadership focused on what is happening in local communities? After all, it's the neighbourhood that is the most basic unit of where people live and can share their lives most directly with others and the earth. I like the *New Parish* definition of 'place.' It's "big enough to live a lot of life in, small enough to become a known character in its unfolding drama."[18] Therefore, local places are where people live and where most people can best share their gifts to see real change grow from the ground up.

This book hopes to spark imaginations, values, practices, and strategies to see lasting change happen in and through local communities. It's for those who are stuck and weighed down, but also for those just beginning their adventure. It's a journey I live as well as share. This book has been for me too.

Unashamedly, this book focuses on the potential of local community leaders. I've been in enough global, national, and regional meetings to know that what is most talked about in board rooms, hotels, and conferences isn't often what makes the most difference on the ground.

Introduction

There is too often a disconnect between brilliant theories for Tarshish and what actually works in practice in Nineveh. In so many ways I've lived that tension, bridge building between local community life and important ideas. For over 30 years I lived and served as an activist Minister based in three neighbourhoods in three continents that faced crushing injustices and complex forms of urban poverty. I've also led and been part of research, denominational, international development, and even UN networks trying to end poverty and usher in God's Shalom. It's not that the ideas discussed at that level can't be helpful or the people making the cases inadequate, it's just that those ideas and resources very rarely connect with the people who can do something about them. This needs to change, and I hope this book can be part of making those connections work both ways.

This book also hopes to spark deep community growth and change. I'd love to see this book help guide a new generation of local community leaders and those who love them. It's for both emerging and established community leaders who love their neighbourhoods and recognise that many of the current models of church, charity, and community building are no longer sustainable or regenerative.

There is a growing number of people who are ambivalent to organised religion, politics, education, and charities, but still want to make a local difference. This is especially true for people in inner cities and outer urban estates who have often not had functioning churches, politics, or schools for generations now. I hope this book can be like fresh flowing water for you and helps your community bloom. Insights and practices here do often draw from my Christian faith, but I hope these are accessible to all who need them, no matter your religious identity.

The most important conversations to me are those that help release the unique potential of local leaders to see their community grow and change for themselves. I hope this book can contribute to that hope and that reality.

In many ways this book isn't hard research. It's more like a work of practical mysticism, detecting insights in community change-making as my journey unfolded. That is the underlying methodology here, more so than a well-thought-out research methodology.

No Wastelands

This creates limitations as well as strengths. My own memory can play tricks on me and the stories and scriptures I share have other perspectives available. Despite these limitations, I hope this book can offer accessible, practical, and inspiring insights to those who long to see local communities thrive, and that my experiences might spark something in you. Sometimes the personal can also be universal.

I have therefore organised this book around its central metaphors, particularly those associated with growing 'seedbeds of Shalom' as a response to local communities that can seem like 'wastelands.' I begin each chapter with personal, community stories before exploring scriptural traditions and insights that pick up on that chapter's metaphor. I end each chapter with some practices to try and some group questions so this book can be a practical resource to community leaders. These are the parts:

Part A. Beating the weeds (as best we can)
Explores what can choke the life out of our communities and how hope can keep these at bay, at least long enough to see change and growth start to happen from within neighbourhoods.

Part B. Sowing seeds of Shalom
Explores what the idea of Shalom can mean and its implications as a guiding vision for nurturing what is possible in our local communities.

Part C. The soil we need
Explores Jesus' famous parable of the four soils and what this can mean for preparing deep and transformative community change.

Part D. Sustainable roots, branches ready for fruit
Explores how three essential qualities can become like root systems able to feed and sustain three different approaches to change from within local communities.

Part E. Work with the seasons (and not against them)
Explores how four traditional Celtic seasons can inform the timings and priorities of local community change efforts.

Conclusions and Challenges
Offers four case studies I have experienced to connect with the themes of this book and spark possibilities of your own.

Wherever you are placed, I hope this book can help you grow seedbeds of Shalom where most only see wastelands. Surely these times require this above all else.

Nurturing gratefulness has become a key practice that helped me find my way into this book and my life calling generally. No matter how dark life has gotten for me over the last few years, there are people, events, and gifts that I can pause and take time to appreciate. A full heart is unstoppable, and joy emerges that makes life worthwhile. This book project is certainly no different. I am grateful for so many who have made it possible to hold this book in your hands. These include:

> The local community members who gave permission for their stories to be told here.
>
> My family, who often paid bigger prices for my vocation than I ever have. Anji's love and support of me has been unwavering over the decades and this book in so many ways is part of the fruit of our lives together. Our children, Amy and Aiden, now have their own lives in different cities, but their passion and giftedness inspire me. While it has become fashionable to complain about Ministry kids' lives, I am proud our children have grown to share their unique ministry lives of their own.
>
> Much of this book was written when I was on sabbatical. I would write most mornings and walk most afternoons over a three-month period between December 2022 and March 2023. I am grateful for friends and family in Australia who hosted me there, as well as Seedbeds, Newbigin House, and our church teams in the UK who picked up extra responsibilities to make this possible. I'm also thankful for a grant from The United Reformed Church's Global and Intercultural Ministries (Mission) to help toward funding my airfares.

There has also been a brilliant publishing team. Brian McLaren, Dave and Sally Mann helped shape the book from the start. Stephen Parker's editing and insights have made my thoughts legible. Proofreaders Paul and Lizzie Ellis, Dave Mann, and Jonah Bateson, and designers Amy Van Eymeren and Chris Grech helped make this book inspirational and ready to be in your hands.

I especially want to thank my Mum and Dad. For over 20 years I have lived overseas from you, yet you have always held us in your hearts and freed us to pursue our dreams. I hope I can pass this tradition on to my kids and extended family around the world too.

Part A.

Beating The Weeds (As Best We Can)

This part of the book explores the weeds that choke the life out of our communities and how hope can keep these at bay, at least for long enough to see change and growth start to happen within our neighbourhoods.

There are four chapters grouped together here, with a chance to stop and personally reflect at the end of each chapter. At the end of this whole section, I recommend group and individual practices and offer discussion starters for those using this as a workbook.

Chapter 1: Weeds That Choke Potential

They spout empty words
and make covenants they don't intend to keep.
So injustice springs up among them
   like poisonous weeds in a farmer's field.
Hosea 10:4

'Joe' loved football and had a rare talent. A young boy at our local primary school in Winson Green when Anji was a social worker there, he would score goals with ease on the makeshift asphalt school football grounds. However, he quickly got frustrated with other kids, and when he started to fight them, it got scary.

But Joe was not your average English schoolchild. He had been traumatised as a child soldier, escaped his war-torn land with his Mum, and was suddenly planted in this small local school. Knowing his passion for football, surely there was an opportunity here. We live within two miles of both Aston Villa FC and West Bromwich Albion FC home grounds, two of the oldest and most famous professional football clubs in England. Anji found a connection with Aston Villa FC, and once they saw his potential Joe was asked to try out for their academy. The barriers, however, were enormous. The academy, frustratingly, was many miles out of town and since his Mum didn't drive, Anji had to drive him there. Joe was one of the few players of colour and he had trouble understanding the coaches. His home life was chaotic, he lost track of time, and not remembering when training was, missed too many sessions. Despite his enormous potential, he was cut from the academy.

We had to find another way. Our neighbourhood has produced some of the most prodigious footballing talents in the past. We knew Joe was just the tip of the talent iceberg here. So, we began making connections with West Bromwich Albion (WBA). Steve Hopcroft, who grew up in Winson Green and was head of WBA Academy Recruitment at the time, came to visit us and hear our stories. He knew the talent was here too and had scouted Saido Berahino. Berahino was a small, eleven-year-old refugee kid from Burundi, who Steve saw playing with adults while driving past our local Black Patch Park. Berahino went on to not only be the top scorer for WBA, but also played for England. He even scored the winner for the 'Baggies' at Old Trafford against Manchester United!

When Steve heard of our experiences in Bangkok with football and Joe's story, he wondered if a new junior club could be started here:

> 'There aren't any football clubs here anymore and Black Patch Park is now a dumping ground full of old tyres and construction rubble. The changing rooms have been burnt down. I can find the local coaches and administrator for you, if you can help us access the players for a trial day. Let's see what happens, but could we start a new club together?'

We systematically approached every primary school in our neighbourhood. Our pitch was simple: can we present at their school assembly the opportunity to trial at WBA's Academy? Most quickly agreed. When the kids heard of the opportunity, they loved it and started to dream.

However, when trial day came, we didn't even know if anyone would come. With a handful of our local kids and neighbours who helped us get the word out we drove our van the two miles to WBA's Academy, but held our breath. As we got closer, we could see lots of Mums pushing buggies, trails of children behind them, skipping toward the Hawthornes. Where are they all going? By the time we arrived an hour early to help set up and meet the WBA scouts and coaches, it was mayhem. Over the next few days over 1,000 children showed up for our first free trials for what became 'Soho Albion FC.' I became the club's first chairman and WBA sponsored us so playing was free and accessible to all who had the talent and desire.

Though we started the first season at a park on the edge of our local community, the second season saw Black Patch Park begin to be recovered and renewed as our home ground. Soho Albion FC took off quickly with great local coaches, winning many junior league and cup titles, and eventually over twenty players from our club signed for the WBA academy.

In so many ways this is the archetypal pioneering approach.

1. Discover local talents, passions, and assets.
2. Connect them together.
3. Mobilise for new opportunities.

However, after a few seasons, we noticed a strange thing happening - none of our players, and few in the club itself, now lived in Winson Green. Parents and caregivers from further afield would consistently travel for miles in their cars and on public transport to help their kids have a shot at fulfilling their dreams. These families, in more stable housing outside the local community, were the ones with time and resources to dedicate and prioritise this opportunity. Despite huge talents and this amazing pathway into football, many of our local young people and their families just couldn't make it to training regularly enough or get to the matches outside of Winson Green.

It's tragic to me that Joe, with his passion, talent, and skill, didn't make it into a Soho Albion FC team, never mind WBA. It is too predictable that Joe, having to keep moving houses and schools, lost his way and is now in trouble with the law. Currently we understand he is in jail. Every system and support structure failed him. I know few will succeed like Berahino, but we know we haven't got this right yet. We're now exploring another model of football with local schools. What is pivotal to this story, though, is that how local talents access and embrace opportunities are key challenges to name early in a book like this. We are up against invisible powers that make simple solutions out of reach.

Failure needs to be named early here too. It is too common that dreams are choked to death before they've even been glimpsed. Like pernicious weeds that attach themselves to the most vulnerable shoots and strangle them before they can start to shoot up, there are forces working against our local communities. We have to name and identify them to help take their power away. This task of discernment, however, can quickly overwhelm us. Like Jesus' parable of the weeds among the wheat (Matt. 13:24–43) it's hard to know what is happening and what are the causes. The needs of urban places, where most of humanity now lives, especially seem to grow ever more complex. It's much easier to turn away and numb ourselves with something that makes us feel better than to dive into the depth of local suffering, poverty, and injustice. The curse of distraction, bugging us to turn our attention away from what matters most, is the most common of all modern pandemics.

Consider just one person you know personally who has been doing it tough lately. In your imagination try to see their face and look into their eyes. What do you imagine they are feeling right now? What are the worries and struggles racing through their mind? What's brought them to this place? Reflect on how they have so often been let down by family, or multiple systems, or services, or all of the above. Think about the impact that these failures have had on this one person's ability to respond in healthy ways.

Add to this our deeper understandings as people of faith and we see the difficult relationships that a person can have with broader cultures, class systems, races, genders, church, and spirituality. Even at a quick glance like this, the complexities can overwhelm us and create a deep sense of despair. If it took generations of poor policies, practices, and a lack of faith and imagination to get one person into a state like this, what can we do now to help them out?

How about whole neighbourhoods? An even darker cloud can intensify further if we consider the places where the most suffering people live. Take an aerial view of almost any urban place where the multitudes of the most let-down people have been herded together. These are more than just individuals gathered, they have developed into organic systems which experience the full force of unseen powers and principalities crashing like angry waves over whole population centres. It's no wonder that these places can be written off as wastelands.

Consider the three neighbourhoods where I have lived with my family, intentionally wanting to make a difference. Whether it was Klong Toey, an urban slum in Bangkok with 100,000 people packed into one square mile. Or a multi-racial neighbourhood in Melbourne with a majority of residents who fled violence and persecution as refugees. Or here in the UK where I live now in Winson Green, inner-city Birmingham, where ten years of austerity stripped bare any real safety net. For over thirty years now I have been intentionally embedded in tough urban places with my family, and I know that keeping the wolf of despair at bay is a constant challenge. I know the feeling that the odds seem stacked against change, no matter how hard we might try.

My colleague in Seedbeds, and community-building legend in East Ham, Dave Mann, loves to show a video clip to emerging community leaders of fleas in a jar. These fleas can naturally jump enormous distances out of the jar. The equivalent of whole skyscrapers if they were the size of humans. However, if the lid is put on the jar, they get used to that barrier. So much so that even if the lid is taken off again, they just won't jump out. They are limited to jumping to that now invisible level. Joe's story was like that in so many ways, held back by invisible barriers. So many of our local leaders experience this too. They may have huge potential but expect to fall short before they even try. Even if the raw talent is noticed, all too often there is a failure of follow-through by people and communities around to realise that potential. Few of us have the focus, tenacity or resources to chase them down long enough to catch them. Not least because we can unintentionally limit ourselves and others in a way that squeezes out the change that is possible before we even start.

As stories like Joe's become more common, feelings of despair can grow. A 2020 UK Gov poll reported that only 35% agreed that "in Britain today everyone has a fair chance to go as far as their talent and their hard work will take them." 44% agreed that "where you end up in society is largely determined by who your parents are."[19] The invisible weeds of class are choking opportunities and the dreams for change. When generationally considered, the numbers got worse: "Just 30% of 18–24-year-olds think that everyone has a fair chance to go as far as their talent and hard work will take them, in comparison to 48% of those age 65 and over."[20] This despair grew throughout the Covid pandemic. A year later a similar study found "56% of the UK adults think the coronavirus outbreak has increased inequality in Britain: 33% say by 'a lot' and 23% by 'a little'."[21] We can easily give up hope even before we've started out. It is easy to despair and write off whole population centres as wastelands.

The ancient Scriptures can help us understand why so much potential in people and places goes unfulfilled. One of the Bible's metaphors for places that are desolated and neglected is that they are taken over by weeds. This was sometimes literal, but was also a powerful metaphor. Lands of Israel's enemies, for example, in Zephaniah 2:9, are said to be: "a place of weeds and salt pits, a wasteland forever" (New International Version).[22] I can relate to this as it often feels like invisible weeds have choked the life and potential out of the people and have taken over the places I love, leaving them desolate.

The prophet Hosea contends that injustice 'springs up like weeds' when false promises are made. Local communities can only grow and flourish at the speed of trust, so distrust grows poisonous weeds to choke this life out.

> They spout empty words
>   and make covenants they don't intend to keep.
> So injustice springs up among them
>   like poisonous weeds in a farmer's field.
> (Hosea 10:4)

The poisonous weeds of injustice grow in an environment of distrust and suspicion. This environment makes even the most fertile grounds unfruitful. False promises, 'empty words,' are so common, even from well-meaning politicians, institutions, and churches. For example, a quick succession of new launches and programmes that are not followed through can soon create a toxic, untrusting atmosphere. This distrust is why local people can fail to believe opportunities are worth pursuing and why injustice and inequalities can quickly overwhelm whole communities. 'Nothing works around here.' 'We've heard this before.' 'Why should this be any different?'

Weeds of false hope can grow, even with good will and intentions. We know, for example, that a few years of funded community work will not reverse decades of systemic failure, yet short-term staffing contracts and projects by churches, governments, and charities are still the norm. Few prepare generational plans that can then be developed by the local communities themselves. This is not just distrusting of local communities, but short-term expectations plant further weeds that give false hope and choke out long term, local fruitfulness. Like water and sunlight, a quick sprinkling of even the good things of life over weeds can somehow provide nutrients that cause even greater desolation and destruction. Feeding the weeds can, in fact, help create wastelands.

However, these weeds are more than just the result of self-inflicted, distrusting environments. Weeds can also have a life of their own. An 'enemy' can plant these weeds. Jesus tells a parable about wheat and weeds where, "his enemy came and sowed weeds among the wheat and went away" (Matt. 13:24-25). There are vested interests in the systems that work for the few and not the many. At a basic level in a supply-and-demand-based economy, we know that keeping housing stock low pushes existing housing prices up. If high quality and affordable new houses flooded the market, existing homes would lose value, current homeowners would be furious, and the banks that loaned the mortgages would fall. Whole economies would collapse. Few governments would risk surviving this scenario and so the invisible barriers that stop secure housing in our neighbourhoods continue. Unseen forces, stealthy 'enemies,' benefit from unjust systems and they need more wastelands so that their harvests are worth more. An 'enemy' who 'goes away' after sowing weeds often gets away with it. They don't have to live with the weeds among the wheat as it's not their problem. Keeping wastelands as wastelands is a calculation made by societies, despite the harvests that are possible there.

I am not unaware of these complex, overwhelming forces of destruction and the fact that rooting out these weeds is far more difficult than we can imagine. Yet I've seen the wheat among the weeds, and I still believe that a *No Wastelands* agenda is possible for every local community. Indeed, as a person of faith I believe it's God's cry. In Jeremiah, for example, we hear:

> Many shepherds will ruin my vineyard and trample down my field; they will turn my pleasant field into a desolate wasteland. It will be made a wasteland, parched and desolate before me; the whole land will be laid waste because there is no one who cares. (Jer. 12:10-11, [NIV])

Will we care with God about what is happening to our places? I hope we can. For me, I know I can't walk away. This is too personal for me now. There are far too many 'Joes' in my life. I have found too that those of us who don't flee but learn to strategically embrace the pain have some things in common. It's not our ideology, personalities, organisations, theologies, politics, or even temperament. Diverse people have stayed to face the weeds and find the wheat, from every theological and political stripe. What are the common factors I see? When confronted by the plight of people we know personally and the places we live in together, we feel like there is a shared pain and responsibility that their problem is also our problem. When our ideal bubble bursts, when we experience our ordeal, we're often only left with a sense of call that beckons us deeper into finding that new deal. There is a gift of stubbornness that says we've come too far to turn back now. Where would we go now anyway?

This theme of responsibility is in so many ways the real essence of leadership. My favourite quote from Dietrich Bonhoeffer, the German theologian and Nazi resister, says simply:

> We have learnt, rather too late, that action comes, not from thought, but from a readiness for responsibility.[23]

Where does this sense of responsibility come from? It is certainly personal and communal, but it's often experienced as a series of miraculous interventions and signs that have been noticed and nurtured. I believe these flickers come from God's heartbeat, breaking through to us if we pay attention. I hope this book fans into flame these sparks of responsibility and change that God has given and is within you. Seeing the weeds without flinching, growing a willingness to learn what is possible for the wheat beyond good intentions, and making a lasting difference are all worth persisting with. May the arts and practices of place-based change-making outlined here help you through the many traps that lie in waiting, break the many chains of futility holding you back, and open you up to more hopeful and compassionate living. You'll notice these themes echoing throughout this book. This is no small thing.

Personal Reflections

1. Who are the people and places you know and love that have not fulfilled their potential yet?

2. Why can just 'creating opportunities' not be enough to see long-term change?

3. What 'poisonous weeds' helped thwart those you love from fulfilling their potential?

Chapter 2: Invasive Weeds That Choke The Harvest

The kingdom of heaven may be compared to a man who sowed good seed in his field, but while his men were sleeping, his enemy came and sowed weeds among the wheat and went away.
Matthew 13:24-25

What are the weeds that choke the life out of local dreams? How are weeds different from wheat in Jesus' parable? Weeds can come from the outside of communities as well as those from within, but what they have in common is that they thwart harvests. They are not fruitful and can cause harm. For example, Giant Hogweed is one of the most dangerous weeds here in the UK. It can grow out of control, not only overshadowing native plants or crops, but endangering the health of wild animals and people. It doesn't mess about!

> It produces a phototoxic sap which causes injury upon contact with results including burns, blisters, scarring and leaving disfiguring marks upon a person's body, hands and face, as well as affecting animals and pets.[24]

As these invasive weeds grow, so do the destructive results. This is true for our local harvest fields too. If we can identify them, they lose their power to run amok through our local communities. One of the characteristics of invasive weeds is how fast they can take over places. For example, Milk Thistle:

> These highly competitive and persistent plants rapidly invade abandoned fields, roadsides, and disturbed sites. One of these plants can produce about 6,000 seeds that can remain viable for nine years. You can imagine the difficult task of trying to control this weed![25]

My time in the UK has especially focused my attention on three dangerous, invasive weeds that leave 'disfiguring marks' and 'take over' local communities like Winson Green. These three weeds are forms of discrimination and prejudice. As a straight, white male, I have been slow to see the extent of the destruction these weeds cause or recognise the extent to which I benefit from them. I have needed help to see things more clearly and resist being the 'enemy' who keeps sowing these weeds and restricting the potential of my neighbours. Thanks to some brilliant friends taking time with me I have learnt to see these three weeds in new ways. I sometimes use a plural form of each word as I discuss these three insidious weeds. I hope this expresses how they appear in many ways. And they grow. What might be 'unconscious bias' at one end of the spectrum can grow into an organised supremacy movement at the other. Sometimes prejudices join forces to hold communities further back. Given our starting point – that all people and places can flourish – these three forms of discrimination are especially destructive in thwarting potential. If wastelands are to grow into seedbeds of shalom, we can't ignore the weeds of class, race, and gender discrimination.

Classism

One of Jesus' parables named 'thorns' as "the worries of this life, the deceitfulness of wealth and the desires for other things come in and choke the word, making it unfruitful" (Mark 4:19 [NIV]). We will consider this parable more closely in a later chapter on soils, but here we simply note that the weeds of classism are attached to status, envy, and the control of the elite. People and places are valued according to where they sit in a social and economic hierarchy. It's a pyramid-shaped ordering of society, where power flows up to the apex. It is exactly the warning that Samuel gave the Hebrew people who wanted a king like other nations:

> "This is how a king will reign over you," Samuel said. "The king will draft your sons and assign them to his chariots and his charioteers, making them run before his chariots. Some will be generals and captains in his army, some will be forced to plow in his fields and harvest his crops, and some will make his weapons and chariot equipment. The king will take your daughters from you and force them to cook and bake and make perfumes for him. He will take away the best of your fields and vineyards and olive groves and give them to his own officials. He will take a tenth of your grain and your grape harvest and distribute it among his officers and attendants. He will take your male and female slaves and demand the finest of your cattle and donkeys for his own use. He will demand a tenth of your flocks, and you will be his slaves. When that day comes, you will beg for relief from this king you are demanding, but then the Lord will not help you. (1 Sam. 8:11-18)

In a Judeo-Christian view of creation, all people and places are lovingly made by God. The diversity in the natural world is divinely declared to be 'good.' All people are equally 'made in the image of God' (Gen.1 & 2) and their addition to the natural world makes it 'very good.' However, in the biblical story, the intended harmonious relationships between God, people, and places are broken and disconnected. Exploitation grows between people and places, and this is seen as a tragic departure from God's plan. Systems emerge that expedite exploitation from one class to another, and make it persistent and generational, like the appointment of kings and other elites; this is especially warned against. The exploitation of whole groups of people or places is an anathema, and laws are often given by God to protect the most vulnerable and to reset society so all can start again. The Jubilee laws (Lev. 25), some of the most famous, ensure no place or person is left behind. It's no accident that Jesus, the promised 'Prince of Shalom,' alludes to these laws in his inaugural sermon in Nazareth (Luke 4:18-19).

Australians like to think of ourselves as egalitarian, 'fair go for everyone,' kind of people. We reckon that family, place, background, accent, or job shouldn't impact your value as a person or your life opportunities. It's certainly morally and legally wrong for us to discriminate against a person on the basis of their class. I found out the hard way that most of the world doesn't think or act like this. Being a working-class Australian with a PhD and a portfolio of leadership responsibilities who has chosen downward mobility can seriously mess with classist people's minds. I'm their worst nightmare. They don't know where to place me in the class or caste pyramid. This was true in Thailand and here in the UK! Am I above or below them? Am I a toff or a convict? It doesn't matter if I am more knowledgeable about a topic I have spent decades studying, for some here in the UK I sound like a 'Chav' or a 'Lout from the colonies' and it's just too humiliating to be outshone by the likes of me. They are not quite sure, however, where my 'place' is that I must be 'put!' Cheap 'convict' jokes have been the most common way to dismiss me. Here, more than once I've been pulled aside and quietly told I need to learn deference with my superiors. I must admit, I know I need to do this sometimes to get things done, but I'm not very good at it. When class prejudice happens, my first instinct is to smirk. That some think they are 'superior' because of a title, status or class position, and not the quality of their ideas, often makes me giggle out loud. That doesn't help us move forward and looks like I'm taking the piss further. Even after 20 years living outside of Australia there is still a *larrikin* in me that can't stomach preposterousness and wants to send it up.

In reality, few Australians are as egalitarian as we think we are. We've learnt how to quickly determine where others sit in importance and value to us. We take short cuts to identify what, or who, we should value. Pre-occupations with brands, celebratory status, and pay scales have undermined our supposed egalitarian ideals. We may not have royal families, but we have A-listers and status symbols in abundance.

It can be alluring too, to feel superior. In the past, Aussie comedy traditionally made fun of the pomposity of elites. Somewhere, somehow, things changed. So much new comedy is different – making fun of vulnerable people so the comedian looks good, and the audience feels superior. This doesn't seem like clever satire to me as much as bullying.

2: Invasive Weeds That Choke The Harvest

Reality television follows the same playbook – making fun of vulnerable people.

Still, the UK's ever-present class system was one of the great shocks to me entering life in the UK. I thought that it was historical, that no one today really believes a small group of people is superior because of their family backgrounds and bloodlines. Surely no one still truly believes a power elite are born to rule the majority? Recent royal events, however, have been taken very seriously here, with lavish displays. The Queen's Jubilee celebrations and funeral, followed by the coronation of King Charles III, have all been nationally and generationally significant milestones, although these events, and what they represent, are not without internal critique.

Sally and Dave Mann helped me understand classism in the UK in profound, new ways. From their many generations of family life and ministries in one East London neighbourhood, as well as their connections around the world, they see, understand and experience classism like few I know. Sally also teaches sociology at Greenwich University and knows the technical side of class oppression and exploitation. Sally explains that, like all discrimination, it is rarely overt or justified out loud; it's more about silent, unexplored assumptions. Most just think class hierarchies are the way things have to be for continuity and stability. However, it is no secret where the UK's wealth and power can be found. A relatively small number of families never let go of generations of unearned privileges, entitlements, and vested interests. Today's systems continue to ensure these remain for future generations of elites too. It doesn't seem to matter that many of these privileges come from tarnished, ill-gotten gains from slavery, colonisation, or brutal oppression.

How governance works here reveals the deep classist assumptions in the UK. The Royal family and the House of Lords, for example, still have roles based purely on hereditary succession and connections. The royal pomp and ceremony can be moving, but Charles didn't merit his role as Head of State and Commonwealth. It was his family privileges, entitlements and royal class that assumed he should have those roles. Seats in the House of Lords are also set aside to certain hereditary landowners, none of whom are elected. Families that send their children to private schools like Eton or universities like Oxford and Cambridge expect class privileges too. The vast majority of UK Prime Ministers have come from this very narrow gate of educational institutions. Although other Western countries have this disease to an extent, they tend to have more diversity among candidates for powerful roles, which is just not the case here. Class matters too much because too much is at stake for elites and their offspring.

The church ties itself up with classism too, hitching its wagon to elite families. The Church of England even has seats set aside for their Bishops in the House of Lords. Only two countries in the world set aside parliamentary seats for clergy: Iran and the UK. It's no accident that most mainline denominations have their most influential Ministry training centres in Oxford and Cambridge. Networks, prestige, and connections matter for those who want to maintain a place in elite circles. Charity and not-for-profits are not immune either since the largest grants come from establishment philanthropic trusts. Accessing trust funds via old school ties is still the way to go.

Sally's views are hard to negate. Few here ask where this narrow access to incredible wealth and power comes from. The centuries of stripping and collecting the assets from other classes, and even whole continents, is rarely considered. Elites gain and keep power because of their exclusivity and ability to pass privilege to the next generation. Few want to think deeply about it, even if this disparity of wealth destabilises societies like few other factors.

Inequality and instability increase where small elites control resources. This is true at global as well as local levels. The World Economic Forum, for example, makes clear:

- Global inequality has worsened, with the richest 1% grabbing nearly two-thirds of the $42 trillion of wealth newly created since 2020.
- Inequality is destroying society and it is not inevitable; it is a choice that reveals us as lacking in both empathy and imagination. [26]

Our leaders need to imagine new economic processes and structures to create a fairer, more equal world, and to save our planet.

How does classism act like a weed, strangling life in our local communities? Certainly, part of the challenge is to unravel how the lack of access to resources, power, and decision-making is at work. Think for a moment how natural wastelands occur as rivers are diverted away from their original pathways. In Asia, the fight for access to water is one of the great battles for survival. Precious water for drinking and irrigation is diverted from one nation and stored far away to be used for another's energy supply. This is the result of the choices of the powerful over the needs of the weak. There may be enough resources for all to flourish, but not when they are diverted, siphoned, and stored in bigger and more elaborate dams and reservoirs in the hands of a few. Greed is never satisfied and impacts what is possible in local life globally. At a local level, barren 'ghettos' and 'postcode lotteries' became accepted, and even needed, to perpetuate a system which works to favour the elite. Classisms take us a long way away from God's purposes of shalom, of harmony between God, people and places. There will be no class system in eternity.

Classism also impacts where people decide to live. Why go, or remain, in places and positions not valued by broader society, where there are limited opportunities for us and our children? Anji and I were warned by English Christian friends that moving to Winson Green was a mistake for our son Aiden. Inadequate schools and healthcare, never mind gangs and violence, would stunt his growth and opportunities. 'Why not shop around for an outstanding state school and move near there?' It felt like they were really saying, 'Did we really love our son or not?' This kind of classism becomes a self-fulling prophecy for local communities. If a place is only made up of families who can't live elsewhere, the impact on schools, health care, and opportunities is inevitable. Classist assumptions perpetuate wastelands.

As it happens, our son Aiden has benefitted from growing up and fighting for justice as part of local communities in Klong Toey and Winson Green. We were warned about both places and criticised by church-going folk for our choices to live there. Aiden was born in

Klong Toey and moved to Winson Green as an eleven-year-old. He is unconventional in lots of ways but living in these communities made him so much better prepared for life than if we had tried to cocoon him in a nice suburb and relate only to people who liked him and were like him. The places he was raised means that he sees life differently. He found his passion in the Change Makers programme and left Winson Green for East London to pursue his dream as a filmmaker, where he also runs a not-for-profit 'East London Community Films' helping diverse young people access the film industry. His connections with Change Makers alumni helped him quickly join another local community. He currently lives with fellow alumni Helen and Donald Fernandez in Silvertown. He's only 19 at the time of writing but has the world at his feet because of where he lives and has lived. As you shall see later in this book, as residents in Winson Green we were also able to help influence the quality of local schooling, healthcare, and opportunities that other residents now enjoy in ways not possible without such intentional relocation. Proximity matters. Where we choose to live is one of the biggest decisions we make and one that reveals our relationship to class. To break the cycle of wastelands requires an intentional resistance to classisms; a change that many families, even Christian ones, are not prepared to make.

Perhaps a more insidious weed is the elite group practices that are mimicked in our neighbourhoods, even the poorest ones. Even crumbs falling from the table can be fought over. Local institutions, including schools, churches, and community centres, close their doors to keep 'the hordes' at bay, protecting their own privilege. Perhaps this weed, the fear of people from a 'lower class' and exclusion of those who most need help, seems like a survival tactic. But in the end it slowly overgrows and overtakes the best in our community life. At a practical level, if you call police in an elite neighbourhood, they will be there in minutes. Do the same in a poor neighbourhood like ours and we feel lucky if police show up at all. 'Divide and conquer' is still the best way for power elites to keep ruling and so there is no urgency for systems, laws, or policies to protect our local people from this dynamic.

Temptations for young people to leave local communities and to seek their fortunes by trying to join elite classes is understandable. If this is where the resources are and you can't beat them, why not join them! As we shall see, aspirations, dreams, and hope are important. Asset-stripping the best individual talents from local communities, a kind of brain drain, keeps poor communities poor. The long weeds of classisms just keep being fed and growing. Sure, some individuals can escape and win for a time, but these are the exceptions to the rule. The game is rigged. Credible visions to both fulfill potential and be able to remain local, or return to a poor neighbourhood, is one of the great challenges of community building.

Classisms can strip local talent, as well as withhold the flow of resources, destabilising and weakening community life. Power elites absorb useful talents and isolate the ones deemed in excess to requirements. These weeds of classisms strangle the life out of communities, even those with the best potential. This weed of discrimination and prejudice must be resisted at all costs if wastelands are to become seedbeds of shalom.

Racism

The weeds of racism choke multitudes of local communities around the world.

Discrimination against people of colour has been assumed for millennia in Western countries, and it has spread. White privilege and supremacy, coupled with violence and militarism, compound class structures and create some of the most traumatic living conditions the world has ever seen. Inner city ghettoes, urban slums, and squatter neighbourhoods multiply around the world today. Only a tiny fraction of these areas are majority white. This continues to happen to such a degree that poverty and injustice today can be said to have a common pigmentation. A recent UN report focused on:

> ...the inextricable link between racism and poverty, stressing that the continued socio-economic vulnerability of minorities is frequently the result of historical legacies, such as the impact of slavery and colonization, and state-sponsored discrimination. These historical imbalances continue to profoundly affect discriminated groups, causing successive generations to inherit the disadvantages of their predecessors.[27]

Racisms completely undermine the equal value of all people, made in the image of God. As a white Australian, I know we have failed to resist this weed. Australians often think of our nation's founding vision as a kind of working-class paradise, but from the beginning this never included black people. Certainly not our First Nations, the oldest continuous living cultures on the planet, whose sacred lands were brutally taken without recognised treaties. Systemic attempts at genocide, both culturally and physically, including 'stolen generations' policies to 'breed the blackness out' of indigenous people, ultimately failed. However, participation as citizens and inclusion in the census was only confirmed in the 1962 referendum. Even so, voting rights were inconsistent. In some Australian states and territories Indigenous Australians could vote from early days, but many were denied until recent times. It was not until 1984 that Aboriginal and Torres Strait Islander people gained full equality with other electors under the Commonwealth Electoral Amendment Act 1983.[28] While we are now one of the most culturally diverse nations, the White Australia Policy, where people of colour were not allowed to immigrate, was only repealed in 1978. For most of our colonial history it's literally been illegal to migrate to Australia if you're not white. Even today, those who seek asylum from persecution and flee to Australia are locked up, taken to remote islands, and treated as illegal until they can prove otherwise, despite our nation's internationally signed refugee obligations. The fact that these are invariably people of colour is a part of this tradition and consciousness. This is not just history. Living memories and current experiences traumatise the present and future.

I have needed help to understand racism's treachery and how deep the roots of these weeds go. Some of the most formative gifts in my life have been connections with indigenous Christian leaders. In Australia the likes of Uncle Ray Minniecon, Aunty Jean Phillips, and Uncle Billy Williams patiently took me on a journey where something like scales fell from my eyes. In New Zealand the likes of Monty and Linda Ohia and the Te Ho Ora movement inspired me to see what was so special in indigenous people's cultures, including education, language, and politics. I've seen how colonisation's racisms can be named, shamed, and resisted. This is a great hope for me.

2: Invasive Weeds That Choke The Harvest

In the UK, I have been profoundly influenced by African-Caribbean leaders who have explained the traumatic legacies from slavery and colonisation. Bishop Mike Royal has been an especially important influence on me. He is a proud English Jamaican with Ghanaian heritage who loves his West Indies cricket. Despite his hectic schedule with different enterprises, churches, and speaking commitments, he helped us start Newbigin Community Trust and re-start Lodge Road URC and The Greenhouse at Barnes Close, providing invaluable wisdom in governance roles. We also designed and co-lead two Masters units in Social Entrepreneurship with Nazarene Theological College, accredited by the University of Manchester. Mike now leads Churches Together England.

Mike lived not far from me in Handsworth and so we loved meeting up together for a drink at The Black Eagle pub, our 'proper local.' Here, Mike taught me about the experiences of the Windrush Generation, post-War migrants from the Caribbean, who have endured decades of racist practices in the UK. This generation gets their name from one of the first boats, the HMT Empire Windrush, which docked in Tilbury, Essex in 1948. It brought 492 passengers from a number of Caribbean islands including Jamaica and Trinidad and Tobago, to help fill post-War labour shortages. But in 2018 it emerged that the British Government had not properly recorded the details of the people who had been granted permission to stay in the UK, and many were wrongly deported.[29] Mike's outrage was palpable. He would quickly become animated, patiently trying to catch me up on the ongoing legacy of racism at the heart of the British Empire.

> 'The Brits needed to rebuild the cities here after the war. The cities were in rubble after the Blitz here in Birmingham. The call went out to the Commonwealth and so many from the Caribbean answered the call. We call them the Windrush Generation because some came on the ship HMT Empire Windrush, but this ship became a symbol of all who came. Many had been from slave families taken from Africa and wanted a new life. We weren't met with gratefulness, but fear. Even the churches wouldn't let us join in with worship services here, so we had to start our own. Now, when some of

these old folks go back to the Caribbean for a holiday, the UK government won't let them back in because they don't have the right paperwork! Outrageous!'

In the summer of 2020, George Floyd, an unarmed black man, was murdered by police officers in Minneapolis who knelt on his neck and choked the life out of him. Mike and Viv Royal hit the streets of Birmingham to protest, and Anji and I joined them in the city centre. The Black Lives Matter movement took off around the world. Given the time of pandemic lockdowns, it was amazing to see so many people out and standing together in Birmingham's city centre. Was this a turning point in the fight against racisms?

I also began to connect and share life with more neighbours from Caribbean and African backgrounds. I met Ash Lewis through Soho Albion FC and, where the majority of parents and children were from Black heritage. During football training, we would talk for hours about their struggle and life experiences. Ash went on to work with us at Seedbeds and then became elected as a local councillor. He loved Black History. I especially loved that we had so much positive UK Black History to connect with in Winson Green! I learnt about 'Handsworth Revolution,' the debut album by local reggae band Steel Pulse, and how they, with Bob Marley, introduced reggae and Black protest music to the world. We even had famous Black activist Malcolm X visit nearby Smethwick in 1965. We screened a documentary of his visit at our church, made by one of our friends, and packed the venue out. We have been a neighbourhood hotbed, ready for change, for a long time!

What disturbed me most, was the violence so many Black neighbours had endured. Handsworth and Winson Green have experienced race riots on more than one occasion. Most of those I spoke with had personal or family experiences of police brutality, which is tragic on so many levels. I also learnt that two local gangs had fought each other here, the violence escalating with guns and knives. I kept hearing about the damage 'Babylon' was inflicting on our local Black community. At first, I thought this must have been an especially vicious gang or organised crime syndicate. They seemed to have their paws in everything, everywhere! Talking with Mike Royal and Ash Lewis in the Black Eagle pub put me straight. Babylon was more than particular individuals. It was a power that was interpreted from ancient biblical times. There was a literal city called Babylon whose ruler Nebuchadnezzar captured Jerusalem and took many of the Hebrew leaders captive (Jer. 52:10–11). The exiled Hebrew leaders longed for Zion again (Ps. 19, 137). In New Testament times, Christians appropriated the imagery of Babylon and held on to the promise of its fall (Revelation 14:8). And now, in my city of Birmingham, West Indian reggae bands like The Melogians sang these Psalms as their own experience. They used 'Babylon' to name invisible powers of exile and colonial oppression in their own experiences. Claiming this narrative as their own, they knew one day the oppressor would fall (Jer. 51:37). 'Babylon' then became shorthand for a kind of a 'principality and power' that oppressed Black people today, but would one day also fall.

Mike convinced me to watch *Babylon on Fire*, a documentary about the rise of West Indies cricket in the 1970s and 80s. One image stands out to me. On a hot day at the Melbourne Cricket Ground in 1975, an angry, red-faced crowd – more like a mob – spat racist abuse at the Windies team while aggressive fast bowlers Dennis Lillee and Jeff Thomson dismantled their batters and crushed their spirits. Australia won the series 5-1, but it felt like I just witnessed a lynching in my hometown. Remarkably, these moments of 'ordeal' on the MCG also birthed a resistance movement in West Indies cricket in a 'new deal.' Led by Clive Lloyd, the West Indies found their own set of brutally fast bowlers who, with brilliant batting, dominated world cricket for the next two decades. Interviews with cricket players and Black activists showed how Babylon was set on fire through this team as much as their cricket matches. Australia's dark racist underbelly had been revealed. Not long after, with the fall of the White Australia policy, Melbourne would become a thriving multi-cultural city.

Sexism and Gender Discrimination
To limit and discriminate against people because of sex, gender or sexual orientation is another destructive weed that our local communities can't afford to let grow. Like classisms and racisms, this set of discriminations have a life of their own and leave few communities untouched. I

include not just the discriminations of misogyny and sexism, but also homophobia and transphobia. Like the other weeds, these ones can best be detected by the absence of certain groups of people in decision-making roles. Only a minority of people are straight and male, yet we dominate most decision-making bodies around the world. Our local communities need everyone's gifts to flourish, including women and all LGBTQ+ people. When we disqualify some people, consciously or unconsciously, on the basis of sex, gender, or sexual orientation, we damage our local ecosystems and do great harm to those who are excluded.

Invisible, old, white, male power networks so often influence the fate of local communities. This is because politics, resourcing, and priorities are mostly set by old white men. Even where they are in a numerical minority, they exert majority influence within local communities. I am learning to question this; to ask, for example, whose decision about finances is this? Nearly always I am directed to a distant committee made up exclusively of the male, frail, and pale. Despite direct requests, Anji and I have rarely been able to address these committees directly. If we can get our community's requests on the agenda, it is often only when an older, white man offers to represent us and advocate on our behalf. We rarely get a positive outcome. There is a community organising saying I am reminded of: 'If you're not at the table, you're probably on the menu.'

This is as true in the church as elsewhere. One of the most important and articulate voices in the UK church for justice in urban estates, Bishop Philip North, will not ordain women, or even receive communion from them. That is outrageous to me! It's women in so many of these communities that keep life going, against all odds. The least we can do is recognise their leadership, share life with them, and not insult them by excluding them publicly.

Again, I have been grateful for those with lived experience of these discriminations to help me see things more clearly. Some of these have been young people who have come to work alongside us, despite being previously excluded from the church because of their gender or sexual identity. I have learnt that while so many churches say 'everyone is welcome here,' they then do a bait-and-switch and point out that, in reality, LGBTQ+ folk are not fully welcome as fully themselves. Over the years we have got to know a number of young, gay Christians this has happened to. They threw themselves into joining a church, taking part in a small group and giving all they had. However, when their sexual identity was discovered, opportunities for them to share their gifts and leadership were suddenly closed down. In every other area of their lives they were leading their fields but were devastated and hurt when told that God doesn't want them to serve as they are in the church. The rate of deaths by suicide among LGBTQ+ people with faith is climbing. Would it be healthier if these churches had more honest signs that said something like, 'Some are welcome here, but not all'?

I have been on a journey to be a better ally and work against homophobia since my move to the UK. The huge cost of marginalisation on LGBTQ+ people just couldn't be ignored. Take this research, for example, that shows the vulnerabilities adolescents face:

> Overall, 25% of LGBTQ youth in our sample reported experiencing unstable housing at some point in their life. LGBTQ youth who experienced housing instability reported considering suicide at twice the rate and attempted suicide at more than three times the rate of LGBTQ youth who had not.[30]

We met and offered housing with so many young people like this. Rejection by families is common. Self-loathing, trauma, and shame seems such a common part of so many 'coming out' experiences. The church, however, is often part of the problem. When I attended a large church planters conference with a majority African denomination in London, for example, one of the participants called for the stoning to death of gay people 'because that was what the bible clearly said.' The crowd cheered and as one of the guests on stage tried to calm them down with explanations, the denial, fear, and threats of violence was palpable. What struck me most in that moment was that if this was an average crowd of 500 adults then perhaps as many as 50 people would have had their sexual identity personally targeted. How would they have felt in that atmosphere? A crowd of people they respect, and who represent God, saying God wanted them executed? My mind raced to church youth conferences I had attended over the decades that were many times that size, where homophobia was preached from the pulpit. I thought of the thousands, if not tens of thousands, who were shamed and traumatised in similar ways. I know life for sexual minorities across the world can be far scarier than it is in Australia, the UK, or Thailand, but the church is often at the forefront of this. That any LGBTQ+ people want to even *talk* with a Minister like me is an act of grace on their part.

LGBTQ+ people don't need my blessing, nor have I ever been asked for my opinion, but this kind of experience was so common that I needed to reconsider where I stood. Neutrality was not helpful or even possible anymore. I think I understood very early on in my life that people can be born with different gender and sexual orientations. In Thailand this was so common and celebrated that we just got used to a spectrum of gender. However, I had assumed the bible prohibited these diverse sexual orientations being actioned, other than between a male and female in a marriage like mine. I had heard it often said that gay people should stay single and celibate, for example. When I began to actually look at those verses, and there are only six of them among 23,145 verses in the bible, I was shocked that the interpretation I had heard did so little to consider their context. Those wanting to 'hold on to traditional readings' were also being very selective in the passages they wanted to keep at face value. What about Leviticus 20:13 which seems to call for stoning?

Here is the full list of the six so-called 'clobber passages':

1. Sodom & Gomorrah   Genesis 19:1-38
2. Levitical Laws   Leviticus 18:22; 20:13
3. Pederasty in Corinth   1 Corinthians 6:9-11
4. Pederasty in Ephesus   1 Timothy 1:9-10
5. Strange Flesh   Jude 6-7
6. Cult Prostitution   Romans 1:25-27

The question for me on these texts was not whether to take the bible seriously or not, but how to do this on this issue. For example, a man once had a tattoo of Leviticus 20:13 etched into his arm but failed to recognise the prohibition of tattoos in Leviticus 19:28. This shows how bizarre 'biblically based' homophobia can get! There are ethical issues

2: Invasive Weeds That Choke The Harvest

here – how people discern what is right or wrong is for them to do – but how we can have integrity in interpreting the bible and not let our 21st century 'culture wars' dictate our interpretations is crucial.

Two important principles quickly came to mind when it came to interpreting and translating these particular biblical passages for today. The first is what we call 'dynamic equivalence.' What is the original intention of these texts in context and what can they mean for us today? Our modern English word 'homosexual,' for example, is less than 150 years old and is not what would have been originally used here in Hebrew or Greek thousands of years ago. What was being prohibited then? Were these verses actually prohibitive of loving, consensual, committed couples in any modern sense?

The second principle, as a Christian, is that there are many genres of bible verses and some of them are superseded or fulfilled by Jesus. We don't interpret poetry for example in the way we interpret purity laws. We believe Jesus is the best revelation of what God is like and for doing God's will. Jesus is also alive today and so Christians read the bible for action from the perspective of Jesus and with the guidance of the Holy Spirit. This is the so-called 'What Would Jesus Do?' ethic, but also requires us to discern 'What Is Jesus Doing?' What is Jesus calling us to do in these passages of Scripture today?

It was also important not to do biblical reflection like this in isolation. I found safe and prayerful conversations with others. We helped Red Letter Christians UK get started and one of my abiding memories of Tony Campolo on this tour in 2019 was him patiently going through those six verses in our Newbigin House backyard after our seminar day with a crowd of people. A brave documentary called *Fish out of Water* explored these six verses too from diverse theological stand points.[31] In the documentary, a young woman was sincerely searching: can she be gay, in a committed relationship and be a Christian? When she hears from all the sides, she concludes that these six verses are not talking about her: she can be accepted by God for who she is and share that love in marriage. It's not the purpose of this book to go through these verses here; others are far more articulate than me, but that is where I have landed too.[32] First, these verses were not talking about prohibiting any modern understanding of same sex marriage, as the 'dynamic equivalency' is more like prohibiting rape and sexual abuse. Second, Jesus would not discriminate against LGBTQ+ people, in fact he came that all may have life "a rich and satisfying life" (John 10:10) and calls me to seek the same.

I am conscious that for many Christians, even those reading a book like this, these scriptural interpretations might mean they write me off, and this book. If, in their minds, I can't interpret these verses correctly, how can I be a real Christian? That has already happened to me here in the UK and has impacted our connections and work with some significant Christians, organisations, and churches. I do wonder why, however, that it is these six verses needing to be interpreted in a certain way that have become the touchstone of orthodoxy? What is it about sex and gender that makes this the test to include or exclude people, even straight people like me who simply want to be an ally? Jesus did not even raise these relationships in all his known teaching and yet many Christians today insist this is the hill worth dying on. It's worth noting that previous generations of Christians also felt that 'the Bible was clear' about supporting slavery, prohibiting divorce, and that leadership is male only, but very few Christians would support excluding people based on those interpretations now. Interpretations of biblical texts can and should change over time, especially in the light of the primacy of God's love for all. One of the reasons I identify as a Red Letter Christian is because I believe we must not weaponise the Bible, but take it seriously, reading it from the perspective of Jesus as the highest revelation. Some Bibles illuminate the words of Jesus in red to highlight that we don't have a 'flat-earth bible' and seek to follow Jesus above all. Sally Mann, who currently leads Red Letter Christians UK, put it this way:

> When I focus on the words and life of Jesus, my Christian faith asks me to confront whether I am willing to attempt to live by the teachings of Jesus, not just whether I say I believe certain doctrines and can make good arguments to defend them.[33]

Those who identify as Red Letter Christians hold a variety of interpretations about these six verses and same-sex marriage, for example,

2: Invasive Weeds That Choke The Harvest

but we agree that all people need to have a safe place to grow, free from prejudice. I believe the tide has turned here too.

Anji was way ahead of me on this. I am afraid I was much slower and too calculating in my public support. In a strange way, Anji and I ended up being safe people to talk to about these concerns privately. We still rarely raise our views in public forums as we'd rather support LGBTQ+ folks speaking for themselves, but privately, Christian people will come to us, confused and wanting some direction. The vitriol towards LGBTQ+ people they either were, knew or loved, just didn't seem right and their understanding of the Bible just didn't make sense anymore. Many were walking away from the faith because of it. Those younger people reading here and perhaps those outside the church may not get the fuss, nastiness, or what is at stake here. Any discrimination or prejudice toward themselves or their LGBTQ+ friends just seems wrong to them. It's more complex for Christian leaders, many of whom fear losing their jobs, livelihoods, and/or donors if they change their mind on this issue and embrace a more inclusive theology. Of course, this is nothing compared to the pain inflicted on those who are LGBTQ+. But, as some Christian ministers consider this issue, they have to take into account the potential loss of a calling they love if they publicly change their stance. Few actively want to step into that without some reassurance. I draw on my particular Christian denomination to try and take the air out of the high stakes and emotions here. Churches of Christ has an ethos: "In essentials unity, non-essentials liberty, and in all things charity." I think charity and compassion is a baseline to hold on to here. But let's not forget the hurt being done as we take our time on this. Churches are losing too many people to discrimination and prejudice; local communities are missing out on gifts, and most importantly, the wellbeing and lives of precious people are being put at stake. Helping find compassion for all, benefits all. After all, the bottom line is that 'God is love.'

I am blessed to belong to a church movement that offers same-sex marriage. The United Reformed Church has had its battles on this, but as URC Ministers, Anji and I could officiate at our friends Laura and Rachel's wedding. We first met when they were students at Springdale College, Birmingham and when Laura and Rach got together, they reached out to Anji and I for support and guidance. To stand with this Christian couple on their wedding day in June 2023, leading a Christian service, was one of the most beautiful and grace-filled moments of my life. There was not a dry eye in the outdoor chapel. It felt like even God cried with joy that day. Potential that could have been lost to faith was being released into a new life together. The weeds of prejudice and fear don't have to win.

Gender-based discrimination and prejudice takes many forms and chokes the life out of too many in our local communities. Misogyny, the male equivalent of white supremacy, especially destroys the potential of local communities like few other weeds. One report said that gender-based violence is a "global pandemic" and that:

> Global statistics on violence against women show that, on average, 35% of women have experienced either physical and/or sexual violence by someone who is an intimate partner or sexual violence by someone who is not a partner. Furthermore, as many as 38% of all murders of women are committed by male intimate partners (WHO, 2013, p.2). And this is just the tip of the iceberg. This figure does not even account for all the other forms of violence against women such as sexual harassment and abuse against girls under the age of 15, the damage to children and extended families, and the anguish and psychological trauma that can last for years.[34]

The cycle of violent male abuse and then absence is such a common story, undermining the growth of so many in our neighbourhoods. It undermines community building too. One of the main reasons our housing advocacy work is so troubling is that when women and children flee domestic violence there are few houses for them. More than 4,000 families are stuck living in temporary accommodation in Birmingham.[35] 'Bed and breakfasts' and hotel rooms host thousands of women and children in Birmingham, all waiting for permanent accommodation. This undermines any sense of community and connection that can be built to help restore their lives.

2: Invasive Weeds That Choke The Harvest

Why does this violence happen so often to women and children in our neighbourhoods? Oscar Lewis, as early as 1966, noted that a "Culture of Poverty" emerges within places facing injustice and that one of many common characteristics to emerge was that:

> There is widespread belief in male superiority and among the men a strong preoccupation with machismo, their masculinity.[36]

This does not excuse the violence, but it can only be fully understood when we understand how this kind of violent sexism intersects with classisms and racisms. If you feel like your manhood has been crushed, then finding a way to prove masculinity becomes more tempting, no matter the impact on those around you. Insecure men hurt women and children, and this leads to shame and guilt. Some men never seem to grow up to face responsibilities and consequences. They stay perpetually immature, as boys. They keep moving on but can't run from themselves. Not all men take on the Culture of Poverty in places like Winson Green, but positive adult male role models can be hard to find. It's another reason why sharing life and modelling alternatives, up close and personal, is one of the most important responses to poverty we can provide.

Despite the myriad biases and forces against them, female leadership in local communities is a common, life-giving feature. The grandmother who holds the siblings together. The single mother getting four children off to four different schools each day. It's most often female teachers, social workers, and health and charity leaders who are holding things together and getting things done in local institutions. In the absence of many functioning males, local communities need to trust their local female leaders with their most precious life decisions. It's frustrating, then, to see how many of these remarkable local female leaders are treated by those outside the local community. The next level regional, national, and global institutions often miss their genius. Even Anji, who is a force of nature and hard to ignore, has returned from meetings deflated because her ideas were simply passed over by elderly white males who had no experiences, expertise, or interest in our communities. This dynamic impacts access and opportunity both for female leaders and their local communities.

Gender-based discriminations and violence diminish and marginalise people – the very people with the gifts we need to mobilise to see local change happen from the ground up. Everyone has talents and we can't afford to miss out on anyone's contribution. It can get messy and complicated, but being willing to work proactively against discrimination, and being for all people and places, can be a joy too. I love seeing confidence build and participation grow. Our household in Newbigin House has often had people with a spectrum of sexual orientations living together. Gay, straight, single males and females, as well as us marrieds, have often lived together. We've often hosted women and children fleeing domestic violence as they wait for staff to come back from their weekend to find emergency accommodation. Our Fresh Expression congregation, hosted at Newbigin House, often has the full LGBTQ+ spectrum sharing a meal and worshiping together each Sunday. The care, acceptance, and participation of sex workers, perhaps the most exploited of all, is common here too. It gets complicated very quickly for me. I often feel like I'm the old clueless dad in a sitcom or a reality TV show just trying to keep up. This wasn't what we set out to do, nor the church we thought we would plant. Yet, to provide a safe place for all to heal, build confidence and contribute has, perhaps, been one of our best offers to the life of our neighbourhood. It does, however, feel like a drop in the ocean of what is happening and what is needed here.

These three weeds can also collide, divide, and feed on each other. The Brexit debacle in the UK was an example of that. 'Take back control' was the slogan that resonated with those who felt like their parents and ancestors once had control of Britain, and by the UK leaving the European Union that would happen again. Not that most of the working class, and especially not racial or sexual minorities, ever had control over most of their lives in the way the Brexiteers imagined. Far from it! However, the elite-established white majority males felt their control slipping and needed to get it back before it was too late. Brexit was an opportunity to take some of it back. As I write, there is definitely a growing 'buyer's remorse' from even the most ardent Brexit supporters. The economic and cultural impact, coupled with the pandemic, has been significant. The blaming of minorities continues. 'Divide and conquer' continues.

2: Invasive Weeds That Choke The Harvest

In 2023, the latest rhetoric for this is 'stop the boats,' something I am afraid was learnt from Australian politics.

Control, however, is an illusion. There is always something beyond our influence. We can't keep blaming those far away from us, whether in Brussels (for the EU) or London (for the UK). This is why a focus on local community change is so important. This is the arena we live in, invest in, and if we work together can influence the most. Returning to an age where elites rule plebs nationally is not so golden after all. It's up close and personal that we can glimpse the wheat from the weeds.

It's also worth noting these three weeds can impact one person's life journey. A Black, gay, working-class woman, for example, simply has so much more to struggle against than if she only had one of these characteristics.

What can be troubling, is when all three weeds compete against each other in a kind of discrimination Olympics. For example, I have seen conflicts escalate between Black working-class men and white upper-class women. Who has it tougher? Who is more discriminated against? It can get ugly quickly. Of course, the power elites love it when minorities fight each other. Divide and conquer is an old and effective tactic where they become the adjudicators and only winner in these Olympics.

What do these invasive weeds have in common? They divide, isolate, and enable conquering. I've seen the impact of these three types of weeds in Winson Green and around the world. Isolation and loneliness take away the potential power, health, and resources of a community. We know this is true in physical health. One recent UK Government study found that "social isolation significantly increases a person's risk of premature death from all causes, a risk that may rival those of smoking, obesity, and physical inactivity."[37] This is true for everyone, but the same study highlighted that,

> loneliness among vulnerable older adults, including immigrants; lesbian, gay, bisexual, and transgender (LGBT) populations; minorities; and victims of elder abuse. It also points out that the literature base for these populations is sparse and more research is needed to determine risks, impacts,

> and appropriate actions needed... [because they] tend to have more loneliness than their heterosexual peers because of stigma, discrimination, and barriers to care.[38]

Division and isolation destroy family, social, and community life. Is it also the other way around?

> Last year, a Pew Research Center survey of more than 6,000 U.S. adults linked frequent loneliness to dissatisfaction with one's family, social and community life. About 28 percent of those dissatisfied with their family life feel lonely all or most of the time, compared with just 7 percent of those satisfied with their family life. Satisfaction with one's social life follows a similar pattern: 26 percent of those dissatisfied with their social lives are frequently lonely, compared with just 5 percent of those who are satisfied with their social lives. One in five Americans who say they are not satisfied with the quality of life in their local communities feel frequent loneliness, roughly triple the 7 percent of Americans who are satisfied with the quality of life in their communities.[39]

If local community life is to flourish, discrimination must be rooted out. These weeds are not an exhaustive list either, but I know these three can create 'devastations' and 'wastelands' of our communities like few others.

What confronted me most in the UK is that these three weeds are also in me. What role do I, male, pale, and getting frailer, have to offer that doesn't help these weeds grow? It's also so tempting for me to use these weeds to get things done as my own 'authority' and 'old boy' networks still hold power. I have learnt to feel at home among the rich male, frail, and pale world at times, but this source is not the long-term solution for our communities if they are to thrive.

At one point I must admit I thought I should withdraw from public life. It's time now for women and those younger with minority backgrounds to shine and I'm just getting in the way. I worked hard to hand over leadership of organisations I founded here. Red Letter Christians UK, Newbigin Community Trust, Greenhouse at Barnes, and Newbigin

House Fresh Expressions all had their first paid leadership sit with brilliant women who are taking these organisations further than I could. I do think I need to have more of a back row seat now, and keep trying to release others, but I also realised that by diminishing ourselves we do no one any favours. Not the established elite (who'd be glad we're gone) nor emerging leaders (who'd experience us as a passionless shells). If we have power and privileges, especially ones we haven't earnt, then we really need to ask – who benefits most from them? We must be proactive in this. I turn to Jesus again, and his model of self-emptying for the sake of others reconnecting. Paul the apostle puts it this way:

> Do nothing out of selfish ambition or vain conceit. Rather, in humility value others above yourselves, not looking to your own interests but each of you to the interests of the others. In your relationships with one another, have the same mindset as Christ Jesus:
>
> Who, being in very nature God,
>   did not consider equality with God something to be
>   used to his own advantage;
>
> rather, he made himself nothing
>   by taking the very nature of a servant,
>   being made in human likeness.
>
> And being found in appearance as a man,
>   he humbled himself
>   by becoming obedient to death—
>   even death on a cross!
>
> (Phil. 2:3-9)

Just as Jesus sacrificially invested in others, so I want to invest everything I have in our local communities. This is the infinite cause that animates me. Connecting real people in real places is where just redistribution of power can happen. We can't do this by ourselves or from a safe distance. God entered the human experience in Jesus and formed a community. This is one reason why local churches are so crucial in practical ways. John Perkins, who gave us the name Seedbeds, calls for Christians to 'relocate' to live and reside in under-resourced neighbourhoods and 'reconcile' with people and places in community; only then can true 'redistribution' happen:

> And as we commit ourselves to just redistribution in terms of creating a new economics in broken communities, we can see how Jesus, through us, offers himself. The body of Christ becomes the corporate model through which we can live out creative alternatives that can break the cycles of wealth and poverty that oppress people. When this happens, the quiet revolution is winning the battle for the community...[40]

These 'Three Rs' became the key themes of the Christian Community Development Association that has seen renewal from within hundreds of local communities around the USA.[41] What has been exciting for me is that as a resident, investing in a particular place, I have just as much stake in the wellbeing of my local community as others here. The 'weeds' here impact us all in some ways. I still want us to invest in others, but if we work on these 'Three Rs,' then all our gifts can still be valued, including our own, and justice can flow in personal and practical ways. We will consider more about hope of connections as an antidote to the weeds later, but here I want us to consider that for those of us with privilege our role needs to be more than just 'doing'; it's 'being' a sign of hope. Where we personally invest and locate our privilege and resources matters if the weeds of division and discrimination are to be kept at bay.

Personal Reflections

1. What 'invasive weeds' have you experienced that choked you and your local community's potential for life in all its fullness? How do you feel about that?

2. When have you or your family benefited from systems or structures that have given you an advantage over others? How do you feel about that?

3. Can you identify with John Perkins' 'Three Rs' of 'relocation,' 'reconciliation,' and 'redistribution' typology? Why, or why not?

Chapter 3: Weeds As Signs Of Life In Wastelands?

Fears are like weeds. They grow wild if left unattended.
– Leigh Bardugo

Not all weeds are bad. Wastelands are often understood as places that used to have life and purpose but have now become toxic and abandoned. Perhaps the most famous wasteland of all is Chernobyl. The tragic 1986 nuclear disaster turned a once prosperous city into a ghost town, resulting in a 2,600km exclusion zone. A strange thing has been reported from there recently. Weeds have started to grow again. Now, lush forests, and even wolves, bears, and boars, have returned to the site of the old nuclear reactor. It was discovered that:

> When it comes to vegetation, all but the most vulnerable and exposed plant life never died in the first place, and even in the most radioactive areas of the zone, vegetation was recovering within three years.[42]

There was life there in Chernobyl the whole time. We just couldn't see it until the weeds appeared. The cover of this book has a plant growing up through the cracks of concrete. Most probably these would be weeds that had been dormant.

There are 'invasive weeds' planted from 'the enemy' for destruction, but I need to say a few words about other weeds that might naturally grow as we engage in community life. These emerge to let us know life is still there. These weeds may not be what we want to see harvested, but they have a purpose and may even confirm that we are in the right place. Their presence tells us that what might seem like a wasteland is not after all, because life is there. Take the weed Goldenrod, for example.

> Goldenrod has gotten a bad reputation—it is often confused with ragweed, a notorious allergen. In reality, goldenrod is a beautiful addition to your yard and lures pollinators like butterflies and honeybees, which may in turn pollinate your vegetable garden, giving you a better harvest.[43]

I have spent most of my adult life seeking change in local communities and I have found that three 'Fs'– Fear, Futility and Frustration – reoccur within me and the communities I am part of. I now think of these three Fs as 'native weeds.' Though they are found everywhere, they are particularly strong in fertile places that have been marginalisesd, where people have felt pushed to the edges and left behind. Each of these native weeds grow alongside good shoots. They grow in natural, normal, and understandable ways, but unless we pay attention to them, and are persistent in keeping on top of them, they will choke out the hopes we have for our communities. They exist naturally, but we can outgrow them. Unlike the weeds of prejudice and discrimination, these 'native weeds' as it were, have some unexpected value. Not least is that they can help us know that a harvest is possible.

Fear is worth paying attention to.
If we notice fear, we can confirm we are in the right place. Where there is no opportunity for fear to grow, there is no opportunity for faith to grow. Fear can grow whenever we go to try something good and think we will look stupid, get hurt, or be disliked. Fear can grow inner insecurity, and harden to become an external shell of pride to protect oneself. To weed out fear takes some doing. Especially if we have been hurt by trying something good, purposeful, or meaningful in the past, only to see it shot down in flames. Especially if we don't really know

what to do and the complexity baffles or overwhelms us. When someone near us is in pain, it is normal to fear what is next. Fear is common because it's a natural instinct. It keeps us at the ready, but it can stop any change emerging before it raises its head. This is true everywhere, but in situations where there are powerful, vested interests in keeping life the same, it can quickly get dark and complex. Oppression and injustice don't happen in vacuums. Some people benefit from them and are unlikely to want to give up those privileges easily. These people have real power and can isolate and hurt us. We have a right to fear.

Fear, therefore, should be embraced. It's normal, it's natural, but it matters where we go with that fear. If we can face fear, we will grow our capacity for change with others. Eleanor Roosevelt put it this way:

> You gain strength, courage and confidence by every experience in which you really stop to look fear in the face. You are able to say to yourself, 'I have lived through this horror. I can take the next thing that comes along.' You must do the thing you think you cannot do.[44]

Will we allow fear the room to grow in our brains, bodies, and neighbourhoods, or can we name it with friends and together stand up and address it? Resisting fear is a common theme in the bible. I once read that the bible says a variation of 'Fear not' 365 times.[45] It's almost as if the Holy Spirit knows we need to be reminded of this each and every day. Finding compassion, which literally means 'suffering with,' helps deflate fear and cast it out.

> There is no fear in love, but perfect love casts out fear.
> (1 John 4:18)

Fear faced with others loses its strength. Whenever we feel fear rise up, we know we need love's courageous intervention. Fear can bring us together; it can bond us with others like few other experiences. Over the years, fires, violence, disease, threat of eviction or deportation could have torn our local communities apart. However, rather than withdraw and isolate ourselves, so often our communities have stepped forward together in love. I mentioned the Wind Rush Generation and the fear it created for so many neighbours of Caribbean heritage. What I didn't mention was the brilliant way the local community came together and the beautiful monuments and art installations that have popped up around our neighbourhood to celebrate this generation's contributions. We have one by our canal. A kind of palpable pride emerged when it was unveiled. It was made from metal, a ship with sails that say, "Black History is British History." It contains images of Black contributions to British life, from Roman times to today. Even when it was defaced with a spray-painted 'N' word only a few weeks later, love still casts out fear, and the graffiti was quickly removed.

Fear can help us act. Fear of change can be addressed by asking a deeper question: What would happen to us if a particular source of fear stayed with us, and change didn't happen? Then what? Sometimes this can be the nudge we need to do something, however small, today. In movies about time travel, people often worry that changing the smallest thing in the past will radically alter present realities. But barely anyone in the present imagines they can radically change the future by doing small things today. What about the potential effect of small changes, made with love? Could small acts of kindness, performed in the face of fear, alter our future trajectories? That is not science fiction, that is good news. We can use fear to motivate us to see real change, even small ones at first, and not let the status quo win.

Futility is worth noticing too.
When we feel futility, we know we are in a place where empowerment needs to be released. How can we grow and flourish if we think nothing can change, so why try? I've heard sentiments like this everywhere I've lived: 'Nothing changes around here. We always get shat on from on high.' Sometimes it can even have a cultural or religious justification: 'It's God's will,' 'this is our karma,' or 'this is just our lot in life.' This feeling is often raised for good reasons. As we have seen, much is stacked against our communities in the most complex and sinister ways. So many institutions and relationships just don't work for us. Change seems unlikely when we name all the many networked barriers against it happening. I've made a fairly strong case that the weeds are turning too many of our communities into wastelands. However, the weeds don't have to choke the life out of us. It is amazing what is possible when

power and love join together in collective action. Martin Luther King once said:

> Power without love is reckless and abusive, and love without power is sentimental and anaemic. Power at its best is love implementing the demands of justice, and justice at its best is power correcting everything that stands against love.[46]

There are those who hear the word power and think only of oppression over other people. Power in this sense, however, is the ability to make the right things happen. We will consider hope soon, but futility is broken by knowing the power we have when we act in love. This is more possible when faith reassures us where the Big Story ends. It is ultimately futile to invest our lives in systems, corporations, structures, and practices that perpetuate injustice and oppression. We may feel futile in the face of them today, but they will not last. One day all other powers will be gone. Only what we do in faith, hope, and love will prevail (1 Cor. 13).

Frustrations occur when we get impatient for change.

Like fear and futility, frustration is an important sign of life. Similarly, it matters where we go with it. Without healthy connections, frustration can turn into destructive rage. One of Change Makers' founders and decades-long youth worker, Tim Evans, has a favourite quote. It's an African proverb: "The child who is not embraced by the village will burn it down to feel its warmth." This is the cost of disconnection writ large in many of our neighbourhoods, but frustrations are a sign that something is wrong here and there's an urgency to do something about it. This can be a deep motivation for change. Frustrations need focus if they are to be a force for good.

Sometimes we have physically shook in meetings when we knew action was desperately needed but the power brokers have joined forces to avoid taking any risks. Rage is the wrong direction here. If we shout out verbally, burn bridges, give up too soon, go silent, or even get violent, we will lose out. Frustration can get the better of us. The problems we want to solve often took decades and generations to create, so a kind of revolutionary patience is required. This is not passive waiting.

Like the other weeds this one can be mulched and turned into fertiliser to enrich our growth. Steve Chalke once wrote:

> Vision and frustration are two sides of the same coin. Those who have vision must also live with frustration. My experience is that frustration is part of the job. So here's to all the frustrated visionaries. Let's make some progress today![47]

I have outlined just some of the weeds that help create wastelands. This is the local community, the world as it is for so many, right now. These weeds can also become internalised and become a part of us personally and choke the life out of us. For some, what looks like a weed-ravaged wasteland is too daunting and depressing. Abandonment becomes a common response to such places. We do need to ask ourselves if the cost of facing the weeds in apparent wastelands and seeking to beat them is worth our efforts? There is clearly a price to pay, but is that price too high? My experience is that a simple abundance emerges making such an intentional life worth living. We can come alive facing challenges. The bigger the challenge, the bigger the life that surges within us. If we can hang in there through the 'ordeal' then not only a 'new deal,' but a new life is possible that far outshines the 'ideals' of this age. We can bloom where we are planted by God.

For many too, facing these weeds as they are in our patch will raise another important question. What on earth can we really do? Most of the rest of this book will explore this in the most practical ways possible, but what I need to say here is that we can give in to the weeds too readily. They are strong, but they are not invincible. There is always a decision or action possible, no matter how small, but only if we can find some hope.

Personal Reflections

1. Which of the three weeds, 'fear,' 'futility,' and 'frustrations,' do you most see in yourself and your local community?

2. How can these weeds be 'hopeful signs of life' for you and your local community?

3. Are there some next steps to tend to these 'native weeds?'

Chapter 4:
Treating Weeds With Hope

For I know the plans I have for you, declares the Lord, plans for welfare [Shalom] and not for evil, to give you a future and a hope.
Jeremiah 29:1

Hope makes a difference. Even a little burst of hope can keep us growing toward dreams being realized, to enjoy harvesting the way the world can be, locally and globally. Acting in hope can make possible what is seemingly impossible now. For what is inevitable now, was once considered impossible. The perspective of hope, therefore, matters like few other resources if wastelands are to change. How can hope start to treat this complex web of weeds in our local communities?

Japanese Knotweed is one of those weeds whose very name strikes fear, futility, and frustration in the heart of any property owner in the UK. It can "grow up to three metres in height, spreading rapidly and pushing up through asphalt, cracks in concrete on driveways and even grow up into cavity walls and drains, in its quest for light and water."[48] Japanese Knotweed is, however, not actually a problem in Japan. It has natural enemies in the form of bugs and fungi there. Here in the UK these natural enemies simply do not exist, allowing it to grow and spread freely.

What are the natural enemies of the weeds we see in our neighbourhoods?

No Wastelands

I have found that it is hope. It is hope that can treat and contain weeds in their many forms. Hope, however, is often the quality most missing in our local communities.

One of the more remarkable expressions of hope is in the book of Lamentations. This book, written in the midst of agony, finds a crucial new key.

> The thought of my suffering and homelessness
> > is bitter beyond words.
> I will never forget this awful time,
> > as I grieve over my loss.
>
> Yet I still dare to hope
> > when I remember this:
>
> The faithful love of the Lord never ends!
> > His mercies never cease.
>
> Great is his faithfulness;
> > his mercies begin afresh each morning.
>
> I say to myself, "The Lord is my inheritance;
> > therefore, I will hope in him!"
>
> The Lord is good to those who depend on him,
> > to those who search for him.
>
> So it is good to wait quietly
> > for salvation from the Lord.
> (Lam. 3: 19-26)

It is not easy to find the new key of hope in wastelands.
Finding hope within our slum neighbourhood in Bangkok felt especially tough. We were confronted with the daily reality of HIV-Aids, child malnutrition, and premature death. It often caused us to cry out to our God, who promised that a better world than this is possible. Sometimes all we could do was pray along with the Psalmist who cried again and again, 'How long do we have to sing this song?' These prayers of lament often preceded the emergence of hope.

4: Treating Weeds With Hope

When Lesslie Newbigin ministered in Winson Green he felt "the commodity in the shortest supply is hope…there is a famine of hope."[49] That is our experience too. Suffering and despair can easily overwhelm us, strangling any last tingle of hope we have for something better. You can see rubbish on streets, or lack of money, but the kinds of poverty in Winson Green or Klong Toey that are most vicious are not just about lack of cash – it's the lack of hope to see that a better life is possible.

I have seen that even a little bit of hope can light up a way. Whenever I see hope rise from within any of our Change Makers I know a shift has taken place. Survival mode thinking is so common; embracing an opportunity to even think about a preferred future is a breakthrough. I don't mean to say anything is possible if you just wish it hard enough. That is delusional. It's just that even the smallest sign of hope can alter trajectories, and once hope gains momentum in a person or place it can be unstoppable. To put it another way, change doesn't happen without hope. Without hope our feelings of fear, futility, and frustration overwhelm us; we will never get past them.

What do we mean by hope? The ancient story of Rahab in Joshua 2 helped me to define a biblical understanding of hope. She was in a dark place. As a sex worker trying to keep her family alive Rahab was especially vulnerable, but now even worse, her fragile home was in a city under siege by the Hebrew army. The life of her city slowly drained away as the quiet anticipation of violence by the surrounding army came closer. It was then that Rahab spotted three Hebrew spies. The instincts to act in fear, futility, or frustration must have been strong, but she had nothing to lose. Rahab acted in hope. She took the spies in, hid them in her roof and then lied to the King about where they went. She sided with the incoming revolution because she said she had heard of how their God had freed the Hebrews from oppression in Egypt. Hope began to rise in her. If God could do that with the Hebrews, maybe God could free her too? With that hope, Rahab then made a deal with the spies for her family.

> 'Now then, please swear to me by the Lord that you will show kindness to my family, because I have shown kindness to you. Give me a sure sign that you will spare the lives of my father

and mother, my brothers and sisters, and all who belong to them—and that you will save us from death.'

'Our lives for your lives!' the men assured her. 'If you don't tell what we are doing, we will treat you kindly and faithfully when the Lord gives us the land.' (Josh. 2: 12-18 [NIV])

Rahab helped the spies escape and the 'sure sign' they came up with together is one of the biblical words for 'hope.' Rahab chose a rope or a cord as a sign. The Hebrew word here is *hwqt tiqvah* and it is one of fifteen Hebrew words that can be translated 'hope.' Rahab helped the spies escape down red 'ropes' (*hwqt tiqvah*) and the 'sure sign' was that those same ropes were to be put up in her windows as 'scarlet cords' so the invading army would know to spare that house (Josh. 2:18, 21).

The Hebrew spies were good to their word. When the Hebrew army saw the red ropes, they honoured their promise, and Rahab's family lived. In fact, they not only survived, but had an integral part to play in the coming of the great Liberator Jesus. Rahab is named in the Gospel of Mathew's genealogy of Jesus, so she is part of the link that made salvation possible for the world (Matt. 1:5). Indeed, Rahab is named alongside the Patriarchs as one of the exemplar heroes of our faith (Heb. 11:31). If anybody understood hope as a rope taking the initiative to pull God's promises into the present, then Rahab did.

This idea of hope is buried deep within the experience of lament, oppression, and injustice. The Psalmist describes God as "the hope (*hwqt tiqvah*) of the poor" (Ps. 9:18). It's this sense of a rope that can connect, pull, and bring into the present the good and promised future God intends. This metaphor of hope as a cord or rope is also taken up in the New Testament, when the writer of Hebrews encourages readers to "hold fast to the hope set before us" (Heb. 6:18 [NIV]). As Christians we believe this hope is ultimately found in the Risen Christ who defeated death and is the first fruits of the good, fulfilled creation. This good future is glimpsed and drawn into the present through the Risen Christ (1 Cor. 15).

T

his is how I can experience hope too. It's more than just wishing that things can get better. Once I glimpse what is possible, as a kind of whispered promise, then I can see signs of a transformative power in the present. Hope is a kind of unexpected grace. If I'm quiet enough, I'll hear the whisper of hope, I'll hang in there, and I'll find that these events will come to pass; these promises will come true.

Cathy Ross, a CMS missiologist, wrote thoughtfully during the Covid pandemic about hope and focused her reflections on the book of Lamentations. She argues silence is "urged" here before hope comes.

> It is good that one should wait quietly for the salvation of
> the Lord.
> It is good for one to bear the yoke in youth,
> to sit alone in silence
> when the Lord has imposed it
> (Lam. 3:26–28 [ESV])

Ross writes:

> This is not a passive silence but a dynamic silence remembering God's love and therefore having hope (Lam 3:21, 40–42)…If the spine of lament is hope then perhaps it is in the silence that we can allow ourselves time to reflect and to be. Silence allows us the time and space to sit and to remember, to be patient, to exhibit courage, repentance and prayer for restoration.[50]

Theologically, God's hope is like a cord that pulls creation and humanity's good future into the present. The world to come will be without any of the parasitic powers of evil that lead to decay and death. We can live in the anticipation that one day all things will be put to right because Jesus defeated these powers. A stillness is required for that reality to be noticed and awakened in us. We can quietly gaze upon that stunning vista of the transformation that is to come, while at the same quietly confronting the dark valley in front of us. To overcome despair and receive hope like this is a special gift. One that is received in stillness within and works itself out in daily realities. That is the nature and task of hope.

Hope comes when we sense the possibility and potential that goes beyond immediate reason. It comes when we see signs of a break in the cycle of despair and poverty; when we know dominoes can fall. When just one person stuck in their addiction finds some freedom, they can step out to help and join others. Hope has momentum. Ultimately, it is the Holy Spirit who gives hope to respond to futilities, fears, and frustrations and helps us see that a different outcome is possible. Hope is not mere wishful thinking. Let's find that rope and hang on!

If you do one thing, do this: ignite hope. Look up from survival mode and intentionally invest time and space in preparing for a better future. The change your talent offers will simply not happen if you don't allow this kind of imagination into your life. Start small, take even a few minutes a day to be still, imagine a preferred future in as much detail as you can and allow hope to sprinkle your life. Sure, join in with others, but only when you personally have that hope growing inside you can your life be lit up to see that change happen.

Finding hope to beat the weeds by taking our own story seriously.

For many years, a big part of our work has involved training local leaders to affect change within their own communities. These currently operate as a programme called Change Makers.[51] Here, we find that hope starts to flow when we start to take our own stories seriously. Our scars can actually become healing forces in our lives and vocations. That there is a kind of divine work of art being made within us and our role is to help detect it and nurture that miraculous life. The apostle Paul wrote, "We are God's workmanship, created in Christ Jesus, to do the good works he prepared in advance for us to do" (Eph. 2:10 [NIV]). This is the hope that we can see realised in us and those around us. To help do that, we have found that three discernment questions, with supporting exercises, help us find the signs of hope. Where have we been? Where are we going? Who can I go with? In this chapter we will focus on the first question that helps us take our unique story seriously.

Discovering and sharing timelines is an exercise that has helped successive cohorts of Change Makers to quietly find their unique hopes and dreams amidst the weeds. This exercise is influenced by research into leadership by Robert 'Bobby' Clinton at Fuller Seminary. He studied the lives of thousands of biblical and Christian leaders and found some common, and often overlooked, themes and patterns. One significant insight was that he noticed that very few leaders actually "finish well." Most started well but peaked too early and didn't fulfill their potential. The iconic leaders, however, those who "finished well," experienced what Clinton called a "convergence" phase. He says:

> During Phase V convergence occurs. That is, the leader is moved by God into a role that matches gift-mix, experience, temperament, etc. Geographical location is an important part of convergence. The role not only frees the leader from ministry for which there is no gift, but it also enhances and uses the best that the leader has to offer. Not many leaders experience convergence. Often, they are promoted to roles that hinder their gift-mix. Further, few leaders minister out of what they are. Their authority usually springs from a role. In convergence, being and spiritual authority form the true power base for mature ministry.[52]

We all long for this kind of integrated life that flows out of who we are. A life well spent is one where our best time, energy, gifts, and strengths are given in relationships and causes that really matter. We find our sweet spot; passion and a kind of unforced authority grows and makes a real difference within the people and places around us. Hope-full lives fulfill potential. A life of hope overcomes the weeds in wastelands.

The opposite of a convergent life is a segregated one, where we never get to focus our best talents and spend most of our time and resources doing what we're not built for, in pursuit of something that doesn't matter. A life where weeds overcome the life of hope in a wasteland.

The weeds win too often in our communities. Too much potential and talent for integrated living is left unfilled. It's a tragedy when anyone's unique gifts are not shared freely, but it's also true that the wider world needs those gifts to be whole. Who can calculate the price of that unfulfillment?

Convergence is what we and our Change Makers need and can eventually experience, but there is no way to fast-track a leader into that experience. I often see the weeds we have discussed in the eyes of so many of these potential leaders, nominated by their communities, to join a Change Maker cohort. We see their potential, but they often find it hard to believe this kind of flow and growth in their lives is possible. For hope to flow it takes a relentless patience and a long-term view. It takes time to see this 'who we are' and 'what we do' integration coming together, especially for those who are currently in survival mode and develop a kind of 'learned helplessness.' Many cease to believe they have the autonomy to make decisions, and look to others to do that for them. A preferred future is something others choose for them. There are many authoritarian leaders and professionals who are more than happy to use disconnected, unintegrated people in our local communities for their own ends. Belonging can be another costly burden, not a liberating force. Beating the weeds and finding hope therefore is an endurance sport.

Hearing Change Makers share their timelines is inspirational. Any reading of Robert Clinton's books sees his fascination, almost obsession, with timelines. It's often taking a step back to see the bigger picture in our lives that makes a difference. When we see how far we've come, where unique passions have been used, we start to see confidence grow. For survivors of multiple griefs and trauma, for example, this moment can be liberating. They have overcome so much and are still standing! Many would not have their resilience. Some of the most precious assets a local community can have are held by people who carry histories of brokenness being healed.

When I lead Change Maker programmes, I typically spend a full Saturday morning on timelines. We have each participant go away quietly for an hour or so with a pile of Post-it notes and write one critical incident, influence, or relationship on each one. It can be books, mentors, key events, locations, songs; anything that might have had an influence on their lives from birth to the present day. Then we ask them to put all these Post-it notes in chronological order and look for 'chapters' and stages of life, as well as life convictions. Some even do a soundtrack to their lives as they look for themes and patterns. After a few hours ruminating on their lives alone, they then share these timelines with the cohort as honestly and boldly as they can. The participants then discover amazing insights together. This kind of self-awareness can be brutal for some, but something awakens within them that can't be stopped: participants begin to own their own stories.

What I'm trying to do is help people face who they really are, not who they wish they were or who their families or cultures wished they were. We simply fail at being people we are not. We are searching here for what the mystics call the 'true self' and not the calculating 'false self.' The false self is not who we really are, it is fragile and easily offended. The true self, however, is who we really are and is an indestructible and unoffendable force for good.

We have found that very few Change Makers have previously shared their full story with anyone. When they do, and as they listen empathically to others, a kind of mystical bonding can happen. These are no longer competitors in a leadership programme, but comrades seeking their own revolution together.

We also use a tool called 'StrengthsFinder' as a kind of warm balm at the end of that day.[53] This Gallup-researched inventory helps leaders find their top strengths and discover how these can work together with others' strengths to see good happen. A few weeks before the retreat we have participants complete an online survey of 177 paired statements that helps measure the participants' talents and their natural patterns of thinking, feeling, and behaving. The online tool then categorises these into the 34 CliftonStrengths themes.[54] We then have our friend and StrengthsFinder specialist, Alysen Merrill, analyse these and share the results with the group. Each person has a unique set of five top strengths, and these can grow if celebrated and focused on. We don't have to worry that we are not good at everything. No-one has all the strengths. The idea is that by focusing our energies where we are strong, we can best engage what is wrong in our world. Everyone feels animated about themselves and what they have to offer after Alysen spends time with us!

Connecting with 'true self' is about self-awareness and centredness.

It's a kind of anchored connection that helps stop us drifting into unhealthy waters. To come back to our central theme here, finding our unique strengths and taking our story seriously, enables hope to keep the poisonous weeds at bay.

Hope within Change Makers

Perhaps you feel overwhelmed? Perhaps you want to give up before you start? The things that choke our neighbourhoods and make them feel like wastelands are complex and multifaceted, and it would be dishonest of a book like this to try and avoid these realities. This very understanding gives us an insight into how resilient so many of our neighbours are. That so many are still standing, and any are ready to grow, is a kind of miracle. I have found change is not impossible, even for those who could be choked by poisonous classisms, racisms, sexisms, and gender discrimination. It just takes more than we might think. I want to finish this chapter with some stories of hope from our Change Makers. Each has beaten their own unique web of weeds and are making a real difference with their lives in places some only see as wastelands. None of them work alone. The Change Maker programme uniquely requires its participants to come with at least one other from any given community. Hope within neighbours can be an unstoppable force

Hope within James

I first met James when he entered the Chapel at Winson Green prison in 2016. He was in the regulation grey tracksuit, and was white working class in his early 20s. He hadn't walked from the nearby small Victorian-era cell, designed for one but accommodating two, like many, but from one of the newer blocks further away, that would be the centre of a riot and soon be burnt down. By any standard, this was an overcrowded penal system.

I remember James, or Jay as we then knew him, as having the energy of a caged tiger, which contrasted sharply with the numbness and blank stares of so many of the other guys who shuffled to chapel that Sunday morning. Jay was impatient for us to get the worship service started and he had a song he wanted us to sing. He was frustrated that we weren't moving fast enough; was this a sign of life? Could I see a glimmer of light in his eyes? He pestered us. 'Do you know Tim Hughes from Gas Street Church? I love his songs. He's a friend of mine.' Jay was a ball of energy, talking intently with all who would listen. As I got to know Jay over the years, I would see that the failure of so many people, systems, and services during his formative teenage years in Essex could have traumatised him for life. Add to this his own responses to all this pain, and it was no surprise that he was in that cold, dark, caged place. To write Jay off, however, would have been to sell Jay short. He was still standing; that glimmer of light in his eyes could have been real. Where did that come from? Could fear, futility, and frustrations be in trouble here? If Jesus can use a few pieces of fish and bread to feed the multitudes, then what was in Jay's hands to give? Of course, many in jail hit rock bottom and in desperately wanting out, need connections and keenly accept any help on offer. I liked Jay from the moment I met him, but was Jay ready to shine brightly or was he just trying it on with me too?

Jay actually did know singer-songwriter Tim Hughes. You might know Tim's song, *Here I Am to Worship*. It was once named by *Time Magazine* as the second most sung song of the year after *Happy Birthday*! Tim, his wife Rachel, and their children moved to Birmingham at a similar time to us and we had mutual friends who introduced us. They had planted a new church – 'Gas Street' – in the city centre with the Birmingham Diocese. We joined the first day it opened in their permanent building, as so many of our initial plans, including church participation, were skittled at that time. With lots of new and inquisitive neighbours, we would join the Gas Street services, walking along the famous 'tow paths' of Birmingham's canals or driving them in our mini-bus from our home less than ten minutes away. The brilliant energy and creativity of the rapidly growing Gas Street church often felt like a different universe to Winson Green, but it was a healing balm with friendships and partnerships quickly growing.

Gas Street Church had a healing effect on Jay too, before he was recalled back to jail while on probation. Jay had originally wandered into the first temporary home of Gas Street with a friend from his probation hostel around the corner. It was here he experienced Jesus in a remarkable way.

Back then, the church met in a bar just off the famous Broad Street night club strip before their move to the permanent site on Gas Street. The church people just embraced Jay and took him into their lives. Even when Jay was recalled back to jail, Tim would stay in contact. I would also pass messages between them, from church to prison and back again.

One of the sparks of light for Jay was that he had a dream and passion to start his own business. He would light up as we talked about this in visits and chats after chapel services. Out of these encounters and relationships he even had a name for his business: 'Eeverse,' as it would represent the changes from darkness to light, negativity to positivity that he was experiencing even in prison.

Jay's release from prison, however, was not easy. We all helped as much as we could, including setting him up in a supported house nearby. Numerous Gas Street people, including Tim and Rach, had him over for dinner. Jay's highlight of the week was Gas Street Church meetings and connecting with new people too. We would also see Jay most weeks, often at Newbigin House for community meals. At one level it was looking good, but his first year of 'freedom' took him to dark and confusing places, including alcohol and drug misuse. The shock of being out, the medication draining his energy, and isolation left him depressed and sleeping for most of his days. Not being allowed regular access with his young daughter was especially hard.

Jay needed more and I was worried how long he could hold up in his sleepy state. I could also see he had so much to give. He was determined to get Eeverse going and had a window to get things right. I therefore nominated Jay onto our first cohort of Change Makers, the emerging leaders programme. I hoped this could help find his passions and channel his energies, build connections and release his potential.

It didn't start well.

During the first residential evening session, Jay kept falling asleep, as he was so heavily medicated. I could see other participants looking at Jay, and then at me, quizzically. I still remember the breakthrough moment, however, in the morning that he told his story through the timeline exercise. His experiences were traumatic, but disclosing what had happened to him to the group was brave, and it opened him up to new possibilities. Later that Saturday we had Alysen Merrill do StrengthsFinder with the group. Jay was quite resistant at first, refusing to be boxed in, but Alysen was firm, caring, and found a connection. It turns out that Jay's top five strengths combination was rare; he was one in many millions! Jay's face slowly lit up with hope.

The next morning Jay came down to breakfast glowing. He said,

> 'I've had the best night sleep I've had in years! I feel awake now! Normally I struggle to doze off, thinking about all that's wrong with me. But yesterday, we spent hours talking about what is right with me!'

Jay grew a wide web of supportive friendships and connections that held him and his dreams as they unfolded that first bumpy year. He made an inspirational pitch of his proposed Eeverse street clothing range to the Change Maker resource panel to complete his programme. This was the first time we held this panel, and I was worried we wouldn't get the right people to give constructive feedback, offer coaching, provide connections or cash grants, and help our young leaders with the next stage of their enterprise or project. I shouldn't have been anxious, as we ended up having eight brilliant people on the panel including Tony Campolo, the prolific sociologist, author, and Christian activist. Tony said Jay's proposal was as good as any he had seen in his Eastern University's MBA programme in Philadelphia. All eight panelists affirmed the worth of Jay's ideas and offered support and connections.

Jay's hopes took off over the next few years and he grew his skills, capacities, and character. There were lots of ups and downs, but at time of writing, Jay not only leads Eeverse Clothing, but also runs a not-for-profit that advocates and raises funds for mental health.[55] He speaks in churches, conferences, schools, and even addressed leaders of the Home Office about mental health and imprisonment. Jay takes his own story seriously – both the wheat and weeds, the hope and the hardship. His assets of brokenness, connected to hope, are transformative not just for him but for all who meet him. My heart especially sings when I see Jay with his daughter at Gas Street.

Hope within the Clark Brothers

I am inspired by Basil, Alex, and Owen Clark. From mixed heritage backgrounds, they were often split up at different points growing up and put into care. Their personal stories are distinct ones, but all moved from survival to thriving before our eyes. I especially remember meeting them during the pandemic and asking them for help in imagining what might be possible with the URC Lodge Road building. As we sat in the chapel for the first time with about a dozen other locals, they tentatively shared some of their dreams. Basil and Owen were passionate musicians and knew so many more, but they had nowhere to meet, play, or teach others. Could this be a place for them? Alex was a graphic artist and painter who was recovering from cancer. Could this be a place to teach, learn, and celebrate the visual and musical arts?

As soon as Lodge Road was available to us, Baz and Alex went to work. They not only helped to make the place safe and usable but were trying out their gifts too. Art and music soon followed. People loved them and their gifts.

Both Alex and Basil were then nominated to Change Makers. They shared their timelines and discovered their strengths at the first residential at The Greenhouse at Barnes Close together. We had just taken up this derelict Cadbury family mansion on the foothills of the nearby Waseley Hills and, with their help, restored that building and five acres of grounds into a retreat centre able to host over 30 people at a time. With others in their Change Maker cohort, they pitched an idea at the end of the programme for a purpose-built creative arts space at Lodge Road Church Centre. Their idea was to transform the large upstairs storage room, filled with decades of church junk, into a space for music, arts, and recording, complete with a new kitchen and office.

It would be a big job, not least because the ceiling was falling down in sections, decades worth of church junk was piled up so high that it was almost impossible to enter, and the old kitchen sink had dark brown sludge through it and a funky smell. I've never seen so many broken overhead projectors, electric organs, plastic chairs, and damaged old hymn books before. None of these were usable, but still stored here, just

4: Treating Weeds With Hope

in case they might come in handy one day. The resource panel could see the merits of the pitch, but was it really possible?

Remarkably, that week, my old youth pastor in Dingley, Arthur Cherry, felt called to donate $10,000 Australian dollars for a local project. Would £5k be enough for this dream? It was certainly a start and a sign of hope. A local builder, Milan, was willing to oversee the project if the local community was willing to help provide the labour. A local hardware store gave a 60% discount on the materials and paint we needed. Baz, Alex, and my son Aiden spent months with Milan clearing the space out, fixing the ceiling, painting it, installing a kitchen, and making it accessible via outdoor side stairs. Today, Baz's band 'Mind Funk' record their own songs there and support people with mental health playing in the band, using music as healing balm. Art is created there by local children. We've even had guitars crafted there and they will hopefully be completed one day! Baz, Alex, and Owen are at the centre of it all. Shalom is on its way.

What made the difference? I saw first-hand how hope, fused with passion and purpose can make dreams work. The Clark brothers offered their talents and saw quick wins that resisted the weeds that affected others. Their dream eventually grew to access targeted resources from outside the community and they developed a specialised place within the community. If you are in Winson Green, please come to one of the community celebration nights that includes food, art shows, karaoke, steel pan drumming, and songs by Mind Funk.

Hope within Louise

I first met Louise Jones at Gas Street Church while she was still an undergraduate arts student at the University of Birmingham. At first, Louise came across as a bit nervous and she had quite a pronounced stammer. Blonde and bubbly, Louise had an obvious passion for Jesus and justice and wanted to explore where to make a difference in the world. After coming to my 'Make Poverty Personal' Gas Street Group, and coming to visit us in Winson Green, something clicked for Louise. While many talked about the poor, few of Louise's peers were willing to personally cross barriers to meet them and share life. Too risky?

Not enough of a priority? Too awkward? Louise met Anji, and she immediately had a few ideas for Louise to get started with. 'God loves you and Anji has a wonderful plan for your life' is a common saying here. Within months, Louise was caught up in Anji's whirlwind by volunteering to lead youth groups, kids' clubs, and community meals. With her much-needed stability, Louise became loved by the kids and caregivers alike. Eventually Louise relocated into Newbigin House to live with us, including during the pandemic lockdowns. We got to know Louise quite well!

What most broke Louise's heart was the plight of so many young girls in our neighbourhood. They had so much potential, but often arrived at primary school hungry and flustered. Growing up with a stutter, Louise knew school kids can be cruel to little girls. It was part of her own story. She also began to grow in her respect for local caregivers. She could see how stretched so many were, often needing to go to more than one school each morning. It was a miracle the kids got there at all. Louise noticed, however, that in the rush to get to school some of these girls had unwashed smells and matted hair that slowly began to ostracise them from other kids. Hunger pains until lunch time limited the kids' concentration. Louise could see destinies undermined before they had even begun.

Louise was nominated onto our second Change Maker programme. While her life story was not as colourful as other emerging leaders in her cohort, she could detect God's heartbeat in her for young girls in her neighbourhood. A plan emerged. Louise pitched 'Beauty and the Feast' to the resource panel as a way of responding to local parents' needs. The parents would drop their girls off early at the Newbigin Community Hub on the school premises. There they would be part of Beauty and the Feast, having breakfast together and learning grooming skills, practicing on each other. It was positive rather than shaming, open to all girls, and soon had a waiting list.

Beauty and the Feast had many positive knock-on effects. Not only did young girls grow in confidence and strength, but the parents felt less flustered, and the school could see the results too. Hope was growing everywhere, including in Louise. Recently she completed an MA in

4: Treating Weeds With Hope

Theology (Humanitarian Aid and Development) with most units from our Seedbeds Learning (School for Urban Leadership).[56] This helped her secure a new role as Programme Director at Newbigin Community Trust, helping form the new local high school where she will be based from September 2023, as well as being part of the leadership team for Red Letter Christians UK. Louise is making a local and national difference, mobilising others for Jesus and justice.

In so many ways, Louise could go anywhere. It's a gift that she chose to face her fears, downsize her world, say no to other options, and be fully planted in Winson Green. It's a gift not just to Winson Green, but to Louise herself. Living with passion and purpose is a rare thing and something that so many of her peers miss out on. The relocation, reconciliation, and redistribution that Dr Perkins called for is beautifully illustrated in Louise. Sometimes the destinies we redeem are our own.

I know the weeds can be outgrown. Hope from within local communities can be their natural enemies. Especially if we take our own stories seriously.

Personal Reflections

1. What most strikes you about the potential of hope?
2. Who have been signs of hope for you in your local community? Why?
3. How can you nurture more hope in you and your local community?

Part A. Practices To Try

Here, as in the end of every section of the book, you will find a set of practices to experiment with and some questions to consider personally or in a group setting.

Given the power of the timelines, I would love you to explore how you can take your own story seriously. God uses our whole lives to draw us to Him. We look at our past to see the fingerprints of God, so that we can see how He is forming our future. This is a summary of Bobby Clinton's insights that can help us think about our own timelines:

1. When God calls a person, He calls them for a lifetime of service.

2. Few people finish their lives well. Most peak too early, bomb out or expect too much too soon.

3. God uniquely shapes each person to make a unique contribution in the world and wastes no experiences we have.

4. There are two tracks God works on. These tracks are 'who we are' and 'what we do,' or 'what God does in us' and 'through us.' To finish our lives well these two tracks need to increasingly come together.

5. Some general phases can be discerned that leaders who finish well go through. These are like chapters in the unfolding story of our lives.

6. One key is to learn from each phase and make good decisions in 'boundary' times, ready for the next phase.

A. Timeline exercise (personal) (1 hour)

1. Brainstorm all the key events, circumstances, people, and incidents in your life. Write each on a single Post-it note, so you end up with dozens and dozens of Post-its, each with one item on it. Make sure you include

- Key people in your life (relationships)
- Key mentors or influences – living or dead, positive or negative (ideas, authors, songs, books, as well as formal mentors, friends, authority figures)
- Key events, including those that are painful and joyful
- Key places and what they taught you

2. Place these Post-it notes in a rough chronological sequence on a larger piece of paper.

3. Make a note of any 'seasons of life' that emerge as you do your Timeline. Name the seasons of your life (e.g. age 0-20: Heart Development, 21-25: Breaking Down/Darkness). Perhaps you can label these with a colour (e.g. aged 35-37: Red for Rawness). Group the Post-its and write the label for the season of life on the poster board above those Post-its if you can.

4. If you have time, personalise your timeline – artistically or with your name or however seems important to you.

B. Share your timeline in a small group or with a mentor (15-30 minutes each)

As you prepare your timeline for your small groups:

- Make a verbal note of any emotions that surface as you share your timeline (e.g. 'Talking about this makes me feel sad all over again,' or 'I can feel anger towards this person still,' or 'I still feel anxious about sharing this event,' or 'I still feel joy remembering that day.')

- Identify a few key 'must share' events, incidences, decisions, relationships

As you share, keep a notepad with you and make a list of the following as they occur to you and as the group mentions them.

- A list of people you may still need to ask forgiveness from

- Positive or negative patterns

- Where God has worked before

- The passions, values, and life lessons that have emerged because of your experiences

- Gifts that seem to have surfaced along the way

- Any doors that may have closed to you along the way, and what this says about who you are and what you are passionate about

- Any 'Birthright Giftings' (see Parker Palmer, *Let Your Life Speak*)[57]

You may find that you feel vaguely unsettled, discontent, or unhappy for a few days following your timeline. These emotions can surface when we revisit the past. Take care of yourself – eat, sleep, relax, interact with other people – and continue to present issues, as they come up, to God.

C. Personal Question: What are we learning about ourselves and others that can help grow our capacity for change? (30 minutes)

Spend some time identifying what motivates you given your unique life story. Record ways your passion and purpose has flowed or been hindered.

Group Questions:

1. What are some of the 'weeds' that have held you, or people you know, back? Why are these weeds so stubborn?

2. In what ways have you experienced hope or signs of hope?

3. Who do you know who has the potential to be a person of hope? How can you help to incubate their growth?

4. If you were to take a step of faith toward a dream, what could it be? Try that step out and share your findings with a friend.

Part B.

Sowing Seeds Of Shalom: What Can God's Vision Of Shalom Mean Locally?

This section explores the idea of Shalom and its implications as a guiding vision to nurture what is possible in our local communities.

Chapter 5: Place-making And The Seeds Of Shalom

The Lord will surely comfort Zion
  and will look with compassion on all her ruins;
he will make her deserts like Eden,
  her wastelands like the garden of the Lord.
Joy and gladness will be found in her,
  thanksgiving and the sound of singing.
Isaiah 51:3 [NIV]

In 2016, Peter and I carefully walked through Black Patch Park in Winson Green. It wasn't what he was expecting of a local, council run park. Piles of car tires, construction rubble, and a funky odour covered most of the grounds. The changing rooms and pavilion had been burnt down years ago, only leaving a concrete slab with sprawled metal and brickwork jutting out, stained with half-finished graffiti. The housing around Black Patch Park had been demolished long ago and it was hard to see its outline now. I pointed out, across the road, where the allotments for community growing had been and where we would walk next, but they had been abandoned and held few signs of life now. Factories that had once hugged the park were now mostly closed and crumbling, haunted shells of industry long gone too. Peter looked down, carefully scanning where his feet were landing.[58]

No Wastelands

Before we walked further, we stopped where two brooks converged in the middle of the park. I had hoped that Peter's organisation might want to help renew our neighbourhood by building new housing here. His face had turned white, 'What a wasteland' he muttered. I shouldn't have been surprised, but despite what his eyes showed him, I could only see potential here!

I explained:

> 'This is no wasteland. In fact, these two brooks have been sacred boundary markers since ancient times.'

I talked quickly about all this park had meant for people here, including the birth of Charlie Chaplin in the trailer of the famous gypsies, King Esau and Queen Henty.[59]

> 'His son Michael Chaplin comes to celebrate this most years just there, in that pub opposite the Soho Foundry. That is where James Watt first manufactured the steam engine and ushered in the industrial revolution.'

This place had such a rich past! But I could see the future too, and how community housing and new schools would reimagine this local area, especially now an old tramline was back in use and it only took eight minutes to get into Birmingham City Centre. I could see festivals and football returning to 'The Patch.' I could imagine faith being expressed in new ways here again.

Peter slowly began to join in with my enthusiasm, but this was a long way out of his comfort zone. By the time we stood in the middle of the abandoned allotments I could see a small light flicker within him, but I was burning with ambition for my adopted neighbourhood. Or should I say the neighbourhood that had adopted us.

I'm not sure why I could intuitively see potential in this local place. Why was this a place more than an empty space? Why was I so concerned about the wellbeing of the natural and built environment here, and not just the people I had got to know?

I don't believe this dream for Winson Green was an accident. Nor is there anything special about me. As I look back over my life experiences, I detect six crucial influences that have shaped me. Each of these informed my approach to life, and I'm grateful for them all. Many others have missed out on these voices.

Firstly, early nature and nurture informed my interest in places.
Some of my earliest memories, being born and raised in Dingley, are of Dad building homes on chaotic building sites, building kitchens in our garage, or sitting in his study designing homes. Dingley, and the broader South East of Melbourne, had a housing growth spurt in my lifetime. Building and designing homes was more than a job for Dad. He came into his own on these projects and built lots of homes in Dingley. We lived in at least nine places there. Dad says the highlight of his working life was designing, building, and running a 30-bed nursing home. The highlight of Mum's working life was being a real estate agent in Dingley. Showing people around, getting value for money, helping people find a home that suited them was a joy for her. My brother too was a real estate agent for a time. I didn't inherit much practically from Dad, though I was a bricklayer's labourer for a time, and felt real pride in seeing something built and useful for generations to come.

Looking back, I guess all those discussions and decisions around the table and in the car did rub off on me. In the three countries that we have lived and served, our homes and work-centres have all been either bought and/or developed. We knew having a local place to be based was an important way to be known and get to know others in our neighbourhoods. We even bought a Buddhist Temple in Springvale for A$168,000 as a way of establishing our project's roots there before we left for Bangkok. We sold it for A$420,000 just a few years later, using the money to buy and kit out an old factory in Dandenong for community life and training. Dad did the designs for this and, with volunteers and a donor, made the dream come alive. I haven't always expressed it enough, but I am so grateful for the people and local places that raised me.

Second, my faith came alive in a Christianity that connected with all of life, including God's love for the whole cosmos.
So much of the Christian faith I initially encountered seemed conservative, narrow, boring, judgmental, and irrelevant. We sang old hymns from another age, anxious about getting individual souls to heaven in a future spiritual life. John 3:16 was an often-quoted bible verse, where "God so loved the world" would enable us to end up in "eternal life" once we died, if we only "believed." Preachers and evangelists would drive it home: 'You don't think you're going to die do you? You could get hit by a bus on the way home tonight and then where would you be?' As a child, this life-after-death rhetoric didn't make me want to become a Christian, but it did make me very careful crossing the road! As I became a teenager, I figured that if God was real then there had to be more to faith than a middle-class subculture that I didn't fit into, waiting until I died. In my mid-teens I experienced a powerful encounter with the Holy Spirit that unleashed a desire to make a difference. Surely this God, who is real, was interested in life *before* death? Little did I know then that the 'world' I'd heard preached about in John 3:16 was not the naughty, 'worldly' people needing 'saving,' but it was the 'cosmos,' the whole of creation, that God loved and started to renew through Jesus. It would take me some time to realise that matter mattered to God.

Then in our early twenties, Anji and I met the 'radical disciples!' Growing up in Melbourne in the 1980s and 90s gave me access to some of the most innovative, intelligent, and prophetic Christian leaders Australia has produced. Often identified as the 'radical discipleship movement,' there was a sense that 'radical' (from the Latin *radix*) meant 'going to the roots' of what our Scriptures originally meant and connecting these insights with the 'roots' of contemporary injustices. These connections called for courageous, faith-filled, prophetic actions. One of the first radical disciples I heard speak in Melbourne was John Smith from God's Squad who started a community to reach outlaw motorcycle gangs, like Hells Angels, in culturally relevant ways. He would turn up to speak at our church in biker leathers on his Harley Davidson and preach with passion and intelligence like I had never seen before. Smithy's captivating stories grabbed me and gave me a lens for seeing the Scriptures, and the

5: Place-making And The Seeds Of Shalom

world too, that has influenced me to this day. I can still vividly remember a Strength to Love Conference in the early 1990s, with John Smith preaching that Jesus' central call was concern for 'God's Kingdom.' Jesus used the phrase over 111 times in Matthew, Mark, and Luke, and it meant 'God's will being done on earth as in heaven.' Smithy preached that being 'born again,' a phrase Jesus only used once, was a metaphor for entering the Kingdom of God (John 3:5-7). Following Jesus meant more than just being 'born again' for the next life, it meant standing up for Jesus and justice in this life and forever. Smithy lived this out too. Not just in his love for outlaws in Australia, but he had once spent time in prison in the Philippines, facing down militia wanting to bulldoze slum homes there. 'After all,' he noted, 'most the New Testament writers ended up in prison too.'

Smithy was just one of many in the radical discipleship movement at that time. Athol Gill was a bible scholar and started the 'House of the Gentle Bunyip' in inner-city Melbourne. Tim Costello prophetically connected faith and local politics and ran for Mayor of St Kilda. John Stewart, from World Vision Australia, shared a holistic faith where 'God, people and earth connected.' Ross Langmead, a real companion for UNOH and later my PhD supervisor, sang and taught about 'living for shalom.' Shirley Osborne would sit for hours on the steps of Flinders Street Station in central Melbourne and share her wild stories of God's love. Dave Andrews would visit us and share how he took following Jesus' command to 'sell all we had and give it to the poor' seriously and how he did that twice to serve the poorest in India and Brisbane! The wonderful thing for me was that at conferences like Strength to Love I could not only read works of significant Christian thought leaders, or listen to them speak from a platform, but they'd sit around for hours with us eating, debating, and telling stories. They valued our initial, fumbling attempts in Springvale. I had found a tribe to belong to.

Over time, there was a whole raft of international radical disciples who we got to visit or who visited us. Not least people like Mick Duncan and Darryl Gardiner from New Zealand, and Ched Myers, Tony Campolo, Ron Sider, Walter Brueggemann, and Shane Claiborne from the USA. Many people in the UK urban mission scene inspired us, including Steve Chalke, Elaine Storky, Dave Cave, and John Vincent. This in turn led to me connecting with Majority World Christian voices including CB Samuels, Jayakumar Christian, Desmond Tutu, Rene Padilla, and others who called for a more integral and holistic mission, with many involved through what became Micah Global. A number of these leaders became close friends, mentors, and collaborators. What this tribe had in common was a Christian faith that challenged lifestyle, systems, and all relationships through Jesus. This included relationships with the land. I didn't hear that call very clearly at first, I was more interested in discipleship, community building, and justice seeking, but it was there waiting for me and grew in importance over the years.

Third, indigenous views of the world saw land and place as more than spaces to fill.

Injustice in Australia has a clear and present face: our Indigenous Australians. If we were going to take seriously Jesus and his call for Shalom in this life, then we had to find a way to connect beyond the weeds of racism that divided us. In 1996, I was on a 'Jilba' led by Indigenous friends Marciel and Reg Lawrence. A Jilba is a kind of walkabout, a journey of discovery. It was for me. We visited Indigenous communities around the Murray River on the border of Victoria and New South Wales as part of an effort with Churches of Christ to listen and better respond. The original name of the Murray River is 'Dhungala,' and it winds its way through the traditional Indigenous lands of the Yorta Yorta, Wamba Wamba, and Barapa Barapa people. These original inhabitants and custodians have lived for tens of thousands of years here. Few of our Ministers took up the opportunity for this Jilba. Instead, Maori leaders from the Whakapapaiti Leadership College in NZ, some of our Burmese neighbours, and members of our newly planted Rainbow Church in Springvale came. We were all shocked by what we saw, heard, and felt. It's one thing to read about horrendous atrocities, attempted genocide, stolen land and generations, but it was quite another to go and hear first-hand accounts on the land where it had happened. Jim Bear Jacobs, a North American first nation man, says:

> You people of European descent tend to think of events occurring on a timeline. An event that is distant on that timeline is distant from you. But we indigenous peoples think

of events primarily occurring in a place. Whenever we are near that place, we are near that event, no matter when it happened. For us, places hold stories. Places become sacred because of the stories they hold.[60]

'God alive and present in creation' became an awakening for me. It soon made sense that stewardship of land matters because God lives there. God hurts when land is hurt. Over the years the connections with Uncle Ray Minniecon, Uncle Graham Paulson, Aunty Jean Phillips and the World Indigenous Christian Gathering opened up a world to me. The work to start the Sir Doug Nicholls Leadership Programme in 1998 especially excited me. Named in honour of the famous Indigenous Australian Minister, footballer, and Governor of South Australia, we saw indigenous Christian leaders from New Zealand, USA, and Canada sharing alongside Australian Indigenous leaders on a nationally accredited, alternative pathway to Ministry Endorsement. This Churches of Christ training course was recognised by other denominations too. To be part of the team to help make this possible, and to be a fly on the wall and listen to inspirational insights as well as the heavy burdens these leaders face, felt like important work. It was complicated, too. Colonisation had different degrees of impact on different peoples and lands. The connections we made through this group, especially on residentials together, changed our lives, not least mine.

When UNOH started Surrender Conferences in 2003, seeking to mobilise a new generation of radical disciples, we made sure Indigenous voices were up front and centre. While many attendees came to hear renowned speaker-activists like Jackie Pullinger, Elias Chacour, Tony Campolo, Shane Claiborne, Mike Duncan, or Mike Frost, they left inspired and challenged by Indigenous voices. I would never see land the way same again. I had learnt that a web of life connects everything; this ancient wisdom has wide ranging implications for us all.

Fourth, we couldn't ignore the environmental crisis and the connection with local places.
The interconnectedness between the environment and our local communities may seem obvious now, but that hasn't always been the case

for me. I previously thought environmental concerns are a privilege for those not in survival mode. Yet, in the rise of the eco-justice movement, especially from young people unwilling for creation to be ignored, I found a connection too.

The first conference I led in the UK was called 'The New Parish' and was a collaboration with the US authors of the book of the same name. Paul Sparks, Tim Soerens, and Dwight J. Friesen joined local Christian activists from all over the UK to connect with likeminded people and share insights at the historic 'St Martin's in the Bullring' in Birmingham, in October 2015. One of the key themes was that by taking local places seriously we can encourage human flourishing, preserve ecosystems, and ensure sustainable development for present and future generations. We can't keep living the way we do; a renewed focus on locality can be a key part to finding environmental solutions.

Take, for example, the rapid rise of biodiversity loss. One of the most frightening environmental statistics for local communities is that it is estimated that around one million plant and animal species are currently at risk of extinction, primarily due to human activities such as habitat destruction, pollution, overexploitation, and climate change. This statistic is alarming because biodiversity loss has far-reaching consequences for ecosystems and communities. Local communities depend on diverse ecosystems for various essential services, including clean air and water, fertile soils for agriculture, natural pest control, and climate regulation. When species disappear, these services are disrupted, leading to negative impacts on human health, livelihoods, and overall wellbeing.

Biodiversity loss also affects local cultures and indigenous communities who have deep connections to their environments. This is not just a loss for Aboriginal tribes in Australia, but, as we have seen, it destroys the heritage of significant local green spaces like Black Patch Park in Winson Green. The disappearance of traditional practices, knowledge systems, and cultural identities tied to specific species and ecosystems adds to the sense of loss and threatens cultural diversity.

Furthermore, the loss of keystone species, which play critical roles in maintaining ecosystem balance, can trigger cascading effects that impact other species and disrupt entire ecological systems. This can lead to their collapse and further exacerbate environmental problems, including food and water, making it increasingly difficult for local communities to adapt and thrive.

Addressing biodiversity loss requires concerted efforts to protect and restore habitats, regulate harmful practices, promote sustainable land and resource management, and reduce our ecological footprint. Preserving biodiversity is not only crucial for the health of local ecosystems, it's also for the resilience and long-term sustainability of local communities.

The New Parish conference helped me realise that if I live more fully in my local area, I can contribute to environmental sustainability in several important ways:

1. **Reduced Carbon Footprint**: By focusing on local living, we can reduce our carbon footprint. Consuming locally produced food and goods means less energy is required for transportation, reducing greenhouse gas emissions. Supporting local farmers and businesses also promotes sustainable practices and reduces the reliance on long-distance shipping.

2. **Preservation of Natural Resources**: Embracing a local lifestyle encourages the preservation of natural resources. By minimising consumption and waste, we help conserve resources such as water, energy, and raw materials. Additionally, supporting local initiatives for sustainable land use, conservation projects, and protection of local ecosystems helps maintain biodiversity and ecological balance.

3. **Stronger Community Connections**: Living fully in a local area fosters a sense of community and social cohesion. Engaging with our neighbours and participating in local activities strengthens community bonds. We can meet people accidentally, more regularly and without planning. This can lead to collaborative efforts in implementing sustainable practices, sharing resources, and collectively addressing community challenges.

4. **Local Economy Support**: When we prioritise local businesses and products, we contribute to the vitality of the local economy. This, in turn, helps create jobs, boosts entrepreneurship, and enhances the overall wellbeing of the community. Supporting local artisans, farmers' markets, and locally owned businesses promotes sustainable economic development while reducing the environmental impact associated with large-scale industries.

5. **Cultural Preservation**: Embracing and appreciating local traditions, cultures, and indigenous knowledge helps sustainable living. Preserving cultural diversity is intertwined with protecting the environment as indigenous communities often have deep connections and sustainable practices rooted in their cultural heritage. By respecting and learning from local cultures, we can promote sustainability and foster a more inclusive society.

Living more fully in a local area empowers us to make choices that align with our values, promote environmental stewardship, and create a more sustainable future. It is about recognising the interconnectedness of our actions with the wellbeing of the local environment, economy, and community.

Fifth, a lack of land rights and secure housing undermines the fullest coming of God's shalom.
We learnt this painful lesson in two of our previous relocations. In Springvale, the district once considered the most dangerous in Melbourne, the community came together and the neighbourhood was renewed in so many ways. Drug use went down, the diverse restaurants that people used to make fun of now became treasured, the young people from places like Vietnam, East Timor, China, and Cambodia began to improve their schooling and job prospects. There was an upward mobility for some extended families who wanted to remain. Instead of staying in the old weatherboard homes they once rented, they began to buy them, knock them down, and build mansions on them. Others with money soon joined them. This was classic gentrification.

However, not all the boats floated with this tide. The price of rents and houses skyrocketed and pushed out many long-term residents. We had to sell that Buddhist Temple in Springvale so that we could follow our friends further out to places like Dandenong. Had we been partly responsible for gentrification? Had we not benefited from it? These were uncomfortable questions to face.

In Klong Toey, Bangkok, community development was thwarted because there was no security of land tenure. Land that was once considered swamp land was, after 50 years of settlement, now considered valuable. This meant bulldozers could demolish neighbourhoods that had been settled for decades, taking back land for the Port Authority of Thailand to use as they saw fit. During many of our 12 years there, rumours swept through that a new shopping mall, casino, or apartment estate would be built over the top of our neighbourhood. This prevented local investment then, and it continues today. Why invest in the built environment, in local housing, schooling, and basic infrastructure if they could be bulldozed tomorrow?

These two issues, gentrification and housing security, became central findings in my PhD research. The rapid growth of informal settlements, like Klong Toey, is a global phenomenon that impacts one third of urban people. Desmond Tutu famously said, "We can't just pull drowning people out of the river. We must go upstream to see who is pushing them in." Meeting Chris Elisara from the World Evangelical's Creation Care Network at a Micah Gathering in 2015 helped me work this through. Chris is passionate about natural and built environments and is a kind of lobbyist into global networks, including the United Nations. A New Zealander by birth, he had moved to Philadelphia to study with Campolo at Eastern University and was a key part of the New Urbanism design movement. We hit it off immediately. We joined forces and started the Urban Shalom Society that ran Summits and the journal New Urban World. A key goal was to go 'upstream' and get involved in the United Nations Habitat call for a 'New Urban Agenda' (NUA). In my mind if all the nations of the world would sign up to NUA this would help prevent or at least thwart the rapid growth of slums.[61] I also felt that in Winson Green, probably our last relocation, we needed to put housing security on top of our agenda. This included buying a home there, to be invested as residents ourselves, but also to try and find ways to develop the built environment with and for local people.

Sixth, having gone 'upstream' I could see where I could most make a difference.

I recall being in Singapore in 2017 helping run the first faith-based UN Habitat 'Urban Thinkers Campus' with Urban Shalom Society. I was on a break, chatting with Tim Costello. Tim is one of the heroes of the faith and officially a 'National Treasure' in Australia. Few have influenced my thinking on power and transformation as much as Tim. We talked for hours about levers of change. What makes a real difference? Tim had been to a lot of UN events in his role with World Vision Australia and was kind enough to be a keynote speaker at our first UN-recognised event that tried to bring people of faith together to talk about the future of cities. I was at the UN Habitat III in Quito, Ecuador the year earlier and sat next to Chris Elisara when all the nations agreed on a more secure, sustainable, and inclusive urban world at the UN General Assembly with the New Urban Agenda. I was now helping run this follow-up event, to help prepare for the next UN meeting. However, I was becoming disappointed that nothing seemed to happen, despite all this conversation and significant costs in time and money.

The world's press hardly covered any of these massive UN agreements about the future of cities, never mind Christians. Tim's answer to where he had seen the most significant change happen surprised me. It wasn't in these kinds of global agreements.

> 'It was when I was Mayor of St Kilda and a Baptist Minister there. We secured housing for local people and enabled the local heritage to thrive with those people.'

It was at the local level that I too wanted to give some of my best energy.

Before former US president Barack Obama entered politics, he was a community organiser on the tough streets of Chicago. He once wrote this about an alternative calling for him:

> I can't help but wonder sometimes what would've happened if I'd stayed with organising, or at least some version of it. Like many local heroes I've met over the years, I might have managed to build up an institution that could reshape a neighbourhood or a portion of the city. Anchored deep in a

community, I might have steered money and imagination to change not the world, but just that one place or that one set of kids, doing work to touch the lives of neighbours and friends in some meaningful and useful way.[62]

I knew I couldn't be US President, but this sounded like a pretty good alternative to me!

Renewing places, as well as people, has become a central part of our calling over the decades, with our growing sense that God is alive in places. This was informed by the circumstances of relocating to Springvale and then Klong Toey, but we suspected Winson Green was the arena we would see this happen in new ways and see how far we could go. We had a growing passion to see God's salvation released in the places we lived. Eugene Peterson put it this way:

> In the Christian imagination, where you live gets equal billing with what you believe. Geography and theology are biblical bedfellows. Everything that the creator God does, and therefore everything that we do, since we are his creatures and can hardly do anything any other way, is in place. All living is local—this land, this neighbourhood, these trees and streets and house, this work, these shops and markets.[63]

Why could I see the places and the people in Winson Green had huge potential; that this was not a wasteland; that my own wellbeing was intrinsically tied to the wellbeing of my new neighbourhood? I think God had been priming me my whole life for such a time as this. If I couldn't see this by now, then I was simply blind! I am conscious that others saw this long before I did, with far less prompting. It's also true that not everyone has had my experiences, met the remarkable people I have, or experienced the incredible places I have been to, but I hope that by outlining these influences, you too are ready to see your neighbourhood as a sacred place in new ways.

God's Big Story: Shalom, People and Place!

Cities are especially contested places today. There are so many competing dreams. We can't simply consume other's dreams or leave a vacuum. What then do we, as Christians, have to offer for a preferred future?

The biblical vision of 'shalom' became a key understanding for me and needs to be unpacked further. Shalom can be considered as 'the seed' that lays dormant, ready to grow and bear fruit, even in the most challenging of local places and environments. It can be understood as a vision, but not one we have to try to manufacture or manipulate people to follow. We *detect* this vision of flourishing, more than try to invent it. Without a vision like this we will perish. Getting people together can be a recipe for disaster if there is no worthwhile purpose to it. Eugene Peterson's paraphrase of Proverbs 28:18 puts it this way:

> If people can't see what God is doing,
>   they stumble all over themselves;
> But when they attend to what he reveals,
>   they are most blessed.
> (Prov. 29:18 [The Message])

God's unfolding revelation of Shalom needs to be explored further if we are to fully grasp its life-giving potential. At its heart, Shalom means **the promise of God, place, and people living in harmony together.** This vision can be understood as the bible's central story. Once you see this thread, you can't unsee it!

Our creation story starts with the Creator (God), Garden (place), and Adam and Eve (people) living in harmony together, but soon these relationships are disconnected (Genesis 1 and 2). The call to restore Shalom is taken up by Yahweh (God) choosing Abraham to form a new nation (people) on a promised land (place) to be a blessing of Shalom to the whole earth (Gen. 12:1-3).

While the Hebrew nation has ups and downs in this pursuit, God's prophets keep the dream alive: Yahweh's Shalom (God) in Israel (people) is tied up to the wellbeing of the city (place), whether in the promised land's capital city, Jerusalem – which literally means 'city of shalom' (Isa. 65) – or even when exiled in Babylon (Jer. 29).

Jesus' vision is often expressed as 'The Kingdom of God' in the first three Gospels, where Jesus' disciples (people) are taught to pray that the Father's kingdom and will (God) is done on earth as in heaven (place) (Matt. 6:9-13 and Luke 11:2-4).

Shalom ripples explicitly through John's Gospel connecting all together throughout the universe. 'Theo' (God) so loved the 'cosmos' (place) that he gave his son that 'who-so-ever' (people) can live to the full 'forever' (John 3:16). Indeed, the very reason Jesus came on earth was to bring 'life to the full' (John 10:10 [NIV]). The resurrected Jesus finds the disciples hiding fearfully in a locked room, but charges them with this call, "[Shalom] be with you. As the Father has sent me, so I am sending you" (John 20:21). As they follow the risen Jesus, in the power of the Spirit, sharing the Creator's good news (God) in all the earth (place) with all the nations (people), the promise of Shalom is being fulfilled.

Then we see the growth of the church across the world. Responding to the God of Glory (God) calls neighbours to gather and multiply (people) in cities (place) as a sign of this promise, with correspondence captured in letters to God's churches in Rome, Galatia, Corinthians, etc. These letters by Paul and other apostles are written to specific 'people' in specific 'places' for God's glory, to see Shalom come among them.

The final scene of the bible in Revelation 21 has a reworking of Isaiah 65's promise of God's new Jerusalem, where heaven and earth join together. This time death is removed.

> I heard a loud shout from the throne, saying, 'Look, God's home is now among his people! He will live with them, and they will be his people. God himself will be with them. He will wipe every tear from their eyes, and there will be no more death or sorrow or crying or pain. All these things are gone forever.' (Rev. 21:3-4 [NIV])

All destructive relationships have gone. Even death leaves the story. Only everlasting harmony between God, people, and place remains. This promised ending should not surprise us. God, people and place are meant to live in harmony together from the beginning.

With this big story and vision in mind, let us focus on one New Testament text to show how this vision of wholeness can be a seed of hope in our local communities and local leaders. But first, take the time to pause and think through these questions, right where you are.

Personal Reflections

1. What do you see when you see your local place?

2. Who has most influenced your understanding of the purposes of God in your neighbourhood?

3. Of the six influences on Ash about the importance of place, which ones can you most and least relate to?

4. Have you seen the connections between God, people and place in the Bible before like this? Why, why not?

5. What could you do to love your local place more?

Chapter 6:
'Fear Not!' - Seeds Of Shalom And Resisting Fear

The thief comes only to steal and kill and destroy; I have come that they may have life, and have it to the full.
– Jesus, John 10:10 [NIV]

A bible story that helps create hope and vision for change within me is the shepherds' encounter with the angels recorded in Luke's Gospel. This text is typically read in the lead up to Christmas, but it's more than a Christmas story. It has three phrases within it that can particularly help us all, like the shepherds, anticipate the good purposes God has in and through our local leaders and our communities.

It is worth noting that in biblical times shepherds were marginal people. They were often, as this story says, sleeping out in fields at night, not in homes. They were often hired hands, known to be scallywags and not to be trusted. Jesus himself needed to clarify that he was a "good shepherd" and not like the "hired hand" who ran away at the slightest hint of danger (John 10:11-18). That God's angelic beings, a whole army of them at that, would choose these labourers to reveal God's purposes for the world and call them into action, would have seemed strange to establishment leaders. Why not work through the important and powerful people, top down? Yet, this encounter is so consistent with a

God of justice, hope, and compassion who works from the ground up. If the shepherds were among the first to receive the Good News and pass it on, then there is hope for all our local communities without exception.

Please read Luke 2:8-20 slowly and consider these three phrases over the next three chapters.

"Fear Not!" (v. 10a [ESV])

Faced with a sky full of angelic beings, on the verge of the greatest night in human history, did the shepherds understand what was going on?
Fear is a natural, reasonable, and important emotion here. So much was unprecedented. So much could go wrong. So much could hurt. Fear alerts our body to danger. Whether it's seeing angelic beings or feeling vulnerable on our streets, it's not wrong to feel fear, but it matters where we go with it. The natural reactions to fight, flight, or freeze are sometimes not enough. Those instinctive reactions to hide, numb, avoid, or do violence don't serve us well in the end. Deeper responses are required if our local communities are to find the freedom and peace we all need. If we are to experience God's promised Shalom we need to face the fears of the unknown and step bravely into this destiny.

It should not surprise us that angels say "Fear not" to the shepherds. Fear is an integral part of anticipating God's purposes of shalom; it's a common occurrence in the Scriptures. For example, after the execution of Jesus, the disciples hide, locked away in a secret room "for fear of the Jewish leaders" (John 20:19 [NIV]). Jesus personally entered that room which was thickly drenched in fear. When the disciples saw the resurrected Jesus for the first time in their midst, they heard his first words clearly: 'shalom.' It was more than a greeting. They must have felt even more fear that he had found them there, hiding together. Jesus then 'showed them his hands and side,' the marks of torture before his death. This really was the risen Jesus Messiah. Having calmed their fears, only then does Jesus commission them:

> Again, Jesus said, "Peace [shalom] be with you! As the Father has sent me, I am sending you." And with that he breathed on them and said, "Receive the Holy Spirit. If you forgive anyone's sins, their sins are forgiven; if you do not forgive them, they are not forgiven." (John 20:21-23 [NIV])

Jesus becomes present with the disciples in the midst of their fears. Indeed, they are to take on the mission of Jesus, to go as Jesus was sent, starting from that locked room. This calling will cost most of them their lives too. It's not that fear is unreasonable here, but the Holy Spirit knows we need to step over the threshold of fear before we can surrender to God's purposes. To step through fear is to glimpse our destiny and to be awake to God's work in that specific moment. So much is outside our control. It's only in God that fear can genuinely be appeased and Shalom experienced. It's important to note then, that 'the Great Commission,' the purpose statement of the early church in John's Gospel, included Shalom given in the midst of fear. These are integrated, central concerns for God and should be for us too.

I have found that the courage to resist fear and find Shalom can be contagious. The shepherds on the hill and the disciples in a locked room didn't face these fears and or experience these promises alone. This has been true for me. I have sometimes felt like I am in a group of disciples in a locked room, or among those shepherds on an exposed hillside. I have needed the company of braver souls than me to face down my fear. This has been my experience around the world.

In Winson Green, January 2021, deep in lockdown, I was fearful for our Gwen. She is like the grandma we never had and gave the neighbourhood the big hugs we all needed. By January 2021, around 100,000 people within a few hours' drive of us in Birmingham had died because of Covid. At the time of writing over 230,000 have died with Covid-19 given as the reason.[64] As a housemate and volunteer pastor at our local church, Gwen worked tirelessly in advocacy and caring for neighbours. We created a special office for Gwen as we resurrected Lodge Road United Reformed Church. Most weekdays, long lines of residents waited patiently to see her for help with their benefits, housing, immigration issues, or all of the above. The local police gave us special permission to stay open during lockdown, so we were one of the few organisations left standing in our local community, and this made these lines even longer. Gwen was nearing retirement age and was one of the first people who had been 'jabbed' with the vaccine. The UK Government had gambled all its chips on 'herd immunity' that vaccines would bring, and so we just kept carrying on.

It was a shock, therefore, when Gwen tested positive for Covid. Then, when her breathing started to fail, an ambulance came to Newbigin House to pick her up. I remember watching Gwen slowly shuffle through our front gate and, with help, get into the back of the ambulance. Would I ever see Gwen again? I felt powerless. I wasn't even allowed to get in the back of the ambulance, to be with her in her time of need, like she had for so many. More than that, I felt a fearful dread of what was to come. I burst into tears as the ambulance drove away.

Gwen, however, had a deep peace. She felt loved by us all and felt that her time had not yet come. We hurried, worried, and prayed, but Gwen sensed God would bring her back safely to Newbigin House and Lodge Road. Many people entered City Road hospital with Covid and never returned to their loved ones. Gwen, however, did return, eventually recovered, and continues to love those who most need help in our neighbourhood. Gwen said of this time:

> 'I knew not to fear, God had this and even if I died, I was doing the right things for God.'

Gwen gave us all courage to carry on and seek Shalom with our neighbours.

I had a similar experience in Kyiv in October 2022. Since 2018 I've helped design and teach an MA programme with colleagues and students at the Ukrainian Evangelical Theological Seminary in Kyiv. After the Russian invasion of February 2022, six Russian missiles hit their campus. They were not to be deterred and rebuilt the places the bombs hit and decided to re-open the campus. Dave Mann, my friend and colleague at Seedbeds, and I both felt it important to be there in person for that important moment, to teach and stand with our friends.

6: 'Fear Not!' - Seeds Of Shalom And Resisting Fear

Despite knowing it was the right thing to do, I felt all kinds of fear at the prospect of travelling to this intense warzone. UK and Australian Governments warned travellers not to go to Ukraine and travel insurance was impossible while Russia continued to bombard Ukraine with drones and missiles. I don't have a death wish and I'm not keen on pain, so why put ourselves in harm's way if we don't need to? Yet, the niggle continued and a surge of support from Dave encouraged me. Of course, I needed to talk with Anji. What would happen if something went wrong? She would be most impacted. Anji smiled, 'I wondered why we just paid up your life insurance? Seriously, we've trusted God our whole married life, why stop now?' We also didn't want to be a burden on already busy colleagues on the ground in Kyiv. As we discussed backwards and forwards, they were clear that they would understand if we didn't want to come, but it would make a huge statement to students, faculty, and supporters if we did. Dave and I decided to go.

It was quite a journey to get to Kyiv. No direct flights were possible there this time. My trip from Birmingham to Kraków was long, but straightforward with a bus ride to Luton, airport hotel, and an early flight. I even enjoyed a stroll, luggage in tow, around the historic old quarter of Kraków and washed down some tasty pork ribs with a local Polish beer. Waiting for the train was no hardship either, with a cappuccino in a shopping centre that could have been any city in the world. Things got harder at the border. I wrote my reflections and thoughts down as I travelled:

> "I'm at the Poland-Ukraine border, changing trains. We've been waiting over an hour now. It's after 10pm and it's started to really pour down on us, with the temperature plummeting. Must be about 800 of us lining up, soggy coats and bags, right around the corners. Conscious of families with small children returning and how determined they all look. Also that lots of kindness is being shown. The shared light-blue plastic poncho, for example, is on brand Ukraine and very much appreciated.
>
> A few hours later a lady in front of me in a bright-yellow fluffy coat starts rifling through her soggy bag. She pulls out an umbrella. 'Now she does this?!' I smile out loud.

It's interpreted by her friend and soon others around are smiling too. Small mercies.

Eventually lights come on in the shack we are waiting in front of and the line slowly shuffles closer to have our passports and papers checked. Sharon has organised lots of diverse papers and I'm grateful they are in order and easy to access as I move closer. I just hope this doesn't take too long as the train is due to leave soon. What if I'm rejected? Or miss this train? Where would I stay tonight? I shuffle forward with more intent. In the end I only needed my passport and once stamped, I made it through passport control and ran onto the platform. I make it to my seat on carriage five with four minutes to spare. It's warm inside and I have plenty of room as my two colleagues' seats are empty, needing to drop out at the last minute. I have 14 hours till Kyiv."

During that journey my mind raced to other borderlands: Birmingham-Sandwell Councils in our neighbourhood and the complex campaigning for a new high school and secure homes there; the England-Scotland borderlands where we walk the St Cuthbert's Way and finish on Holy Island with Change Makers; the Thai-Burma border and our recent time in Mae Sot with the Civil Disobedience Movement activists piloting the Change Incubator programme.

What do these diverse borderlands have in common? Suspicions, often complications and inefficiencies, even danger. For me, also a sense of call to the edges where centres of power often have little control. Creativity, cooperation, and innovation seem more possible here. Unlikely people bond together.

Safely on board the train, I contact friends and family praying for me. My daughter Amy sent a text that her friend recently visited Kyiv with Doctors Without Borders. I replied, 'I think a doctor might be a bit more useful here than a theologian right now! Can only give what's in our hands to give though!'

There are small televisions throughout the train carriage showing repeated cartoon-driven messages, silently, but with Ukrainian subtitles.

6: 'Fear Not!' - Seeds Of Shalom And Resisting Fear

Some seem to be adverts for items like headache tablets, but some others are 'duck and cover' public announcements in the case of missile strikes. It's getting real.

I settle in for the overnight train journey, and listening to Billy Bragg, start to doze off and ride into the dark unknown. What will tomorrow bring beyond the borderlands?

It was a relief to see colleagues in Kyiv, but teaching in a war zone wasn't easy either. Denis, one of the Ukrainian lecturers, tried to reassure me at one point, but 'Don't worry about the 'boom, boom" probably wasn't the best way to do it. I wasn't too worried until then! I had heard thuds in the distance earlier and assumed it wasn't anything. 'They are just getting rid of excess missiles.' There was quite a 'Boom, Boom' in the afternoon session that shook the classroom and I looked across at Denis. He just shrugged, looked at the app on his mobile that warns him of danger and mouthed it was fine. He carried on translating, not missing a beat. The others smiled at me. The new normal.

That morning Wes White explored the nature of 'sin as against God's shalom' on Zoom from Glasgow. He encouraged us to reflect on the current realities, even over the last 24 hours. 'What isn't as it ought to be?' Denis talked about hearing news of the dreadful killing of a local pregnant woman, and the day-to-day reality of life shivering with cold in his apartment without electricity, Putin's latest deeds to terrorise the people of Ukraine. 'Not as bad as missiles, but sure, not as it ought to be.'

I snuck into the library during the break and started talking with the Principal, Ivan Rusch. He was a bit teary, pointing out what had happened to the library through the shelling. All the windows had been blown out, the walls and doors punched through. 'Now, students are back studying here! I'm so emotional.' I could still see shrapnel marks on the ceilings, but the library was functioning again. 'The Ukrainian army lived here for a while. They protected our library!' I know, with the rise of the internet, libraries are out of fashion, but there is something precious about the smell and space of a room full of books. Worth protecting indeed.

No Wastelands

On my final evening, Ivan stood in the seminary car park with Dave Mann, who had arrived from London for his week of lectures. My teaching completed, it was such a relief to see Dave again and to go out for dinner. As Ivan drove the car to Kiev central, we heard about what it was like to stay in Kiev when others fled. Every part of the road trip had stories.

> 'We decided no one will be hungry in this neighbourhood and so we worked to make that building over there work for food and for accommodation for older people who couldn't leave…. We had to buy a bus to help evacuate people. One of our student's body was found, but it was cut up by the Russians and spread over different places and his mother was distraught at the funeral held there. That forest is where we served communion to our troops… This whole road had fighting. See where a rocket landed.'

Ivan could fill books with these stories and his theological insights. I hope he can.

At a restaurant in downtown Kyiv we meet Fyedor, the seminary's key theologian, who had lost both his wife and son over the last year. There was no room for the four of us in the traditional Ukrainian restaurant they liked, so we walked into the civic square. Destroyed Russian tanks and cars were exhibited. It was dark because of the lack of electricity and it was hard to see much, but people were out and about. We found a special restaurant that only sells food from Kyiv. Dave and I ordered Borsch and 'The Best Chicken Kyiv.'

I wish I had recorded our conversations. Both men faced their fears and shared how they had suffered for staying in Kyiv when others fled. Not all Christians in Kyiv took up the command to 'fear not.' There was frustration from Christians who stayed in Kyiv. Many Christian men left when they were most needed. The worship leader, for example, who left as early as possible and now wanted to zoom in to teach 'how to worship God in war.' Or the Christian ministers who paid for forged passports to get out illegally. Was Jesus was talking about them in John 10:12-13? When the wolf came to attack the sheep, they found some to be the hired hands? In contrast, Ivan and Fyedor are passionate, honest, practical, and deeply theological in their approaches to this context of suffering. Ivan, who did his PhD on Newbigin, now explores Newbigin's public theology in a context of war. Fyedor explores political theology and the 'red lines of nationalism' as identified by the prophets. Both are inspirational and I hope the world can get a chance to hear what Dave and I heard that night. We need it! Their kind of courage can be contagious.

I asked them how we could be better allies and advocates. Ivan looked up at me across the table:

> 'Presence matters. Many of our own people are not here. Your presence here is healing for us.'

I'm not sure how true that will end up being, but I know being there was right and overcoming my own fears for these historic movements are some of the most important times in my life. We had a sense of Shalom together around that table, even in the midst of a war zone.

The angels needed to help the shepherds overcome fear before the promises of God were revealed. The shepherds didn't overcome fear alone. They needed each other. We need courageous community leaders too.

What is a genuine antidote to fear? We have talked about hope in previous chapters, but there is love and joy too. "Love expels all fear" (1 John 4:18). When God loves people and places through us we can even risk ourselves in sacrificial love. God so loved the cosmos he gave. Joy, also, helps us respond to God in the most difficult of circumstances. Needing to appease fear, the angels point to joy in their announcement to the shepherds. Fear can be a sign of life, but we need to move past it too if Shalom is to be experienced.

Personal Reflections

1. When have you most experienced fear? What happened? What was it like? How did you survive?

2. What are you most afraid of if you gave your life more fully to God's purposes in your neighbourhood? What could go wrong?

3. Why is overcoming fear worth the effort, even if it doesn't end the way we plan?

Chapter 7:
'Great Joy' - Joy And The Seeds Of Shalom

Living the hope of the city.
Oh we dance and sing
As we're living the hope of the city.
Oh the Spirit blows,
And we're finding God
> *In seeking justice,*
> *In celebration,*
> *In many small groups,*
> *In signs of life in rich and poor.*

Oh we're working, oh we're living for Shalom.
– Ross Langmead[65]

I am bringing you good news of great joy for all the people: to you is born this day in the city of David a Savior, who is the Messiah, the Lord. This will be a sign for you: you will find a child wrapped in bands of cloth and lying in a manger.
Luke 2:10b-12 [New Revised Standard Version]

The shepherds' fears are calmed in part by a promise and a sign. The promise was that this Good News would bring great joy. The sign, though, is often misunderstood by us today. The promise and sign both need a little unpacking if we are to see their implications for us.

No Wastelands

I love our neighbourhood at Christmas time; our 'live nativities' have become a feature. We have live sheep, goats, and a donkey. Our alpacas even dress up as camels for the wise men and their shelter on the school field becomes the stable. Hundreds of residents move around the block for different moments in the nativity story and sing carols together. It is particularly dramatic when our Mary and Joseph, with all their animals and the crowds behind them, knock on various doors of our neighbours asking for a place to stay. This is always a moment to hold our breath. Did the neighbour remember this was organised? Are they home? Will we scare someone who then makes trouble? Eventually the door opens, and we hear a gruff shout of 'No! Go away! There's no room in the inn!' We all breathe a sigh of relief, laugh, and sing a carol.

The 'no room in the inn' tradition, however fun and positive it is for us today, undermines our understanding of what was the shepherds' sign. Consider what actually happened. The shepherds recognise the angels' reference to "the city of David" as the small peasant village of Bethlehem. This was not obvious to outsiders as most would have thought of Jerusalem as David's City. Bethlehem, though, was where the shepherds were from themselves, and Joseph's hometown that he needed to return to for the Roman census. He had family there, proud of their hospitality and royal lineage. He would not have needed to book into a cheap hotel and end up in a stable. Family would have put him up.

Kenneth Bailey does important cultural work for us here. He argues that peasant homes were set up in three sections. At one end, the animals had a space to be brought inside for safety reasons each night. The middle was the family area that people lived and slept in. It included an adjoining wall with an opening for feeding the animals and to help the family keep warm. At the far end was the guest room or 'inn.' Luke is careful not to use the word for commercial inn or hotel, but a guest room for hospitality. There was no space in that guest room, because other family must have been there, so Mary and Joseph are most likely in the middle room, with the house's family. The strips of cloth and the baby in the manger, in the wall between animal and family room, were together a sign that the baby was in a peasant household. It was safe for the shepherds to go there and see this good news because the baby was one of them! They need not be frightened of breaking into a powerful elite's birth.

7: 'Great Joy' - Joy And The Seeds Of Shalom

The angels anticipated this anxiety and told the shepherds they would find the baby wrapped (which was what peasants, like shepherds, did with their newly born children). Furthermore, they were told that he was lying in a *manger*! That is, they would find the Christ child in an ordinary peasant home such as theirs. He was not in a governor's mansion or a wealthy merchant's guest room but in a simple two-room home like theirs. This was *really* good news. Perhaps they would not be told, 'Unclean shepherds-be gone!' This was *their sign*, a sign for lowly shepherds.

With this special sign of encouragement, the shepherds proceeded to Bethlehem in spite of their "low degree" (Luke 1:52 [King James Version]). On arrival they reported their story and everyone was amazed. Then they left "praising God for all that they had heard and seen" (Luke 2:20). The word 'all' obviously included *the quality of the hospitality* that they witnessed on arrival. Clearly, they found the holy family in perfectly adequate accommodations, not in a dirty stable. If, on arrival, they had found a smelly stable, a frightened young mother, and a desperate Joseph, they would have said, 'This is outrageous! Come home with us! Our women will take care of you!' Within five minutes the shepherds would have moved the little family to their own homes. The honor of the entire village would rest on their shoulders and they would have sensed their responsibility to do their duty. The fact that they walked out, without moving the young family, means that the shepherds felt they could not offer better hospitality than what had already been extended to them.[66]

This is the joy of the Gospel – ordinary people are included and their God-given gifts valued, recognised, and mobilised. The Greek word here for 'joy' is *xará* which means, 'to extend favour, lean towards, be favorably disposed,' the awareness (of God's) grace and favour; joy is 'grace recognised.' Joy comes from recognising gifts.

Spotting joy in local people is a kind of art form that can unlock transformation in whole communities. Many approaches to change start with asking what is *wrong* with people and communities. What are they upset about? Then they move to how to fix those needs and deficits with appropriate, often professional services. The results are so often unsustainable without significant outside resources, and rarely work. However, when we start with what is *strong* in people and communities, what gifts they recognise in themselves, and fan those strengths into flame, then long-term change can come from within. This is why we take Change Makers through the StrengthsFinder process, as it helps them to identify, focus on, and enjoy what is best about them.

I learnt that joy is often the key in Klong Toey. You could look at our neighbourhood, about 100,000 people in a square mile, and feel overwhelmed by the sheer misery of each household. Disease, exploitation, and real suffering was everywhere in some form or another. However, if you could spot joy in people, then things would change.

Anji has a finely tuned 'joy-detector.' She can spot joy a mile away and home in on it before anyone can blink. One day our neighbour Kuhn Poo came to Anji shaking with anxiety. Kuhn Poo was a brilliant cook and would sell her delicious and inexpensive meals out the front of her home, just across the small lane from us. Everyone loved her food, including us. Kuhn Poo's food created so much joy. But Kuhn Poo was upset that day because the government had removed subsidies from rice and the price had skyrocketed. Wages had not gone up, so now Kuhn Poo could not afford to sell her meals at a price neighbours could afford without losing money on every plate and going into debt. And when you get into debt in Klong Toey, you get into debt with some ruthless, dangerous, underworld people.

> 'Anji, could you get me a job with some of your *Furang* (Westerner) friends? We're desperate.'

At that point Anji could have fixed the deficit that Kuhn Poo had with a phone call to friends, but Anji knew the joy Kuhn Poo's cooking brought to herself and so many.

> 'You're such a great cook. Why don't you teach people how to cook? How about starting a cooking school for tourists?'

At first Poo was reluctant, but Anji specialises in filling people with hope and dreams when they don't have hope in themselves. First, Kuhn Poo experimented with visitors from Australia. She'd take them out to our

7: 'Great Joy' - Joy And The Seeds Of Shalom

local market and introduce them to delicacies like cockroaches, bugs, and frogs cut open with their hearts still beating. She'd then take them back to her little house and teach how to make intriguing, traditional, and quick Thai meals.

Visitors loved the authentic Thai experience that offered so much warm hospitality and created so much joy. Within six months the cooking school became the number one thing to do in Bangkok on Trip Advisor. Number two was visiting the Grand Palace. The cooking school expanded. It got larger premises a few doors down, a van, and employed lots of local people to help. Some would go on to start their own small businesses.

Then Anji convinced Kuhn Poo to create a cooking book to sell to customers. Shelly, a friend from Melbourne, was a brilliant photographer and spent weeks taking photographs of the food and the people. Anji and Kuhn Poo painstakingly worked out recipes and identified inspiring stories of people in Klong Toey. Of course, the title, *Cooking with Poo*, was genius. The book was entered into the Frankfurt Book Fair, the biggest book fair in the world, and won an award for the 'oddest book title of the year!' Comedians all around the world picked up on this and news reports from the BBC and others emerged. Jamie Oliver, the famous British chef, even did an episode with Poo where you can see the apron that says 'I cooked with Poo and I liked it.'[67] The book became a global phenomenon and Poo sold over 50,000 copies. By the time we left Bangkok, we saw how locally-gifted income generation could free whole neighbourhoods and saw this as a model for others. We couldn't have done this by finding someone with a name that sounded funny and starting a cooking school with them. We started with what was strong, what brought Poo joy, how Poo brought others joy, and the rest sorted itself out.

Unfortunately, shortly after we moved out of Klong Toey and transitioned to Birmingham, tragedy struck. A fire burnt down Poo's home and cooking school kitchen. The neighbours, some who had become jealous of Poo, blamed Poo and those pesky visitors who would come. They also saw a chance to get some quick money. Police were involved. Would they close down the cooking school? Had we been running the cooking school for Poo, this event would have been the end of it. There could be no recovery for a Western-owned programme there. However, this was Poo and her husband Kai's social business. They carefully, and in culturally appropriate ways, rebuilt trust and ensured everyone had what they needed. There was a deep resilience that comes from joy and empowerment from within.

Amy, Aiden, and I visited Klong Toey in July 2022. We stayed with Poo and Kai and brought friends to cook with Poo in her cooking school. Covid had decimated most of the Thai tourist industry, but here was Poo bouncing back again, taking customers on a joyful journey of a lifetime, empowering fellow residents. Services can run out of steam, but joy cannot be kept down.

Our new home in Birmingham soon provided another example of detecting joy. The Firs and Bromsford estate, in East Birmingham, is often maligned as a wasteland, but some of my most joyful experiences in the UK have been here. Indeed, this neighbourhood has become one of the best exponents I have ever seen of finding joy that changes lives and places. This local community helped shape Change Makers from the beginning and two of our Change Makers Alumni, Phil and Claire, have been instrumental in Firs and Bromsford's transformations through joy. Both have led colourful lives and used their experiences to create joy for others. When I say colourful, I mean that Phil was literally in a circus!

Joy can especially be found and expressed in the annual Firs and Bromsford community pantomime. 'Pantos' are a British institution and Phil directs and narrates them, teaching the parts to the local community. Claire is often the star of the show. We always bring busloads from Winson Green and arrive early at their community hall. As the lights go down and the music fades, suddenly Dame Molly (aka Phil) appears. Splendid in a Mother Goose costume, he quickly has us in stitches, cracking joke after joke that mostly go over the heads of the children gathered and sets up the storyline. The show itself then starts. Whether it's Jack and the Beanstalk, Aladdin, or Cinderella, familiar and traditional characters emerge. Tim Evans and Paul Wright, who are instrumental in both building community in this estate and founding

7: 'Great Joy' - Joy And The Seeds Of Shalom

Change Makers, always play the villains with relish. As ugly stepsisters, for example, they seriously frighten some kids, but have us all laughing till we cry in the end. Claire then comes on as the hero and saves the day in the finale.

This Panto isn't just entertainment; it uses local gifts to find and celebrate joy together. Indeed, it's become an annual tradition and a catalyst for community change. They have even had community Easter and Christmas plays using their streets as theatre. Phil's Change Maker pitch was for a History Centre and Cafe on desolate land that could both honour the local past and create a place to connect for the future. Claire has become a 'local street connector' and door knocks seeking out ways each resident can share what gifts they have in their local community. Momentum is being built as they use what's strong to fix what's wrong.[68]

We are not supposed to just exist and survive on this earth. We're made for more than that. God's purposes are for fullness of life (John 10:10) and so joy is how we can respond to signs of God's goodness on its way. It's that 'ping' in our hearts that goes off, becoming aware of all that we are grateful for.

My daily routines changed over lockdown. Conscious that my nights were getting later zoning out on Netflix, I became exhausted not going out. I began to get up early to reset my body clock and started most days naming at least three things that I was most grateful for. I can easily see what's wrong in life and can start the day with a head full of criticisms. Instead, I found something changes in my heart and mind when I begin the day with 20 minutes nurturing gratefulness.

During those Covid lockdowns and isolations, when so much was disrupted in so many ways, you would think gratitude would be hard to find. Surprisingly, with less action, it often took me over an hour to recount all the acts of kindness by neighbours, people offering their gifts, conversations over zoom, backyard discoveries, books I had the chance to read, dreams that were starting to come true. I rarely woke up feeling grateful in the middle of the pandemic, but this small practice became a habit that helped fill my heart, free my imagination, and open my eyes to pay attention to those around me as the new day unfolded.

Gratefulness became a key practice that helped me find my way into the joy of this next stage. No matter how dark life has gotten for me, there are people, events and gifts that I can pause, savour, and take time to appreciate. A full and joyful heart is unstoppable.

There is a saying, 'hurry and joy can't live in the same home.' Over the years I have met so many local church, charity, and community building leaders who are exhausted and stuck in survival mode. Hurried and complaining, like hamsters running on a never-ending wheel, they become cranky and cynical. I've been one of these at times. This is understandable, but that's no way to spend a life. I wonder what would happen if we could slow down and become better at joy-detecting? John Mark Comer explained it this way:

> Corrie ten Boom once said that if the Devil can't make you sin, he'll make you busy. There's truth in that. Both sin and busyness have the exact same effect – they cut off your connection to God, to other people, and even to your own soul.[69]

For me, at least, the willingness to consciously slow down, try not to pack out my day and consciously pay attention to moments of joy has helped with all my connections.

I completed the 280km Camino Portuguese pilgrimage from Porto, Portugal to Santiago de Compostela in Spain, March 2023. At the end of 'the Camino,' there is a place many pilgrims go to called Finisterre (literally 'the end of the world'). As I sat on rocks there, watching the wide Atlantic Ocean from the western most point of Spain, I was mesmerised by the ocean birds diving for fish. They'd go up so high, then, like a spear, speed down through the air, breaking the surface of the water, diving deep, and coming up with fish. I felt a challenge. Could I consistently go higher to gain better perspectives, pick my spots to focus better, and gain momentum to go deeper and find my destiny? I felt I needed to limit my priority-goals to five and let go of the many others I was interested in until I finished these. Finishing this book was one of these! What I was doing here was giving myself every chance of experiencing joy. Eliminating 'hurry,' I can find signs and promises in life too.

The angels announced there is 'Good news of great joy,' and as they invited the shepherds to this joy, so too are we invited into joy today. What is this good news that brings ultimate joy? What is that ultimate grace that gives our heart a 'ping'? Recognising joy helps recognise our life and destiny.

Personal Reflections

1. What are you most grateful for?
2. Where have you most noticed joy? What have been the promises and signs of that joy for you?
3. Where do we miss joy? Why?
4. What could be the next step in uncluttering our lives and becoming less busy? What can you say 'no' to so you can say 'yes' to the most important priorities and experience joy?

Chapter 8:
'Shalom On Earth?'

If people can't see what God is doing,
　　they stumble all over themselves;
But when they attend to what he reveals,
　　they are most blessed.
Proverbs 29:18 [MSG]

God's promised Shalom is a central theme of this book. These are the seeds we want to sow and bear fruit in our lives and local communities. In Advent, we especially prepare for God entering into the human experience to bring this "on earth peace and good will toward [all peoples]" (Luke 2:14 [New King James Version]). We are reminded that God's purpose is for all to fully experience His 'Shalom' – a sacred harmony between God, people, and the earth.

In the original Greek, the word for 'peace' used in this text, *eirēnē*, is more than 'lack of violence.' Often translated 'peace,' and deriving from *eirō*, 'to join, tie together into a whole,' the idea is that there is a proper *wholeness*. That is, all essential parts are joined together as they are intended. This *peace* is essentially God's gift of *wholeness*.

The shepherds, however, didn't actually speak the New Testament Greek that Luke records! They spoke a form of Hebrew, and if the angels were to communicate clearly with these shepherds, they would have needed to use the Hebrew word '*Shalom*.' Hebrew is a very earthy language and Shalom is more than a single word concept. It's about the whole purposes of God coming true. It's a time when God, people, and the earth live in sacred harmony together.

The shepherds knew the daily reality of life under Roman occupation. Shalom was limited. The Roman Empire was just the latest in a long line of oppressor-rulers. God's people were anxious for real life to start and have no end as God had promised. This new life without ending was promised in the Hebrew history, law, and prophets. For example, we see Isaiah 65 promises very new physical and social realities that the Hebrew people expected to inherit.

> 'For I am about to create new heavens
> and a new earth;
> the former things shall not be remembered
>   or come to mind.
> But be glad and rejoice for ever
>   in what I am creating;
> for I am about to create Jerusalem as a joy,
>   and its people as a delight.
> I will rejoice in Jerusalem,
>   and delight in my people;
> no more shall the sound of weeping be heard in it,
>   or the cry of distress.
> No more shall there be in it
>   an infant that lives but a few days,
>   or an old person who does not live out a lifetime;
> for one who dies at a hundred years will be considered a youth,
>   and one who falls short of a hundred will be considered accursed.
> They shall build houses and inhabit them;
>   they shall plant vineyards and eat their fruit.
> They shall not build and another inhabit;
>   they shall not plant and another eat;
> for like the days of a tree shall the days of my people be,
>   and my chosen shall long enjoy the work of their hands.
> They shall not labour in vain,

> or bear children for calamity;
> for they shall be offspring blessed by the LORD—
> and their descendants as well.
> Before they call I will answer,
> while they are yet speaking I will hear.
> The wolf and the lamb shall feed together,
> the lion shall eat straw like the ox;
> but the serpent—its food shall be dust!
> They shall not hurt or destroy
> on all my holy mountain,'
> says the LORD.
> (Isa. 65:17-25)

Here, God promises sustainable and resilient life, in a particular place, including proper work and health, where the most vulnerable people and the land itself are empowered and healed. What God intends is that the spheres of heaven and earth come together to form a new creation. Indeed, this is a central promise of what God will do through the Hebrew people. The shepherds, and many more, waited long for this Great Day to come. When would this happen for these shepherds and their people? When they hear from the angels that the promised Saviour-Messiah is being born not far from them, then it's these kinds of promises that are expected to come true. These promises are not about other-worldly, disembodied evacuation plans to heaven, as many of us imagine when we hear the words 'salvation.' Indeed, Isaiah 65 talks about old people dying, but having lived a "full life."

Christopher Wright has helped me understand the biblical thread of Shalom as salvation. He explains the biblical narrative as the story of God's promised Shalom being realised. From the beginning we see three relationships in harmony: Yahweh (God) with Adam and Eve (people) and the Garden of Eden (earth). Then, Yahweh (God) seeks to restore the breakdown of relationships through Abraham (people) and the Promised Land (earth) that would spill out to the whole cosmos. Then, Jesus comes as the promised 'Prince of Peace' to bring harmony for the whole cosmos through resurrection. The role of the local church before Jesus' return is to serve as collaborators with God in this *missio Dei* (mission of God), and cooperators in the redemption and renewal of all things.

As Christopher Wright summarises:

> Fundamentally, our mission (if it is biblically informed and validated) means our committed participation as God's people, at God's invitation and command, in God's own mission within the history of God's world for the redemption of God's creation.[70]

To partner with God establishing Shalom with all the peoples and places of the earth is the very reason local churches exist.

Shalom is not the only biblical word for these purposes of God coming true. The motifs of Shalom, eternal life, salvation and Kingdom of God are all important threads in the Gospel's rich tapestry. We unstitch them at our own peril. I hear too often from church and community leaders who try to isolate life to outsource different responsibilities: Church for souls; Hospitals for bodies; Government for politics. God's dream for us, however, refuses to be demarcated and unpicked like that. Indeed, one of the most important contemporary Lukan scholars, Joel Green, argues that:

> Throughout, the Lukan narrative focuses attention on a pervasive, coordinating theme: salvation. Salvation is neither ethereal nor merely future, but embraces life in the present, restoring the integrity of human life, revitalizing human communities, setting the cosmos in order, and commissioning the community of God's people to put God's grace into practice among themselves and toward ever-widening circles of others. The Third Evangelist knows nothing of such dichotomies as those sometimes drawn between social and spiritual or individual and communal. Salvation embraces the totality of embodied life, including its social, economic, and political concerns.[71]

The biblical witnesses do use different metaphors for the coming of God's 'Shalom,' 'kingdom,' and 'salvation,' but these are all ways of saying that God's intended peace and love is fulfilled in relationship between God, people, and place. It is a vision for the here and now that is never ending.

8: 'Shalom On Earth?'

In recent years, the theme of Shalom has been taken up as a vision for change. The Christian Community Development Association, describes Shalom this way:

> When God created the heavens and the earth, he wove it all together like a million silk threads forming a dazzling garment never before seen, each thread passing over, under, and around millions of others to create a perfectly complementary, tightly-woven interdependent, amazing whole. This wondrous webbing together of God and man and all of creation is what the Hebrew prophets called shalom. Shalom is a word packed with hope for a broken, bruised, and wounded world. It speaks of wholeness, right relationships, justice, salvation, and righteousness, all of which can be missed when we read the English word "peace." God's intention for every community is that his shalom would reign.[72]

Similarly, Cornelius Plantinga's book, *Not the Way It's Supposed to Be*, defines Shalom this way:

> ... the webbing together of God, humans, and all creation in justice, fulfilment, and delight... shalom means universal flourishing, wholeness, and delight—a rich state of affairs in which natural needs are satisfied and natural gifts fruitfully employed... Shalom, in other words, is the way things ought to be.[73]

This was God's original design for his creation – not that we live in scarcity, poverty, or in minimalistic conditions. Instead, he desires that we enjoy the fruits of his creation and the fruits of our labor because we bring him glory by doing so.

Perhaps my favourite Shalom bible passage comes from Jeremiah where the key leaders of Israel are in exile in Babylon and are called to "seek the [Shalom] of the city where I have sent you ... in its [Shalom] you will find your [Shalom]" (Jer. 29:7 [NRSV]). Peterson has a wonderful definition of Shalom here:

> Make yourselves at home there and work for the country's welfare. Pray for Babylon's wellbeing. If things go well for Babylon, things will go well for you. Welfare: shalom. Shalom means wholeness, the dynamic, vibrating health of a society that pulses with divinely directed purpose and surges with life-transforming love. Seek the shalom and pray for it. Throw yourselves into the place in which you find yourselves, but not on its terms, on God's terms. Pray. Search for that center in which God's will is being worked out (which is what we do when we pray) and work from that center.[74]

Perhaps few have done as much scholarly work defining Shalom for practical outworking as my friend and colleague in Urban Shalom Society, Andre Van Eymeren. He outlines some of the aspirations and indicators of Shalom living and calls this the 'Shalom/Flourishing Framework.'[75] These include:

- **Basic needs met:** This includes shelter, food, water, safety, and security.

- **Belonging to place and to people:** For many, particularly in the West, this idea of belonging to place has been lost. Globally, as more people migrate to the cities from traditional lands this will become an increasing issue.

- **Contributions valued:** The ability to contribute is core to our sense of wellbeing. To know that we have something of worth and value to give back to the community.

- **A life of purpose:** Each of us have skills, abilities, gifts, and perspectives. To live well we need the opportunity to express these things.

- **Lament & Celebration:** That a community could hold grief and joy.

- **Growing sense of spirituality or meaning:** Being involved in something outside of themselves – some call it a spirituality, others a sense of meaning.

8: 'Shalom On Earth?'

What these visions of Shalom have in common is a deep connecting and joining together in practical ways. If God's vision for Shalom is where God, people, and place live in harmony together then we need to see our neighbourhoods as part of the means of redemption. In this context, place matters as much as God and people.

I am conscious that places have chosen me more than I have chosen them. This is especially true for Springvale, Klong Toey, and Winson Green. New opportunities have also come out of relationships once rooted in these places. For example, one of the first people to come and live with us in Springvale was a young Burmese activist named Kyaw Soe Moe. I met him as he was moving into our neighbourhood in 1995. A small, quiet, and gentle man, he had been Buddhist monk at different points of his life, and he had that serenity about him.

However, he had also been one of the student activists leading the 8.8.88 uprising against the brutal dictatorship in Burma. When the Military hit back with a massacre and put a price on his head, he had to flee to the jungles. He acted as medic for a time and then was exiled to Melbourne as a refugee. Kyaw opened our eyes to the atrocities happening in Burma and over the years we stood with exiles in campaigns, social enterprises such as the 'Free Burma Cafe,' and resettlement programmes. When we moved to Bangkok, we even got to meet Kyaw's family in refugee camps near the Thai-Burma border and were able to assist many Burmese refugees transitioning to Western countries including Australia and the USA.

Kyaw eventually became a social worker, got married, and had kids. He still lives in Springvale, and decades later, we've kept in touch as the ups and downs of Burma's fight for democracy against Military oppression unfolded. This included the Coup in February 2021 and brutal crackdown on the Civil Disobedience Movement (CDM) and democratically elected National Unity Government (NUG). We also piloted the Change Incubator programme to help young CDM leaders in Myanmar start their own enterprises and community projects.

This programme had humble beginnings. Kyaw had organised a Zoom meeting with NUG leaders and I heard first-hand from a Civil Disobedience Movement worker who had fled to the jungle. I knew the CDM worker's name, but taking his picture wasn't possible at the time. His testimony massively impacted me and made me determined to offer something in solidarity, even if it was feeble. I couldn't turn my back. Inspired, we began developing the Change Incubator program.[76]

We did most of the programme online over three months, then gathered as many of the 50 participants as we could in person for the final two weeks on the Thai-Burma border. After the final 'pitches' to the Dragon's Den-style resource panel, evaluation, and prize-giving session on the last day in Mae Sot, a participant came up to me. Swam Yee had been the Incubator trainee looking after me with medicine and coconut juice while I had been impacted by food poisoning. He was an engineer by profession, with wife and kids still in Myanmar who he missed, often playing Richard Marx's, *Right Here Waiting*. He was a key leader in the Department of Labour before the Coup. We had agreed his project to train vocational school founders and leaders was a critical one that the NUG Ministry of Labour and Seedbeds could work on together going forward. I gifted him our manuals and projector I brought with me to help him make an immediate start

In the final session, just before we left, Swam Yee said, "Did you remember me from the Zoom?" Then it dawned on me and I double-checked our Seedbeds website for the article I wrote and screen grab I took of the name. "You're the reason we're here Swam Yee! That Zoom is what convinced me we couldn't turn our backs and needed to stand with you with this programme." He interpreted my response to the crowded room and everyone clapped and cheered! Sometimes the work of the Spirit is about paying attention! Sometimes just meeting your neighbour and welcoming them into your home can change destinies decades later. Shalom can connect and cross borders when we least expect it. Focusing on our neighbourhood doesn't mean we forget the rest of the world. Indeed, it can open it up.

8: 'Shalom On Earth?'

Biblical visions for our future are important foundations for our work in neighbourhoods. If we build our work on fears, illusions, or superstitions then our lives are easily wasted. As I try to evaluate my years of urban ministry, there is a scripture that quickly comes to mind. It's about how our work will be tested by fire and only what is good and true will last (1 Cor. 3:12-14). So much of my service was not built with gold, but 'wood, hay, and straw' and will be lost. I do believe that all truth is God's and only what has joined with Jesus remains, the rest will be forgotten. Where have I joined in with God's incoming Shalom, and where have I only been distracted or compulsive? These are tough, but important, ultimate questions to consider.

The shepherds responded to the Angels' announcements and got to meet the promised Good News of Great Joy in the person of Jesus. This baby was like their babies. Jesus was one of their own. They shared the joy. They even become the first evangelists sharing the Good News.

We especially long to see how the person Jesus grew up to become as the 'Prince of Peace' and what he gained for us will be realised amongst those who suffer now. Jesus' resurrection is the first fruits of this new creation. This is the hope for the world, that through Jesus all things will be reconciled. God's Shalom is coming. Joy is coming!

As I write this, I am conscious I need a good refilling with God's joy and Shalom. I'm on sabbatical in Melbourne and about to go to Kyaw Soe Moe's birthday in Springvale. Covid hit the people and places we love and serve hard. Like many, the last few years felt like driving up a steep hill with only a whiff of fuel fumes left in the tank. Depleted, but in the hands of God, just keeping on going can be enough sometimes. Despite so much fear, we have seen signs of hope that God's Shalom is coming. We have experienced joy in unexpected times. It's this hope that can get us on the right pathway for the right changes.

Personal Reflections

1. Which definition of Shalom resonates most with you?

2. Where have you seen Shalom most activated? What was it like?

3. If you were to describe God's purposes in the world, what word do you find most helpful?

4. If you were to take one step towards a more Shalom-filled life, what would it look like?

Part B. Practices To Try

Finding seeds of Shalom within myself and my community, believing that there is a preferred future for me and my local community, doesn't come easy. It is not intuitive, but it is possible. I have found that articulating a personal vision for my life can help me begin. We have developed a couple of exercises in the Change Makers programme to help participants have a better sense of who they really are, and not who they wish they were. From this, they are in a much better space to detect seeds of Shalom within themselves. I normally do a variation of three exercises and hope at least one sticks. I wonder if they could help you too.

A. Imagine four eulogies at your own funeral

The idea of visualising our own deathbed or funeral is an ancient way to detect our convictions and values. From St Ignatius to Stephen Covey, this imaginative exercise has for centuries been a way of confronting our mortality. When we look back at our lives from the viewpoint of our own death, we can find fresh perspectives missed in the stress of our daily grind. I often ask Change Makers to visualise their own funerals and imagine listening to four eulogies. What would we want the most important people in our lives to say about us, about what we did, and how they experienced us?

The four voices I encourage participants to imagine are: a family member; a colleague; a person who lived in poverty; and Jesus. I include the voice of the poor because, as Jesus' parable for the End of Age in Matthew's Gospel (Matt. 25:31ff) reminds us, how we treat others, especially the "least of these," is actually how we have treated Jesus.

Can I encourage you to pause and take time to do this now?

It can be a bit unnerving, but imagine seeing a crowd ahead of you and realising it is a graveside gathering or a wake. Imagine realizing that it is your funeral. Now, imagine going over to listen in as four people take it in turns to stand and speak about you. Listen to what they might say: your closest friend or family member, someone who have worked with, a poor person in your community, and finally Jesus. What has each one made of your life? What are you hoping they will say?

During Change Maker programmes, overcoming a fear of death isn't as big a deal as you might think for participants. Sharing the positive words that they have imagined is the most difficult part. 'You'll think I'm a big head! I can't say that.' Yet, when people do this, it clarifies their deepest convictions like few other exercises I know. It reveals what is important to them, the core values they hold, and what they have overcome. It's worth trying at least!

B. "If you could not fail...?"

Another exercise is a seemingly simple one that my first mentor, Steve Addison, asked me to do in Melbourne around 1992. It's an especially good back-up for those Change Maker participants who spent the whole time being freaked out by their own funeral and couldn't think or connect clearly with their preferred future as a result. The question goes something like this:

> 'Given who you really are, if you could not fail and if money was no option, what would you spend your best time, energy, and resources doing?'

For Christians, I often phrase it like this:

> 'What would you do for the glory of God if you knew you could not fail? What would you invest your best time, energy, and resources in if money was no barrier?'

I try to encourage participants to go away by themselves, be still, and allow all their internal doors and windows to be flung wide open. At this stage it's best not to get too caught up in any particular methodology. Simply focus on what you would do if you could. Sometimes whole destinies have emerged at once. Others find just a few verbs. When I first did this, the idea of Urban Neighbours of Hope came out almost fully formed.

> 'If I wanted to be a missionary anywhere else in the world, there are mission societies and agencies ready to sign me up. But because I want to be a missionary in Melbourne there just isn't a vehicle. I want to start an incarnational missionary movement for the West as well as the rest.'

One of the biggest challenges can be to feel like we have permission to dream like this, and to not critique too quickly what comes to mind.

Another version of this exercise comes from community organisers. Leaders like Barack Obama cut their teeth in community change asking people:

> 'What are you most angry about the way your world is today? What do you want your world look like?'

I found that allowing people to get in touch with their biggest frustrations before they go on to see possible solutions can really help. I first did this exercise with Citizens UK's Pete Brieley during a community organising workshop with Change Makers. He went around the circle asking, 'what are we most angry about?' Anger is not actually something I am conscious of most of the time, but then suddenly it hit me. Housing. My own experiences in a slum where homes were not protected, in my Melbourne transition, in Nineveh Road, and now with so many neighbours forced into transience. This seed grew as we kept knocking on doors for community-led housing and fair social renting.

Yet another version comes from the Appreciative Enquiry practitioners. Andre Van Eymeren helped found the Urban Shalom Society and one of his gifts was to take Urban Shalom Forum participants from cities around the world through this process. While this exercise is aimed at communities, a similar process can be used with individuals. It has four stages, but the first two evaluative stages can be used in isolation and can be really helpful:

> Discover: 'When you are at your best, what gives you life?'
> Dream: 'What could be if you did more of that?'

Andre leads folk to go on to a 'Design' and 'Destiny' phase, thinking through steps that might realise this intention and the eventual outcome.

Alone, or in a group, have a go at one of the variations of these questions. They can help us unearth the seeds of Shalom that lie within us. We can even imagine how they might grow to impact our neighbourhoods. All these exercises are kinds of brainstorms to free imaginations from limitations. I would encourage you to take some time investing with others in these kinds of tools.

C. Write a personal mission statement

It's reported that Carl Jung once said,

> 'The world will ask you who you are, and if you do not know, the world will tell you.'

To avoid this, it helps to develop a personal mission statement. I have done this exercise hundreds of times with participants across the world and know the investment in time is always worth it. I never wanted people to join UNOH, for example, only to get caught up in our existing vision and values. I wanted each new recruit to bring their best gifts and passions to our cause, if we were right for them. There is research about talent retention that was important for me here. Just because an organisation might have strong and clear culture, it doesn't mean that the right people will automatically stay and make a long-term contribution. A strong organisational mission needs to be matched by people with strong personal vision. In fact, a person with strong personal vision can keep going even in an organisation with a weak sense of mission, as they can find a way to make it work. However, if a person has a weak sense of personal mission, no organisation can make up for that up for very long. People feel squashed or oppressed by the 'fanatics' around them. What works best is if there is a strong personal mission that connects in harmony with a strong organisational mission.

A robust personal mission statement helps clarify what is important to you, gives you a sense of purpose and priority, taps into your God-given passions, and helps describe your identity that will be expressed in your various roles. Often Change Makers say it helps give them confidence to say 'no' to good opportunities which are not the right ones for them.

There are many ways to write a personal mission statement. However, most have three core elements. I have found these really helpful to focus and pull together what is important:

First, what central and infinite 'cause,' vision, or dream do you see as worth pursuing with your life?
If everyone could access that X factor, it would make the world a much better place. We can especially detect this from our timeline and other exercises that bring passion and convictions to the surface. It has to be impossible and worth giving our full selves to make

happen. For me it's about the 'fullness of life' that God's promised Shalom brings as harmony between God, people, and place emerges. I'm in my sweet spot when I'm working towards that happening in big and small ways. For some people, the 'cause' may well be more specific like healthy families, justice, or access to health care. I have found that we don't really choose our cause; the cause chooses us. "We detect," said Victor Frankl, "rather than invent our missions in life."[77]

Second, what three 'strengths' can you bring to the table to help make this dream a reality?
You can find these strengths in the funeral exercise, key verbs in 'do whatever' exercises, strengths in StrengthsFinder assessments or 'assets' in your own Appreciative Enquiry. Sometimes I've noted that Christians can identify spiritual or supernatural gifts as well as acquired skills and natural abilities. The trick here is to come up with as many 'doing words' as you can and intentionally whittle it down to only three. The whole process of why you'd pick one over another can help to discern what is most important to us. Over the years, I have changed these words in my own personal missional statement. For many years it was 'mobilise,' 'form,' and 'equip.' More recently, influenced by StrengthsFinder and honing my focus, I have identified these three strengths for myself: 'connect,' 'develop,' and 'release.' The point is not to perform only these actions forever, but to have three that are easy to remember and give the best direction for what you want to be doing most of the time.

Third, 'who' is it that you want to focus your best attention on?
Our cause may be for everyone, but we cannot focus on everyone, all the time. We have to find our way in and a group of people to prioritise and focus our best attention on. For me, it's around 'urban people and places.' My call to engage rapid urbanisation and place-making is a long story, but the willingness to focus on neighbourhoods, as well as the people in them, grew in focus over

the years. This focuses on where I live, and who I live in proximity to. For some Change Makers, the focus may well be on groups who have experienced the same injustices they have. For others, it may be a particular community or subculture beyond them. Again, brainstorming lots of options and coming up with who you most love, who most needs the dream of Shalom to become a reality, can help.

A challenge emerges next in pulling these three parts together. Can you put these three elements into an inspiring statement of intent? There are many different ways to pull these ideas together in a memorable sentence. One of the simplest ways is to make these three areas into a statement. That is, your three 'strengths' verbs – to a focused 'group' – for the 'cause' of something wonderful. So, for me:

> 'My mission is to connect, grow, and release urban people and places into God's promised fullness of life.'

Another way is to describe the world you want to live in first and then how you plan to contribute to that. For example,

> 'I want to live in a Shalom-filled world where God, people, and place live in harmony together, through connecting, developing, and releasing urban people and places into fullness of life.'

Others love to write down a dream or a kind of manifesto, or to have a symbol. It doesn't really matter how you do this, but find a way that can help you keep focusing in on what matters most.

Many people resist writing down a statement like this, but even more people resist living by one. 'Doesn't it close down my options? I want to be free to follow my heart!' say some. It is true that we can only find out what we love, and can be great at, through experience. Holding personal mission statements lightly at first, and being open to refining it over time, can still help.

For others, the real barrier is the belief that we can't really choose to focus our lives in this way. Choosing a life seems like an extravagance reserved only for rich and powerful people. 'I'd have to win the lottery to be able to do that!' However, once you have a clear statement of intent about what is worthwhile to you, and the direction you want to go, it is amazing what is possible. Sometimes we only get to do this a little at first, but as we grow in experience, so too can our authority in living this out further. I'd go so far to say that without some sense of personal vision, such a life isn't even possible, even if you win the lotto! Most lotto winners are not prepared to focus their resources on what matters to them. Cash, even millions, can quickly get squandered.

Our lives are worth more than billions in cash. To have a mission statement, a centre to return to, helps us know when we are off course and when we are making the most of what we are given in life.

The previous ideas have been mainly designed for individuals to do alone and then perhaps share in groups. There are other powerful ways that communities can work together to unearth the precious seeds of Shalom that exist within them. Next, I offer a few ideas for groups. They are best undertaken in an unhurried and creative way. Try to make spaces where everyone gets to join in.

Group Exercises:

1. Our neighbourhood as it could be: What would our neighbourhood look like if God's purposes fully came here? Draw pictures, images, words, or phrases of what could happen if life was lived to the fullest by all here. Place these at one end of the room. Try to group themes and read them out.

2. Our neighbourhood as it is: What is stopping our place now living up to its potential? Why are they happening? Draw pictures, images, words, or phrases of what is happening here to stop Shalom. Place these at the other end of the room. Try to group themes and then read them out.

3. Our neighbourhood strengths? What are the gifts, strengths, or actions we have among us that are signs of hope for us? Draw pictures, images, words, or phrases of what could happen to release these strengths in our community. Place these in the middle of the room. Try to group themes and then read them out.

4. Are there some small, next steps we could do to move our neighbourhood close to becoming that place of Shalom, where God's purposes are fully present?

Personal Reflection on Part B

1. What are you discovering about place-making and God's purposes? Which one text, story, or insight did you find helpful? Which one text, story, or insight did you find difficult?

2. Could you identify any fears as you seek God's purposes in your local community? If so, what were they?
If not, why not?

3. The theme of being a 'joy-detector' emerged. What role do busyness and hurry, gratitude and joy have in your life? Where do you most detect joy in you and your local community?

4. A central theme of this book focuses on the meanings and implications of God's promised 'Shalom.' How would you describe Shalom? What can its potential mean for you and your local community?

5. There are a number of personal exercises and a community practice in this part of the book. What did you discover about God, people (including you), and place as you explored these?

6. What is possible for our local community because of God's promises of Shalom for us? You might be inspired by this song written by Ross Langmead, and perhaps come up with something like it for your own community:

Part B. Practices To Try

Living For Shalom

Seeking the health of the city.
Oh you know it's hard,
As we're seeking the health of the city.
Oh but we can't stop
'Cause we're seeing God
In every greenshoot,
In every squatter,
In every network,
In every prophet for the poor.
Oh we're working, oh we're living for Shalom.

Feeling the pain of the city.
Oh those broken dreams!
And we're feeling the pain of the city.
Oh, God knows it's real.
You can feel the cross
Weigh on the homeless
And unemployed ones
And new arrivals —
On all the outcast and the poor.
Oh we're working, oh we're living for Shalom.

Living the hope of the city.
Oh we dance and sing
As we're living the hope of the city.
Oh the Spirit blows,
And we're finding God
In seeking justice,
In celebration,
In many small groups,
In signs of life in rich and poor.
Oh we're working, oh we're living for Shalom.

© 1990 Ross Langmead (www.rosslangmead.com)

This tiny place played a central role in the story of the Celtic Christian movement that transformed Britain and much of Europe during what we now call the Dark Ages. Lindisfarne, often called just Holy Island, was a missionary base, a learning centre, and a model village of what was possible. Walking in the ruins of where all this happened, I reveled in the rich atmosphere of the place. We stayed in Ray Simpson's then home, right in the middle of the small village on the island and woke up to views of the famous Lindisfarne Castle from our window each morning. Ray had founded the Community of Aidan and Hilda and had welcomed us into the community. I have mentioned Saint Aidan before, but Hilda was also a fascinating character whose hospitality and leadership transformed the world in her times. I had joined the Community of Aidan and Hilda, first as an explorer and then later as a member, but this was my first visit to the legendary Holy Island. These moments with Aiden on Holy Island gave fresh, if very cold, air to our lungs. It also proved to be an encouragement to not give up on our dreams.

It had been a tough first six months for us Barkers as we started our new life in Britain. Most of our initial plans had started to unravel. Aiden was bravely facing a new school, but struggling to fit into the strict regime. Anji was creating a community hub in a local primary school, but was only just holding on and had trouble hiding her misery; grieving Bangkok. I had been invited to set up a new 'Centre for Urban Ministry' with a theological college, but it looked like it could be overturned as the college underwent a re-branding and restructuring process. We had also vastly underestimated how much our move and setup would cost, and our money started to run out. Our rented house in Winson Green was freezing cold with the gas often leaking and electricity going 'around the meter' in dangerous ways. Even worse, the landlord refused to fix anything. Because we had no previous 'official' landlords for decades, we were forced to pay six months' rent in advance. Without the threat of withholding the rent, our landlord just refused to make things safe. This was not unusual for landlords in Klong Toey, but we did not expect this in Winson Green. We began to wonder what we were doing here. Were our dreams dead on arrival? Had we missed God's will? Was I a fool for getting my family into this mess?

Part C.

The Soil We Need

Here, I explore Jesus' famous parable of the four soils and what this can mean for preparing deep and transformative community change. As before, this is split into different chapters, each with personal questions to address. This whole section is concluded with a series of suggested practices and group questions.

Chapter 9:
Soils And Enchanted Worldviews

The earth where King Oswald died seems to have been soa[ked] in his sanctity and to have become a seedbed. A sick horse [and a] sick girl were cured by touching the soil upon which Oswa[ld met] his death; the soil from that spot seemed to have power to m[ake] grass grow greener, to resist fire and to heal all sorts of peop[le who] were touched by it.
– Ray Simpson, (Celtic Daily Light, August 7.)

Whoever is devoid of the capacity of wonder, whoever rema[ins] unmoved, whoever cannot contemplate or know the deep shudder of the soul in enchantment, might as well be dead f[or he] has already closed his eyes upon life.
– Albert Einstein

Other seeds fell on good soil and brought forth grain, some a [hundredfold], some sixty, some thirty.
Matthew 13:8 [NRSV]

My first visit to the Holy Island of Lindisfarne was a revelatio[n] in more ways than one. It was late Winter 2015, and I was with [my son] Aiden, then 12 years old. He was named after the Celtic Saint w[ho] relocated to this tidal island at the invitation of Northumbria[n King] Oswald in 635 AD.

9: Soils And Enchanted Worldviews

Visiting Holy Island that weekend helped answer some of those questions. Some courage was found to face a new stage. In those holy soils we found fresh life.

Holy Island, and Celtic Christianity in general, offers a kind of enchanted worldview, alive to a hope that can be nurtured and discerned through the Holy Spirit. So much of the modern Western worldview relies too heavily on the rational, calculating mind, but there is a reality far beyond what we can see and measure. To the Celts, the so-called 'supernatural world' lies hidden just beyond a veil; it sometimes pokes right through, and it influences us more often than we realise. God, angels, demons, and miracles are all part of both biblical and Celtic imaginations of what is real. Any worldview will impact how we behave. It's like an operating system in a computer. A modern Western worldview, for example, often leads us to become preoccupied with machine-like control, management for results, because the material world is all that is real. This view, a kind of functional atheism, can be found even in Christian leaders. It leads to impossible expectations that pressing 'levers of change' is all that is needed to see our communities transform. However, this kind of control, especially in fast morphing and moving urban chaos, is simply an illusion. In contrast, Celtic Christianity offers an understanding beyond what we see. To return to our central metaphor, this worldview can be good soil for intentionally nurturing interconnectedness between all the ecosystems for life and fruit in our local communities. Entering a more enchanted worldview could not be more important for those who long to see God's justice, and see joy flow into the complex agonies of urban life. Especially for those who are not sure they can keep going, as we were during those early months in the UK. Certainly, entering this worldview helped us imagine a move forward, a step at a time.

During my stay on Holy Island, I experienced three aspects of a Celtic Christian that helped prepare a kind of good soil within me. These insights, and the practices developed from them, would grow resilience and hope over the years ahead.

Listening for the Spirit in Prayer

One of the first buildings constructed by Saint Aidan on Holy Island was a Chapel for prayer. Early Celtic missionaries had a focus on discerning prayer. Deep within the rhythms of Celtic life together were practices that helped missionaries pay attention to what the Spirit is doing. Once discerned, they would follow, no matter what the cost. This intentional and relentless seeking of God's will was a transformative impulse that changed the world.

At the centre of this life together was an enchanted worldview that could see and hear the oneness of God's cosmos. The dichotomy of 'seen,' which is taken seriously, versus the 'unseen,' which is optional, is so common in the modern Western worldview. This falls short of the fullness of reality. We know there is an interconnectedness of all things. As Christians we are not pantheists, that is, holding the belief that God 'is' all things. However, we are panentheists, and believe God is alive 'in' all things. Evil is still alive in our fragile world until Christ comes again, but God is present in all things. It should be no surprise, therefore, that ancient cultures, including the Celts, should look for ways to consistently connect to this reality. Dreams, visions, miracles, and angels, all calling for steps of faith and valour, seem to be common experiences in the life of Celtic missionaries in their faith adventures. These breakthroughs didn't happen in a vacuum. They happened because Celtic missionaries were relentlessly awake to what was going on in worlds they could not always see.

On Holy Island, I was immersed in this unity of worldview where prayer, discernment, and walking sacred paths seemed to join seamlessly together. As I prayed in Ray's home early one morning, observing the castle on the end of the rocks from his window, a renewed dream emerged. A mystical sense of calling emerged to live a deeper life in Winson Green, but to also connect more broadly to community leadership development around the world. It was a call to say 'no' to everything else other than that focus. It seemed as if the heavens themselves were cheering us on, calling for more focus.

One of the reasons I became part of the Community of Aidan and Hilda was because I need to keep being awakened to this enchanted worldview.

Part C.

The Soil We Need

Here, I explore Jesus' famous parable of the four soils and what this can mean for preparing deep and transformative community change. As before, this is split into different chapters, each with personal questions to address. This whole section is concluded with a series of suggested practices and group questions.

Chapter 9:
Soils And Enchanted Worldviews

The earth where King Oswald died seems to have been soaked in his sanctity and to have become a seedbed. A sick horse and a sick girl were cured by touching the soil upon which Oswald met his death; the soil from that spot seemed to have power to make grass grow greener, to resist fire and to heal all sorts of people who were touched by it.
– Ray Simpson, (Celtic Daily Light, August 7.)

Whoever is devoid of the capacity of wonder, whoever remains unmoved, whoever cannot contemplate or know the deep shudder of the soul in enchantment, might as well be dead for he has already closed his eyes upon life.
– Albert Einstein

Other seeds fell on good soil and brought forth grain, some a hundredfold, some sixty, some thirty.
Matthew 13:8 [NRSV]

My first visit to the Holy Island of Lindisfarne was a revelation to me in more ways than one. It was late Winter 2015, and I was with my son Aiden, then 12 years old. He was named after the Celtic Saint who had relocated to this tidal island at the invitation of Northumbrian King Oswald in 635 AD.

This tiny place played a central role in the story of the Celtic Christian movement that transformed Britain and much of Europe during what we now call the Dark Ages. Lindisfarne, often called just Holy Island, was a missionary base, a learning centre, and a model village of what was possible. Walking in the ruins of where all this happened, I reveled in the rich atmosphere of the place. We stayed in Ray Simpson's then home, right in the middle of the small village on the island and woke up to views of the famous Lindisfarne Castle from our window each morning. Ray had founded the Community of Aidan and Hilda and had welcomed us into the community. I have mentioned Saint Aidan before, but Hilda was also a fascinating character whose hospitality and leadership transformed the world in her times. I had joined the Community of Aidan and Hilda, first as an explorer and then later as a member, but this was my first visit to the legendary Holy Island. These moments with Aiden on Holy Island gave fresh, if very cold, air to our lungs. It also proved to be an encouragement to not give up on our dreams.

It had been a tough first six months for us Barkers as we started our new life in Britain. Most of our initial plans had started to unravel. Aiden was bravely facing a new school, but struggling to fit into the strict regime. Anji was creating a community hub in a local primary school, but was only just holding on and had trouble hiding her misery; grieving Bangkok. I had been invited to set up a new 'Centre for Urban Ministry' with a theological college, but it looked like it could be overturned as the college underwent a re-branding and restructuring process. We had also vastly underestimated how much our move and setup would cost, and our money started to run out. Our rented house in Winson Green was freezing cold with the gas often leaking and electricity going 'around the meter' in dangerous ways. Even worse, the landlord refused to fix anything. Because we had no previous 'official' landlords for decades, we were forced to pay six months' rent in advance. Without the threat of withholding the rent, our landlord just refused to make things safe. This was not unusual for landlords in Klong Toey, but we did not expect this in Winson Green. We began to wonder what we were doing here. Were our dreams dead on arrival? Had we missed God's will? Was I a fool for getting my family into this mess?

Listening for the Spirit in Prayer

One of the first buildings constructed by Saint Aidan on Holy Island was a Chapel for prayer. Early Celtic missionaries had a focus on discerning prayer. Deep within the rhythms of Celtic life together were practices that helped missionaries pay attention to what the Spirit is doing. Once discerned, they would follow, no matter what the cost. This intentional and relentless seeking of God's will was a transformative impulse that changed the world.

At the centre of this life together was an enchanted worldview that could see and hear the oneness of God's cosmos. The dichotomy of 'seen,' which is taken seriously, versus the 'unseen,' which is optional, is so common in the modern Western worldview. This falls short of the fullness of reality. We know there is an interconnectedness of all things. As Christians we are not pantheists, that is, holding the belief that God 'is' all things. However, we are panentheists, and believe God is alive 'in' all things. Evil is still alive in our fragile world until Christ comes again, but God is present in all things. It should be no surprise, therefore, that ancient cultures, including the Celts, should look for ways to consistently connect to this reality. Dreams, visions, miracles, and angels, all calling for steps of faith and valour, seem to be common experiences in the life of Celtic missionaries in their faith adventures. These breakthroughs didn't happen in a vacuum. They happened because Celtic missionaries were relentlessly awake to what was going on in worlds they could not always see.

On Holy Island, I was immersed in this unity of worldview where prayer, discernment, and walking sacred paths seemed to join seamlessly together. As I prayed in Ray's home early one morning, observing the castle on the end of the rocks from his window, a renewed dream emerged. A mystical sense of calling emerged to live a deeper life in Winson Green, but to also connect more broadly to community leadership development around the world. It was a call to say 'no' to everything else other than that focus. It seemed as if the heavens themselves were cheering us on, calling for more focus.

One of the reasons I became part of the Community of Aidan and Hilda was because I need to keep being awakened to this enchanted worldview.

9: Soils And Enchanted Worldviews

Visiting Holy Island that weekend helped answer some of those questions. Some courage was found to face a new stage. In those holy soils we found fresh life.

Holy Island, and Celtic Christianity in general, offers a kind of enchanted worldview, alive to a hope that can be nurtured and discerned through the Holy Spirit. So much of the modern Western worldview relies too heavily on the rational, calculating mind, but there is a reality far beyond what we can see and measure. To the Celts, the so-called 'supernatural world' lies hidden just beyond a veil; it sometimes pokes right through, and it influences us more often than we realise. God, angels, demons, and miracles are all part of both biblical and Celtic imaginations of what is real. Any worldview will impact how we behave. It's like an operating system in a computer. A modern Western worldview, for example, often leads us to become preoccupied with machine-like control, management for results, because the material world is all that is real. This view, a kind of functional atheism, can be found even in Christian leaders. It leads to impossible expectations that pressing 'levers of change' is all that is needed to see our communities transform. However, this kind of control, especially in fast morphing and moving urban chaos, is simply an illusion. In contrast, Celtic Christianity offers an understanding beyond what we see. To return to our central metaphor, this worldview can be good soil for intentionally nurturing interconnectedness between all the ecosystems for life and fruit in our local communities. Entering a more enchanted worldview could not be more important for those who long to see God's justice, and see joy flow into the complex agonies of urban life. Especially for those who are not sure they can keep going, as we were during those early months in the UK. Certainly, entering this worldview helped us imagine a move forward, a step at a time.

During my stay on Holy Island, I experienced three aspects of a Celtic Christian that helped prepare a kind of good soil within me. These insights, and the practices developed from them, would grow resilience and hope over the years ahead.

9: Soils And Enchanted Worldviews

On my own, I can easily fall asleep to the hum of an overly rationalistic Western worldview without noticing the realities going on around me. The common 'roots, rhythms and relationships' of our community have kept me at the table of discernment, seeking to do God's will, giving me the confidence to keep stepping out in faith again and again.

I can easily see the surface, but there is always something deeper going on. If I will only take the time to listen to the Spirit with my 'soul friend,' in community, then the Spirit's shy, calm voice can be heard and followed wholeheartedly. My soul friend with the Community of Aidan and Hilda, since 2015, has been Geoff Holt. He meets with me regularly and helps me discern what is happening in and through me, as well as what could be next. A kind and gentle man, he connected with this vision and prays with me each month. I have found that returning to prayer is a constant centre.

Listening for the Spirit in Places

An enchanted worldview sees places as alive and needing to be nurtured into resurrection hope. Holy Island is more than a space to visit, it is a place alive to God. Celtic missiology includes a strategic place-making thread. It can be particularly important for urban Christians today. Yes, there was an instinct to retreat to marginal places as monks and hermits, but many Celtic Christian communities were close enough to strategic cities to shape and inspire them.

The Holy Island of Lindisfarne, which can seem so remote to us today, was intentionally founded by Aidan at the time when boats were the key form of transport. It was situated on the North Sea, one of the biggest connecting superhighways in Europe. Aidan also placed his community within striking distance of the key seat of Northumbrian power and decision making at Bamburgh Castle. From there, Saint Aidan influenced the future of the whole lands of Northumbria.

In fact, many of today's largest post-industrial cities in the UK were founded by Celtic missionaries as they sought to build 'villages of God.' Saint Mungo, for example, began his monastery beside a busy river and it would later become the city of Glasgow. We can see Saint Chad's pioneering ministry in the Mercian and Middle Saxon Kingdom in the ninth century, impacted where I now live in Birmingham and the West Midlands. This Anglo-Saxon Kingdom was centred in what became Lichfield near two significant Roman roads, close by to the seat of Mercian power at Tamworth. There was an intentionality about where and how Celtic missionaries placed themselves. At a time when few human beings lived in towns and cities, Celtic missionaries took people and their places seriously.

Places were not simply a platform for work and ministry. They were alive with possibilities for good and evil. St Chad, for example, when preparing Lichfield for his base in the Mercian Kingdom, spent "40 days in prayer and fasting to clear the site of evil spirits and to establish a strong connection between heaven and earth in the place chosen to house the Christian community."[78] This sense that places could become 'thin,' in that there was little there separating heaven and earth, echoes the prayer of Jesus for God's will to be done 'on earth as in heaven.' These are visions far beyond the modern idea that places are just spaces to fill and use for our own purposes.

Places were alive with a unique hope worth discerning. The search by some Celtic missionaries for their 'resurrection place,' for example, was not uncommon. This is where the Celtic missionary believed that the place they were called to be planted would also be the place where they died and rose again at the return of Christ. All would be finally put to right, and that all the work done in Jesus' name in that place would be fully experienced as heaven and earth fully joined together as God dreamed they would. This was not a short-term vision, but stretched out to the horizons, even beyond death.

I became aware that I desperately wanted that sense for Winson Green, and maybe Winson Green wanted that for me? If many considered Winson Green a wasteland, how could it become a 'village for God,' a sacred place that pilgrims might one day feel is a 'thin place?' Was Winson Green my 'resurrection place?' Holy Island itself seemed to be healing me and refreshing my vision. One of the meanings of the names for Lindisfarne is 'healing island' and I felt this tangibly.

Places can choose us more than we choose them. This has been true for me. The neighbourhood of Springvale in Melbourne was our first relocation in 1992. This multi-cultural, multi-racial, and multi-faith community drew Anji and I to be planted there for over a decade. My sense of call to Klong Toey, Bangkok, began with an unexpected sense that I was 'home' in that slum and squatter neighbourhood of 100,000 people in one square mile. The transition to live and serve there for 12 years changed our lives. Our third relocation to Winson Green, inner-city Birmingham, began with a surprising internal tug in a visit. At the time I had expressed this in saying, 'if I could live another life, I'd love to spend it here.' Paying attention to that thought began a joyful agony to be planted here. We have been here since 2014 and it has required everything we'd learnt previously. In all three cases I sensed an invitation, confirmed by community discernment, that enabled us to be planted and buried in a place. In all three places, it took time and a lot of wrestling with weeds, but eventually we saw good fruit grow. To this day I feel like these places are holy ground to me in ways other places are not.

I love the definition of *New Parish*. It's not just ownership lines marked on a map. Rather, it's a place "big enough to live a lot of life in and small enough to become a known character in the unfolding drama of that place."[79] To follow the Spirit's guidance to invest with faith, hope, and love in such a place is worth our smallest and largest sacrifices. Sometimes, you just need to know the dream is not dead yet. That a place that called you hasn't yet finished its work with and in you.

Listening for the Spirit in People
Celtic missionaries took connections with people seriously, especially people they didn't know. Hospitality played a central role, and encounters with strangers were often a mystical experience for Celtic missionaries. They were often based in places intentionally set up for encountering Jesus through hospitality with those traveling, injured, or wanting to learn. These were mostly not people who could return the favour, but 'the stranger' who in the biblical tradition was often associated with angels or even Jesus himself. To them, Jesus' parable in Matthew 25 had a special resonance. Jesus was unexpectedly served in 'the least of these:'

those who were sick, without home, hungry, in prison, or naked. The Greek word for 'hospitality' literally means 'love of the stranger,' and this was a central concern of Celtic Christian community life. More than safe and distant service provision, the compassion of Celtic missionaries often made them vulnerable to those most in need. Discernment in how best to love meant that the hospitality and welcome they extended could be as unique as the people they met.

That weekend on Holy Island I also experienced Graham and Ruth Booth's hospitality. I'd met Graham briefly before as he was a Guardian of the Community of Aidan and Hilda. In so many ways I was a stranger to him and Ruth, but he listened to my musing and grief and stood with me in prayer. Being deeply rooted in Winson Green with neighbours, but connected to the world to develop local leaders, became a theme and thread as we talked and prayed into our situations. This was a thread helping weave the tapestry of why we had come to the UK. This is what our lives were being prepared for. We must find a way to take the next step!

While deeply planted in a place, Celtic missionaries would also connect widely to touch the lives of people in other places. On the road, serving people in remote towns and villages, they would also become the ones needing hospitality. There was a deep sense of what Bonhoeffer called 'place sharing' where the Celtic missionary gave and received love to others 'through' Jesus, as if Jesus was in-between every encounter between them and other people.[80] This kind of regular, vulnerable faith sharing was only possible because of the hope they discerned in the encounters they had with people. Graham did that for me that weekend.

Sacred soils in places like Holy Island seem viscerally special, but more mundane soils can be re-enchanted too. Well at least in our own imaginations. All the earth is the Lord's and God is present in even the most cast-off place, so all places are sacred. It's just that we struggle to recognise it.

Pilgrimages to Holy Island have become a regular part of my life. I regularly lead groups of pilgrims to walk St Cuthbert's Way in the Scottish borders and end with the trek across the causeway to Holy

9: Soils And Enchanted Worldviews

Island. Many emerging leaders from Winson Green have made this journey with me – and some have even been televised!

Over the past few years BBC Songs of Praise have filmed two stories about us in Winson Green, fascinated with how we attempt to express God's love here, as well as by our alpacas.[81] In 2022 one of the producers, David Waters, made contact again and explained that they were doing an Easter special on Holy Island. He knew we took Change Makers and others regularly there. Would we come up again and be part of the programme? I didn't need an excuse! We quickly brought together some Change Makers and panelists and set off. It was beautifully filmed and two of our Change Makers, Claire and Kay, shared their mystical experiences with emotion and thoughtfulness. The presenter, Sean Fletcher, asked me why we kept coming given 'it couldn't be more different to inner city Birmingham.' I talked about the 'big skies' and feeling the 'resurrection of Jesus,' but my mind raced back to that first experience on Holy Island with my son Aiden. There was a sense that we had 'brought back' what we had experienced to Winson Green. The same Spirit's presence that is so easily recognised and felt on Holy Island waits for us in less obvious ways, back in Winson Green. Experiences in 'thin places' with fewer distractions and the imagination of history can help give us confidence to sense the same Spirit in places brimming with different kinds of life.[82]

Returning from mystical moments in sacred places can be difficult, but a practical first step became clear to me on that first visit to Holy Island. What would help us feel more planted in Winson Green? We needed to focus on our own housing. One of the first things I felt called to do on return from Holy Island was to work to secure a new home for us to live in and help us be further planted there. This was no easy thing. Landlords were buying up any cheap housing in the area and quickly renting them out. It was almost impossible for individuals who wanted to live in Winson Green to buy a home. We had trouble even getting an agent to look inside a place as any houses that came on the market were sold 'sight unseen' to investors and landlords. This was a systems and policy failure that impacted who could live and invest locally in Winson Green.

I doubled my efforts to buy a small terrace house there, so that we'd have a long-term stake in the community and be able to put roots down. I felt we still had a small financial window for this to happen. Anji and I were both 45 and, if this was my 'resurrection place,' then we could still get a mortgage to buy a home and pay it off by the time we had retired from our working life and avoid it being a burden to our kids.

Finally, I got us in to see a place. When Anji and I were shown a middle terrace house right in the middle of the most densely populated part of Winson Green, we knew it was perfect for us. It was over one hundred years old but had a fully renovated kitchen and bathroom. Downstairs was knocked through so it was open and upstairs had two bedrooms and a box room that could fit a bed. Importantly, no one lived in it so it couldn't get complicated waiting for people to move out, as 'upward chains' can stall house sales for years. At £95,000 it was also one of the few homes in our price range. We put an offer in and waited. Months went by. After many phone calls I started to go and sit in the lobby of real estate offices until the offer was agreed. That eventually happened. Then I needed to do something similar at the lawyer's office with the signing of legal forms. I felt like my strategy was to wear people down until this house sale got over the line and it wasn't offered to a private landlord. Eventually I outlasted them all and we moved into 85 Markby Road in June 2015. I held my 46th birthday party there. This process took many months, and our personal money was just about gone, but we were now putting roots down, investing our future in Winson Green in a practical way.

I had also left Holy Island with a sense that God wanted us to lead again. To invest in starting organisations that could help us connect locally and go deeper, as well as spread more widely for training. Could we reopen the large, disused vicarage in Winson Green to the local community? Would it help give us an organisational presence, as we'd originally planned? Despite countless trials along the way, over the next year we set up and started Newbigin House, Newbigin Community Trust (a registered charity), and Newbigin School for Urban Leadership (a not-for-profit Community Interest Company). We lead these to this day. These were formative times. All of this would help us become known local characters in Winson Green as our adventures were often visible.

Keeping alpacas and walking them from Newbigin House to the local school each morning might have helped too! These would later be shown on BBC1's *Songs of Praise*. When one of our alpacas escaped, millions viewed the 'Llama Drama' on TikTok. Sometimes we become 'known characters' in ways we least expect.

Like so many Celtic Christian communities, we began to envision Newbigin House as a kind of 'seedbed of hope.' We had a core live-in community, but also took in emerging leaders who were learning the ropes in urban ministry. Identifying local leaders, we would help incubate new programmes and ministries, including Newbigin Community Trust, that offered community meals, parks, housing, youth and children's groups, and support campaigning groups for residents. That quickly grew to hundreds of guests each week at Newbigin House. We were bursting at the seams and needed more space. Soon God provided connections at a local school and church who offered us buildings that we could base and grow programmes in, like a community café, music and arts, and homework clubs, as well as church services with new Christians. Today, some of my most strategic work is helping other urban neighbourhoods become seedbeds of hope through our leadership development ministry we now call, appropriately enough, Seedbeds. Here we offer Change Makers emerging leaders' programmes and Masters modules in Urban Ministry. All of this grew out of the resolution to return to Winson Green, and to seek to go deep and incubate life and connections from Newbigin House.

At the heart of all this work, however, is the simple call to make connections, discover talents, and bring people together to mobilise them. The isolation and loneliness that characterises much of the urban experience can only be transformed by human interaction led by the Spirit. These connections can be mystical, life-giving, and hope-raising experiences; if we are awake to the possibilities and risk backing them.

As Aiden and I returned to Winson Green from Holy Island, I didn't know all this would happen. I just had a sense of the very next step. In reality, all that had changed at that time was the resolve within me; the confidence to keep going.

Before Holy Island, I had felt buried by failure and circumstance, but somehow now felt I was planted in a particular place for a particular reason. Resolve, however, is no small thing and not to be underestimated.

Are Hard Soils worth the work?

I first shared our dream to start 'Seedbeds' with John U'ren in 2014 when we were still in Australia, preparing for the UK. He smiled and let out a laugh. In many ways John is the godfather of the radical discipleship movement in Melbourne. His opinion mattered to me and so I listened intently as he asked: 'Are you trying to reverse Jesus' teaching on the soils? Are you going to see hard places take seeds and grow fruit?'

John was alluding to one of Jesus' most famous parables that is often understood to be about the readiness or lack of receptivity for Kingdom growth. As noted in the previous chapter, God's Kingdom, salvation, and God's Shalom, can be understood as nearly synonymous – Kingdom come, Gods will on earth as in heaven. Therefore, this parable relates to whether God, all people, and all places can live in harmony together in God's reign.

Let us consider this ancient parable. In Matthew's Gospel 13:1-23, Jesus tells a story about a farmer who throws seed onto different grounds. Not much of the seed finds the right soil to grow in. At a time when the growth and production of grain provided the staple diet of bread and kept people alive, this farmer seems to be wasting one of their society's most valuable assets. Like many parables, Jesus' teaching delivers a principle through comparison and contrast. Unlike many parables, Jesus gives an interpretation with this one (Matt. 13:8-23). Much-needed grain would eventually die if the seeds were thrown on hard paths, or stones, or among thorns and thistles; likewise, not all hearts and lives are ready to experience the seed of God's Shalom in their lives. Those hearts and lives that are ready can multiply God's goodness in remarkable ways, however, only if the sower perseveres. The main point is that perseverance is worth it!

Some important questions arise for us out of this parable, as John U'ren was alluding to. This is especially true for those of us in contexts that can seem difficult. Not least is the question: are there places that are, in fact,

9: Soils And Enchanted Worldviews

'wastelands?' Can nothing really be done? Is sowing seeds in places like Winson Green a waste of time and energy? Are some places like paths, like rocky ground, or are thorn-infested, with there being no point in even trying to plant seeds of Shalom there?

Another member of the Community of Aidan and Hilda helped me find understanding here. Peter and Dorothy Neilson became my Pastoral Supervisors. Peter offered a reflection on this parable in light of an experience he had at Princeton University in America. Princeton had acquired a small farm through the inspiration of Dr Nathan Stucky (Nate) that they called the 'Farminary.' Nate was a farmer and a youth leader who went on to study theology. He worked with students on the farm to help them discover how God works in our lives by observing God's presence in creation. Nate handed out this parable of the 'Sower and Soil' to the group of Ministers visiting, including Peter. They all 'knew' what it was all about and 'jumped' to 'well-trodden' interpretations, ready to preach their sermons.

Nate however, had a challenge for them:

> After listening to all our spiritualising, Nate challenged us to see it differently. In his words, we tend to hear the story in terms of 'three losers and one winner.' Maybe our farmers will recognise that proportion in terms of how harvests can be ruined by pests and weather and even changing market preferences – many factors not under our control, however hard we work. Hopefully not three to one, but harvests are not guaranteed.

> Nate went on to tell of some research into first century farming, and to suggest that Jesus' first hearers would have heard the story quite differently. As the farmers spread the seed – 'broadcasting' was the word for that kind of sowing – some would fall on the different kinds of land, just as Jesus said. However, the farmer would know that over time, the path would be turned over, the rocks would be removed, and the thistles be rooted out. In time the land would become fertile and become the soil that produced the good crop.

The parable was no longer a story of static attitudes set in stone, but a progression towards the fruitful soil.[83]

Interestingly, the sower is not ridiculed for trying to grow a harvest in such diverse soils. The sower is willing to give opportunity to all kinds of terrain and to see what can grow over time. Through persistence the harvest does come in the end and multiplies far more than expected. Similar points are being made in what we can call the Kingdom or Shalom parables that follow. Keep going and growing 'weeds among the wheat' until the final harvest (Matt. 13:24-30, 36-4). Don't despise the small start of the mustard seed for it will eventually grow way out of proportion to the size of the seed (Matt. 13:31-32). We may not at first see what yeast can do, but without it the bread won't rise (Matt. 13:33). Soils of all kinds can in fact be prepared for a future fruitfulness.

The cost of persistence is highlighted. Like a man who "sells all he has" to buy a field that has treasure buried in it, or a merchant who "sold all he had," we can't be half-hearted if we know the worth of God's Shalom in a local community. Matthew finishes this parable with diverse "fish of every kind" being swept up in the net of God's Kingdom, but "at the end of the age," it is angels who will separate out the fish. What do these parables have in common? I think the themes here are about the costs of persistent inclusion. From little things, big things emerge. Premature judgments about the likelihood of fruitfulness, or giving up, work against God's promised Shalom. These parables are warnings about writing places and people off before their time.

What then, can we learn from the parable of soils? Not least, that some areas and people in our 'patch' might feel like concrete paths, but not all the areas or people, and not always.

In December 2022, I was on Sabbatical and got to visit John U'ren again, this time at his home in Melbourne. He was keen to update me on all that was going on in Melbourne including Tim Costello's remarkable progress against the huge gambling industry and the recent Royal Commission findings. He gave me his copy of Tim's memoirs, *A Lot with a Little,* and urged me to read it. He had been following our progress in the UK with interest too. John kindly barraged me with insightful questions. I was able to let him know how far Winson Green had come and that we now called our community leadership training organisation 'Seedbeds.' This book, *No Wastelands,* is in part inspired by our conversations. I also got to express how grateful I was for all John's love and support for Anji and I over the decades.

John was in his 90s when we met this most recent time, and quite frail, but he stood up and hugged me tight. I know I shouldn't seek the approval of others, but John's acceptance of me meant a lot. It was actually the last time I saw John in person. He died peacefully, surrounded by his family, in June 2023. However, what he sowed in the lives of so many, including me, lives on.

Personal Reflections

1. What are the sacred moments of listening to the Spirit you have had in life? What was it like? Did you take the 'next steps' to action them? Why, why not? What happened?

2. Of the Celtic traditions of Prayer, Place, and People, what helped you most to listen to the Spirit to grow in faith? Why?

3. What has been your accepted understanding of the 'Parable of the Soils?' How is it similar or different to the ideas of 'broadcasting' sowing to help all areas become fertile eventually? How do they connect?

4. When you think of your neighbourhood 'patch' which of the four soils can you see? Where and why?

5. What could you do to help cultivate all soils in your place to be fertile for God's Shalom?

Chapter 10:
Hard Paths -
Lacking Awareness

When anyone hears the word of the kingdom and does not understand it, the evil one comes and snatches away what is sown in the heart; this is what was sown on the path.
Matthew 13:19 [NRSV]

What do we do with these barriers to growth that Jesus talked about here? What does the 'good soil' have that other types of terrains, like paths, don't have? How can we persevere to see harvests and fruitfulness grow? This ancient text gives us some surprising starting points, but we do need to reflect further on what the dynamic equivalents might be for us today. To push the parable a bit further, too, I wonder if there is anything we can do to help our hard grounds become good soil, ready to produce a harvest? Can 'wastelands' be transformed into 'seedbeds' if we know what we are looking for? Like all of Jesus' teaching we must be careful to start with ourselves first before looking out to people and places beyond us.

The ground that the good seeds fall on are 'hard paths' and that means to 'not understand.' To not 'understand' here is not simply a cognitive, objective appreciation of the facts. The invitation to join God's new reign is not simply a passive assent to an idea or a doctrine.

It's deeply connected to the heart, mind and right action. The Greek word used here is *suniemi* and literally means 'sent' (*hiemi*) 'together' (*sun*). It's about connecting with an insight beyond what we already know and integrating that into the right things to do. To 'understand' then has an ethical dimension more than just appreciating an idea or concept. The person who is like 'hard ground' simply can't make the connections. Jesus says that the invitation made it to the person's 'heart,' but no further. It was quickly 'snatched away.'

I certainly know I can miss connections by not being awake enough to see what is happening in front of me. I am one of those people who can easily 'hear and not really listen.' Even in the most tragic of situations I have the capacity to simply go on autopilot and fast-forward till I am interested again. I remember years ago in Springvale I sat in front of a fire in our backyard listening to a Cambodian friend. He was smiling and animated and I laughed along with him. He had quite a thick accent and normally I would need to concentrate hard to understand what he was saying, but hey, there was a fire to stare into, I was stressing over something else in my mind and I was sure he was being funny again. Unfortunately, I was asleep to what was happening. My friend was disclosing his experiences under Pol Pot and the brutal murders of his family as part of the genocide in Cambodia. He smiled to cover his embarrassment; his emotion was actually rage. I woke up in time to ask him to share it again, desperately apologised for misunderstanding, but the moment had passed. I was, in that moment at least, a concrete path lacking understanding.

I'm not sure if you've had experiences like this too. We can sleepwalk through our lives and miss out on what is happening in front of us. Our minds can get caught in a repeating loop of reliving our past or rehearsing for the future, but this can be a loop of doom for us.

How do we awaken to the incredible connections and understandings ready and waiting for us when it's easier to stay asleep? Just being aware of our lack of awareness can help us start to awaken. Catching ourselves in the loop and then redirecting that concern back to God, ready to be awake for the now can help too.

10: Hard Paths - Lacking Awareness

The Enneagram has been an important self-awareness tool for me. Identifying core motivations for both health and dysfunction has helped me become aware when I am losing my way. As a 'Nine' my common go-to under pressure is to try to keep harmony at all costs. I'm at my best when I engage and am assertive in making peace. I can empathise, see other views and bring people together. However, I can be at my worst when I'm avoiding conflict, disengaging, and doubling down to try to please everyone. This can leave me resentful and simmering in a kind of coma. Of the 'seven deadly sins,' a Nine has 'sloth' as our key temptation. There are times when all is too much for me and all I want to do is 'veg out' and escape from my reality. I can become that 'hard path' others walk over, and miss out on growing the good seeds of life. When I notice this, I can awaken to what is happening and find ways forward. Often this means getting up and doing something difficult – a hard conversation, task, or event. Sometimes physical activities – like walking – help me get out of my head and into my body. This awakens me to the fact that what I'm trying to avoid is not as bad as what is happening to me in avoidance. I don't have to be a 'hard path' to be walked over.

Anthony de Mello writes extensively about awakenings and awareness. For him, the very meaning of spirituality is awakening.

> Spirituality means waking up. Most people, even though they don't know it, are asleep. They're born asleep, they live asleep, they marry in their sleep, they breed children in their sleep, they die in their sleep without ever waking up. They never understand the loveliness and the beauty of this thing that we call human existence.[84]

What the 'hard path' person can be then is one who doesn't take responsibility for themselves. Doesn't risk their own actions, but blames others.

> The person who is asleep always thinks he'll feel better if somebody else changes. You're suffering because you are asleep, but you're thinking, "How wonderful life would be if somebody else would change; how wonderful life would be if my neighbor changed, my wife changed, my boss changed".[85]

Knowing we can't change others, we can then start to be awake to what we can change. Here is one of de Mello's exercises:

> Put this program into action, a thousand times: (a) identify the negative feelings in you; (b) understand that they are in you, not in the world, not in external reality; (c) do not see them as an essential part of "I"; these things come and go; (d) understand that when you change, everything changes.[86]

Part of waking up to understanding then moves us to start living as we see matters. De Mello argues that this is not selfish as we might feel. It is staying asleep that is selfish and wanting change from others that is selfish.

> The selfish thing is to demand that someone else live their life as YOU see fit. That's selfish. It is not selfish to live your life as you see fit. The selfishness lies in demanding that someone else live their life to suit your tastes, or your pride, or your profit, or your pleasure. That is truly selfish.[87]

Owning our own feelings, desires, and aspirations, both good and bad, helps us wake up. If we are awake then we can see too what others have to offer. No one is always stuck as a 'hard path' unable to be fruitful in our local community. Over time change is possible, but awakenings and awareness matter.

Parts of our local communities can feel like 'hard paths,' not awake or aware yet. This is not just true of people, but systems and structures too. How true is this for political parties, church denominations, charities, or even sports clubs? Too often, they stay blissfully unaware of reality and will not face the impacts of vested interests; they sleepwalk into their decline. Hard conversations and decisions, for example, are often avoided until it is too late. Competing internal powers emerge and forget their overall original missions. Learning how to have hard conversations and see conflict transformed is a gift most local communities miss out on. Hardness of hearts and lives result. Seeds of Shalom have trouble growing here. The patient and courageous work of local organisational reform and renewal from the inside out is also a gift few local communities experience.

10: Hard Paths - Lacking Awareness

Hard paths can be broken up in time. Seeds can start to grow life in the cracks.

Why is it easier to be asleep than awake? The increased options to numb our pain are at least part of the reason. All major faiths and wisdom traditions believe that coming to terms with suffering is an important part of living this life. However, with increased access to drugs, alcohol, entertainment, social media, and all kinds of other distractions, we can try to avoid this reality. Disadvantaged communities have been inundated with the cheapest and nastiest numbing down strategies of all, and few can resist. The mantra of parents to merely 'stay out of trouble' doesn't help. When their kids obey, often they become passive zombies who rarely go outside. Surely numbing will impede this generation's growth. Risk, suffering, pain – these are all important teachers on the way to becoming awake to maturity and understanding. We numb these experiences at our own peril.

Hard paths can be broken down by breakthroughs of connections. Local communities offer us an antidote to fake anaesthetics by opening us up to others and their pain. In genuine community we can be awake to our own pain too, and find deeper connections. The art of hospitality can also be such an antidote to isolation. A wholehearted welcome, sharing food and laughter together, can be a tonic for even the hardest hearts.

This parable warns that people and places can be hard-hearted, spend their whole lives asleep to what is happening around them and never fully awaken. I often meet people who have lived a long life, but not a full life. They missed their moments to grow and be fruitful and they now cast a cold shadow of bitterness on any others who dare try to enter their closed, dark domain. Desperate for others to fail to prove their point, they have lived a hard-hearted half-life, following a cold, dark path until the inevitable end.

In contrast, we can meet those rare older folk who live in the moment, took risks that gave them life, and are still life-giving with people around them. I know what kind of older person I want to be. I know too, that I could be either if I'm not awake now to what is going on around me in every moment. It's never too late to break the concrete barriers down.

Personal Reflections

1. Have there been times when you have been like a 'hard path,' unawake to what is going on around you?
   What was it like?

2. What are your temptations to keep lacking 'understanding' and being 'aware' of what is happening?

3. Have you experienced local organisations or community groups that have felt like they are 'hard paths'?
   What was that like? What could you do?

4. Have you experienced 'cracks in the concrete'?
   What was it like to become aware and glimpse what is happening and might be possible?

5. What can you do to better be awake, aware and present in the moment?

Chapter 11:
Stony Fields - Lacking Grit

As for what was sown on rocky ground, this is the one who hears the word and immediately receives it with joy; yet such a person has no root, but endures only for a while, and when trouble or persecution arises on account of the word, that person immediately falls away.
Matthew 13:21-22 [NRSV]

The 'rocky ground' in Jesus' story is a person who initially has joy, but they are like soil that is too shallow. Such a person 'has no root' and the seed that comes their way cannot grow long enough to be fruitful.

In the same way, we can easily become excited by a new possibility, but not have the follow-through to realise it. Over the years we often get people who say, 'I'd love to do what you do!' We get excited about their enthusiasm and find ways to help them join in, sometimes including living with us. That initial 'joy,' however, can quickly disappear before any 'rootedness' happens. The willingness to 'downsize' our worlds long enough to give our best energy to local people and places is always tested. I often find it's the most naturally talented and confident people who find the discipline of rootedness the hardest. Scanning the horizons of opportunity, some folks get bored too easily and chase one cause after another and never get to experience any real transformation. Sometimes just 'showing up' at the right time can make all the difference.

I learnt a lot about the importance of 'showing up' when we lived in Bangkok. Many say they are committed to people or places, but when the going got tough too many Christians would go missing. I clearly remember our own temptations when civil unrest occurred in May 2010.

Since early March, tensions had been rising. Bangkok's main commercial hub had been blockaded by Red Shirt protesters after exiled and former Prime Minister Thaksin Shinawatra's assets had only been partially released. There had been over 50 deaths and thousands injured in Red Shirt grenade attacks and clashes with army and police during this time.

We had some close calls ourselves. Ben Rowse (a brother of Urban Neighbours Of Hope Melbourne worker, Hannah Rowse) was about to step onto a train at Saladeng BTS station when four grenades went off. He was rushed to hospital and after a night there stayed in Klong Toey ready to continue work in Burma with just cuts and bruises. I was due to pick up my laptop from a computer repair shop just near this station at the time the grenades went off. My computer wasn't ready in time and I was spared the trip and danger. Chris McCartney, another UNOH worker, heard shots fired and saw people fall to the ground, while he kept riding his motorbike. On the morning of May 19, my mum was with my son Aiden at a local shopping mall when suddenly shots rang out and bombs went off nearby. They eventually found a person to help them across the road and found a tuk-tuk to take them to my office. This was all happening about a five-minute motorbike ride from our home.

At a neighbourhood level, there had been a deep divide. Even our house church had strong supporters of both Red Shirts (pro-Thaksin) and Yellow Shirts (anti-Thaksin). The Red Shirt barricades of tyres, sharpened bamboo poles, and barbed wire had been in place in central Bangkok for more than two months, with battle-ready soldiers on the streets, even near our kids' schools. Skirmishes and explosions on the edge of the protest barricades had been common, but an atmosphere of quiet, anticipatory dread fell across the rest of the city until it all exploded early on May 19.

11: Stony Fields - Lacking Grit

The most violent, bloody climax imaginable was about to happen and you could feel the dread in the air. Just a few minutes from our slum house, a mob was using grenades, M-16s, and machetes to fight the army and loot 7-Elevens, luxury shopping malls, and banks. By midday the crazed mob were getting closer and closer to our slum by the minute. The memory of looking up from where I was, at the Klong Toey Community Centre, seeing plumes of smoke rising up into the sky from nearby business buildings is an image that stays with me. Along with the adults and children gathered there, I was transfixed as army helicopters started to land on the very top of one of the closest skyscrapers: the burning Channel 3 building, rescuing TV execs and staff from the fires, with looting and rioting going on below.

The Red Shirt protest leaders had surrendered after the army crashed through their protest areas in downtown Bangkok with tanks. Now their supporters, some armed with M-16s and grenade launchers, were moving across the city to exact revenge. Banks who had held on to Thaksin's assets, media outlets that had not fully supported their cause (including Channel 3), and some of the largest shopping malls were set alight and turned to rubble.

UNOH workers, including myself, quickly gathered together with our children at the community centre, trying to work out what was next for us and our neighbours. Even getting in and out of Klong Toey was difficult now and there was a rumour that Red Shirts were coming to burn our slum down. The young men who I normally coached football with had grabbed baseball bats, machetes, and even a golf club to guard the two main entrances to Klong Toey.

Perhaps these apocalyptic images of social conflict exemplify why the transformation of slums should be so important for all people today, including Christians.

We know currently over one billion people live in slums (one in six people) and this could double in the next 20 years. Indeed, over 2.6 billion live in Majority World cities today. With nearly all the population growth over the next 100 years in cities, the Majority World is unprepared for an extra seven billion people joining them.[88] The world's poor live within touching distance of the rich and famous, and are nurtured and informed by the same media marketing bombardment, yet they remain without the wherewithal to access these lifestyles. This is a toxic cocktail of guilt and resentment. Guilt that they and their children have not been smart or able enough to have what 'everybody else has,' and a deep, burning resentment of 'everybody who can.' From this perspective, the looting and destruction of Bangkok's luxury shopping malls only a few kilometres from slums should not be a surprise. Christians surely have something to offer here.

How and why the rural and urban poor became radicalised as Red Shirts was also a warning. At first glance, it made no sense for so many poor to leave what they were doing and put their lives on the line for Thaksin, one of the richest people on the planet. For this is not an 'uprising of the poor,' but an acting out on behalf of a billionaire. Even while in exile and with his official assets seized, Thaksin bought Manchester City Football Club and a Greek island. Populism, polarisation, and post-truth became noted strategies in Western politics in recent years too with Mr Trump and Mr Johnson using Thaksin's playbook to gain power and cause mayhem.

Some of Thaksin's success can be explained by Thailand's patron-client relationships where a benefactor is sought to look after them. Thaksin offered to be a kind of mega-benefactor for the poor. For example, Thaksin paid 500 baht a day plus food for each Red Shirt protester that signed on each day and a further 1500 baht a day for those on frontline 'security.' He further promised that if they won their cause against the government there would be homes and cars for everyone who wanted them. This was part of Thaksin's appeal while in office too, though very few of his populist schemes actually worked for many people and he certainly made more money in office than as a private citizen. The sheer amounts of money on offer and the idea of such a benefactor was hard for some of my Klong Toey neighbours to reject, but it was almost impossible for many of those in rural areas like the northeast to reject.

What other options are there to find the 'good life'? Messianic figures able to manipulate the masses for their own benefit should be expected as poverty and the number of urban slums increases.

11: Stony Fields - Lacking Grit

There are only so many helicopters that can whisk people to safety. In a world with so many urban poor, no one can be immune from the chaos.

As the UNOH team sat around our regular communion table in classrooms of the Klong Toey Community Centre late in the afternoon of May 19, we were deeply aware of two primal impulses: fight or flight. The impulse to flee was being echoed from the Australian government and some of the parents of our team. It's a harrowing thing to read an SMS from your embassy saying they have already evacuated, and basically 'good luck, you're on your own now.' As a parent with two of our children with us (Amy aged 13 and Aiden aged six) as well as three children of UNOH workers, I was also deeply aware of the potential trauma that staying could have on them.

But there was also the impulse to overstretch our role and try to be heroic in reckless ways unhelpful to the cause. Should we join our footballers, for example, with the baseball bats and fight the mob coming toward us? What good could we really do in this urban chaos?

In the end, while we prayed together around that table, we all had peace in staying. While all workers were given the freedom to leave, we all decided to stay together that night at the community centre so no one was isolated and so that we were in our slum. What we had to offer was our solidarity in Christ. Of course, what would it say about the Jesus we say we follow if we left our neighbours when the going got tough? Some of us did venture out to give moral support to our friends on the frontline at different points during the night. As rioting continued, over 50 more people died and hundreds more were injured.

As the sun rose early on May 20, I did have a baseball bat in my hands at an entrance of the slums, but it was for fun, playing around with some of the footballers who had stayed awake all night. The Red Shirts had not come much further. Though there were attempts to light fires, all the fires had been put out in time and no damage was done. We lived to stand with our community another day.

As six-year-old Aiden rose that morning, I tentatively asked, 'How are you going there mate?' He looked up from a mattress on the floor in one of our classrooms and said, 'Great Dad. When can we do it all again?'

With a smile I joked back, 'Next time there's a riot, Son.'

Amy and I went for a motorbike ride to survey the damage and look for something for us to do that day. 'If I get shot,' Amy said matter-of-factly, 'I'd like to only get shot in the arm. Because it wouldn't hurt that much, but gee I'd have a great story to tell with it!' We found a movie theatre open and with all the team went to watch the latest Shrek movie as if nothing had happened.

Our kids are now adults and are finding their faith and unique callings. They have witnessed some awful, real world things, but they don't think authentic Christian faith is boring or irrelevant. They have seen that Christian fidelity requires we stand with people as the crucified and risen Jesus stands with us and on the side of the poor. That faith is active and alive may well cost us more than we bargained for, but is worth it to see our lives count for something. Faith in action is rarely convenient, but anything less than the giving of our lives undermines the God who "became flesh and blood and moved into the neighbourhood" (John 1:14 [MSG]) and who calls us to "come follow me" (Matt. 4:19; Mark 1:17). Urban chaos will subside, but how we live for Christ within it lasts forever.

In modern language we often call 'going missing' a 'lacking grit.' There has been a lot of recent research about the nature of grit. American psychologist Angela Lee Duckworth, for example, says that "Grit is passion and perseverance for very long-term goals" and that "Grit is sticking with your future, day in, day out, not just for the week, not just for the month, but for years, and working really hard to make that future a reality."[89] We all need a bit more of this kind of grit!

I know I can lack grit under certain conditions. I love seeing good ideas become a reality and can quickly get obsessed about the latest one. My daughter Amy thinks I have Attention Deficit Disorder along with Dyslexia and so 'hyperfocus' can be both a curse and a superpower for me. I have begun to understand that I love the design, pilot and testing phases of any project, but once developed and stable, find it hard to maintain. I can also have trouble letting go of lost causes (people and programmes) and think, if I can just find a new way forward, we can make it work.

11: Stony Fields - Lacking Grit

Therefore, I have learnt the hard way that I am a person who needs a good team around them if new programmes or projects are to grow to have a life of their own. If it depends solely on my enthusiasm, we will eventually lose momentum and then precious resources of time, funds, and energy can be wasted as the project peters out. It's one of the reasons having a 'patch' that is 'large enough to live a lot of life' resonates with me as I can stay rooted in one larger place and connect and cycle through with diverse people and projects over time. That passion for place keeps me rooted in my catalyzing gifts. I know if I were forced to do the same thing, over and over, day in and day out for years on end then something would die inside me. The challenge of the rocky soil for me is discerning when or how to let go and when to just keep going.

Grit then isn't just a stubborn refusal to quit something. Realising our own limits is a good thing and saying 'no' with empathy is an art form worth learning.

I do meet people who enjoy the comfort and confidence of doing the same old things, over and over, but it's to everyone's detriment. It's their own detriment because they're not giving time to what they are made for and they miss out on their talents. It's for the detriment of others because we miss out on their talents and may end up doing what they could be doing better. If our best actions don't release our passions toward a worthwhile goal then it's not grit that keeps us growing, it's a kind of arrogance or selfishness. If we're not 'rooted' in reality, then we can't grow to share our fruits.

Patience is one fruit of the Spirit that Paul identifies in Galatians 5:22-23. It's not passive hanging on, but the kind of long-suffering defiance that outlasts opposition, even persecution.

When I think of grit I certainly think of my friends in Ukraine. Originally, I met this group when I was invited to teach Masters units at the Ukrainian Evangelical Theological Seminary (UETS) in Kyiv, 2018. I loved connecting in person there and found the whole school and city alive with potential. There was a real interest in more holistic understandings of Christian faith and it felt like we had brothers and sisters in the cause. Little would I know then that Russia would soon invade.

No Wastelands

When I visited and taught at the school after the invasion in October 2022, I saw Kyiv full of such determined people. What we had talked about previously had been actioned in the most courageous ways. UETS is the grittiest school imaginable. In facing down a superpower hell-bent on their annihilation they make these kinds of statements:

> Mr Putin
>
> You may bomb a concert hall
> But our music is not there
> You may flatten a hospital
> But our strength is not there
> You may twist an election
> But our will is not there
> You may steal our loved ones
> But our love is not there
> You may take out a tank
> But our courage is not there
> You may destroy stadia
> But our spirit is not there
> You may kill a comedian
> But our joy is not there
>
> These things are off limits.
> They are deep within.
> You cannot touch them.
> We carry divine DNA.
>
> As do you. We pray you find it.
>
> (Inspired by Tatiana)

My friend Andy Flannagan wrote a book called *Those Who Show Up*. It was a title inspired by *The West Wing* TV show line that states "decisions are made by those who show up." Andy explains that so many political decisions that impact communities are made in boring meetings by those who consistently 'show up.' As a leader in 'Christian in Politics' encouraging Christians to engage in the political process, including joining political parties and running in elections, he has experienced this firsthand.

11: Stony Fields - Lacking Grit

He wrote:

> History is made by those who show up. It always has been. Decisions are made by those who show up. Not necessarily the smartest, not necessarily the most qualified, not necessarily those of the best character, not necessarily those who may have gleaned some divine wisdom, but by those who… simply show up. It is sobering, but perhaps also empowering.[90]

All of us can join local groups and 'show up.' If we are faithful, consistent, and do what we say we will do, we will become one of the most valued members of that group. Our local political parties, school boards, 'friends of' parks, and so many more groups are crying out for such people. We can make an amazing difference if we focus our enthusiasm and 'show up.'

We can meet, and be, local people who are not shallow, have deep roots, and keep growing. They can overcome even dramatic 'trouble' or 'persecution' because they have a fire deep in the belly for something much bigger than themselves that they see as worthwhile. I have had the honour of meeting such people most of my life.

I know the temptation is to write off stony fields, but I also know stones can be picked out and broken up. Stony grounds are not built to last and no local community is only made of stones. Showing up, even if it's just to pick out the stones, is worthwhile in the long term.

Personal Reflections

1. When has there been a time you felt like giving up? Did you stay or go? Why?

2. What does 'showing up' look like for you?

3. How can you tell the difference between needing to let go or dig deeper?

4. What could you do next to build your sense of 'grit' for your local community?

Chapter 12:
Thorny Grounds - Lacking Trust

As for what was sown among thorns, this is the one who hears the word, but the cares of the world and the lure of wealth choke the word, and it yields nothing.
Matthew 13:22 [NRSV]

Some people and places are choked by a 'thorny' lack of trust. They might be great, innovative and committed individuals, but they quickly hurt each other if there is little trust between them. If trust is absent, change is almost impossible. Who and how we trust matters a great deal. It is at the heart of how 'thorny ground' resists God's Shalom.

Robert Putnam has been an important academic voice for community building. It was Putnam who made the argument that 'social capital' is essentially the amount of trust available in a community or society. He wrote:

> A society that relies on generalized reciprocity is more efficient than a distrustful society, for the same reason that money is more efficient than barter. Trust lubricates social life.
>
> Networks of civic engagement also facilitate coordination and communication and amplify information about the trustworthiness of other individuals.[91]

No Wastelands

The idea that local communities grow at the speed of trust can help us detect blockages. When gifts are freely given and shared, when we have an abundance mindset that there is enough for all, then flourishing can happen quickly, 'lubricating' change in remarkable ways. However, if these kinds of trust are absent, community life is quickly choked. It can take decades to grow trust, but seconds to lose it. Scarcity, insecurity and distrust make change almost impossible.

Jesus specially named two places as areas of trust: 'cares of the world' and 'deceitfulness of wealth.' These two pinpoint where our confidence and trust is based. The powers of anxiety and money should not be underestimated as brutal forces, with a life of their own, to create mistrust. They can bring down even the best of us. I have seen how these two challenges can choke and take out even the most impressive ideas and community leaders.

I have been especially vulnerable to the thorns of worry and money in transitions. That is a time when we often have choices to make about what's next, and who and what we trust in. One of my favourite sayings to pioneers who are in transition and discerning what is next, is: 'You can have security or you can have freedom, but you can't have both.' Interestingly, a survey of existing Pioneer Ministers found that in the choice between money and freedom, most said freedom was more important.[92] I agree with that. I have lived on 'faith support' most of my adult life, since I began full-time urban ministry with Youth For Christ Melbourne in 1990. This is where people who know me, trust me, and believe in what I'm doing, commit to fund me a regular amount each month. It was the traditional way to fund missionaries; inspired, in part, by how Jesus and his apostolic community were 'supported' by three women "out of their own means" (Luke 8:1-3 [NIV]). Our support has gone up and down over the decades, and sometimes I've needed other work to top it up. We've also tried to live on a basic monthly living allowance (currently pegged to the 'Real Living Wage') and share in community.[93] This has enabled me to take risks and follow possibilities in ways that would not have been possible if only my current role or project was funded, and not me personally. It also meant we haven't had to compete with local organisations for grants or financial support because we were funded independently.

12: Thorny Ground - Lacking Trust

It has meant that our presence does not take finances away from the existing local ecosystem. Having personal backers as one stream of our income has helped us win trust, freely choose focus, and not be understood as financial competitors. Groups like Stewardship still offer this to pioneers today, but it has become less common.[94]

Finances and resultant worries in life then are still common thorns that can undermine trust. One observation from my sabbatical in Melbourne in 2022 was that few of those who had started out in ministry with Anji and I remained in Christian leadership. Not all of our peers continued to be part of a church, others no longer identified as Christian. It seemed as if a whole generation of us had 'heard the word' but it had been 'choked out.' The older generations, some of the great lions of the faith, were getting frailer, retiring, or had died. Few were ready to take their place in churches and Christian organisations and pick up responsibilities.

I know the reasons are many and complicated, but here are some of the thorns that I think impact the confidence, trust, and viability of Christian leadership. The boomer generation of leaders was such a large and larger-than-life cohort, and the kinds of organisations they left behind were often not fit for purpose for the next generation. The way many Christian churches and charities are governed and run, for example, can crush the spirits of today's leaders. Last generation's excesses, compulsions, and sins have strangled the next generation with administrative red tape to keep people safe and reduce risks. Few have the administrative support to keep on top of this. Expectations on too few or on too many fronts, can be unrealistic for those wanting to serve in Christian organisations and raise a complex, modern family well.

Formative experiences that created opportunity and awareness for radical faith have mostly been curtailed too, meaning that the Christian world in Melbourne has shrunk in many ways. For example, the kinds of youth missions and youth groups I grew up with have mostly gone now. How many Christian teenagers are encouraged to start their own drop-in centre or youth club or to visit prisons today, as I did with Youth For Christ Melbourne or Theos? These activities are deemed too risky for young people now.

Larger churches sweep up young people, inviting them to attend 'youth services' that are much safer and more common. The next generation may come for a while, and many have experienced a lot of 'joy,' but have mostly been left unchallenged and moved on and out.

The Christian world in Australia has severely shrunk as a result of all this; with older people more fragile and younger people absent, meaningful Christian leadership opportunities have become limited. With few exceptions, there are insufficient people to fund a full-time minister in most churches. For example, "National Church Life Survey (NCLS) data shows that over the last four decades the proportion of Australians attending church at least once per month has more than halved from 36% (1972) to 15%."[95] There are significantly fewer local churches now and they are getting smaller with 47% having less than 50 people attending weekly church services in 2016. Since then, Covid may well have taken a quarter of these attenders out and many more churches have become less viable. In 2016, only 5% of churches estimated they have over 500 in weekly church services and most of these were in narrow 'Bible Belt' suburbs.[96] Risk-taking and trusting others, the oils that keep organisations moving, is almost impossible in such fragile times. There are so many other ways young Christians can find meaning and purpose and not put up with often petty and oppressive Christian institutions. For example, consultancies, enterprises, and welfare services are needed and are often better paid with less hassle and more freedom. There are a lot of thorns here. These are just hypotheses for some of the changes I noticed on sabbatical reconnecting with friends.

What has been happening in Christian churches can also be seen in other local organisations. Larger, national charities, offering less risky, professional service provisions 'to' and 'for' local communities have become common. The onramps for local young people to cut their teeth in local community building efforts has often been outsourced and replaced by professionals. Learning how to be a good, voluntary 'member' and 'citizen' has mostly been lost. There is work and there is leisure; there is time for little else.

Being a 'consumer' rather than a 'citizen' has become all encompassing, but it enslaves and chokes the life out of us. Ivan Illich outlined the

12: Thorny Ground - Lacking Trust

disaster of this move for communities and people. He wrote:

> In a consumer society there are inevitably two kinds of slaves: the prisoners of addiction and the prisoners of envy.[97]

Addiction and envy undermine trust in others and the potential to experience Shalom in people and places. These are not easy to root out.

Perhaps those of us on the frontline most easily see the repercussions of this drift to consumerism. Systems often work best for the centre and fail those on the edges. On the margins, we see and experience these failures first-hand. They often crush the people we love and serve, including us. This is especially true for Christian organisations, denominations, and churches who can be more anxious and functionally atheist than most. It's not just policy and politics, but theology and spirituality too.

Who and how can we grow trust over consumerism? Finding deeper theological frameworks and freedom of conscience to pursue trust and meaningful community building is important work.

We certainly need a better theology of generosity if we are to undermine these thorns. It seems like there are two poles. *Stinginess* at one end where funds are strictly private and rarely shared or risked. For example, recent research in Australia found:

> Over 73 per cent of top income earning churchgoers (earning over $158,000 per year) give less than 0.6 per cent of their income. The average churchgoer isn't much better, giving only 0.7 per cent of their income.
>
> According to the Australian Taxation Office, the average Australian taxpayer gave 0.32 per cent of their taxable income in tax-deductible donations in 2012-2013.[98]

No wonder we are struggling to support good work when so much is kept to ourselves. *Prosperity* is at the other end, where those with faith only give to the few in order to get back more (and are often exploited). Benny Hinn is but one example, earning over US$200 million a year and squandering it on lavish living.[99] We have seen a concentration of wealth in certain ministries with massive excesses.

While at first sight it can seem generous to give to such ministries, it is based on a false formula that to get money for yourself you give to such ministries. That Christians would exploit others for gain like this is horrendous. Even good aid and charity organisations can do something similar, making impact claims that are more beneficial to the egos of their donors than what has actually happened locally. Even benevolent giving can become consumer driven today. As Ivan Illich reminds us, "the corruption of the best is the worst."

For me, the stories of miracles of loaves and fish are important places to start to address this. In the face of so much need, faced by multitudes in a seeming wasteland, "Jesus replied, 'They do not need to go away. You give them something to eat.' 'We have here only five loaves of bread and two fish,' they answered" (Matt.14:16-17 [NRSV]). The disciples don't feel the same as Jesus about the hungry multitudes in a wilderness. Late in the day the disciples start to display what Parker Palmer calls "the scarcity assumption."[100] The disciples see the needs and problems around them, and the limited resources they have. There is a lack of trust in the multitudes, but also in Jesus.

Jesus' question, 'What do you have in your hands?' challenges those instincts and the story flows in a new direction. Jesus had an 'abundance' approach to life. When we look at urban people and the communities we serve, we can, like the disciples, get resentful, fearful, or overwhelmed by unmet needs. However, we can also join Jesus in taking an inventory of strengths and what can be offered. As Asset-Based-Community-Developers would say, 'use what's strong to fix what's wrong.' Jesus never did anything for anyone that they could do for themselves and never created dependencies. Indeed, his miracles only happened within the context of cooperation, empowerment, and the dignity of the most vulnerable. In the hands of Jesus, their combined loaves and fish are abundantly enough.

Walter Brueggemann, the great Old Testament scholar, describes a kind of conflict going on traced back to the Genesis stories and especially Hebrew oppression under Pharah. He writes:

12: Thorny Ground - Lacking Trust

> The conflict between the narratives of abundance and of scarcity is the defining problem confronting us... The gospel story of abundance asserts that we originated in the magnificent, inexplicable love of a God who loved the world into generous being. The baptismal service declares that each of us has been miraculously loved into existence by God. And the story of abundance says that our lives will end in God, and that this well-being cannot be taken from us.[101]

Trust needs to be evident in letting go of our own 'loaves and fish' if abundance is to win in our neighbourhoods. Will our small resources be wasted on the crowds? Will we miss out? However, the alternative of defaulting back into the scarcity mentality is ultimately an even bigger risk. It's not just that the multitudes in front of us will eventually find out what we are hoarding and then turn on us, but we become diminished. Our joy is choked out. If we can release what we have in faith, at the speed of trust, miracles are possible. Moving from scarcity to appreciating what we have together in our hands for abundance, is one of the most needed shifts for us to learn today.

To see deep Shalom emerge in a place can take generations of trust-building work and there are no guarantees that we will see this happen in ours. Longevity and patience then are crucial to curtail the 'cares of the world' and 'lure of wealth.' As Dave Andrews, an elder of community building from Queensland, says: 'Some of us start out seeking to do good, only to end up doing very well!' Dave, however, is an example of someone who has resisted this and stayed rooted in the West End of Brisbane for many decades. He is open and honest about his hurts, especially at the hands of Christian organisations, but continues to inspire as a brilliant Christian speaker, trainer, and writer, as well as a local and global activist. Dave wrote these wisdom maxims that I have kept returning to over the years:

> Be continually converted to Christ. Constantly relate to reality through Christ.
>
> Be accountable to one another. Answer the hard questions as honestly as you possibly can.

> Don't be responsible for everything, but be responsive to everyone.
>
> Never react; always respond; as constructively as you can.
>
> Don't try to do big things; try to do little things with a lot of love.
>
> Extend love unconditionally, but trust only conditionally.
>
> Don't have high expectations; have high hopes with low expectations.
>
> Cultivate seeds of hope in the grounds for despair.
>
> Never forget – there's no salvation without grace, and no grace without suffering.
>
> Always remember – that strength is made perfect in weakness.[102]

How and who we trust matters. If we put our trust in the mirage of wealth, or in economic markets as consumers, we will have the life choked out of us through envy and addiction. In the abundance of God, however, there is enough for all, including us and our local communities. Trusting this God in people and places creates possibilities for even the wildest wastelands to experience the flourishing of God's love and Shalom.

12: Thorny Ground - Lacking Trust

Personal Reflections

1. Where have you seen a low level of trust in your local community? In what ways has that dynamic been like thorns for you?

2. How does scarcity and consumerism connect?

3. How can trust and abundance connect?

4. What can you do to grow trust in you and your local community?

Chapter 13:
Good Soils - Praxis Understanding And Action

But as for what was sown on good soil, this is the one who hears the word and understands it, who indeed bears fruit and yields, in one case a hundredfold, in another sixty, and in another thirty.
Matthew 13:23 [NRSV]

This parable has a surprising and hopeful ending for us. The yield the sower sees is way out of proportion to what they sow. A traditional yield at that time was seven to eleven times. Here we have a hundred, sixty, and thirty times. These yields:

> are magnificently unusual, the excess of the anticipated Garden of Eden when God's empire is established in full ... Such yields anticipate the final establishment of God's just reign, which will provide abundant resources for all and will destroy the cycle of poverty.[103]

The promise of Shalom is possible in good soil. It's there and worth the consistent work.

If we can keep sharing life and God's dream of Shalom with people and places it can multiply beyond our wildest dreams.

No Wastelands

Our local community is no longer shallow or fallow, but instead grows deep roots of awareness, grit and trust, and keeps growing into fruitfulness. Our neighbourhoods can overcome even dramatic trouble or persecution because they connect together for a dream much bigger than themselves that they all see as worthwhile. There is a supernatural abundance of life that can flow from them if we are patient and gritty and show up. Sometimes, even we can be such 'good soil,' 'fruitful' people ourselves. This is the soil ready to be a seedbed of Shalom.

At a basic level, soil still represents potential for life today. In a negative sense, if the overall quality of the earth's dirt is too low, then life as we know it will die because plants and animals won't grow and can't live without it. That has a knock-on effect that includes the death of humans. Humans can't live without good dirt; this has always been so. Indeed, our creation story in Genesis 2 has a play on words with this. The Hebrew word for dirt (Adamai) becomes the name of the first human being, Adam, as God picks up the dirt and breathes life in it. God then sets Adam and Eve to the calling of looking after the earth/dirt. Our first picture of Shalom has dirt front and centre.

What makes for good soil? Good soil is teeming with life containing millions of microorganisms that are decomposing, dead organic matter, along with oxygen and water. Animals such as earthworms can live in the soil and aid in the process of enriching the soil. Soil can be improved by adding more nutrients, which can be done by composting or leaving more roots in the soil year to year.

I have learnt a lot about soil from Ernie who leads one of my favourite projects in Winson Green called 'Warm Earth.' They are based at a local primary school's paddock with our alpacas. He is a kind of genius, working with volunteers and the students to ensure all the food waste from the primary school is turned into usable compost and gas. A key part of the process is literally making the earth and waste warm and ready for composting so that plants can grow in their many raised seedbeds. These plants are then sold to neighbours for their gardens, and this helps fund Warm Earth. From little seedbeds, with naturally enriched soil, big things come. Meaningful work and learning, environmental sustainability, and joy are as much a harvest as the plants themselves.

13: Good Soils - Praxis Understanding And Action

I have had the honour of meeting many people who are like 'good soil' in my ministry life, but they are often found in unexpected places. It's often the wild places that can be the most fruitful. We have seen with other soils that initial joy may be shown, but no long-term fruit. There has been a kind of socio-political dimension to this with 'deceitfulness of wealth' undermining the potential harvests. Neighbourhoods facing injustice, in contrast, can come together to connect in remarkable ways because they have nothing to lose. What they often have in common is that they can be open, multiply a lot with a little, and recycle their experiences with help.

Take Glenda for example. She is one of our members at Lodge Road Community Church in Winson Green and was nominated on our Change Makers programme in 2022. Glenda is a single mum and was worried about taking up the nomination on account of her physical disability and special needs, but she was willing to trust us and have a go. I'm glad she did. Not just for herself, but because she provided one of the most inspirational moments of our time together.

We were on the Holy Island of Lindisfarne for the final residential of Change Makers together with Cohort 8. We walked barefoot at low tide from the mainland, along the Pilgrim's Posts, to Holy Island itself, helping us to experience in our bodies the weekend's theme of 'resilience.' This is a pilgrimage route that has been taken over a thousand years, from Celtic times. Something spiritual always happens in this thin place as we walk barefoot, touching the mud in the traditional way.

We needed to start early that Saturday so the tide would not come in while we walked. It normally takes about 90 minutes or so to walk the three miles to the Island, and we had three hours left before the tide would come in. It was a cold and slightly misty November morning and the weather kept changing, but all was well as we stopped at the first Pilgrim's Post to pray for God's blessing and awakening. Glenda had been nervous about this pilgrimage, spending months discussing with us if she could do it or not. There she was, however, well prepared in coat and hat. She even had a staff to help her walk.

We set off, holding our silence, open to God speaking to us. We all walked alone, doing our own pilgrimage until we met together at the first Refuge about one-third of the way across the estuary.

Some participants are like buzzing bees, not just going from post to post, but going wider, exploring and looking under rocks and seaweed, and end up making it to the first Refuge within ten minutes. Not Glenda. She took her time, not just because her disability slowed her walking speed, but because she was savouring the whole experience. As we broke our silence and shared what we experienced at the first Refuge, Glenda's response was confidence. 'I've experienced a deep peace here I've never experienced before.'

The last two-thirds of the pilgrimage normally creates more of a social vibe. Participants share and walk together, meandering from one post to the next. The weather this time, however, closed in. The temperature suddenly plummeted, it got dark, and rain pelted down on us. This led some participants to move faster to both warm up and get across to the Island and out of the weather as quickly as possible. Not Glenda. By halfway she'd started to struggle with fitness and slowed right down. Every step was a struggle and breathing became a problem. Glenda's friend Sue walked with Glenda for company and encouragement and as I looked back, they seemed to be navigating fine through the mud.

Past the middle of the pilgrimage there is a particularly dark, black, and muddy section that can be quite deep in places. Sue and Glenda got through these together by going around the darkest and deepest patches. However, they had slowed down. I could see others had made it to the Island in under 80 minutes, but Glenda and Sue were just over halfway. I got to the second Refuge, two-thirds across, and tried to keep an eye on everyone spread out between there and the island.

That's when I heard my name called on the wind. 'Ash, Ash, help, help!' It was Sue. As I looked back, I could see Glenda flat on her back, like a turtle, arms and legs moving, but unable to right herself. It took me ten minutes to run back and a million thoughts went through my head. Had she had a heart attack? Can she walk? Will the tide come in? Do I call the Coast Guard? Glenda was still on her back when I arrived.

13: Good Soils - Praxis Understanding And Action

She had twisted and hurt her right knee, but with some help was able to stand upright. Then with an arm around Sue and I, she was able to tentatively start walking again.

We had been on the pilgrimage for just under two hours now and were not two-thirds across yet. We only had an hour of good walking left before the tide would come in. At this slowing pace I didn't think we'd make it. Each step was hurting Glenda and I wasn't sure if I could carry her if she stopped. I started to look for ways from the Pilgrim's Way to the adjacent road and to higher ground. Glenda wouldn't have it.

'I need to finish this pilgrimage!'

'You don't need to do that Glenda, you've done amazingly well and this tide is coming in now.' I pleaded.

'The tide can wait! I'm finishing this!'

An hour later we were still going, step by painful step. All the other participants were safely on Holy Island by now, but now the tide was streaming in. In some sections, the water was up past our waists, but we kept going. Soon the sun came out, and we could hear the others, cheering Glenda on.

The last 100-metre section had shallower water, just over our ankles, and the loud clapping and encouragement of the others kept Glenda going. When she made it to dry land, she was mobbed by all the participants of Cohort 8.

'I told you I could do it!'

I was relieved, but also inspired. How often do we take the risk out of scenarios and experiences? It may make things easier for us, but doesn't allow others, or ourselves, to grow. Here Glenda found a confidence in herself and sense of achievement well beyond her expectations.

When Glenda pitched her project at the graduation of Change Makers, she made mention of this moment. She also gave a rallying cry that people with disabilities are not invisible, that they can beat expectations, take on challenges and make a difference.

Glenda's project pitch was to set up a weekly group using our alpacas for people who have disabilities and their supporters as a way of connecting with God, people, and creation. Few of the resource panelists that day didn't want to support her in that venture. Few were left dry-eyed by Glenda's passion and idea. The Alpaca Whisperers group has made a great start and currently engages about twelve people each week.

Any resilient good soil in me was probably most forged in Bangkok. When we faced multiple dilemmas arriving in Birmingham, and none of our plans survived impact, we drew on our experiences back in Bangkok. There, I had been stricken by dengue fever, dysentery, typhoid and typhus, and June 2002 was probably the worst. As I lay in Samitivej hospital, my fourth hospitalisation in our first four months in Bangkok, that old hymn *I Surrender All* returned to me and I could not get it out of my head. Here I was lying in a foetal position, in a fever, the now familiar IV drip needle irritating the top of my hand, my palms and the soles of my feet cold and bright red, and with a headache like someone was hammering away inside my skull to the rhythm of my pulse... and humming, 'All to thee my blessed saviour ...' I am sure the nurse thought I was delirious. I didn't care, as at one point I felt like my life was draining out of me and we found out later that my platelets – the stuff that holds the blood together – were free falling from a normal of 400,000 to 38,000.

For the first few days the doctors thought it could be dengue fever, but then they also became worried about a virus in my heart. The diagnosis, however, seemed to change with each shift of doctors. At one point it was a relief to be definitely diagnosed with dengue fever. At least we knew what was wrong and that I would eventually get better.

Unfortunately, the insurance company refused to pay for the last hospitalization, over A$3,400, claiming it was all 'pre-existing,' due to a bad hot dog I'd eaten at a soccer match, way back in May, which had given me dysentery. I had eaten the dodgy hotdog a few weeks after our initial insurance had lapsed and prior to us signing up again for more health insurance. When a fax from the insurance company was brought to my bedside saying they refused to guarantee any treatment I could not help but be amazed at what damage a hot dog could cause.

13: Good Soils - Praxis Understanding And Action

Dengue fever symptoms four months after I ate a hot dog! It didn't make sense and added to our helplessness.

Anji made the long trip from our Bangkok slum to the hospital each day with Amy, and was starting to wear down. The next few days are blurred, as all I could do was just lie in bed feeling like a truck had hit me – and not the slow-moving ones in a Bangkok traffic jam either. I do remember Anji's crying pleas on the phone to the insurance company that 'a hot dog can't cause dengue.' The diagnosis, however, kept changing each day and between my mum in Australia and Anji here in Bangkok, the insurance company received a lot of angry and frustrated phone calls. Later we found out that while Anji was doing all this running around and chasing the insurance, she had dengue fever herself.

At one point my fevers stopped for about twenty-four hours, but as my platelets were still dropping the doctors were concerned that I could have a virus in my heart which could mean six to eight weeks in hospital. The insurance was still not willing to pay for the treatment. If one week in hospital was A$3,400 what would eight weeks cost – with surgery? Anji, who was showing the dengue rash by this time and was getting weaker by the day, was getting nowhere with the insurance company.

The doctors suggested we fly back to Melbourne for treatment. This would mean that my hospitalisation and treatment would be free, because we had an Australian Health Care Card and could use our existing return ticket. Going home early, however, was not something I wanted. Our neighbourhood in Klong Toey was doing all they could for us, providing meals, looking after Amy at times, even offering their blood for transfusion – so I didn't want to turn back now and let them down. To be honest, it would also have been a blow to my ego. 'Tough missionary finds it too tough!' But with Anji lying half-conscious on the sofa next to me and Amy doing her best to stay still, watching Popeye cartoons in Thai on TV, what choice did we have?

My vocation as a missionary in a slum flashed before my eyes. What if I don't have the health for this?

Just as it all seemed too much, I sensed God break through the silence.

Keith Farmer from Sydney rang saying he and John Bond from Perth had activated a prayer chain for us. Combined with our existing supporters, I realised that this meant that every state in Australia had churches praying for us, believing God wanted us here. My brother activated worldwide prayer support too. Steve Addison, my mentor for over a decade, also rang and helped me to put things into perspective. 'God has led you all this way. Trust him with whatever is next,' he encouraged. 'I surrender all,' I whispered to myself as I put the phone down. I gave back this Bangkok ministry to God – it was his after all, not mine. I had to surrender all the ego and identity I had placed in it. If God still wanted me here, then it was up to him.

My headache was right behind my eyes, so, unable to read, I listened to a tape by Franciscan priest, Richard Rohr. He was talking about how 'liminal space,' the space in which God does his transforming work, was like standing in a doorway between two rooms. It is when we are in a no-man's-land and see beyond our illusions and assumptions, to what is real and true about the world and us. His quote from Thomas Merton seemed just for me: "Faith, patience and obedience are the guides which must help us advance quietly in the darkness without looking at ourselves."

After replaying this quote and then writing it in my journal, I whispered, 'Lord, please give me this grace.' In an instant I felt I could trust God and look beyond myself and my own control. I could trust God in the threshold between my old life in Australia and whatever new life God was opening up for me, however long it took. We would continue to follow what guidance God had been revealing to us. Even if we had to go back to Melbourne for a time, I knew God's presence was with us, opening up new possibilities even through this darkness.

In Thailand, smiling is often used to keep face and calm things down. So it was a bit disconcerting when the doctor came in on about the fifth day saying with a big grin, 'If your platelets get below 40,000 it is very dangerous. You can start bleeding from the ears and mouth and then the brain and then you die within twelve hours.' Then the big, beaming smile!

13: Good Soils - Praxis Understanding And Action

Anji and I laughed along. Then Anji asked, 'How low are Ash's platelets?'

'Oh, 38,000 but don't worry! It is definitely haemorrhagic dengue. See the rash on your arms? You don't need to go to Australia. Just don't cut yourself, lie still and you'll be fine,' the doctor said and left the room. Anji and I just kept laughing, otherwise we would have cried.

A few days later, having laid still and avoided shaving, my platelets went back to normal and the insurance company eventually admitted my now fully confirmed dengue wasn't caused by a bad hot dog. We were able to go back to our home in Klong Toey and mum came from Australia to stay with us and help us as we recovered.

One night a few days later, Anji and I watched the romantic comedy, *Keeping the Faith*. Jake Shrame (Ben Stiller), a rabbi, and Brian Finn (Edward Norton), a priest, had been friends since childhood. They were reunited with their other childhood friend Anna (Jenna Elfman) who had turned from being a tomboy into an attractive top executive. Both Jake and Brian fell for her. Of course, this was more complex for the priest. After Brian made a fool of himself by propositioning her, finding out that Jake and Anna had secretly been an item, he confided to his older priest mentor about nearly giving up the priesthood for a woman.

'I'll tell you something. If she'd kissed me back, I don't think I would be sitting here now. I'd have given it all up. She didn't but I kept thinking about what you said in seminary—that the life of priest is hard and if you could be happy doing something else, then you should do that.'

The older priest laughed, puffing out his cigar smoke. 'Ah ha, that was my recruitment pitch. Not bad when you're starting out because it makes you feel like a marine. But the truth is you can never tell yourself there is only one thing you could be. If you are a priest or had a woman it is the same challenge. You cannot make a real commitment unless you accept that it is a choice you make again and again and again. I've been a priest over forty years and I fall in love at least every decade.'

'You're not going to tell me what to do here are you?' Brian smiles.

'No, God will give you your answer.'

God was giving me my answer too. This scene spoke to me about free surrender but also the responsibility that flows out from it. Richard Rohr calls it 'contemplation and action' and named his centre in the US after it. Out of the grace found in the surrender of contemplation flows the grace to be response-able. Few of my friends survived their teens and early twenties as Christians. They simply couldn't make the choices for Christ again and again and again as the passage of life unfolded. Surrender was in, but being response-able to Christ's ongoing call for action – well, that was something different.

When we arrived in Bangkok, the average missionary in Thailand lasted less than three years, barely long enough to be fluent in Thai, so I was aware of these first hurdles. It's like Christ is saying, 'I won't give you a crown until I know you won't hock the jewels.' The Thai people are so precious to Christ, that only surrendering to Christ and overcoming hardships will help introduce Christ properly. In 2 Corinthians 11:23-33, the apostle Paul writes of the hardships that made him a minister of Christ. He lists those of imprisonments, escapes, tortures, hunger, nakedness, being left adrift at sea, and facing death. It is these experiences of weaknesses and his willingness to continue on in the Kingdom cause that give him credibility as a Gospel worker; not his contacts, superficial results, or academic credentials. "If I must boast, I will boast of the things that show my weakness."

Bangkok and Birmingham are international cities with state-of-the-art hospitals, shopping malls, good communications, and education systems for people like us. Compared with Paul, Christ, or even contemporary Christian leaders in more isolated contexts or war zones, Anji and I have few hardships. We have, however, received a grace to serve Christ in particular places and this grace is discovered from our own weakness.

There can be no 'once for all surrender' when our hearts and minds struggle for control, desperate to drown out the soft whispers of the Spirit saying, 'I am worthy to surrender all.' Although the illness interrupted our timelines for language learning and starting new projects, we were determined to continue to serve Christ in Klong Toey slum as long as God gave us grace to be there.

These moments were burnt deep into my soul. Had we left Bangkok then we would have missed all that God did in us and through us in Klong Toey over the next 12 years and continues to do through locals to this day. I had similar experiences in our first few years in Birmingham. We needed to keep turning up and finding our way to be fully surrendered disciples of Jesus here. I reminded myself that if it was easy, it would have been done before and even the great Leslie Newbigin struggled to make a difference here in Winson Green! I knew patient endurance and constant surrender can slowly change the soil in my heart, giving it life.

The good soil Jesus commends is teeming, full of diverse life. The supernatural multiplication of Shalom that it produces is not the result of clever strategy and policy. Rather, it comes from unexpectedly small starts, relentless determination, and trust. I love it when the good soil comes together as everyone wins. Shalom is on its way.

Personal Reflections

1. When have you seen abundance come from the soil of your neighbourhood? What was it like?

2. What role does perseverance have in your life?
   What would have happened if you had quit too soon? Stayed too long?

3. Why is perseverance, patience, and showing up worth the effort?

4. How can you and your local community help create more fertile soil for Shalom's harvest?

Part C. Practices to Try

Toward an incarnational spirituality - entering your C.A.V.E daily.

Part C of this book provides us with deeply spiritual life challenges. To develop soil ready for Shalom growth requires imagination, character and formation. I'm going to offer a whole set of suggestions that work for me. They take time and persistence. This goes against the quick, consumer-driven forces in our lives. For many, there is a kind of motorcar analogy of spirituality. We can easily feel like we are running on empty and need to be filled up quickly just to keep going in life, never mind our calling. Different Christian traditions have different fuels to offer. If we just worship enough, pray enough or read enough we'll be full again and have enough to keep going. Have you ever felt like you could not stop to 'fill up' or that no fuel station had what you needed? Actually, many spiritual practices have felt more like an addiction cycle to me. They give an initial buzz and a filling at first, some 'initial joy,' but over time I needed more and more to get the same buzz to feel 'normal.' After a while I go 'cold turkey' and move on in search of another fuel.

An important understanding that has helped me is the theological term 'incarnate' that has enabled my activist self to come together with my spiritual life, like a dynamo for my inner life. The more I ride my bike the more the dynamo turns and creates light. It's not that I can't stop, it's just that my activism can become the fuel for my spiritual life. These insights were part of my maturing as a distinctly Christian activist. My PhD research about incarnational approaches, with my supervisor the late Prof Ross Langmead, has continued to integrate my calling.

To 'incarnate' is to 'enflesh' or to 'make real.' In Christian theology, we talk about Jesus being the 'Word made flesh' (John 1:14). There is a kind of spectrum of understanding how this idea of incarnation can apply to us.

At one end of the spectrum are those who say the incarnation was a one off, Jesus was unique and his approach has nothing to do with us. It's all about a transaction on the cross that we are to receive spiritually. Jesus bought our souls a ticket to heaven. However, to me, this makes a mockery of the physicality of Jesus' life and resurrection. Why would God come and defeat death as a human in creation, if matter didn't matter?

At the other end of the spectrum are those who say we are to copy Jesus' Incarnation and become both a Messiah and a sufferer, exactly the same as those who are suffering around us. Since Jesus didn't just pop down from heaven for the weekend, but moved into the neighbourhood, so must we go and relocate our lives. We simply can't 'save and be safe' at the same time. Required Messianic complexes aside, the pressure incarnational activists can put themselves under can be crushing and unsustainable. Can I fully identify with my neighbours' suffering the way God did through Jesus of Nazareth? Can I 'save' the way Jesus did?

Ross Langmead showed me another way to understand an incarnational approach. It can be a distinctly Christian approach to mission and spirituality that is more than a spiritual analogy or less than a particular methodology. If to incarnate is a motif then our discipleship of Jesus can be inspired, integrated, and informed.

We can follow, join and participate with the incarnating God to see creation healed.

We are not the incarnating God, but we can enflesh hope. Finding ways to nurture movements can help us develop that much-needed character to stay put long enough to grow roots and fruits. Some of these themes have been explored, but here we describe a needed movement in us:

- Control to Surrender: Waking up to our limitations and responsibilities.

- Space Invading to Place Sharing: Showing up as a resident not a service provider.

- Scarcity to Abundance: Trusting God's presence in local people and places as enough.

Becoming good soil is not wishful thinking. There is a lot of current research that reveals what helps and hinders the growth of personal capacity to be change makers. One finding is that consistent, daily routines make a real difference. Our daily habits can instinctively move us toward our big hopes, or they can undermine them. How we consistently spend our days impacts how we lead our lives.

It is easy to be distracted away from cultivating hope today. Habits that take us down dark rabbit holes we don't want to follow, has become almost normal for most people now. I'm not just thinking about the many classic addictions like alcohol and other drugs, but the many time-and-energy-sapping distractions too. Consider how many times we touch our mobile phones in a day or get caught late at night binge watching repeats. These habits become cycles that may once have been a cry for connection but can quickly become rewired into the heart of our identity and character. We need a circuit breaker that can allow us to slowly reconnect our best selves with others. It's always extremely challenging to start new, positive habits and routines, but it is worth the effort.

We know that it takes on average 66 days to build a new habit so that it becomes a normal part of our lives. It's important, therefore, to keep returning to a practice until you get over the hump. What starts as a good practice to try can eventually become second nature to who you are if you stick at it. In fact, once the habit is in place, it can seem harder *not* to do the good practice.

How we spend our days is how we invest our lives. To re-wire ourselves for hope, therefore, I like leaders to consider how we start our days and set them up. Do the important practices first with our best energy and we can set up our days well. Wait until we find energy and desire and it will be put off and not done.

There is a science and an artform at work here. Life coach and author Robin Sharma, for example, has consistently called for a 5am club arguing that the body, mind, heart, and soul is built to prepare for the day in those silent and still hours before most people are up and about.[104] Certainly, the Christian faith has a tradition where those who seek change get up early to prepare for it, not least Jesus himself. If Jesus needed to prepare for his day, how much more do I!

During the 2020 Covid lockdown I read Sharma's *The 5am Club* thinking it could help unlock some of our emerging leaders' talents. I got inspired myself and, with nothing to lose in lockdown, tried it out. Sharma says this habit is "hard at first, messy in the middle and beautiful at the end." As I went into our Yurt on the front lawn of Newbigin House, prepared for each day from 5am, something beautiful did eventually happen within me. Sure, it meant that I fell asleep earlier and sometimes needed a nap in the afternoon, but it helped me focus my days and make those small decisions better.

Here is a morning routine that, if you can make it a normal part of how you start the day, can help you find hope and better connect with others each day. It's based on the ancient Hebrew commandments known as the *Shema* found in Deuteronomy 6:4-5, Leviticus 19:18, and confirmed by Jesus as the most important commandments that all Scripture is based on (Mark 12:28-34). Put simply it is about loving God and neighbour with our full selves including our heart, soul, mind, and strength. I have an acronym that I base this routine around to put first things first in our morning routine.

Set your alarm for 5am and put the alarm away from your bed so you have to get out of bed to start your day. Then find ways to cultivate, for two hours, these four areas Jesus said were important.

Here are some ideas for **C.A.V.E** time. They can be done in any order, but making sure attention is given to each area over a week seems important.

Curious Mind:
God has given us a mind that is complex, but we know it's healthiest and able to love when it's growing. To cultivate learning as part of a morning routine helps the foggy thoughts we wake up with, get blown away. Loving God with our mind each morning can help us to better focus, centre, and prepare our day so we can also love our neighbours better.

The Hebrew word *lev* in the Shema that Jesus quotes means 'mind,' but it is also sometimes translated in English as 'heart.' It seems the ancients believed in the connectedness of all things, including the human body, often more than most modern Westerners. We first see the word *lev* used in Scripture in Genesis 6:5-6 where the New Living Translation says that God is grieved about people on earth because "everything they thought or imagined was consistently and totally evil." *Lev* is therefore not merely abstract thought, taking in new information, or sentimentality. This word *lev* is actually made up of two Hebrew characters with one meaning 'house/temple' and the other 'authority.' So in each human body (house), the *lev* lives as central to decision-making, emotion, and conscience (authority). This will to love with all our *lev* includes sensitising what we call our conscience so that we act in ways that please God and are consistent with who God made us to be.

Loving God with our mind/heart can start early in our day. Here are some ideas for stimulating our minds first thing so we can prepare for our day.

- *Devotional reading.* I like to read along with others I know so Ray Simpson's *Celtic Daily Light* as part of the Community of Aidan and Hilda and *Common Prayers* from Shane Claiborne and the Red Letter Christian movement are my go-to devotional books. These give each day a mix of set Bible passages, reflections, and actions together, which connect me in with others around the world who are reading these at the same time. During special times in the Christian calendar I do like to mix it up and David Cole's *Celtic Advent* is my most recent find on these.

- *Specialised reading.* Growing in our understanding of a key challenge we face can also be an important area to read on. Sometimes these are related to my area of academic discipline in theology, culture, leadership, or history, but sometimes it can be a novel or an inspirational book. I read physical books, but also love my Kindle ebook reader. There is access to so much stimulating material now, so focus on one at a time! Giving myself permission to pursue one line of thinking at a time can help me to focus and helps to get my mind going.

- *Listening for stimulus*: Listening to books, sermons, and podcasts can be helpful for someone with dyslexia like me. I do find it hard not to be distracted if I just passively listen, but with a bit of preparation and adding in exercise or walking there can be real benefits. There is so much on offer now that it can be overwhelming and distracting. I find my best listening is when I find key people or themes that are important for me to understand. I try to prepare these the night before, otherwise I can spend my time in this area scrolling through options.

Attentive Soul:

The soul is our inner, true person that goes deeper than what we just think about. The mind can be so busy and full that we lose connection with this precious part of ourselves. To love God and neighbour with our soul is to create intentional space to move beyond the mind's noise and pre-occupations. Here are some ways I've found helpful to find that centred-ness.

The Hebrew word *nephesh* is often translated into English as 'soul,' 'life,' or 'desire.' It is our true self, not just our thinking. So we see in Psalm 42:5 that our mind actually speaks to our soul. "Why are you in despair, my soul? Why are you disturbed within me? Hope in God! For I shall still praise him for the saving help of His presence" (World English Bible). Having a soul is what makes a person alive.

Becoming centred and being conscious of our soul, our true self, is also important to do at the start of each day. Here are some practices I have found helpful to do this.

- *Music:* Listening to music that is calming, soothing, and inspiring can help centre me. I know this is a personal taste, but not all music helps me do this. Some contemporary Christian worship music can help, but some distracts me as I get caught up analysing lyrics. I do enjoy listening to all kinds of music recreationally, but when I'm trying to be centred I have found that Celtic or classical music best quiets my racing mind. I think part of this is that it is sparking my mind, but also soothing it.

- *Stillness, Silence and Solitude*: These are variations on a theme, but help at different times in similar ways. I find stillness when I sit quietly and consciously focus on different parts of my body from top to toe, giving each part to God. I find silence when I use a prayer mantra like Maranatha (Aramaic for 'Come, quickly Lord Jesus'), praying it in four syllables as Ma-ra-na-tha, two breathing in, two breathing out, returning to this word if my mind wonders. I find solitude when I spend extended time without stimuli, focusing only on sensing the loving gaze of Jesus, and offering any stray thoughts to God like I'm pushing them down a river. I often use all three over a 20-minute meditation practice.

- *Gratitude:* We know that if our heart is full of gratefulness we don't drain our lives of hope by taking people, places, or God for granted. Each morning I try to write an A4 page of people, events, situation, things that happened the day before that I'm grateful for. It lifts my day before I start and helps me be more receptive to the good things that come my way.

- *Examen:* This exercise uses activities of our lives as the fuel to still our minds. There are various ways to do this, but one is to simply reflect on the day before, letting it stream like a movie, then to stop and savour that time that 'gave life' to us. Don't try to change or make more of this moment than we should. Just savour that moment and give it to God in thanks. Then, keep going, looking for that moment that most 'took life' from us. Again, don't try to fix it or replay it until we got it right, just let it go to God. Then ask if are there any next steps today.

Vital Body:

Philip Yancey, a best-selling Christian author and speaker, once noticed that all the leaders he knew that were most passionate about fighting hunger and injustice were fat. How could this be? There was a serious medium and message problem. I'm afraid I am one of them. Too many of us activists and leaders are obese and poisoning ourselves with food and drink.

I can relate to this as my physical health and fitness has often been neglected. Of the four areas, this is the area I've least appreciated for the longest time. Deep down I thought it noble to not spend time on myself. There is a common delusion that not looking after ourselves is a sign of holiness and a silent protest at the amount of time and resources some folks spend trying to look good. And I wanted to be holy! Spending time on myself seemed wasted. Going to the gym, getting expensive haircuts or bike rides was for those who had time for the superficial and vain. There are so few hours in the day, surely others' needs are far more important than mine. Besides, if I was honest, I was already exhausted, and the idea of exercise exhausted me further. There is a price to pay for such thinking.

Add to these internal pressures were the external challenges. It is not an accident that obesity and poverty often go together in the West. Our neighbourhoods are often bad for us and undermine our health. Urban air quality and access to affordable healthy food are just some of serious issues we face. Quality food is expensive, time-consuming to cook, and often not available near us in so called 'food deserts.' If we are speaking to or training others and we need to travel to do this, fast food on the road is often our only affordable choice in time and money. Add to that work environments of stress and high expectations of others, where it's much harder to say 'no' than 'yes,' and our health can be in trouble quickly. It's not been uncommon for middle class people I know who have relocated to a poor neighbourhood to put on 10kg in weight the first year they move in. Do this for any meaningful length of time and we can be in big trouble. We want to protest against others, but our bodies will eventually protest against us.

The Hebrew word *meh-ode'* helped me get over myself and take my environment more seriously. It has to do with strength and will, but also 'abundance,' 'muchness,' and 'vitality' of life.[105] It's not about how much muscle I have or how good I can look to strangers. In Genesis 17:6, for example, we see God promise Abraham: 'I will make you extremely fruitful (meh-ode'). Your descendants will become many nations, and kings will be among them!" It is this vitality for and of life that I need, and my community need from me. I need to demonstrate this kind of 'vital strength' that can help me keep going when times get tough, and results don't go my way. Unnecessary and premature death is not helpful for me or my community. If it's taken generations for poverty and injustice to get our neighbourhood in the state it's in, then it will take generations to get it out. I need to be physically up for the challenge and resilient for the long term. Physical health grows our own capacities too.

Loving God and living life to the full includes our bodily strength. Compared to most of our ancestors our lifestyles today are often mostly sedentary. We're not hunting food or protecting ourselves from the elements as most did. Our bodies are not designed to sit most of our days in meetings, at meals, and on computers. Some of us need to be more relentless in our intentionality here than in other areas.

Here are some practices I have found that helped me regain my physical strength.

- *Starting with Exercise*: I bought a second-hand exercise bike I can fold away for £30 from Facebook Marketplace – lots of people get rid of them cheaply. If I start my day with 20 minutes on it, listening to a podcast or music, then I can feel my heart pump and my brain ignite, ready for the day ahead. Push-ups, sit-ups, and other ways to get a sweat up first thing has proven to have scientific benefits for our vitality too. It also means that if my day gets away from me, I know my body already has what it needs. Waiting until the end of the day to do my only exercise or going to gyms rarely works for me.

- *Walking:* The Covid lockdown re-ignited my love of walking. When we were only allowed outside to exercise, our household often walked longer than the recommended hour. There is actually a long tradition of thinkers taking long daily walks. People like Nietsche would walk and ponder, then do their writing. In the summer I love walking in the morning, starting out just before daybreak, but more often it is after lunch. I especially love to walk around our neighbourhood and along the canals here, often praying for people, places, and organisations I love and want to see flourish.

- *Sabbath days*: Having one day without work and ministry is such a gift. As it was first instituted to Moses, it says that I am free and am not a slave. It's not just a 'day off,' which I often have on Saturday, but is a renewal day – like my morning devotion extended over a day – and includes my loved ones. For decades I've done Sabbaths by starting on a Sunday night in preparation and finishing on Monday evening with our household meal. I love how the 'Sabbath Manifesto' has developed ten modern practices for us to use: avoid technology, connect with loved ones, nurture my health, get outside, avoid commerce, light candles, drink wine, eat bread, find silence, and give back.[106] It's the unplugging that I find the hardest, but the most crucial over the last decade. This kind of day helps give rhythm and routine and lets me enjoy all my life. If I miss it, then I know toward the end of the next week, having gone up to thirteen days without a sabbath, others will pay for it as well as me. In my calendar, my Sabbath day is the first day I put in.

Empowering Spirit:

Most people believe in keeping the body, mind, and soul healthy. There are few people who would want them unhealthy, even if they defined them differently to the way I have. This fourth area, however, is a challenge to many self-improvement gurus and church leaders alike. It says that a personal force beyond us is available to us to channel into the world. We can't just wish for our hopes to happen. Hope is not wishful thinking. There is power beyond us that helps us love. The apostle Paul said it this way: "and hope does not disappoint us, because God's love has been poured into our hearts through the Holy Spirit that has been given to us" (Romans 5:5 [NRSV]). This is not power for power's sake, but a way to animate love from the inside out. This Spirit's empowering to love was prophesied for all people to receive. Joel 2:28-29 (NRSV) says:

> Then afterwards I will pour out my spirit on all flesh;
> your sons and your daughters shall prophesy,

> your old men shall dream dreams,
> and your young men shall see visions.
> Even on the male and female slaves,
> in those days, I will pour out my spirit.

As Christians we believe this started on the day of Pentecost when the Spirit came upon all people. This Spirit can empower everyone in their liberation and destiny. Even slaves.

This truth is often experienced more by those on the margins than others. There is an old line that 'the Liberation theologians had a preferential option for the poor, but the poor had a preference for the Pentecostals.' Those Christians who most talk about the intricacies of poverty and injustice often can't relationally connect with those who have first-hand experiences. Certainly, they rarely feel like they can lead those who are facing poverty. However, if there are only a few Christians in a poverty-stricken place, often those Christians self-identify as Pentecostals. Until recently Pentecostalism was not taken seriously and is still often ridiculed by mainstream Christianity. Why would oppressed peoples flock to Pentecostalism then? I'm sure the reasons are many, but there is something about the possibility of empowerment that resonates. There is Good News that rich and powerful people may well 'sell all you have and give it to the poor and come follow' Jesus so we are not possessed by our possessions. To surrender to God and become a servant to all is an important challenge to those born into privilege. However, for those who feel beaten down and oppressed, nothing is more liberating than to access empowerment from God. To lead as you sense God promising your community generates hope. Indeed, this kind of empowerment by the Spirit within us can cause ripples of revolutionary love to flow from the inside out.

For me there are a few exercises that help to access this flow.

- *Visualising:* Taking regular time to imagine in as much detail as I can what I want to see happen has been revolutionary for me. If I can't first imagine it, I often don't have confidence it will happen. I ask the Holy Spirit to help me imagine ten years out and write a newspaper story about what I'd personally like to be like and see happen. I push the dates out intentionally. We mostly overestimate what we can do in a year, but drastically underestimate what is possible in a decade or a generation. I also like to visualise my day ahead and give those planned meeting, events, and relationships to God in prayer. What would this day look like if it was especially great?

- *Empowering People in Prayer Candles*: I can easily get distracted when I pray, so visual reminders of the people I care about and are investing in are helpful. When I light a candle and think about that person and bless them there is a kind of connection I can hold in place. It's not a magic candle or a flaming voodoo doll, but a simple way to help me pay attention to a person that matters to me.

- *Empowering Places with Rocks in Bowls of Water*: I have picked out rocks and small pebbles from my garden. I like to hold one in my hand and think of a place that matters to me. I slowly place these pebbles in a bowl of water, one at a time, and ask for God's blessing on them. I might pray for Newbigin House, or Lodge Road Community Church centre, or The Greenhouse at Barnes Close, and for all the people that will connect with those places that day. I pray for Winson Green and pray for particular places like parks, schools, commerce, the prison. I hold them in my hand as a rock and give them to God for transformation.

- *Focus For The Day*: Generally, the last thing before I start my full workday is to ask God to show me three things that will help make this day wonderful. Is there one thing I could do today that if it came off would make everything else better? Sometimes these events are ones that I know are coming up that day. Sometimes these are personal development activities that I want to do. Sometimes they come from another place. What this gives me is some intentionality for the day.

I can return to it the next day and see what happened. These three activities then form the basis of my journal entry the next day.

The point of this smorgasbord of practices is to prepare myself well for the day ahead. I don't do all of them every morning, but I do use most each week. This helps me engage the people and places I meet that day with as much attention to them as I can. This helps me find the flow and join in. If I can prepare well each morning, then my days will matter more. If my days and weeks matter more, then ultimately my life will be good and meaningful. This kind of hope is personal, but it's not individualistic. The more I cultivate hope in the morning, the more hope spreads into my life.

Come Holy Spirit, awaken us and empower us to invest in seeking the Shalom of the city.

Questions for Group Reflections

1. Which of these three Celtic Christian practices are we strongest and weakest in? Why?

2. How can an 'enchanted world view' help or hinder us in discerning the Spirit of Hope in urban people and places?

3. Which of the 'soils' are you most tempted to be? Why?

4. If you were to give a focus this week to one of these practices that could enable us to listen better to the Sprit's leading and obey, what could that look like?

Part D.

Sustainable Roots, Branches Ready For Fruit

This part suggests that three essential local leadership qualities and three particular approaches can generate root systems able to feed and sustain change from within local communities.

Chapter 14:
Not All Roots And Branches Can Grow The Fruit We Need

They are like trees planted along a riverbank, with roots that reach deep into the water. Such trees are not bothered by the heat or worried by long months of drought. Their leaves stay green, and they never stop producing fruit.
Jeremiah 17:8

I hold my breath a lot on the first Saturday morning of our Change Makers programmes. We seek to make this morning a safe and confidential space for emerging community leaders to be honest about their lives and bond together. It only works if everyone drops their masks, brings their authentic selves to the table, and are willing to share. I try to model this on the Friday night, sharing the devastating loss of my foster son Metus and how my life changed trajectory because of that moment. As mentioned in Chapter 1, the participants then spend an hour the next morning writing key events down on Post-it notes: people, places, music, books, talks, commitments, and any other influences they can think of, one at a time, one Post-it note at a time. They place all these Post-it notes in chronological order from birth to today on a large piece of card. We then ask them to show and tell their 'timeline' with the group for about fifteen minutes. I never know what will happen next.

No Wastelands

I take lots of deep breaths.

'Who wants to go first?' I ask looking around the circle.

Most eyes dart to the ground. Eventually a brave soul decides to look up and get this over with. I am always surprised by what I hear.

'I grew up in care. Never knew my parents. My brothers and I were often separated…'

Some matter-of-factly go through each life event and influence until they get to today. Others have a flair for storytelling, and we have to remind them that it's been 10 minutes and we should move on from Primary School. Every person has a story to tell with heroes and villains. No one gets to a Change Makers cohort without experiencing real suffering. Sometimes these influences have never been shared before. I have been running similar exercises with groups for over two decades and have never had a group where abuse, mental health, and addictions have not been experienced. In the UK, I especially notice the many scars created by the care system when participants have grown up in urban neighbourhoods, and how their start in life is so thwarted. Trauma of many kinds is a common experience. We almost always cry at some point, no matter how tough our outer exterior might be. I cry often too and feel honoured to be in this space with these precious people. To hear remarkable people's life stories and to listen empathetically is a privilege that few ever have.

I wonder sometimes what church or charity leadership recruiters would make of our cohort's sharing. I suspect they would disqualify many of them from any responsibilities and move on to more 'together' people. Little would they know of what lies just underneath the surface of us all. Little would they know about the potential they're missing. These scars, wounds, disappointments, even anger, can be the raw material for community change from the inside out. Lived experienced leaders can heal their communities like few others.

The importance of developing a new generation of local community leaders has grown to become something of an obsession for me. Indeed, the transition to Birmingham was partly to focus my best energy on

14: Not All Roots And Branches Can Grow The Fruit We Need

investing in these kinds of leaders, especially in urban contexts, where most communities now live. I was convinced that if we didn't invest in, connect, and empower these emerging leaders, then outside forces will dissipate and divide them, exploiting and conquering whole classes of people and neighbourhoods. The draining loss of community, and its costs, can only be stemmed by a new wave of leaders from within.

I still remember workshopping the initial idea of Change Makers with about 20 of the most experienced UK community leaders I could bring together in 2015. We were at Newbigin House, and I outlined a model I thought could work based on my own experiences in UNOH, an initial experiment with Newbigin Associates in Winson Green, and an emerging leaders programme I participated in back in Australia. I was nominated onto this Arrow Australia programme in 1997 and participated in it for two years. Only some of the teaching material was helpful for me at the time. I was leading UNOH and most of the cohort led large church or evangelistic organisations. But I felt special being nominated and connected with others like me. Arrow Alumni have gone on to play significant roles in Australian Christianity. Magic happened when high potential, emerging, and diverse leaders came together, shared experiences and learnt together. We have often stayed networked, created opportunities for each other and helped to shape many churches in Australia. What if such a process could be adapted and offered especially to those in our local communities? Could we train emerging leaders in ways that empowered and connected them?

Dave Mann had traveled up from East London for this gathering and listened intently. He had three decades of local community organising and church leadership experience in two of the toughest neighbourhoods in London. When Dave did eventually speak, all listened. He loved the idea of creating cohorts that would connect and grow in self-awareness and develop skills to enhance community capacity together, but he also outlined how their community had experienced the negative effects of existing leaders programmes: 'We send them off, they grow, but they never come back.' Church growth researchers call this phenomenon 'Redemption and Lift' which sounds like a new kind of WonderBra®, but actually describes how personal growth can lead to people leaving the very communities that need them the most.

All of the community leaders in the room had experienced similar things and nodded. Would Change Makers actually weaken our communities by helping take the next generation away? Dave, however, had solutions:

> 'Have them come together in small groups from our communities and pitch their ideas for local change at the end of the programme. That way, even if some do go, our communities will still benefit. They'll enjoy going away together too as some never do that. It will give them confidence to bring back what they are learning.'

This was brilliant. By the end of the meeting, we had an outline of how it could work and five local communities from Birmingham, Luton, and East London were willing to nominate Change Makers in a pilot programme. What, however, would be the content of such a programme? What capacities did we want local leaders to grow in?

Not all roots and branches produce Shalom

The 'Tree of Life' archetype offers a beautiful picture of Shalom. Found in the mythology of many cultures, including the early Celtic ones, it often represents the forces of nature combining to create balance and harmony. The branches *reach up* for the sky, the roots *reach down* into the ground, and are presented as a kind of circle. We know now that all plants need roots reaching down for nutrients and stability. They provide the anchor needed to keep a plant in place and are the lifeline of a plant, taking up air, water, and nutrients from the soil and moving them up into the above ground into the branches and leaves. Branches *reach up* to photosynthesise, the process within a plant converting light, oxygen, and water into carbohydrates (energy). Without adequate light, carbohydrates cannot be manufactured, energy reserves are depleted, and plants die. The ancient Celts intuited this process and saw it as representing the link between heaven and earth, mind and body, and the never-ending cycle of life: reaching higher and reaching deeper.

If the seeds of Shalom are to cultivate healthy growth in the lives of our local leaders and communities, then finding the appropriate *roots* and *branches* needs to be carefully considered and nurtured. There are limits to this analogy, like all analogies, but healthy native trees produce good

14: Not All Roots And Branches Can Grow The Fruit We Need

fruit and multiply because they adapt their roots and branches to their context. As an Australian, I love our huge native gum trees. Even the smell of eucalyptus does me good! Gum trees can survive even in the most dry and desolate places because their root and branch systems are uniquely developed for Australian conditions. The reason they survive is because they became experts in sucking up all the available moisture and nutrients for themselves. Very few other trees or plants outside Australia can grow near large gum trees. In South Africa, for example, they have become such a pest that they take the water of native plants at incredible rates. Indeed, "invasive eucalyptus accounts for 16% water resources due to invasive plants."[107] Just as gum trees dry up and even kill nearby life, growing the wrong capacities and using inappropriate approaches with leaders can kill local community ecosystems. This doesn't make these values or approaches wrong under the right conditions, but just because something seems to work for a middle-class neighborhood, doesn't mean they can help release the unique potential in people and places written off as wastelands. Local communities get tired and cynical of the latest trends guaranteed to fix them. Worse than this, they can develop a kind of dependency culture from these experiences; waiting for others to come in and serve them. Deeper, more contextualised and indigenised responses are needed. The kinds of roots and branches we nurture over time matters if we are to see a diverse harvest of Shalom grow in unexpected places.

The seeds of Shalom should naturally grow native roots and branches in local communities. Perhaps in days gone by, they were easily seen and nurtured. However, as we have discussed, there are many weeds that are counterfeits and invasive. The best way to grow the seeds of Shalom in our communities is to give special attention to nurture the unique, adapting localised and indigenous roots and branches.

What native roots and branches (qualities and approaches) do we need to nurture with diverse, emerging local community leaders? There are far more than we can name, but we have identified three leadership qualities and three approaches that can especially help local leaders and their communities to grow deep and flourish widely.

Roots

We have found three pivotal roots or qualities for community leaders and their communities. When these three are present and nurtured, they provide the stability and energy needed for sustainable growth and life. Miss any of these three for too long and change can quickly fall over and die. These roots are:

- **Compassionate motivation:**
  Local leaders channelling God's tenderness, fidelity, and solidarity in ways that inform the long-term wellbeing of their people, teams, missions and organisations.

- **Innovative instincts:**
  Local leaders finding relevant, practical, even surprising responses to new challenges and opportunities.

- **Resilient endurance:**
  Local leaders rising up after disappointments, finding deeper authenticity, responsibility, and growth from these experiences.

If we can identify and 'dig out' diverse local community leaders who can grow in these qualities, then whole neighbourhoods can flourish and the new urban world we are facing can be influenced and transformed.

Branches

The way that branches reach up for light, creating the photosynthesis energy and life needed to bear fruit, can be likened to various approaches and methodologies. The way local communities go about change matters. Branches in healthy trees reach up and find light, holding up buds long enough to grow and ripen fruit. Not so with branches of unhealthy trees. Some branches struggle to hold fruit long enough to ripen. Others take too much wood out of a tree in one year with vigorous shoot growth. The tree's energy is put into compensating for the lost foliage at the expense of fruit. The fruit from a tree never comes unless the branches are healthy, reaching for light, and ready-made to produce fruit.

14: Not All Roots And Branches Can Grow The Fruit We Need

Not all approaches and methodologies are of the same value in local community building. There are approaches that, like healthy branches, can give local communities a better opportunity to be fruitful than others. We have found that the 'branches' of community organisation, liberative learning, and enterprise development can overlap and intertwine, providing crucial approaches to focus local energy long enough to ripen the fruit of Shalom from within local communities. If real transformation is to happen from within our neighbourhoods, then we need to see more local leaders who can be:

- **Community Connectors:**
  With society fracturing and individuals more isolated, leaders bring people together in local places to discover, connect, and mobilise their gifts and assets. These roles can be informed by 'community organisation' approaches.

- **Community Animators:**
  With injustice and poverty becoming more complex, leaders bring people together to awaken praxis to address injustices inflicted upon their community. These roles can be informed by 'liberative learning' approaches.

- **Community Entrepreneurs:**
  With the State increasingly withdrawing resources from local communities and the Global Markets becoming more volatile, leaders generate local resources, jobs, and opportunities together. These roles can be informed by 'enterprise development' approaches.

Six elements have emerged to become the basic curriculum for Seedbeds local leadership programmes. Time and again participants in Seedbeds programmes have identified, incubated, and then pitched their ideas for community change resourced by the stability and energy that flows from these frameworks. The ripple of growth within these leaders and their projects keeps growing.

As a shortcut way of remembering these roots and branches, we can draw on the tree of life image again with its deep roots and branches climbing into a circle.

C: Compassion
I: Innovation
R: Resilience
C: Community organisation
L: Liberative learning
E: Enterprise development

We will explore these roots and branches of this C.I.R.C.L.E in more detail in the next chapter. Here it is enough to outline them and prepare to engage with what growth might be needed and possible if change is to come from within local communities.

Personal Reflections

1. Have you heard the life stories of local community leaders, what do you feel?

2. What have been some important influences in starting to see your potential released? How can they be passed on and multiplied?

3. What happens when capacities and approaches don't fit our local community? Why could local capacities deepening and approaches reaching higher, help grow fruit 'from within' local communities?

4. What could you do next to support the growth of local leaders' stability and energy?

Chapter 15:
Roots Systems For Sustainability

To be rooted is perhaps the most important and least recognized need of the human soul.
– Simone Weil

Change your opinions, keep to your principles; change your leaves, keep intact your roots.
– Victor Hugo

Large, growing trees develop incredibly deep and wide root systems. They are invisible to the human eye above ground, but often spread two to five times the length of visible branches. These complex root systems are the secret to a tree's sustainability, vitality, and strength. We offer the qualities of 'compassionate motivations,' 'innovative instincts,' and 'resilient endurance' as three root systems that can likewise help local communities and their leaders grow deep and flourish too. These qualities may not be seen easily but are crucial to nurture if genuine growth and change is to happen in sustainable ways from within local communities.

Root Systems 1: Compassionate Motivation

Compassionate Motivation: local leaders channelling God's tenderness, fidelity, and solidarity in ways that inform the long-term wellbeing of their people, teams, missions, and organisations.

Compassion means far more than pity or feeling sorry for people, although sometimes we may start to notice compassion in those emotions. We see compassion starting with God's loving tenderness for all creation, for God is love (1 John 4:8). God's deep longing for healing and the flourishing of the cosmos runs deep. It includes each person's wellbeing but goes much further. God loves the whole cosmos and suffers for its long term flourishing (John 3:16). This is the Creator's deep pathos and passion, which moves to sustained action in compassion. There is a fidelity and loyalty to those God feels tenderness toward, a sense of responsibility for their long-term wellbeing. Jesus said:

> Are not five sparrows sold for two pennies? Yet not one of them is forgotten in God's sight. But even the hairs of your head are all counted. Do not be afraid; you are of more value than many sparrows. (Luke 6:7, [NRSV])

Compassion has feeling and fidelity in action. We can sometimes only have feelings of sadness or pity about people, but not the follow-through of actions that compassion requires. Sometimes we act in useful ways, but our motivation is more about duty or ambition, having lost the feelings of tenderness toward a person that is a crucial part of compassion. Authentic compassion, however, has integrated both feeling and fidelity in seeking the long-term wellbeing of the other. Compassion as a core motivation doesn't take shortcuts to make us feel good or just relieve pain but is willing to 'suffer with' – literally 'co' together, 'passio' suffer – for the long-term wellbeing of others.

Paul the apostle reminds us in 1 Corinthians 13:2b-3 that there are false motivations in change-making that end up being futile.

> If I had such faith that I could move mountains, but didn't love others, I would be nothing. If I gave everything I have to the poor and even sacrificed my body, I could boast about it; but if I didn't love others, I would have gained nothing.

If our local community roots can run deep as compassion and not ambition, pity, fear or ego, it's amazing how change and flourishing can become sustainable, even eternal. "Three things remain: faith, hope and [compassion], the greatest of these is [compassion]" (1 Cor. 13:13). Whatever we then do with compassionate motivations is never wasted and 'remains' in ways that live on after we die.

Compassion should be central to the Christian motivation for change. The Hebrew or Aramaic word that Jesus would have used so often is *hesed*. It can be translated in English as 'compassion,' 'mercy,' or 'loving kindness,' and is used over 240 times in the Hebrew Bible. God's *hesed* is described as intrinsic to Yahweh's very character and nature (Ps. 116:5). Moved with *hesed*, the Lord helps those who cannot help themselves and includes God's motivation in instigating covenant with Israel and freedom from slavery (Exod. 34:6; Deut. 4:31). Proverbs 14:31 explains, "He who oppresses the poor reproaches his Maker, but he who honours him has *mercy on the needy*." *Hesed*, then, is one of the most important terms for Old Testament ethics, drawing on themes of compassion, loving-kindness, and grace to those in need. As Walter Brueggemann explains,

> the subset of covenantal love is derivative commitment to neighbor love, best known in the terse command of Leviticus 19:18: 'You shall love your neighbor as you love your own life.'[108]

At its best, in the Hebrew Bible this mercy and love for those in need has a social vision, "rooted in YHWH's own character, reaches beyond the contained community of faith or of ethnicity to those outside that community who, by their very existence, warrant neighborly solidarity."[109] This includes those vulnerable ones who are refugees (Lev. 19:34), and widows and orphans (Ps. 68:5).

Jesus' mission can be also understood as a mission of compassion, promised by the God of Compassion. As Zechariah – John the Baptist's father – put it when speaking of Jesus, "Thus he has shown the mercy promised to our ancestors, and has remembered his holy covenant" (Luke 1:72). Jesus is a fulfillment of this promise and draws on the ethics of *hesed*, and goes further than his contemporaries. As the Gospels record, he spent a considerable amount of his ministry 'showing mercy' himself. He touched lepers, fed the hungry masses, and met direct needs, motivated by a deep compassion that at times led him to weep over the city (Luke 19:41). It was also a core theme and commandment of Jesus' teachings. In the beatitudes, for example, those who are blessed by God are those who show mercy and are promised mercy (Matt. 5:7). This is based on the premise that God is merciful, that his children should express the same response to those in need (Matt. 5:7, James 1:27). It is no surprise then to see the parable of the Good Samaritan explaining that those who are not moved with compassion to show mercy toward a neighbour in need have failed to do the will of God (Luke 10:25-37). Lack of compassion to those who are hungry, thirsty, homeless, or in jail are acts that Jesus sees as having eternal repercussions (Matt. 25:31-46). Merciful compassion, therefore, is not an optional response for Jesus' followers.

Indeed, "God is love" (1 John 4:8), so there is wisdom and an empowerment that can only come from God. As Marcus Borg points out, *hesed* has also sometimes been translated as "opening the bowels of compassion," which he explains has rich metaphorical associations:

> It is the plural of a noun that in its singular form means "womb." Sometimes the association is explicit: a woman feels compassion for the child of her womb (1 Kings 3:26); a man feels compassion for his brother, who comes from the same womb (Gen 43:30). Compassion is located in a particular part of the body, the loins. In women, this means, of course, in the womb. In men, it is located in the bowels, and explains the otherwise odd biblical expression of bowels being moved with compassion.[110]

15: Roots Systems For Sustainability

This sacrificial and ultimately fruitful love comes from deep places, but it also flows. The Greek word *agape* is often translated as 'compassion' or 'love' in the New Testament and seems to pick this up in new ways. *Agape* is what moved God to heal the cosmos through Jesus (John 3:16) and is the same force that motivates us to do the same: "Love (*agape*) your neighbour as yourself" (Mark 12:31). The importance of self-awareness is crucial here. It's why we work so hard with exercises like timelines and StrengthsFinder, but it goes further. This *agape* does presuppose a love of ourselves, but it also moves through us. In his inspirational novel, *The Pilgrimage*, Paulo Coelho writes about Pedro, a spiritual guide, who helps the protagonist on a quest that includes experiencing *agape* along the way. He explains *agape* as an almost frightening life force with the backdrop of the Camino de Santiago pilgrimage:

> Agape is total love, the love that devours those that experience it. Whoever knows and experiences Agape sees that nothing else in this world is of any importance, only loving. This was the love that Jesus felt for humanity, and it was so great that it shook the stars and changed the course of [hu] man's history.[111]

Do we really desire to experience this devouring force for the sake of our neighbourhood? Can we support local leaders in this experience, even if it doesn't immediately help our organisational machines? This compassion may be experienced as a mystical, emotional, and practical connection that could overwhelm us. It can be embarrassing and hard to explain.

If compassion starts with God and flows outwards from there, how can our capacities for compassion grow? In many ways compassion is more a gift than a skill. A kind of conversion can happen when we put ourselves in places and spaces for compassion to come and transform us.

Che Guevara's biopic movie *The Motorcycle Diaries* vividly illustrates this kind of conversion. Guevara wasn't always an icon for revolutions and activists. He was a middle/upper class medical student before he took an adventure with a friend on a motorbike around South America. *The Motorcycle Diaries* follows this road trip, and like many such films, a dramatic conversion point is experienced in a key scene that would alter the trajectory of Che's life forever.

In the movie, Che celebrates his birthday with staff at the leper colony where he had volunteered as a doctor. They were on one bank, while the lepers were on the other side of the river. In the dark, and against the anguished protests of friends and colleagues Che risks the currents and crocodiles and dives into the water to swim to the other side. His breathing becomes more strained as he swims. Che struggles with asthma, and it is not clear if he will make it or not. As Che gets closer to the other side his patients with leprosy hear the noise and they gather on the bank to cheer him on. As Che rises out of the water exhausted, the lepers meet and embrace him. Che's allegiances and priorities were transformed forever. He was on a different side of the river now both physically and metaphorically. His anxious friends and colleagues cheer back on the other bank too. 'I always knew he would make it' mutters one and returns to his drinks.

It's a funny but powerful scene. Whatever we make of Che's politics, this scene reminds me that compassion is an adventure and requires life-trajectory altering conversions too. If Christians are to fully invest in God's coming Shalom, then life with Jesus should enable us to live in radically different ways. As in the movie, our adventures with Jesus should mean we can't stay on the safe side of the river and simply provide a safe service. God's compassion once embraced and flowing, calls us to overcome barriers and become different people. Not just loving those who love us. These conversions can't be forced or worked up by hype or guilt, but they can come as we embrace, encounter, and live new engagement and insight on the discipleship journey. Like Che Guevara's conversion as he crossed over to be with lepers and become a revolutionary, our lives should be different for meeting Jesus and investing ourselves in God's coming Shalom.

I love the Gospel stories of Zacchaeus who had such a powerful conversion to God's compassion with Jesus. As recorded in Luke's Gospel Jesus says of Zacchaeus "salvation (Shalom) has come to this house today, for this man also is a descendant of Abraham" (Luke 19:9). Zacchaeus had experienced a conversion in a popular Christian understanding of conversion, but it went much deeper. Before he met Jesus, he had power over others as a tax collector but after his conversion he had a kind of eternal authority, while becoming more physically vulnerable.

15: Roots Systems For Sustainability

Before, he was rich, after, he chose poverty. Before, he was alone and up a tree, after, he was accepted into a revolutionary community. Before, he was a spectator watching history go by, after, a player forever remembered in the divine drama in this promised land, going back to Abraham. The Good News is that we can experience these kinds of conversions through God's compassion too. Have we been awakened and converted to this Good News of God's Shalom enough to share it with our lives and our words like Zaccheus was? How can we find the containers to incubate such life? If we join Jesus in seeking first the Shalom in our local communities, what will it mean for us?

It's hard for me to write about the conversions of compassion without thinking about loss and grief. Many vulnerable people I loved most didn't improve their wellbeing, even though I felt I acted motivated by compassion. Indeed, too many got worse, and some had their lives cut short. My foster son Metus, for example, came to live with us in Springvale at 11 years old. We loved him as our own son, but he died confused and alone on the streets when he was only 18 years old. Compassion didn't seem to do any good for Metus. Compassion gave me a broken and bruised heart that I have never fully recovered from. Still, compassion, as painful and risky as it is, doesn't require the right outcomes to be the right way to live. I know that a life without compassion is empty. I know that Metus experiencing compassion made his short life better than if he had not. Somehow, in the economy of God, I have found that compassion never gets wasted. One of the joys of my recent sabbatical back in Melbourne was having dinner at a Vietnamese restaurant in Springvale with my daughter Amy as well as Metus' daughter Christine and her daughter Menau who was about to start kindergarten. Yes, Anji and I became great-grandparents in our 40s! It was real joy to see Amy and Christine talking passionately about their youth work and ways they want to change the world with love and conviction. These moments would not have been possible without our fragile attempts at compassion, no matter how costly that compassion has felt at times. Love 'remains.'

I like St Francis' idea of being 'channels' of God's peace and love. A channel is a passageway, a means of access for a thing, a communication, or an idea. Think of a channel as sort of a tunnel or funnel that moves something directly through. God's compassion can flow like this through us.

Our channels can get blocked at times, but through prayerful silence, solitude, and stillness we can be open again and allow God's compassion to flow again. The morning C.A.V.E. practices I suggested earlier in this book are important here. The roots of compassion grow and deepen in such places and helps the needed oxygen, water, and nutrients stabilize and move up beyond ourselves. Preparing to stand, be open and available for God's embrace in people and places requires alertness. As I wrote in my last book, *Risky Compassion*, it's too easy to be a Priest and a Levite, passing by on the other side, than to be the Samaritan who sees, feels, crosses over, connects, and does something that is helpful.[112]

Compassion then can't just be an individual capacity to build. We have found that when we intentionally and consistently open ourselves up to God's compassion together in community, we can channel God's tenderness, fidelity, and solidarity in ways that creatively inform our relationships with others. This includes the people, teams, places, missions, and organisations we are committed to.

The roots of compassionate motivation draw good nutrients, energy, and much-needed water from good soil into our community ecosystems. Indeed, without such roots, other motivations help things grow for a while, but our hopes can easily dry out, be destabilised and even blown over. If these motivational roots of compassion can grow strong, then so too can our capacity for community change.

Root Systems 2: Innovative instincts

Innovative instincts: local leaders finding relevant, practical, even surprising responses to new challenges and opportunities.

Healthy roots need to explore and adapt to find and utilise what is good in the soil. This is not so much a motivational root, like compassion, but an instinct or tendency to see new changes happen. The instinct of innovation finds relevant, practical, even surprising responses to

15: Roots Systems For Sustainability

new challenges and opportunities. Innovation then is an essential local leadership quality that sees new possibilities and adapts to make the most of them.

An instinct can be understood as a kind of reflex. It can grow sharper if it is practiced and accessed regularly. Local communities often get stuck when their instinct to imagine and pursue a different future is blunted: 'We've always done it this way around here.' Their capacity to think about other options has slowly been diminished, often because local communities have rarely been trusted to experiment or find new ways forward. These roots can wither, become resistant, and be lost. However, this communal instinct for innovation can be learnt and restored.

Without innovative instincts, 'more of the same' in our local urban contexts will generate less and less, for fewer and fewer, until our community's life slowly shrinks and dies. Without growing the capacity for intentional renewal, community life will be slowly sucked out of us. Fragile, we are then prone to be knocked over by outside forces.

When I think of Gospel stories that inspire innovation, I think of four friends who are commended by Jesus for their faith. They believe that Jesus wants to heal and restore their disabled friend, but there is just no room for them in the crowded house to get to Jesus. Powerful people have encircled Jesus and seem to want to dominate Jesus' time and agenda. Jesus, however, sets his own agenda for Shalom and was not dependent on powerful people for approval.

In Jesus' time, sickness, disability and poverty were often thought to be caused by sin or wrongdoing. So, when in this story Jesus focuses his best attention on people with disabilities, a prophetic action is being announced about the priorities of God's Shalom. The text says:

> They couldn't bring him to Jesus because of the crowd, so they dug a hole through the roof above his head. Then they lowered the man on his mat, right down in front of Jesus. Seeing their faith, Jesus said to the paralyzed man, 'My child, your sins are forgiven.' (Mark 2:4-5)

No Wastelands

Can you imagine this scene? I actually think it is supposed to be funny. Everyone is very intense, crowding around Jesus and then… small grains of dirt start falling, landing on people's noses and getting in their hair. People are patting themselves, flicking off the dirt, and looking around. But then bigger clumps start falling and smashing on the ground as people get out of the way. Suddenly, everybody looks up to the ceiling at once. Peeking through the sunlight are four grubby faces, and they start lowering a disabled man by rope. People jump out of the way, and the mat with a man who can't walk lands on the slabs of loose clay in front of Jesus.

Most people would have given up when they saw all the obstacles these friends faced. Too many people crammed into the room Jesus was in. Too many of the pillars of society, the powers that be, monopolising Jesus' time and space. But these four friends were no quitters. Their capacity for innovation had not yet been blunted by the Romans, religious leaders, or collaborators. More likely, the brutal occupation had trained them to consider out-of-the-box solutions, their innovative capacities finely honed by the need to occasionally subvert the status quo. Can't get in through the front door? Can't get Jesus' attention through the windows? How about we climb the roof, rip a hole in the tiles, and lower our mate down into the crowd, all somehow without dropping him and turning the needed miracle into a resurrection. Now that's an innovative instinct!

The friends could have seen that the house was too crowded and gone home. No one would have blamed them. But to do something about their friend's disability, they overcame those weeds of fear, futility, and frustration to find a deeper way forward. These determined roof diggers would have been seen to be fools, but they discovered what was in their power to do. They had an innovative instinct that helped a friend find Shalom.

Stephen Covey talks about the difference between our "circle of concern" and "circle of influence."[113] The 'circle of concern' is all the things we have opinions about, things we feel strongly about. Some of these things we can spend a lot of time thinking and talking about, the latest politics, celebrity gossip and news for example. With much of this, we can't do

15: Roots Systems For Sustainability

very much to change things, we can only be concerned about them. In contrast, 'the circle of influence' is the area we *can* do something about. It's much smaller than our circle of concern. It is those areas of our relationships, abilities, and what we can do about something where we find the innovative instinct.

When I go to Klong Toey and see the Ta Rua church building, I will always think of Ajan Suwat's innovative faith. The congregation had to leave their original building; it was unfair in so many ways how that happened. When we talked about what we could do, Ajan would always say 'God will provide.' I must admit I couldn't see how that could happen. I didn't think there were any buildings big enough in Klong Toey that we could afford. Yet Ajan prayed and found a place he thought would work brilliantly, not just for the congregation but for his family to live in and set up social enterprise, music studio, and educational classes. He could even set up a radio station because the ceiling was so high!

There were two barriers, however. The first was that the house currently belonged to an infamous Mafia boss. The second was we had very little funds. Negotiations might be tough here, especially as the Mafia boss was in prison. All I could say was that I would pray and ask God's people. That's all I could do. Alan Suwat went to work too, finding the homeowner's family and bringing the church together, gathering together what funds he could. Amazingly, a pastor in Australia called me out of the blue and said his church had $10,000 they felt called to give us. That turned out to be the shortfall we needed. Small risks of faith combined to be enough for a great new home for this church that is sustained by enterprises, music, and education. Just as Jesus commended the friends for their faith in finding a way to get the man with a disability to Jesus, I think Jesus would commend the innovative faith of Ajan Suwat and this church. The determination and creative risks taken by this community of faith in Klong Toey are so similar to the roof-breaking freinds. To beat futility and fear requires innovative risks. These are the risks that free us to do what God wants done through us.

The theme of relearning the innovative instinct is one that was introduced to me in the early 1990s and has become formative.

Daryl Gardiner, then with YFC New Zealand, opened up the instinct of innovation to me with this little maxim: 'the mission is more important than the methods.' As new youth and community workers we would be spellbound for hours listening to Daryl share his experiences, stories and insights.

> 'If knitting was best going to achieve change and growth with our Maori and Pacific Islander young people in our context, then I'd drop the youth clubs and camping projects for wool and knitting needles in a second. They are just methods. It's the reason why we do this that matters.'

With typical humour, Darryl implored us to evaluate and find new ways to respond to challenges in our neighbourhoods, but always remembering they need to be based on our overall purposes. I would go on to read and train people in theorists like Edward de Bono and Simon Sinek who helped create a more technical side of creating innovative instincts, but I'd always come back to Darryl and his hypothetical knitting needles. Ironically, years later, I find that one of our most effective methods for bringing isolated neighbours together in Winson Green is in fact a 'knit and natter' group! The wool and knitting needles time has come!

Tim Evans loves to share two inspirational TED Talks about innovation to help prepare our Change Makers to pitch their projects. They are brilliant talks, but it's Tim's ability to help Change Makers make the connections with their own lives and project ideas that make these sessions so memorable and formative.

In the first TED Talk, Simon Sinek's *Start with why: how great leaders inspire action*, Change Makers are challenged to ask, 'Why this project?' 'Why them?' 'Why now?'[114] Sinek describes how at the very centre circle of our priorities should be our purpose or motivation. That is our 'why.' Then we can discern 'how' we can go about that, before focussing on the 'what' to do. Too often our thoughts start and finish with 'what' to do or even the 'how' – attempts to do that better. This is as true for churches and charities as governments and enterprises. Institutionalism forgets why we do something, but community leaders with the local leadership quality of innovation always put purpose front and centre.

15: Roots Systems For Sustainability

Tim is so engaging on this theme that, if you meet Change Makers, one of the first things they will ask you is, 'What is your why?'

The second TED Talk, Ken Robinson's *Do schools kill creativity?*, resonates with Change Makers who have had traumatic educational experiences.[115] In our neighbourhoods, 'control of classrooms' has often had priority over creativity, with lifelong mental, and in some cases physical, scars as a result. We are born creative, but so often this instinct is squeezed out of us by our educational experience. At one point Ken tells the story of a young girl who can't concentrate in school, keeps fidgeting and getting into trouble and so is sent by her teacher to a doctor. The doctor examines her and then says to the girl, 'I just need to step outside for a moment to talk with your mother, you stay here.' As the doctor leaves, he puts the radio on. Once outside the room, the doctor says to the mother, 'Look at your daughter.' She was dancing and swaying to the music. 'She isn't sick, she's a dancer. Take her to dance school.' The little girl's name is Gillian Lynne, and she found her passion in dance to such a degree that she had a wonderful career as a dancer with the Royal Ballet, founded the Gillian Lynne Dance Company, met Andrew Lloyd Webber, and has been responsible for some of the most successful musical theatre productions in history. Robinson explains, 'She's given pleasure to millions, and she's a multimillionaire. Somebody else might have put her on medication and told her to calm down.' As the Change Makers watch, we all cry. So many of us wish we had a doctor like that who could have seen our talent rather than sickness!

I am conscious that many Change Makers live with neurodiversity. This includes me, Anji, and our children. So often the modern, industrial-scale education systems struggle to bring out the best in us. What we have begun to claim is that this difference is not a disability, but an innovation superpower. Given the right time, space, and support, we can see and make creative connections others can't. Put us in rigid and strict environments with topics we aren't interested in, and you will not have our attention for long. We are not sick, we are creative.

Innovation can be relearnt. Edward de Bono's ideas on creativity as learnt skills, for example, can help grow back our innovative instincts. I have taught his Six Thinking Hats process with leaders from inner cities to refugee camps. It's a creative process that helps see good ideas come to life. This is thrilling to me. De Bono writes: "An idea that is developed and put into action is more important than an idea that exists only as an idea." [116]

Innovation often begins when challenges and opportunities are identified. This requires eyes to see and places to freely discuss the hypothesis of what is happening and why. The innovative instinct starts to kick in when there is space to explore the many possible options. The root system of innovation starts to really create value when there is a willingness to focus and action one of the possible options. To incubate, develop, and grow that response via action steps and evaluation, will see a genuinely innovative idea have a unique life of its own.

For the innovative instinct to grow, a community culture of permission needs to be nurtured. Humiliation, blame, and risk aversion, so often experienced at the slightest attempt at doing things differently, can quickly kill off the willingness to step out and experiment: 'I told you it wouldn't work, didn't I.' In Google, I am told, they ring a bell when a worker has tried an innovation and it finally comes to an end. Everyone stops to applaud the worker, their attempts, and their learnings. If high-tech Google workers need this kind of permission-giving and encouragement to risk failing, then how much more so our local leaders? When local people feel like their local community values and encourages them to try something new, even if it may fail, genuine and unique local community change and growth can happen.

Innovation requires some trust, confidence, and compassion to start with. The roots of innovation grow deep in the good soil we have considered. If we nurture the innovative instinct, our local communities can grow stronger than the weeds of false ideologies and fears. The walking-alongside roles of mentors, coaches, partners, and supporters can especially be important here. Sometimes we just need to hear a voice from outside us: 'You are onto something important here. This idea has legs! Keep going!'

Roots Systems 3: Resilient endurance

Resilient endurance: Local leaders rising up after disappointments, finding deeper authenticity, responsibility and growth from these experiences.
Roots provide a kind of anchor for a growing, healthy tree. These roots require the quality of resilience. This is, perhaps, the most obvious quality for sustainable community leadership, but how best to describe this quality has been a challenge for us.

As a Seedbeds team we have gone back and forward on what to name this next important quality for sustainable community change and growth. My initial sense was to call this 'resilience' because I noticed that creative change and deeper authenticity happened after rebounding from setbacks, failures and disappointments. Dave Mann felt that 'endurance' was a more positive and better description of what happens when leaders and communities outlast, overcome, and keep going to see change eventually happen. Dave, who is also a Baptist Minister, loves memetic devices and felt that Innovation, Compassion, and Endurance spelling I.C.E was very cool and easy to remember these root systems together. 'Grit' is another name that could fit here, and we have discussed this in previous chapters along with the importance of passion and perseverance over time. 'Sustainability' was another potential name here, but this actually sums up what all three of these root systems provide in the life of local leaders and their communities. I also like a made-up word from Alistair Campbell, former Tony Blair advisor, popular podcaster of *The Rest is Politics* and bestselling author. In his latest book, *But what can I do?* he shares honestly about his own breakdown and addictions, encouraging readers to ask how we have overcome our troubles? His combination of 'resilience' plus 'perseverance' makes his new word: 'persevilience' that describes this:

> In which case you have shown powers of persevilience. The resilience element is the ability to recover from setback, particularly if you don't merely recover, but end up better and stronger than you were before the setback occurred. Perseverance is more about keeping on keeping on, whatever

the setbacks and difficulties, and however long it takes to meet the challenge or solve the problem you're facing.[117]

Campbell's hilarious attempts to add his new word to the English dictionary has not yet been successful at time of writing. I do, however, think Campbell is describing a quality that is needed by us and other local leaders if to change is to happen.

In the end we went for 'resilient endurance.' Not least because it helps with our memorable C.I.R.C.L.E structure (Compassionate motivations, Innovative instincts, Resilient endurance, Community connecting, Liberative learning, Enterprise development), but we still often shorten this to grit, resilience, endurance, or perseverance. Not yet persevilience! This root system is about a quality of paying attention to expectations and finding ways to consistently overcome challenges and keep going.

If real and deep change were easy, it would have happened by now. Pushing the horizons back helps people not to dismiss small starts and encourages them to keep going long enough to get momentum and not to take setbacks personally. It's a key part of the hero's journey of self-discovery and capacity building. If our local communities and their leaders can grow deep roots of resilient endurance then no matter what is thrown at them, like a tree standing by the waterside, we shall not be moved! We see in Jeremiah this quality in spades, described like this:

> They are like trees planted along a riverbank, with roots that reach deep into the water. Such trees are not bothered by the heat or worried by long months of drought. Their leaves stay green, and they never stop producing fruit. (Jer. 17:8)

Growing deep roots to overcome obstacles is a picture of what our local leaders need if Shalom is to come. These trees outlast the conditions and produce fruit despite drought and heat.

Jesus' story of the persistent widow in Luke 18:1-8 (NRSV) has also been an inspiration for us. She is introduced as someone who needed justice from her accuser, but an unjust judge refuses to hear her case and make a decision. The widow, however, would not be deterred and kept

15: Roots Systems For Sustainability

coming to his house day and night pleading for justice. In the end, the Judge said to himself, "Though I have no fear of God and no respect for anyone, yet because this widow keeps bothering me, I will grant her justice, so that she may not wear me out by continually coming." Of course, this story is about persistence in prayer and "not to lose heart," but this same persistence can also inform and inspire our community's growth and a quality needed from our local leaders.

We often underestimate how long real change takes to happen. There is a line attributed to Bill Gates that says,

> We overestimate what we can do in a year, but underestimate what we can do in ten years.

The endurance for change sometimes requires generations in our communities. For communities in survival mode, long-term thinking and planning seems like a luxury of time and energy few have. Therefore, creating intentional space to nurture this root system is especially important. Like compassion and innovation, it can die before it has a chance to grow. We often quote the African proverb:

> Go quickly, go alone. Go far, go together.

There are warnings too that can rot resilient endurance. If we attach our ego to how well things are going, our emotional life will be tied to a crazy roller coaster ride. If we do well, we are brilliant and high, but if we fail we are losers and low! This emotional fragility undermines trust and momentum. The capacity for resilient endurance learns not to take setbacks and failures personally. Instead, it grows a deep sense of overall call or mission, like a beacon on the horizon we aim for. Even if we have ups and downs, we can look up and see that we are still on the journey to get where we're going. To return to our metaphor in this chapter, resilience is a root system that sustains us in place long enough for growth and fruit.

Resilience also relates to listening to our bodies and knowing their limits. Sometimes I hear leaders suddenly say, 'I'm burnt out and need to quit right now' as if this is a noble thing. I think we need to be very careful about using terms like 'burn out' as a basis for making decisions to leave communities behind. More accurate terms like 'exhaustion,' 'mental ill health,' or 'feeling overwhelmed' help us take more responsibility for our lives and take action to prevent these situations happening in the future. Few people actually burn out totally because of overwork and need to quit communities at that moment. More often we can work in fits and starts, booms and busts because of inadequate motivations, boundaries or assertiveness. These inadequacies have an impact on our bodies and emotions, far more than mere workloads.

Rather than compassion and innovation resourcing us from the ground up, our ego and fear can drive us into the ground. Quitting is tempting but doesn't help here as these inadequacies will follow us. When we take responsibility with something like: 'I'm sorry I haven't listened to my body for a long time and got caught up, driven by my own ego. I know this will impact you, but I need a break. Can you help me?' then resilience is being grown in ways quitting for burn out can never do. Learning to listen to our bodies earlier, checking our motivations, learning clearer 'yeses' and 'noes' help prevent exhaustion and find new ways to go deeper with our local community. Our vulnerabilities can then become gifts not instabilities. Quitting is often preventable and should only be a last resort.

Maintaining resilience challenges me. I am not naturally a high energy person. As I've got older, I have found I need to listen to my body earlier, consider what is driving me and create far more margins in my life over time. My local community needs me to want the marathon with water and rest breaks, rather than full-on sprints and collapse. Wayne Cordeiro's book *Leading on Empty* has been helpful here. He says,

> We don't forget that we are Christians. We forget that we are human, and that one oversight alone can debilitate the potential of our future.[118]

The body can be our friend in letting us know when we think we are too important or not important enough. Pacing ourselves can be a crucial element with this quality, but this challenges too.

Parker Palmer picks up this tension between our limits and potential:

15: Roots Systems For Sustainability

> If we are to live our lives fully and well, we must learn to embrace the opposites, to live in a creative tension between our limits and our potentials. We must honor our limitations in ways that do not distort our nature, and we must trust and use our gifts in ways that fulfill the potentials God gave us.[119]

We have been talking about growing capacities for sustainability in this chapter, but these qualities are not endless. We can't do everything, all the time, no matter how compassionate or innovative we are. Finding our limits is a process that requires us to go to the edge of our potential and often fall off it. Perhaps we do too many things, outside of our giftedness and strengths, for too long. Perhaps we need to discover we need others and can't do everything thing on our own. Perhaps we are climbing up the wrong ladder on the wrong wall and need to come down and start again. Reaching our limits is just the beginning, not the end of the growth process. We don't know our limits until we find them. Of course, many local people never get the chance to test out how far their potential can go. Brene Brown has been an important voice for us in building capacity for resilient endurance in our local communities. She has been especially insightful around the theme of shame resilience' which impacts so many, including so many of our key local community leaders.

> By shame resilience I mean the ability to practise authenticity when we experience shame, to move through the experience without sacrificing our values, and to come out the other side of the shame experience with more courage, compassion, and connection than we had going into it…If we can share our story with someone who responds with empathy and understanding, shame can't survive. Self-compassion is also critically important, but because shame is a social concept – it happens between people – it also heals best between people. A social wound needs a social balm, and empathy is that balm. Self-compassion is key because when we're able to be gentle with ourselves in the midst of shame, we're more likely to reach out, connect, and experience empathy.[120]

This centre to return to is our 'true self,' but found connected to community. Shame is a universal experience, but Brene found that what triggers the experience can also be determined by gender. For women, a host of unrealistic expectations, especially to be perfect, to please, to perform, or to be small, sweet, and quiet; for men, it boils down to one: don't be weak. I think these expectations are amplified living in local communities. In all these challenges Brown explains that the "shame resilience is about moving from shame to empathy – the real antidote to shame." The connections, then, between the roots systems of 'compassion' and 'resilience' are crucial.

Toward the end of our Change Makers residential on 'Resilience' we nearly always quote Teddy Roosevelt. *Time Magazine* used to have the annual Teddy Awards 'to take note of some of the people who performed honorably as winners and losers in the public arena' based on this quote:

> It is not the critic who counts; not the man who points out how the strong man stumbles, or where the doer of deeds could have done them better. The credit belongs to the man who is actually in the arena, whose face is marred by dust and sweat and blood; who strives valiantly; who errs, and comes short again and again, because there is no effort without error and shortcoming; but who does actually strive to do the deeds; who knows great enthusiasms, the great devotions; who spends himself in a worthy cause; who at the best knows in the end the triumph of high achievement, and who at the worst, if he fails, at least fails while daring greatly, so that his place shall never be with those cold and timid souls who neither know victory nor defeat.

It's such an inspirational quote that Brene Brown entitled her brilliant book *Daring Greatly* after this. It finds resonance with our Change Makers because seeking change requires this kind of passionate determination that risks real public humiliation. Local leaders, whose arena is their own local community, live literally alongside their critics, sharing their schools, churches, and sports clubs. The deep roots of resilient endurance may be desperately needed here more than anywhere else! The local community leaders who can rise up after disappointments, finding deeper authenticity, responsibility, and growth from these experiences will see change happen in ways that others can't, or simply won't.

Conflict transformation emerged for us as a key part of building resilience. Our coaching sessions quickly found personal growth created more community conflict as some local people grew and developed while others didn't! So often when it came to conflict, our emerging leaders only had the options of 'stop' or '100 miles an hour,' with little in between. Our friends Carolyn Merry and Martina Hunt, who have experienced conflict in war zones, found ways forward.

They explore different conflict styles and preferences with our Change Makers, and cohorts act these out in amusing and informative role-plays. 'I'm a shark, no wait, maybe I'm a fox' became vocabulary leaders could use to notice what was happening in them and others. Change and conflict often go together, especially where there are vested interests, and so this skill helps resilience like few others. In fact, finding new ways to transform conflict makes resilient endurance possible.

We have always run the final residential of Change Makers on the theme of Resilience at Holy Island. It's the most expensive part of the programme, a challenge to get them there, but always worth it. There is something special about sacred places that help us go deeper together. As we walk the Pilgrim's Posts at low tide, those physical posts stretching deep into the ground are metaphors for the journey we take together. They are visual reminders of the roots we too need for sustainability.

Personal Reflections

1. Of the three root systems (qualities) of local leaders proposed in this chapter, which have you most and least connected with? Why?

2. Compassion can be a critical motivation able to inform and inspire local leadership. Where have you seen this present or absent in your local community? What difference has it made?

3. Innovation can be a critical instinct able to inform and inspire local leadership. Where have you seen this present or absent in your local community? What difference has it made?

4. Resilience can be a critical capacity to inform and inspire local leadership. Where have you seen this present or absent in your local community? What difference has it made?

5. Which of these qualities can you grow in next? How?

Chapter 16: Branches Prepared For Fruitfulness

There is a crack in everything, that's how the light gets in.
– Leonard Cohen

Keep your face always toward the sunshine — and shadows will fall behind you.
– Walt Whitman

Plants convert light into energy, a process called photosynthesis. They will adapt and grow toward light because this process helps to create the energy plants need to survive, grow, and be fruitful. There are different kinds of vegetation and plant life. All have root systems, but how they reproduce can vary dramatically as they grow and evolve to their conditions. How some plants find ways to seek energy from light can be ingenious. How we go about preparing for Shalom fruitfulness requires intentional approaches in finding energy too. The fruit of Shalom we seek can't be produced without strong branches.

What could be our branches that offer leaves and fruit? With our Seedbeds local community leadership programmes, we have found three approaches that can help prepare our local communities for Shalom fruitfulness, far more than others. They are not exhaustive, and in many ways these approaches overlap and intertwine, but they do have their own disciplines worth drawing on. Helping community leaders find, understand, and practice these three approaches has been liberating and grows the energy and capacity for change. We know these approaches can help local communities transform energy from light to prepare for more Shalom fruit, but these approaches must be taken seriously.

Branch 1: Community Organisation

Community Connectors: With society fracturing and individuals more isolated, leaders bring people together in local places to discover, connect and mobilise their gifts and assets. These roles can be informed by 'community organisation' approaches.

When we look at our local urban communities, the fracturing and isolation of individuals can be pronounced. Neighbours can literally die and not be found for months, in some cases years. An extreme example of this happened in May 2023 when a 70-year-old man was found in his Bolton home as a skeleton having died six years earlier. He had been a consumer all this time - prepaid bills and rent kept this happening - but not a living human being.[121] So many of us can live only as consumers if the conditions of 'wastelands' persist. Loneliness, in fact, is a bigger cause of death than a poor diet, obesity, and lack of exercise, while it's on a par with heavy smoking and alcohol consumption.[122] It makes sense, therefore, that those who want to see change from within their community need to become community connectors.

If community connecting was a branch, I imagine it stretching out horizontally to find the light and make the tree wider and stronger. Connecting together can be a way to create energy and power for Shalom. However, there are different ways of approaching community connecting. A common way is to look for community needs and ask, 'what needs can we meet?' then design and offer a service to find people with that need, and then meet that need. People are hungry? Provide a food bank. People are in debt? Provide a debt service. People are illiterate?

16: Branches Prepared For Fruitfulness

Provide a literacy class. People lack God? Provide a course and a worship service. These may well be places to start sometimes, but this can also be counter-productive, creating even more isolation and loneliness. As we explored previously, the service provision model can uplift providers, but disempower and even oppress the provided for. This is especially true when we do for others what they can, in fact, do for themselves.

Jesus was a community connector par excellence. He didn't so much preach a message as connect up a community. It was this community that would be mobilised to go out and change the world. The story of Jesus using what the crowd had – a few fish and pieces of bread – to feed the multitudes also inspires. Jesus uses what people have and, when connected freely in the abundance of God, it can be enough for all to experience Shalom.

Asset-Based Community Development (ABCD) has emerged as an approach with huge potential to see local communities come together and see change for themselves. This approach has especially proved to be crucial for us in moving Change Makers away from their instinct to act 'for' their local communities, to act 'with' their community and setting up opportunities led by overlooked parts of the community. There are key disciplines to learn, but it often starts with seeing what is 'strong' in our communities, rather than what is 'wrong.' It works with what assets our neighbours have in their hands, rather than what they don't, to see change happen.

Tim Evans has been instrumental in the rise of ABCD approaches, not just in his own local community, Firs and Bromford estate in East Birmingham, but also in leading 'Worth Unlimited' (an intergenerational community-building enterprise) across England for 20 years, and in training diverse communities in ABCD at 'Nurture Development.' Tim is one of the founders of Change Makers and often takes key sessions in our intensives and residentials to outline this ABCD approach as a basis to assist Change Markers to shape their ideas for change. Just as 'compassion' is a central quality that also informs the roots of 'innovation' and 'resilience,' so too can ABCD be a central approach that can inform 'community organisation' which in turn will inform the two other 'branches' of 'liberative learning' and 'enterprise development.'

Without exception, an ABCD approach changes the mindsets of what Change Makers pitch at the end of the programme. Instead of waiting for outsiders to come and fix local challenges for them, they begin to take seriously what their local community already has and soon find ways to connect locally to see change come from the inside out.

If community is about a deep sense of belonging that comes from common commitments and values, then the approach and disciplines of ABCD have a lot to teach us. There are some great ABCD resources that can do this, but the book *The Connected Community*, written by Tim's colleagues Cormac Russell and John McKnight at Nurture Development, consolidates some of the best thinking in accessible ways.[123] The book outlines three disciplines of ABCD that are worth exploring here.

Discover: We need to go on a kind of treasure hunt to find strengths in our neighbourhood. It's not always obvious. Those assets, gifts, aspirations, and skills are there, sometimes in plain sight, but often overlooked. They can be found in local individuals, groups, institutions, churches, clubs, associations, and in built and natural environments. There are a variety of tools to help in this discovery: 'one-to-one' interviews, 'asset mapping,' and 'generosity dinners.' This can take time, but once we start to see our communities as glasses half-full, rather than half-empty, sustainable change from within becomes more viable.

Connect: When local strengths are recognised, solidarity emerges and alliances to act together are forged, a kind of community-building magic can appear. If local people can band together in positive ways and grow in trust, an unstoppable force can emerge. This is especially true when we consider 'foundational community functions' like enabling health, ensuring security, stewarding ecology, shaping local economies, contributing to local food production, raising our children, and co-creating care.[124] If local communities can join together on these, then the need for outside resources diminishes. Connections create local power for change. Connecting tools include finding natural connectors, listening campaigns, and community meetings. We may need to cross over dividing walls, but the time and trust-building required is worth the effort.

16: Branches Prepared For Fruitfulness

Mobilise: The buzz that discovering and connecting strengths creates in local communities needs to be focused and acted on, lest it fizzle out. People can grow cynical and despondent if talk, even encouraging talk, doesn't move to action. Finding the right 'wine skin' so this 'new wine' can ferment and mature is therefore crucial. There are many kinds of structures for this, but local participation, ownership, and decision-making are essential. Dave Andrews suggests that Jesus' call in Matthew 10 to go out in 'twos' is so that finding a third person creates the minimum for community building. One person is single, two a couple, but with three you have the first embryo of community that can grow a cause. Three people meeting together regularly to evaluate and plan how to share their talents and passions can be revolutionary. Tools for mobilisation can start off small like this, but some need to grow more sophisticated to reach their potential, including local community meetings, groups, alliances, associations, Community Interest Companies, charities, and campaigns. Finding ways to best mobilise talent in visible, processable and sustainable ways can take some discernment and experimentation but is worth it to bring others on board.

When I think of a Change Maker who connects the community I think of Helen Fernandes. She grew up in the countryside between London and Birmingham but came to East London for a gap year with Dave and Sally Mann. 15 years later she's still there. I love the project she developed as a Change Maker. Helen was teaching at the local school, living and volunteering in Royal Docks. She wanted a way to get local people together, support health, and show off the positive side of her neighbourhood. The idea of a 5km parkrun around the docks emerged. Now hundreds of people run this each Saturday. More than just a run, however, it sparked a role for Helen where she now leads the local Baptist church and the community association. She doesn't teach in the school anymore but has worked with the local community and Oasis Trust to start a much-needed high school. Local talent and resources are being discovered, connected, and mobilised.[125]

My wife, Anji has been a community connector for as long as I have known her. She may not have used those words, but she has grown in the ABCD approach. As I see the way she can quickly find local talents, connect them together, and mobilise them for change, I am awestruck.

One young person might meet her looking for help and before they know it they are running the social media of a charity! Anji has led Newbigin Community Trust (NCT) to become an ABCD organisation and in many ways has lived Barak Obama's alternate calling, building up "an institution that could reshape a neighbourhood or a portion of the city."[126] The motto for NCT is not 'empowering the local community' as if NCT has the power. No, it is 'Empowered by the people of Winson Green.' There is a big difference. What NCT does so well is to recognise that power comes from within the local community. The organisation helps connect and shape that power into sustainable actions.

With society fracturing and individuals more isolated, how leaders bring people together in local places to discover, connect and mobilise their gifts and assets matters. Growing capacities as community connectors is one of the most crucial approaches to learn if change is to come from the inside out. On these strong branches can hang great fruit!

Branch 2: Community Animators

Community Animators: With injustice and poverty becoming more complex, leaders bring people together to awaken praxis to address injustices inflicted upon their community. These roles can be informed by 'liberative learning' approaches.

Branches grow ready for fruit because light can be efficiently transformed into energy. If community animating was a branch, it would be one that stretches up vertically to find light, making the tree taller and impossible to miss. A key role we have found that helps grow energy for change in our communities is when local leaders become animators, agitators, or organisers through liberative learning.

Community animators don't just facilitate community discussions. They create awakenings that lead to intentional actions and reflection processes. Jesus casting out the money changers is a powerful example.

> Then he entered Jerusalem and went into the temple, and when he had looked around at everything, as it was already late, he went out to Bethany with the twelve. (Mark 11:11)

16: Branches Prepared For Fruitfulness

This a critical moment; Jesus had invested in a handful of leaders and connected together a broader community movement of disciples. However, he mostly told parables to crowds and his intentions were not yet public. Jerusalem, under the iron rule of Rome, was a powder keg, ready to explode. Expectations of a violent revolution to free God's people were building. Could Jesus be the Messianic answer to Jewish prayers and prophecies for their freedom?

When Jesus entered Jerusalem, he sought to downplay those expectations, riding a donkey, not a war horse (Mark 11:1-10). The crowd pressed in with their own hopes for Jesus anyway, claiming him as their liberating savior with palm branches and raised voices. How would Jesus respond? He enters Jerusalem, and like those spies of old, looks around on a reconnaissance mission before going back to his friends in Bethany. The next day, his evaluation of the situation clear, he would intentionally protest and clear the Temple of the money changers and others.

There are times to quietly work below the surface and not worry about what others think about us or our intentions. And there are also times that require us to prepare well and stick our heads above the parapet, go public and leave people in no doubt.

Like Jesus, we must pick our moments, plan intentionally and be prepared to pay the price. There is a lot of overlap with ABCD here, but where Connectors grow wider to help grow healthy communities, Animators grow communities taller to penetrate freedom from oppression. Community organisation connects communities, but liberative learning animates grassroots campaigns to address oppression and injustice together, to shift the balance of power toward local communities. Desmond Tutu once said, 'There comes a time when we can't just pull drowning people out of a river. We must go up-stream and find out why they are falling in.' If we think about the challenges in our neighbourhoods, why would going 'upstream' be important? Not everything starts and finishes in our own neighbourhood. The river can be polluted upstream and only by going up there in strength can this change.

Liberative learning especially helps to address outside forces that impact local communities by creating awareness and power from within. Many thinkers and activists have helped to shape this approach around the globe. Some of these include: Tom Paine, Paulo Freire, Henrietta Barnett, Augusto Boal, Mary Parker Follett, Mahatma Ghandi, Robert Owen, Kurt Lewin, Saul Alinsky, Steve Biko, Robert Putman. It was Ann Hope and Sally Timmel's book, *Training for Transformation*, that was especially important to me.[127] This manual provided important summaries of this approach, but also exercises to try with local communities.

The roots of community animating go back to the 19th century in Europe, the United States, South Africa, and South America. The ideas and techniques were developed over 100 years in the tenant empowerment and trades union movements. We see them in the settlement movement, the civil rights movement, the suffragette movement, the community enterprise, and cooperative movements. Other movements for social justice, critical education, and community ownership have emerged. These movements start locally, but can stretch out globally in solidarity and awareness, focusing on the change they collectively need.

Liberation theology has especially influenced my approach to change making through a community animating approach. The fervour for change in Latin America created some of the most important Christian voices for transformation in the 20th century. Gustavo Gutierrez is a good example of liberative learning when he writes of 'praxis' in this way:

> The praxis on which liberation theology reflects is a praxis of solidarity in the interests of liberation and is inspired by the gospel.[128]

This process of liberation begins with the pain of people, but by bringing people together, helps find the causes of oppression and actions in hope of liberation together.

Paulo Freire can, perhaps, be known as the most influential thinker in this approach. His principles have helped unleash movements around the world. He wrote "Liberation is a praxis: the action and reflection of men and women upon their world in order to transform it." Freire devised what proved to be an astonishingly effective way of teaching people to read in Brazil.

> Rather than using a standard textbook approach that followed a pre-set procedure for everyone regardless of local context, his team would visit a community first and identify a small set of words that both were especially meaningful for people in that specific time and place, given the issues and struggles they faced, and also had syllables and sounds that made them a good basis for learning other words. He called these 'generative words'. Using this method his team could teach adults to read the newspaper in about five weeks. At the same time this gave people the capacity to begin to see or name their own social context, and thereby to analyse why things were as they were – to judge or reflect on it.[129]

Helping participants ask questions about what was happening became crucial:

- 'Who made the decisions about this?'
- 'Who will and won't benefit from this?'
- 'How will this change this community?'

Local communities soon found they could act and began to improve things. Freire referred to the learning process that took place as 'conscientization.' A more accessible English term might be 'consciousness-raising' or 'awakening.' This meant, in turn, that people were animated from being 'objects' to 'subjects' and didn't have to be passive and fatalistic about their lives. Indeed, they now had the energy to help shape their life together. This approach to learning was not so much storing up or 'banking' new information, but more animating through 'problem solving.' This was liberating, enabling people, not only to name and reflect, but also to act to change their circumstances for the better. Freire's approach can be considered an influence on liberation theology. This liberative learning approach, that needs local leaders to become more animators than controllers, has huge potential in our local communities.

I hope you can cope with another acronym. If A.B.C.D is an approach for community connecting that is easy to remember for Asset-Based Community Development, then the vowels A.E.I.O.U can do similarly for community animating approaches. These are especially important to remember as we meet individual residents and listen to their concerns before bringing like-minded people together.

> **Agitate:** The Agitate step of the animating conversation is made up of two parts: 1. Finding the issues that affect someone, and 2. Bringing to the surface how it affects them.
>
> **Educate:** Finding how collective action can solve the problem. Educate can be subdivided into three main questions. First, 'what would fix the problem?' Second, 'who can give us what we want?' Third, 'what collective action can you take to force the appropriate powers to fix the problem?'
>
> **Inoculate:** The people in power react. Those in power always react, which is why animators need tools to anticipate and prepare for the counter-offensive in whatever form it takes. Inoculation has two parts: 1. Anticipating and preparing for what the powers will do, and 2. Addressing people's fears.
>
> **Organise:** Organise is about finding ways for people to participate by taking on tasks that are right for them.
>
> **Uplift:** The uplift part of AEIOU is about follow-through, particularly with talking through obstacles that coworkers may face to completing tasks.[130]

In the UK, Citizens UK has been instrumental in 'living wage' campaigns, starting with a community meeting in East London in 2001, when they brought together churches, mosques, schools, and other local institutions to talk about the issues affecting their communities. One issue came up again and again – low pay. Living Wage grew from these struggles:

> At the time the government's minimum wage was just £3.70 an hour. Cleaners working for some of the richest financial institutions in the world were struggling to keep their heads

above water, often working two or more jobs and unable to spend time with their children and partners. And nowhere more so than in London, where housing and childcare costs are much higher than in other parts of the country. Working with community organisers they decided to act, and from that meeting a powerful movement of faith leaders, trade unions and community organisations came together to call on major employers in the capital to pay their staff a London Living Wage.[131]

Over the next few years they organized, agitated, and animated, making the issue so hot that those with the power to make decisions couldn't sit on it any longer. Today the living wage has taken traction, though there is still a long way to go:

> With more than 3.5 million people paid less than the real Living Wage that meets the cost of living, the job is far from done. For people paid the real Living Wage it means the difference between being able to afford the things you need for a decent standard of living, and just getting the government's minimum – things like healthy food, a warm home, and a birthday treat for your children. Over 13,000 organisations across all sectors have joined our movement, including half of the FTSE 100 and household names like the Houses of Parliament, Nationwide, Oxfam, ITV, Chelsea Football Club and LUSH.[132]

We love it when Citizens UK activists come to talk with our Change Makers during their innovation intensive. It fits well with the theme of innovation because it's about finding new solutions to challenges Change Makers face. Most of these activists also have a Christian background and bring their faith to community animating in such brilliant ways. A key challenge is thinking about power. Not just power 'over,' which can be abusive, but power 'with' and 'of' local people facing the challenges. Martin Luther King's quote is often used and makes a real impact:

> Power without love is reckless and abusive, and love without power is sentimental and anemic. Power at its best is love implementing the demands of justice, and justice at its best is power correcting everything that stands against love.[133]

Many of us feel uneasy about power. Especially those of us who have inherited it and/or experienced its abuse. Yet, a key part of animating a community is to awaken its power. This is power from within, power to make decisions about our own lives. This approach seeks to liberate power, rather than control others with it. For example, we can start by identifying what people care strongly about in a community through one-on-one conversations. Other key aspects include building relationships and networks that are strong enough to support a long struggle for change, developing community leaders, and mobilising people to come together to take collective action. All of this is designed to achieve a shift of power and significant social change in favour of local communities.

I still remember my first foray into community organising. Ken Luscombe, from World Vision's 'Urban Advance,' had been encouraging us in this approach and I was on the lookout for ways we could try it in Springvale.

Then, in 1998, it happened. I received a phone call from Charlie O'Campo, a leader with the National Council of Churches in Australia (NCCA). As a Filipino activist, he had stood up to the Marcos regime as part of his Christian faith. He moved to Australia and led NCCA in justice and refugee work. After a few pleasantries, he got right down to it with me.

> 'Ash, did you know that there are 1650 East Timorese asylum-seekers in Australia? Many of them are in and around Springvale.'

> 'Really Charlie? That many? I know a few families here, but had no idea.'

Charlie explained,

> 'Yes, but they all are facing deportation. Rumour has it that it could be soon. The Government doesn't want to process their refugee claims because they would easily prove they have a 'well-founded fear of persecution 'as most fled Timor after the Dilli massacre. Giving them refugee status and sanctuary

16: Branches Prepared For Fruitfulness

would seriously offend Indonesia. As you may know our Government has just signed an oil treaty worth billions with Indonesia.'

'That's outrageous!' I said.

'Would you help the Timorese in your neighbourhood?'

'Sure, but we'd want to take a community organising approach Charlie. Is that okay?'

'Wonderful! Jill at the Red Cross is happy to work with you and has all the names and addresses of families in your area.'

What are the issues you see in this scenario? If I was to take a community animating approach, what should I do next?

There were a few phases to this. First, I got help from the Red Cross to visit as many of the local Timorese as I could with a couple of our UNOH interns. I introduced us as 'local volunteers who had been asked by the Red Cross to do what we can to support you.' We tried to connect and listen to their stories as best we could. This wasn't easy as many only spoke Tetum or Hakka. There were lots of smiles and awkward silences. My daughter Amy was just learning to walk then and as Anji and I shared the parenting I would often visit with her. She became known as the 'White Monkey' and melted the hearts of all who met her. Charlie was right too, so many had been waiting for their claims for many years and had no idea if they would be deported soon or not. All were stressed.

Second, it was quickly apparent some Timorese leaders we met had real capacities as community connectors. Rocky and Maria and their children were especially friendly to us and we planned a community meeting where the local Timorese, as many as we could gather, would connect and see what we could do together. One of the interns, Jon Owen, had a friend from his church that spoke Hakka, and could act as an interpreter. Most of the families we had met spoke this Chinese dialect. We would host the meeting at our UNOH Centre, a shop front near the train station in Springvale. Rocky and Maria would make sure we had a crowd!

Third, the time came for the community meeting came. We worked so hard to get everyone there, but I realised I didn't really know what we'd do in the meeting itself! As I walked from our flat on one side of the Springvale Railway Station to the UNOH centre on the other I prayed vigorously and then remembered an exercise in the Hope and Timmel book. It was simply brainstorming three questions, one at a time:

- What are you most worried about?
- What are the causes of your concerns?
- What can we do together to help?

Timorese families packed out our UNOH shopfront and as we introduced ourselves and the interpreter there seemed to be an air of hopeful anticipation. However, our Hakka interpreter didn't speak the same dialect of Hakka as our Timorese friends and so one of Rocky and Maria's children needed to take over. We had three large pieces of paper, one for each question, and quickly filled them up.

What I found interesting was that there were real concerns about the wellbeing of their children and the stresses this was causing. Also, as many didn't speak English, they didn't feel part of the local community, have jobs, or transport. When rumours of them being rounded up by immigration authorities began, no one knew who to contact to confirm or deny the story, so it kept spreading. We did eventually get to the challenge of gaining refugee status itself, but first there was a long list of very practical day-to-day concerns we could address together. Some great 'quick wins' to get momentum going emerged: English classes, job clubs, monthly outings to tourist sites, indoor football. We also made connections with those who could help us campaign for permanent residency.

Fourth, there were many years of community connecting activities together. These built deep trust, friendships, connections, and community capacities. The English classes went for many years with volunteers and even me trying my hand at times. The job club on Saturday mornings, however, didn't last long, as we rang up Christian businesses we knew and found jobs for all who needed them within months.

16: Branches Prepared For Fruitfulness

Our monthly outings to places like Philip Island to see the kangaroos and koalas were unforgettable, with UNOH providing the bus and the Timorese providing the food. The young men, that the community were so worried about, loved football and the 'Fatboys' indoor football team won their league one year. Many of the Timorese were Catholic so we asked the local Catholic church if the Timorese could hold a prayer service on Wednesday nights in their own language in their chapel. This activity proved inspirational and sustaining for so many. It also meant any news from Immigration could be actioned quickly.

Fifth, alongside local community building, we campaigned for the Timorese to get permanent residency. This decision was at the very centre of what was causing so much vulnerability. The plight of our Timorese friends needed to be seen, felt and heard, especially by those who could make a decision about them. We had to organise strategically and not just protest if the needed decision-makers were to do the right thing. We joined hands with others to make the issue of refugee status for our friends so hot that the Immigration Department couldn't sit on this decision any longer. This was complex, as significant legal, political, and attitudinal changes were needed outside the control of the Timorese. We needed others outside our local community to help make this decision possible.

A helpful community organising tool at one point was a 'force field analysis.' At one end was those who were decision-making insiders against the Timorese staying. At the other end was the Timorese asylum seekers themselves who were desperate to stay. Everyone else was in the middle and many of these were winnable to our cause. How could we move the needle? Who were the insiders who could 'pull' as we gathered as many different networks as possible to 'push' with the Timorese from the outside.

Over the next 10 years two campaigning groups were significant for us. The 'Sanctuary Network' was started by Sister Cath in Sydney, who said that if the Government tried to deport the Timorese, then we will hide them in our homes to avoid their subsequent deaths. Most of the Timorese impacted were in Melbourne, and so with a Timorese friend and Uniting Church Minister, Etavina, I joined the steering group for the local Sanctuary Network. I was quickly connected with lawyers, unionists, church Ministers, and anarchists. Our goal was to make the Timorese seen, and this threat to hide them public and credible. The Sanctuary Network soon got national attention as tens of thousands of Australians, especially from churches and unions, signed up to provide safe homes if the worst came to it. The then Immigration Minister, Philip Ruddick, started to get worried and threatened us with a six month jail sentence if we carried out these plans. The second group was the 'Justice for Asylum Seekers' (JAS) which created public awareness and political pressure like the Sanctuary Network, but also had insider connections in the legal world and in the Immigration Department. Over the years, in big ways and small, we pushed and found people to pull until decisions about the Timorese got across the line. This issue simply became too hot for the Immigration Department to sit on any longer.

In October 1999 Indonesia's occupation of East Timor suddenly ended. This was such a joyous day. Back in 1975, after the Portuguese colonisers suddenly left, Indonesia had invaded Timor, fearful that the ruling Fretilin political party had Communist sympathies. The world stood by as an estimated 200,000 Timorese died through violence or from starvation from 1974-99 under the Indonesian occupation. This was around a third of East Timor's population. As the Indonesians finally left in 1999, East Timor was left smouldering and peace-keepers stepped in. Was it safe for our Timorese friends to return? Did they really want to return, given their kids had been born and bred in Melbourne now, as some had settled for over 10 years?

Jon Owen and I were commissioned to go and visit Timor on a fact-finding tour. One of the fathers had returned to Dili, the capital of East Timor, as he had a construction business and was in much demand in the clean-up and rebuilding. He had taken over an Indonesian house on the outskirt hills of Dili and we could stay and be hosted by them. It was a very strange time. Dili itself looked like a cyclone had flattened it out. People were living in rubble. The UN and other NGOs had a luxury cruise ship docked on the harbour jetty where they lived and worked from. On the mainland, electricity and gas mostly didn't work. One night at our host's house I could hear movement in the shadows of the candlelight. Suddenly red glows and puffs of smoke emerged. More

16: Branches Prepared For Fruitfulness

importantly, there were strangers behind these cigarettes. I could hear the quick panicking tones of our host's voices but didn't understand what they were staying. Later we found out it was family and staff of the Indonesian owners of the house. They had left some things behind and demanded them back. Our hosts got them quickly and the Indonesians left as silently as they came. Surely, this was too difficult a place to send young children!

Sixth, after lots of discussions we ended up advocating that the Immigration Department offer our Timorese friends permanent residency on the basis of their connections in Australia. Our Timorese friends needed to be offered a choice now. While Australian public sympathy was now fully with the Timorese as the atrocities of Indonesian occupation became well known and Australian troops were on the ground, we needed to move now from public noise to quiet diplomacy and process. By 2007, 10 years after our first community meeting in Springvale, all 1650 Timorese had the chance to stay in Australia. Liberation was now possible on all fronts.

While many Timorese went on to have families in Australia, some also returned to Timor and helped in the rebuilding of the new nation. Our original UNOH interns who helped start this organising process grew too. This included Jon Owen who ended up starting UNOH in Western Sydney. After 20 years with UNOH, Jon went on to lead the Wayside Chapel in Kings Cross, Sydney and become a well-known public Christian voice in the media. His decade with the Timorese shaped and readied him for these roles. One of my favourite memories is of him being interviewed by the media at a big Timorese protest rally. Although he was of Sri Lankan heritage, because he looked Timorese and could speak Tetum, they assumed he was Timorese. Jon didn't let them know any different and boldly proclaimed what the Timorese needed! I learnt so much too about power and change. It would connect me with all kinds of diverse coalitions and campaigns over the next decades in Bangkok and Birmingham. Not least was the campaigning for the restoration of Black Patch Park that also led to a new high school and new housing in Winson Green.

There are many connections and overlaps between ABCD and Community Animating. Both, for example, focus on grassroots connections and development as a source of power for change. It is true too that community animating can lead to community development and vice versa. Dave Mann, for example, did a lot of the winning over of local leaders and connecting with policymakers in his first 10 years in Royal Docks in classic community animating style. This groundwork created healthier new community organisations like new schools, local church, housing, and a community association. Then as Helen Fernandes took over from Dave to lead the church and charity, she had the space and local resources to better discover, connect, and mobilise local residents and develop an even deeper sense of community. This stronger community building in turn has created local power to better campaign so that 'nothing happens here without us.' Rather than competing approaches, ABCD and community organising complemented and helped each other. The deep transformations that Royal Docks are seeing wouldn't be happening if only a horizontal approach of connecting the community or only an upward approach of animating against oppression was taken.

We have found that it has been more difficult for Change Makers to develop local campaigns than the two other approaches we explore here. Going 'upstream' and 'pushing back' external forces is important to consider even if the approach they ended up taking didn't take the explicit form of a campaign. However, we have seen some attempts with Change Makers like Stacey Cordery designing campaigns to prevent domestic abuse in relationships. She worked with young people in her neighbourhood in Bonny Downs to help school-aged children be better prepared for relationships. A survivor of an abusive relationship herself, she felt if she could just go 'upstream' engaging early teens with themes about respect and expectations in relationships, she could prevent what she went through. Hundreds of local school-aged children participated in the school with this campaign.[134]

Where injustice and poverty are complex, *how* leaders bring people together to campaign matters. Growing capacities to shift the balance of power in favour of our local communities is a crucial approach to learn if change is to come from the inside out. If these branches can flourish, then great fruit can be grown!

Branch 3: Community Entrepreneurs

Community Entrepreneurs: With the State increasingly withdrawing resources from local communities and the Global Markets becoming more volatile, leaders generate local resources, jobs, and opportunities together. These roles can be informed by 'enterprise development' approaches.

As well as community connecting and community animating, another crucial branch that helps prepare communities for Shalom is enterprise development. If community entrepreneurship was a branch, I don't imagine it would be very straight! I think it would wiggle, wind, and adapt to find light to create energies and resources to bear fruit from the tree. It would find the cracks and gaps to light in even the darkest or dampest environments. The traditional sources of financial resources for our local communities are Governments, businesses, and philanthropists, and unfortunately, each of these have their problems right now. Many local communities become wastelands because resources from these areas are blocked or siphoned off. Community entrepreneurs can find a way! Where resources come from matters, as these sources help to define what fruit is possible. What, then, are the problems with these traditional local community funding sources?

Firstly, Governments around the world are looking to cut taxes and therefore spending wherever they can. This has been exacerbated by Covid spending, interest rates, debt, and deficits. The capacity-building ideas that local communities know they need will therefore often be overlooked by Governments. Our elected representatives are needed to stand up for the most vulnerable people, but local communities can rarely rely on them for what matters to them. Perversely, this is especially the case if local communities stand against the State in campaigning.

Secondly, business corporations primarily seek to benefit their owners with profits. No profits, no business. While there may be roles for corporations to play in local communities, they are not primarily loyal to local flourishing if there is no benefit to them. Can business be trusted if the profit they expected doesn't eventuate? This is especially the case if the corporation can't make money from the local community.

Thirdly, philanthropic trusts mostly fund not-for-profits with grants. They too have their own agenda, often these are about funding to meet a particular need they feel strongly about fixing. No problem, no fixing, no funding. If ABCD says 'focus on what is strong' and community organising says 'give us our rights,' then as well meaning as these grant funders might be, they cannot be relied upon by local communities because outside agendas and people can quickly move on. Sometimes without much notice. Indeed, few philanthropic funding cycles are long enough, most just a few years, to evaluate real change, especially if the process required is generational in nature.

Under some conditions all three outside sources can and should make contributions to the life of local communities. However, they cannot be relied upon long term, especially if local people want change from the status quo. Indeed, some have a vested interest in keeping problems they can solve so their aims are profitable for them. For example, we can see that in the proliferation of gambling industry shops in so many of our local communities. Therefore, the more local communities can generate their own resources, the less dependent they can be. The less dependent they are, the freer they are to choose their own destiny.

We have found that 'social enterprise' and 'Business as Mission' approaches can help resource local growth and change. They often begin and go on to seek to benefit local communities because of where their streams of income come from. They can also find markets beyond our local communities and the gifts of neighbours can be shared with the wider world. This approach is defined by having both a social mission and surpluses used to resource social good, as well as not being primarily funded by the State or donations. This does not mean surpluses can't be used for staff salaries or invested back into building the capacity of the business, but it does mean that any owners do not get dividends or profits.

A social or community enterprise is a business that is driven by a social or environmental mission. It seeks to create positive change in the world while also generating financial returns, often through the sale of goods or services. Social enterprises are innovative and driven by a strong sense of purpose.

16: Branches Prepared For Fruitfulness

They are not content to simply make a profit – they want to make a difference. They use their business model as a means to address pressing social or environmental issues and to create positive change in the world.

One of the things that makes social enterprises so inspiring is their commitment to creating a better world. They see the challenges facing society and are determined to do something about them. Whether it is addressing issues such as poverty, health, inequality, unemployment, or climate change, social enterprises are driven by a deep sense of purpose and a desire to create a better future for all.

In addition to their social impact, social enterprises can also be innovative and forward-thinking. They are constantly seeking out new and better ways to do things, and they are not afraid to take risks to achieve their goals. An important element here is that these are real businesses, generating incomes that have an impact on their staff, customers, and sphere of their industry.

There is also a distinctly Christian version of enterprise known as Business as Mission (BAM). BAM is a way to combine the practical and spiritual aspects of life, by using the skills and resources that God has given us to serve others and share the love of Jesus Christ in the world.

The biblical basis for BAM can be found in several passages in the New Testament, including Matthew 28:19-20, which states that Christians are called to go out into the world and make disciples of all nations. This 'world' includes the economic world as much as culture, politics and religion. Similarly, Colossians 3:23-24 states that whatever we do, whether it be working, or serving, we should do it as though we are doing it for the Lord and not for just for people. This passage encourages Christians to bring their faith into all aspects of their lives, including their work.

BAM advocates believe that by using their businesses to serve others and share the love of Christ, they can make a difference in the world and fulfil their calling as Christians. Many BAM enterprises focus on serving underprivileged communities and providing jobs and economic development opportunities in these areas.

BAMs can be different to social enterprises in that they are often private companies with profits going to owners. Surpluses don't have to be used for the enterprise's social purpose. BAMs don't have to be not-for-profits in the way a social enterprise is primarily designed to generate community resources. What BAMs do have is a distinctly Christian identity, which is not always the case for social enterprises.

Mostly our approach has been more 'social enterprise' than BAM. This is because many of the stakeholders in our enterprises did not start out as Christians, and we wanted these community residents with the gifts for roles to be stakeholders in the enterprise. Many of our social enterprises have had Christians involved and most had partnerships with churches and mission, but that was not what defined them. God's compassion and Shalom was still often experienced, but the enterprise had a local identity as fellow neighbours joined to gather for social good and resourcing.

Paul the apostle was also a missional social entrepreneur, and his BAM approach can be considered an important model. He was a tent maker which "could have meant anything from saddle maker to one who works with goat haircloth."[135] In the first century Roman Empire this would mean being part of a local trade association. This trade not only contributed to the common good, but gave him a local identity and resources to establish local churches pro-bono in four provinces of the Roman Empire (Galatia, Macedonia, Achaia, and Asia) in a 14-year period (A.D. 48–62). While Paul was not against local people giving financially to church leaders, his churches did not provide his livelihood. In a brilliant book on BAM, Mark Russell makes the case that:

> Paul clearly had reasons for why he chose to continue his tentmaking trade. Those reasons are far more sophisticated than a simple need for money. His approach helped him model a lifestyle to his followers that they could emulate, put him in relationship with a vast web of people, and helped him to show everyone that the Christian faith is a way of life and not simply a set of beliefs.[136]

16: Branches Prepared For Fruitfulness

At the heart of this approach was the freedom Paul's enterprise created for him and others. Russell explains:

> Paul wanted to preach the gospel for free, and he wanted to be free to follow God without being controlled by others. The issue of freedom was very important to Paul. He sought personal freedom in paradoxical ways. He gave up his rights to payment to work a physically arduous trade in order to retain the freedom to preach the gospel without external control and free of charge.[137]

Shalom cannot be experienced without liberation. Oppression is simply anti-Shalom. How local communities go about seeking Shalom matters. Uninformed and controlling benefactors, committees, or denominations holding tight the resources can kill compassionated, innovative work (and workers). What the apostle Paul created with his enterprise then is something Change Makers need today: freedom to pursue their unique callings without outsider, institutional control. This empowerment doesn't mean no accountability, that can be built into enterprises, but it does mean high levels of responsibility. Freedom and empowerment need to come with responsibility. Unfortunately, too often Change Makers get all the responsibility for a project and no power and freedom to find the right way to approach it.

Today there is a resurgence in social enterprises. In the UK, for example, there are over 100,000 such enterprises, creating 2 million jobs and generating over £60 billion to UK GDP. This alternative to State, donor, and private sector dependence is creating serious waves.[138]

Social entrepreneurial approaches then can be a powerful force for good in the world, including our local communities. They are driven by a strong sense of purpose, a commitment to creating positive change, and can generate much-needed resources. They can inspire us all to think differently about the role of business in society and to strive for a better future for all. We cut our teeth in social enterprise at Klong Toey Handicrafts in Bangkok. Anji says she started this the wrong way around from most businesses. She started with the potential customers and their needs.

Anji had met and had access to a large network of women who were Christians, in AUS, US, and UK, as well as expats in Bangkok, who wanted more meaningful lives. What contributions could our neighbours, especially those stuck in prostitution, make to these women's lives to make them more meaningful? We knew so many of our local women had skills in crafts and beads. Anji made an initial attempt with our neighbour Bla, who was a walking miracle and like family to us, even being in the birthing unit for Aiden's birth. Trafficked herself, and saving her family from destitution through prostitution, Bla began making necklaces similar to ones Anji saw in Bangkok's plush department stores. I tried to sell these at the back of a church after I preached, and all the profit would go back to Bla and her family. The pilot worked so well that more organised attempts were made, and business grew. It became known as 'Klong Toey Handicrafts.'[139]

Over the years Anji's model for Klong Toey Handicrafts was to keep these handicrafts affordable as meaningful gifts for low-income families. The local women would make twice the minimum wage per hour and be able to work flexibly from home, able to keep looking after their children, and therefore have a genuine alternative to prostitution. A network of volunteers in AUS, UK, US, and Bangkok emerged who would be given a variety box of handicrafts to sell to their networks including schools, markets, women's groups, and churches. They would return the money made as well as whatever handicrafts weren't sold. There was no risk to volunteers. This generated incomes for those in Klong Toey, funded the development of new products, and helped find out what customers liked and didn't like. The handicrafts range grew and shrunk in variety as trends emerged, but as hardly any item sold for over A$15, Klong Toey Handicrafts grew to become known for beautiful, meaningful gifts for thousands of women around the world and connected them with the plight of women in urban poverty in Bangkok. At its peak over A$300,000 of sales were made and 80 local women were employed by Klong Toey Handicrafts. There was even a shop and warehouse in Melbourne, where our volunteer coordinator, Liz, managed sales and distribution. Over the years, Klong Toey Handicrafts morphed and moved.

16: Branches Prepared For Fruitfulness

Today, it's called Roy Rak (Thai for 'Love Beads') and continues to bring income and meaning for all involved. Bla is still involved and it's a joy to meet up with her and feel the pride she has in helping so many women locally and around the world over the last two decades.

In Cape Town, South Africa, a young community entrepreneur named Allan van der Meulen changes the destiny of thousands with his app Zlto.[140] Zlto is, "a platform that uses blockchain technology to increase engagement amongst youth, track positive behaviour via live dashboards and encourage certain behaviour through our innovative rewards systems. The rewards can be redeemed across 3000 stores." At the time of writing this app engages over 200,000 members seeking rewards, has tracked over 2.5 million hours of voluntary work, and benefited over 3 million people in over 3 million transactions. Anji met Allan on a visit there in 2015 and saw the potential to reward positive acts and help those who are cash poor. This included newly arrived asylum seekers and refugees. We invited Allan back to Winson Green to help us pilot Zlto in our community. We saw the talent of local women for cooking and Anji started 'Flavours of Winson Green' with them for cooking and catering. With some of the young people and local shop owners Zlto was set. Rewards points were offered to those who helped Flavours of Winson Green, and these points could be redeemed in local shops. For some asylum seekers this was a lifeline. For others, an encouragement to get out of the house and meet others. Allan has continued to support Seedbeds and has lectured for us in our MA units with Nazarene Theological College as well as in Myanmar with our Change Incubator programmes.

In the UK, Jonny Adams lives and works in Bonny Downs and was in of our first cohort of Change Makers. He had been working with local homeless men with NEWway charity, but saw the need for more meaningful things for them to do with their time than just survive in the night shelter. He also saw lots of local neighbours who were struggling with their gardens. He made the connections and went to work developing a business plan, and his own gardening skills developed through work with the local guys who would join. He pitched his idea to the Change Makers resource panel at the end of the programme and found a contact there for a grant fund to get him started.

Today, 'NEWLife' is a brilliant social enterprise employing men who have been homeless to tend the gardens of many in Newham, East London.[141]

We loved having Jonny and the team come up to Winson Green, showing some of our local guys how to transform the side area of Lodge Road Church. It had been overrun with weeds and construction waste, but became a beautiful courtyard complete with vegetable garden. As Jonny helped this happen, a real sense of Shalom sprung up in the most unexpected places. Not just in the lives, homes, and gardens of his neighbourhood, but in the lives of the men who used to live on the streets and further afield.

Bicycle social enterprises are now key features of local life in Winson Green and Firs and Bromford. Stewart Boyle grew up in Firs and Bromford and connected with Tim and others at Worth Unlimited. He became a staff member and started a social enterprise selling and repairing bicycles. He was nominated into the Change Makers programme and his pitch was to expand it further to include education and mentoring young people in cycling. A Gear Up bicycle club operates now with weekly rides, and lessons on how to ride and access bikes are offered.[142]

We saw what Stewart and his team were doing and looked for a way to replicate it in Winson Green. A local housing group was disbanded and had within it a unit for bicycle repairs and education led by Steve. Steve wanted to continue but needed a new organisation to host and somewhere to base his workshop and the donated bikes. We had just taken over Lodge Road Church and had plenty of space. Initially 'New Routes' came under our Newbigin Community Trust, but soon grew to become its own Community Interest Company.[143] They have fixed and given away hundreds of bikes as well as teaching how to maintain and ride bikes. They help other communities too and go on the road as 'Dr Bikes.' We know many residents have bikes in their shed but can't afford or don't know how to fix them and get them back on the road. I have personally benefited too and love my Thursday afternoon group rides on the canal with a bike they restored for me. This outing helps my mental health like few other activities. These two bike enterprises add significant value to our communities. Yes, they now employ local staff, but they also help our local community get more mobile, fitter, healthier, and help reduce the need for motor vehicles on the road. Shalom is on its way!

Perhaps Seedbeds' most explicit use of this approach has been in Myanmar piloting our 'Change Incubator' with Civil Disobedience Movement participants post-Coup. We have helped hundreds of small enterprises get seed funding and generate an income they could no longer find in their mostly government jobs. We use Osterwalder's Business Model Canvas with its nine building blocks for enterprises: customer segments, value propositions, channels, customer relationships, revenue streams, key resources, key activities, key partnerships, and cost structure. We then have live case studies from entrepreneurs around the world for each of these nine areas. We do most of this online with Google Classroom and Zoom with some participants in the jungle or refugee camps. We also offer a kind of in-person boot camp intensive to bring this together for those who can in a secret location. These have been remarkable times together. The pitches to panel are often remarkable. From restaurants to mushroom farms, to dried meals to drones, local entrepreneurs are doing good and generating much needed funds. The connections with comrades and encouragement from the outside world is liberating. One participant gave this feedback: 'When the coup happened it was like my life ended. After this Seedbeds programme and my enterprise started, it's like I am alive again.'[144]

In many ways the idea of 'pioneering ministry and mission' can be considered a kind of community entrepreneurship. In 2021, Seedbeds joined forces with Church Mission Society, United Reformed Church, and Congregational Federations to form 'Newbigin Pioneering Hub.' I know Missiology can sometimes be clouded by the dark spectre of colonisation. Missionaries have often been used as tools of the Empire and that's the last thing local communities need right now. In more recent years, the idea of 'Pioneering Ministry' has begun to be explored by church and denominational leaders as an alternative to 'Missionary.' I went to work to define what we could mean by this term. To connect with the calling, challenge, ministry, and hope of pioneering can help offer some basic premises and my preliminary definitions.

Could a pioneering ministry be describing your heartbeat too?

Calling: 'A God-given sense of responsibility…'

God is the initiator of pioneering. It's often a mystical experience to connect with God choosing us for a particular part of God's mission. We just can't let it go. This call keeps finding us. Like Isaiah we can only respond 'Here I am Lord, send me' even if all that will be left is a small shoot from a blackened stump (Isaiah 6). Bonhoeffer, the great German theologian and Nazi resistor put it this way: "action comes, not from thought, but from a readiness for responsibility."[145] In so many ways this is at the heart of all good leadership. Brene Brown says, "A leader is anyone who takes responsibility for finding the potential in people and processes, and who has the courage to develop that potential."[146] My own callings to pioneer over the last 30 years were more detected than invented too. In so many ways Springvale, Melbourne (1990-2002), Klong Toey, Bangkok (2002-2014), and now Winson Green, Birmingham (2014-current) were places that chose us more than us choosing them. We begin to love these local communities, see potential and, deep within, want them to thrive. Though it may look different, a deep sense of God given responsibility for people and place is life giving.

Challenge: '…to cross barriers…'

Pioneers experience real obstacles to see their callings realised. The willingness to take initiative and cross cultural, relational, class, and/or geographical barriers are a hallmark of pioneering. God did not just zap us from a distance, but "The Word became flesh and blood and moved into the neighbourhood" (John 1:18 [MSG]). Pioneers often need to take community 'context' seriously as the connections between culture, theology, and methods need to be explored if local people are to have authentic encounters and follow Jesus together in ways that are most natural to them within their community. Who is missing out on encountering and following Jesus together today? The rapid decline of UK church involvement, for example, especially in Urban Priority Areas, raises many questions that require us to connect in new ways. Should working classes, for example, have to become middle class in style and culture to meet Jesus and 'fit in' to the life of congregations? Pioneers say 'no'! 'We don't have a compassion problem' says Shane Claiborne, 'as much as a proximity problem.'

16: Branches Prepared For Fruitfulness

What barriers can we overcome to help local communities be authentically themselves and experience Christian faith together? How can local churches be both relevant and faithful?

Ministry: '…creating new opportunities with local communities…'

Pioneers see differently. They see potential, ready to be released in new ways. Local communities don't need things done to them. Pioneering today is working 'with' local people, joining in with God's work there. 'The Great Commission' in John's Gospel is simply: 'Shalom be with you. As the Father sent me. So I am sending you' (John 20:21). This speaks of entering into the suffering of local people as Jesus did with humans and seeking wellbeing from the inside out. Lao Tzu in 6th century BC put it this way:

> Go to the people.
> Live with them,
> Learn from them,
> Love them.
> Start with what they know,
> Build with what they have.
> But with the best leaders,
> The work done, the task accomplished,
> The people will say,
> 'We've done it ourselves.'[147]

At the heart of the Newbigin Pioneering Hub is to recognise and resource pioneers in their calling as catalytic Christian ministers. We aim to discover, nurture, empower, and release a new generation of Pioneers. This will include helping Pioneers connect with new mission contexts, pathways, retreats, and coaching. We believe we can go further and deeper in our calling as Pioneers if we connect together well. We will form this 'Community of Pioneers' out of those who currently identify as Pioneers as well as those coming through the 'Certificate in Pioneer Mission' we will offer based in Winson Green started in September 2021.[148]

Hope: '...to see flourishing in God's love and Shalom.'

The purpose of pioneering isn't just to get more people attending church services. It's no less than helping realise the promises of God on earth as in heaven, as Jesus prayed. We can anticipate now the promises of new heavens and new earth in our local places which includes all our life together (Isaiah 65). This promised 'Shalom' happens when God, people, and place lives in harmony together. This purpose is what Jesus began and is now the core work of the local church. As Lesslie Newbigin says, the aim of the local church is: "To be a sign, instrument and foretaste of God's coming reign in the place for which it is responsible." We long for every local community to flourish in God's love and Shalom but know so many neighbourhoods are missing out right now. I believe this new venture, and this book, can unearth a new generation of pioneers, ready to be planted personally in local places and able to grow people into new communities of hope, faith, and compassion wherever Jesus has called them to serve. We have hard-won insights from experienced Pioneers that can help form, guide, and inspire a new generation of Pioneers from here.

Our Newbigin Pioneering Hub pilot year started in September 2022 and the first cohort pitched their ideas for pioneering in July 2023. We had 16 graduates from over 10 local communities, but it is early days. We are now recruiting for our second Cohort of 'Newbigin Pioneers.' The highlight of the first cohort was definitely the final pitch to panel. We have used this method of focussing entrepreneurial energy in most of our Seedbeds programmes. Preparing panelists is a key and we can improve on this area. Being an experienced resource panelist can be one of the most satisfying gifts possible. As a panelist you meet people who have prepared and shaped their idea in a local community and a learning cohort, hear their heartbeat and offer what you can.

Here is an example outline of how we do 'pitches to panels.'

1. A Seedbeds trainer compères each session, and each panelist will give a quick introduction about themselves at the start of the session. There will be an interpreter where needed. We aim to have four to five participants pitch in an hour session. We want panelists to stay at least one full-hour session. Of course, they can be in as many sessions as they like!

16: Branches Prepared For Fruitfulness

2. Each participant will have five minutes to pitch their idea for change. In Pioneers these are mostly creating new opportunities with the local community to experience God's love and Shalom. In Change Incubator these will mostly be enterprises that help improve the lives of specific customers and help generate income for their family/community. In Change Makers these are mostly local community projects, but can sometimes be campaigns or social enterprises.

3. There will be five minutes for responses by the panel. This can include offering:

- Constructive feedback
- Cash grants
- Connections to help
- Coaching to offer next stages.

4. The panelist responses are recorded and a full list of participants and their projects (including needs and how to contact them) are circulated by email over the next week. It's not a problem if the panelist doesn't offer anything in the panel time itself. They will be able to connect up with any participant they want and offer after the event. Of course, it is more exciting if panelists offer something in the moment, even if it's something seemingly small to us!

5. Panelists mostly give constructive feedback on Zoom or in person, but if they do offer cash, connections, or coaching we require them to follow through! This can be done through Seedbeds or by direct contact with participants. We want any offers at least started within a few weeks.

One of the Pioneer graduates, Matt Birt, achieved a successful outcome from his pitch, 'Open Table.' Matt is a part of our Lodge Road Community Church and is a staff member with Newbigin Community Trust. He noticed how local people coming into the centre struggled to open up about mental health and other difficulties they were experiencing, especially in a strange place with unfamiliar people.

As a mental health first aider, Matt decided to use a corner of the church's community space to develop a safe area for people to talk, placing newspapers and a community computer there to aid conversations about the news or sport which helps people, especially men, to relax and share honestly. In his pitch, Matt talked about the funds needed to train another mental health first aider to support his work when he is not available, as well as extend partnerships with addiction services, adult social care, and the church's own advocacy services to help with any referrals. He asked for a financial donation of £300 towards the books and training required for a two-day Mental Health First Aid England accredited course. His pitch was successful, and he was awarded £500 towards the training support requested.

What do these examples of community entrepreneurship have in common? They certainly have an ABCD flavour to them as local gifts have been discovered, connected, and mobilised for the common good. They generated jobs, resources, and met customer needs, which creates local power and freedom, which community animators would appreciate. They all found partnerships to do what they couldn't do for themselves and accessed channels to get their product or services to their target customers. They had a business model that mostly generated more funds than expenses, though investment in the form of grants and donations was still needed to get started. Some enterprises needed donations as one of their streams of income. What most inspires me about these enterprises is the dignity they create. These entrepreneurs are in places others call wastelands, but here they are defying the odds and making beautiful change for themselves and others.

We need more local community entrepreneurs and know more can do it too. With the State increasingly withdrawing resources from local communities and the global markets becoming more volatile, how leaders generate local resources, jobs, and opportunities matters.

Shalom can be possible from within even our most troubled wasteland communities, but we need new kinds of local leadership qualities, approaches and roles if this is to happen. More of the same will not do. The roots and branches outlined in this part of the book do not exhaust the possibilities for growing local community sustainability and flourishing. They are however the qualities and approaches we have found most crucial in our Seedbeds story to date, and we are seeing local community leaders finding life, energy, and vitality in their local places. The potential of local leaders to see Shalom emerge from the inside out will be enhanced if these roots and branches are learnt, experimented with, adopted, and multiplied.

Personal Reflections

1. Of the three branches (approaches/roles) of local leaders proposed in this chapter, which have you most and least connected with? Why?

2. Community connecting can be a critical role to inform and inspire local leadership. Where have you seen this present or absent in your local community? What difference has it made?

3. Community animating can be a critical role able to inform and inspire local leadership. Where have you seen this present or absent in your local community? What difference has it made?

4. Community entrepreneurship can be a critical role to inform and inspire local leadership. Where have you seen this present or absent in your local community? What difference has it made?

5. Which of these roles and approaches can you grow in next? How?

Part D. Practices To Try

This part of the book has considered three essential local leadership qualities and three particular approaches that can generate root systems able to feed and sustain change from within local communities. You might want to pause and follow up some of the weblinks to find out more about the programmes we have developed, and listen to the testimonials of some of our alumni. There are links in the notes at the end of the book. Aside from this, are there practices that can help you explore and develop these in your community?

Here are two suggestions:

Generosity Dinners

Hospitality can bring our Tree of Life C.I.R.C.L.E together. Regularly bringing people together in an intentional way throughout the year to connect, discover talents, and share resources can build liberating experiences and set up qualities and approaches. No matter the season, hospitality can remind us of the fruit to come.

There are specific models of hospitality that can help. We have been blessed too with two of the best practitioners of Generosity Dinners here at Newbigin House. Common Change's founder, Darren Peterson, and UK leader, Matt Wilson, led us through a process that continues to bear fruit.

One night in 2017 Matt Wilson led us through a Generosity Dinner at Newbigin House. Matt is a man who wears many hats. I met him through his leadership of the urban mission 'Eden Network,' but he now leads social impact firm Goodlabs Consulting Limited and is an elected Councillor of North Tyneside as well as Chair of Trustees for Common Change.

The Generosity Dinner began with Matt meeting a member of our community, Mark. Mark had arrived quite agitated and flustered as he walked through the front door at Newbigin House. Originally from Manchester, Mark was an ex-prisoner in Winson Green prison, stayed in a boarding house, and struggled with his mental health. Mark desperately wanted to start again, but his past kept catching up with him. He joined about a dozen other neighbours around our dining table.

As people settled down, Matt Wilson explained the night:

> 'As you know, you've been invited tonight to join us for a meal and an experiment in collaborative giving. We'll share a meal, pool resources, and collectively explore different ways we can support and draw alongside people, projects or passions in our lives that could do with a little "awesome." Each of us has contributed a one-time donation into a group pot and as we eat together, we'll come up with ideas of how to share these resources with people that we know could use it.'

Mark was hungry and really looked forward to the meal. He'd given a few pounds to support the cause, but when Matt announced that 'we had over £500 in the pot to give away tonight' he suddenly sat up straight and took notice! Starting with abundance, rather than scarcity, changed things for him. Now he was engaged and excited with the process. When we start to share what we have between us, the seasons can change.

We also shared fun games as we ate our spaghetti bolognaise. Each person was asked what skills, passions, or resources they have that could be shared, but others might not know about. Suddenly gifts in music, art, fixing skills, lawn mowing, camping equipment to be shared emerged. The abundance was growing before our eyes.

Mark's imagination started to whirl too. What could I offer, who could we give to that I care about?

Matt then asked us to:

> 'share a story about someone that you care about that might benefit from the common funds that were pooled together tonight. It's not about a project as much as the people. Think about how much you might need to to do something too.'

One member shared about her work in childcare in the neighbourhood and how so many little children there had autism. The childcare centre was struggling financially to stay open, was pretty bare, and these kids were bouncing off the wall.

> 'If we had some money, could it help create a sensory play area? You know, lots of colourful scarfs and a parachute? I guess we'd need £100.'

Soon other needs flowed too. People we knew in circumstances that they couldn't address by themselves. Helping a single mum with bills that they were struggling to pay, cleaning up an overgrown garden of an elderly friend, some play equipment for Newbigin House's backyard to help all the kids who come here enjoy themselves more, and wreck our lounge room less! Some of these could be helped with the cash, but some with just a little effort.

Mark's mind still whirled as we told stories and brained-stormed even more options. Few of us had £500 to spend on good before! Eventually Mark spoke.

> 'You know, when I was inside I did my time. On day of release you go collect your personal things they've kept. Didn't have much – a phone, charger and few clothes –

but I really needed a bag to hold it all. They gave me a big, clear plastic bag that has 'HMP Birmingham' printed on the side. I needed to catch the local bus outside to sign-on at probation before going back to my room. I'd done my time, paid my dues, but everyone would know where I'd been. No would sit next me. It would be humiliating. Then a prison officer heard my groans and knew what I was thinking. He gave me a black carry-all bag before I was released. I called it my dignity bag. That's what I want to do. Set up a dignity bags ministry for the other guys getting out, so they can have a fresh start. I don't think it would cost much for bags and maybe some shampoo and other toiletries inside to get them started on the right track. Maybe we give the church's address too and invite them for our community dinners?'

We could all see the merit and value. How were we to choose from all these good ideas?

When everyone who wanted to share stories had shared, Matt brought us back to order. We would vote! Each of us had ten points and we could share them across the needs as we saw fit. Some gave all their ten points to one project. Others spread them around. Matt tallied them up.

Mark's idea was a clear winner, followed by the sensory play area. Both were given seed grants. Other needs could also be met by a few of us working together. Mark seemed to grow even taller.

'Dignity Bags' was piloted. It wasn't easy to get the right bags into the right hands, but Mark found a way. Mark was also nominated for the Change Makers programme, so he developed and pitched this idea to the resource panel. His local church took up the ministry, helped fund it further, and now hundreds of Dignity Bags have been given away to men as they leave HMP Birmingham.

Here are the recommended steps by Common Change to try this practice for yourself.

There are some things you'll need to decide before inviting guests:
- The Venue - whether it's a potluck, bring and share or a wine & cheese evening or coffee and desserts, people LOVE to gather around food. Find a venue that can accommodate your guests comfortably – this could be your home or a local coffee shop.
- The number of attendees - your Generosity Dinner can be as big or small as you like. Decide what's manageable. In order to facilitate healthy discussion and keep the process moving, we recommend 10-12 guests.
- Date and time
- Type of meal
- What should guests bring
- Are kids welcome to participate and how will you keep them engaged

Invite your guests:
Think of people in your life who have expressed an interest in collaborative giving, who are looking for creative ways to share their resources, or who you think would be open to experimenting with you. There are many ways to invite guests to a Generosity Dinner – call them up, ask them the next time you see them at the gym, drop them an email, or create a Facebook event.

Here's what you could put in an invitation:
> You are invited to join us for a meal and experiment in collaborative giving! We'll share a meal, pool resources, and collectively explore different ways we can support and draw alongside people, projects or passions in our lives that could do with a little "awesome."
>
> Each guest will contribute a one-time donation into a group pot and as we eat together, we'll come up with ideas of how to share these resources with people that we know could use it.
>
> When: Sunday April 26, 6:00pm
>
> What: Bring and Share Dinner. Please bring a dish to share.

> Where: [Insert Address]
>
> Donate: Click here to find out more about the [...] Community Generosity Dinners. Click Register and Donate and select [Insert Host Name] from the dropdown menu.[149]

There are variations of this meal. This is just one model, but it is tried and tested. The good folks at Common Change can also coach you through it.

G.R.O.W Coaching

> "Spoon feeding, in the long run, teaches us nothing but the shape of the spoon." – E.M.Forster
>
> "I've learned that people will forget what you said, people will forget what you did, but people will never forget how you made them feel." – Maya Angelou

Local community leaders need to discover their own approaches to change and transformation inspired by the roots and branches just outlined. We have found the practice of coaching to be invaluable for these kinds of integrations. It's more an artform than science, however, and needs a flexible, but consistent practice.

There are many models of coaching, but we have found the G.R.O.W. model is simple, reproducible, and can help our programme aims. G.R.O.W stands for: Goal? Reality? Option? Will do? These four questions can provide clear and practical steps that can frame a session.

Coaching can mean different things to different people, but we have found this particular model helps explore the six C.I.R.C.L.E. ideas together. The 'G.R.O.W Coaching Model' helps provide enough flexibility to start with where local leaders are at, but also adapt and move forward, one step at a time. It is a process that helps raise awareness, but also action.

Part D. Practices To Try

For our Seedbeds programmes we have noticed that local participants have three main requirements for our coaching sessions if they are to pitch an initiative to a resource panel. These are:

A. Momentum for Praxis Cycles

Participants can grow into praxis cycles through our coaching. Paulo Freire describes praxis as "reflection and action upon the world in order to transform it." Our actual coaching sessions are mostly on the reflective side (evaluation, thinking, planning, praying), but we want participants to identify 'next steps' to do outside the session (observation, input, study, action) that can then be reflected upon again in our next coaching session, that then requires further actions and so on. If this praxis cycle can gain momentum and go deeper each time, then the participant can grow in being a transformative agent in their community. The four-step G.R.O.W process helps this cycle move forward and not get stuck.

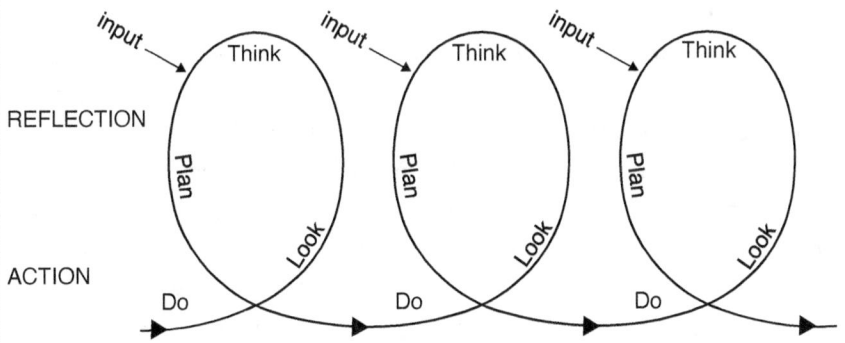

B. Informal and Relational, but Focused

Participants will present a pitch to a resource panel at the end of this coaching cycle. This is the formal goal to focus on, but we want this to be an excuse to be in solidarity together. Many participants will have had negative experiences with formal education and so these coaching sessions need to more relational and informal, an opportunity to connect and enjoy the journey together toward a practical end.

The four-step G.R.O.W model is followed by the coaches, but without notes, and with discussions allowed to wander. Notes can be taken at the end or after the session, especially 'Will do' next steps so the actions can be reflected upon next session.

C. Making the Most of a Coaching Hour Together

We know both participants and coaches have limited time so making the one-hour session as meaningful and practical as possible is important. The session together can be done in-person, while walking, or even online, but needs to be as free as possible of distractions. Trusting the G.R.O.W. process to help the participant is important, so the Coach keeps returning to each of the steps.

The Four Questions of the G.R.O.W model of coaching have consistently helped participants to evaluate, plan, and act for their initiative. These are the four questions:

Goals?

'What are your goals?' Each participant needs to identify and own their goals and concerns that they come to our programme with. Overall a key outcome they will know is that in most of our programmes they need to pitch a meaningful project to a resource panel. However, as sessions progress, each coaching session will have mini-Goals identified from the end of the previous coaching session (the 'Will do' step). I often ask at the start about the goal for our session together, 'what would be a good outcome from this hour or so together?' Clarifying goals at the beginning of each session is an important first step so both participant and coach are on the same page. This first step shapes and focusses the session.

Reality?

'Where are you at in reaching these goals?' Evaluation can come in many forms and if the coach keeps asking 'why' this reality is happening (or not!) the session can quickly go to deeper, even to political and systemic places. The key here is to keep evaluating and moving forward with actions even if plans don't quite work out at first.

We often learn more from our failures than what works. Max de Pree once said, "The first responsibility of a leader is to define reality. The last is to say thank you. In between, the leader is a servant." This step aims to help the participant name their reality and what is really happening.

Options?

'What <u>could</u> you do next that would help move you towards your goals?' We like participants to brainstorm what options they could do next. This can include more understanding (what resources could they learn from?), observations (what do they need to see next?) and actions (what could be tried next?). While it's important that the participant generates their own options, the coach can offer some suggestions too. Free and unhindered thinking about 'options' doesn't mean they will do all these. This step is about the participant working out what could be possible and beneficial.

Will do?

'What <u>will</u> you do before our next session?' This question is about discerning the 'one next thing' to do that can make the most significant difference toward the identified goals. The benefits of the process of prioritising a single key task have been explored by Gary Keller in *The One Thing: The Surprisingly Simple Truth Behind Extraordinary Results*. Identifying the most significant task with a singular focus can help move any project forward. Confirming the date/time/place of the next coaching session and what one to three next actions steps they 'Will do' is crucial. Write these down in your calendar and remind the participant too in a few weeks before the session if you like. This step is about moving forward toward the participant's goal.

Most of our Seedbeds programmes have a final presentation or pitch to a panel. What we want participants to have by then is something that really expresses who they are and what is possible and needed. Coaching helps us get there.

Group Discussion Questions:

1. Who could you join with to explore one or more of the three qualities/roots? Where have you seen compassion, innovation, or resilience build local sustainability? What did it look like when these were present? When were these in limited supply?

2. Which of the three approaches/branches do you most resonate with? Of community connecting, animating, and entrepreneurship, which have you least and most experienced? Who could you join with to attempt to further one of these approaches?

3. Mentoring and coaching are art forms. What have been your experiences of them? What helped and what hindered your growth? Who could you work through this G.R.O.W model of coaching with?

Part E.

Grow In Seasons (Not Against Them)

This final block of chapters explores how four traditional Celtic seasons can inform the timings and priorities of local community change efforts.

Chapter 17:
The Celtic Season of Samhain - Winters Of Our Discontent And Discovery

How many lessons of faith and beauty we should lose, if there were no winter in our year!
– Thomas Wentworth Higginson

That's what winter is: an exercise in remembering how to still yourself then how to come pliantly back to life again.
– Ali Smith

There are limits to what we can do at different times in our personal and communal lives. As we have explored so far, it's important to detect and identify our longer-term hopes and be consistent in our daily practices, nurture the right qualities and approaches. However, if we don't also appreciate which exact season we are in, then we can work against the flow and quickly exhaust ourselves. "There is a time for everything, and a season for every activity under the heavens" (Eccles. 3:1).

In Australia, not knowing the riptides at a surf beach can kill you. It happens every year, including recently in January 2022 at Gunnamatta surf beach in Victoria. A teenager drowned when he was simply swimming with a friend and the rip took him out to sea.

Rips look benign. They are flowing waters that have less waves as there is a deeper channel below the surface that lets the incoming water rush quickly back out to sea. These channels can look much easier to swim in than the bigger waves pounding into shore nearby. However, these are where riptides can take a swimmer out to sea in a few moments. Just trying harder to swim against the rip will exhaust and eventually drown even a good swimmer.

Rips can be useful. If you know what you are doing, there are times to rest in the current and be dragged where you want to be. Experienced surfers, for example, can use the rip to their advantage. By paddling into its fast-flowing stream they then quickly move across to the side of the flow, not against it. If they do that, they'll get 'out the back' before they know it, ready and waiting to ride the next wave into shore, then do it all again. It's much easier to be ready to ride the waves with this rip-flow, than to be pounded by the larger waves you're trying to get out front on. The trick is to know the waters and flows and to make the most of them, not try to fight them.

This can be true for our callings too. If we don't realise the direction of the flow of seasons it can be fatal. We can exhaust ourselves trying to swim against it. Different seasons and flows require different efforts. If you know the flow, and move the right way, we can reach our potential together.

Seasons of life in community and our own calling are similar too. Identifying where we are in our seasons can help us find the right rhythms, the right methods, at the right time, and to grow to where we need to be. How we adapt to the seasons of life will shape and sustain us. Parker Palmer wrote a chapter in his remarkable book, *Let your life speak*, on the importance of this metaphor as opposed to the industrial manufacturing ones we so often use to 'make,' 'build,' or 'develop' our lives.

> Seasons is a wise metaphor for the movement of life, I think. It suggests that life is neither a battlefield nor a game of chance but something infinitely richer, more promising, more real. The notion that our lives are like the eternal cycle of the seasons does not deny the struggle or the joy, the loss or the

17: Samhain - Winters Of Our Discontent And Discovery

gain, the darkness or the light, but encourages us to embrace it all - and to find in all of it opportunities for growth.[150]

Knowing the times and seasons has become an obsession for me. Not just personally, but also for the lifecycle of teams, projects and communities.

I was born and raised in Melbourne, Australia and we needed to be ready for almost any weather, at any time of the year, but the light was pretty constant. Placed in the southeast corner of Australia's mainland, Melbourne's weather can change in an instant. We could have burning hot North Westerly winds straight off the deserts with high 30 degrees, the dust and heat baking us, and then suddenly, there'd be a change of wind direction. A Southerly wind could blow in from Antarctica plunging the temperatures close to zero almost instantly. The band *Crowded House* famously wrote their song *Four Seasons in One Day* about Melbourne. We'd often tell our guests 'if you don't like the weather, just wait a minute!' Melbourne's weather rarely stayed the same for very long in any season. These seasonal influences could explain how innovative, resilient, and ready-for-anything Melbournians often become as a result.

In contrast, the light and weather could be quite consistent through all the seasons in Bangkok. We still needed to adapt in different ways, but placed near the equator, the daily light in Bangkok doesn't change very much over a year. Neither does the relentless heat. It's often said that Thailand has three seasons: 'The Cool Season when it's hot; The Wet Season when it's hot and wet; The Hot Season when it's bloody hot!' In Klong Toey, however, we were packed so tightly together and so close to the elements, that even a few degrees of temperature change or a little more rain than expected could cause chaos. For example, we were so used to steaming hot temperatures night and day, that even getting below 30 degrees would suddenly bring out a scramble for coats and scarves at the local market! Tropical rainstorms could instantly flood local roads, jamming traffic into gridlock for hours at a time. Some neighbours just wouldn't go out of Klong Toey if it rained. Most knew how to conserve energy and knew when was the right time to set out on a journey or rest or work. This does shape the character of Bangkok people too. No matter the challenge, Bangkok people get things done, but just at the right time!

Birmingham's quite distinct seasons were a real surprise. It was more the light than the temperature that threw me off balance. I expected rain, but in summer it can be light for 16 hours a day and twilight after that. I found it hard to sleep while it was still light at 11pm and light again at 5am. Deep into winter it can be dark for up to 15 hours a day and you leave for work and come home again in darkness. In autumn and spring too the light seems to suddenly turn. Birmingham has four quite distinct seasons. In the long dark winter days it can snow and cover the landscape in a powder of white, making even the dirtiest streetscapes look like Narnia. In the long, light summer days it can get into the 30s and we can still be wandering around outside at 11pm without any need of electrical light. The flamboyance of spring with flowers bursting into life and autumn's dropping of multi-coloured leaves helps signal light's transitions. On the edge of Europe, in the geographic middle of England, Birmingham is not far away from anyone. Forty million people live within a two-hour drive of our home in Winson Green. To find the rhythm and flow of when things can happen and why, took me some time. Of course, like most Westerners, I can try to ignore the seasons and carry on regardless. Our technologies do their best to compensate and overcome what goes on outside. The 'spirit of the blitz,' when Birmingham was bombed and nearly destroyed by Nazi bombers, lives on with a kind of 'keep calm and carry on' attitude prevailing. No matter how light or dark, hot or cold, Brummies just seem to keep on going regardless!

There are however, some deeper, more spiritual rhythms here in Birmingham too. Over 1700 years of Christian tradition here has integrated itself with even more ancient, indigenous traditions. I found that if I could join in with this rhythm, recognise the seasons, then life worked better. A kind of flow can be found.

I have especially found the local Celtic Christian roots, rhythms, and relationships helpful to navigate the seasons of weather, but also life and community seasons too. As the Roman Empire began to withdraw from Britain around 300AD, it was the culturally Celtic tribes and peoples that held up the light in the so-called 'dark ages.'

This was not just in writing or learning, but in the Christian faith too. Their expanding number of monasteries became like 'villages of God' that would go on to help re-evangelise Europe. Glasgow, for example, began its life as a monastic centre founded by St Mungo, before it became a village, town, and now city.

It's almost impossible to engage with Celtic spirituality without connecting it to nature and seasons. Those early Celtic Christians seemed to keep whispering to me that if I fail to take notice of the rhythms of life it will be to my own peril. Though daily consistency is crucial, there are times and seasons to act in distinct ways. To go with the flow of the season, rather than fight against them can make a real difference. The subsistence and agricultural-based Celtic world knew this well. If a harvest is to feed the village of God or get to market at the right time, then different areas of work were required at different times. Don't plant seeds in the snow! Make sure you have all hands ready when the fruit is ready to be picked. Don't have fruit waiting around for months rotting. Change Making and community growth is seasonal work too in so many ways.

The Celtic Season of Samhain: When Winter's darkness falls

The Celtic season of Samhain begins on November 1, understood as the start of the Celtic year. It is also the Christian feast of All Saints and associated with the coming of winter and the thinning of the veil between the living and the dead. I wrote earlier of an 'enchanted Celtic worldview' and winter's dark and shadow-driven days here do nothing to dispel this imagination. Most things seem to lurk in the dark at this time of year. It's easy to believe that there are life and beings you cannot see, in fact, you can't see very much in the light for weeks at a time.

A community life can have winter seasons that can be a bit spooky too. There are seasons when endings happen and the earth cools for us. We can double-guess ourselves when our productivity and effectiveness drop, and we can't seem to get things done. We can also discover what is real and what is just wishful thinking. Certainly, we need to let go of all that is non-essential if we are to be in a place to take up what is needed, to be ready for more fruitful seasons. The dark winter seasons can help us, but I know few who enjoy them.

There are ancient mystical traditions about darkness, that offer practices that can help us move through the winter seasons.

The Celtic Year starts in November, just as winter begins here, but it leads quickly into the Advent Season. The modern traditions of Christmas lights and festivities seem to draw from these ancient attempts to cope with darkness. In the Celtic tradition, however, the Advent Season is more than just Christmas. Typically, it begins on the fourth Sunday before Christmas Day and ends on Christmas Eve. Advent is a time of preparation and anticipation, literally meaning 'comings' or 'arrivals.' In the Celtic tradition, we remember three 'comings' of Jesus in these dark times. His first and most obvious coming, is his birth in Bethlehem as a baby. This incarnating God became one of us, and has a personal stake in our salvation despite all that is happening around us. The second 'arrival' is Jesus coming into our lives. Jesus' life in and through us is how God works in the world. Thirdly, there will be a final coming, on that Great Day when all things will be put to right, and he comes again. Holding these three themes together: the Messianic, the Personal, and the Apocalyptic, can be a dynamic and hopeful way to view the world in dark times. The Advent season itself is about discovering that newness can break into our old, tired, expected realties. Jesus' first coming – as a baby refugee who was born to a virgin – could not have been more unexpected. In Jesus' last coming we wait for the surprising renewal of all things and the fulfilment of all God's promises. Bruggemann puts it this way:

> The newness that God wrought at Christmas was sending into the world this Jesus who is beyond our imagination, who brought healing and grace everywhere he went, who forgave and transformed and called people out beyond themselves to a newness they could not have imagined. "I am doing a new thing!" It is easy for us to be held down and held back by the pain or glories of the past. Aid us in perceiving the wondrous new thing you are doing in our world through the birth of Jesus, the one who comes to make all things new. Amen."[151]

17: Samhain - Winters Of Our Discontent And Discovery

At this time in the Christian calendar, I have often felt tired, weary, and fed up with current realities. Hurried, overwhelmed, and even anxious at times, I can drag myself to end-of-year obligations. Advent season asks, however, if I will take a deep breath and join with others in faith, anticipating that the new world Jesus promised is not only possible, but imminent. God's Newness is on its way.

A key date in the Celtic imagination and calendar was the winter solstice on December 22. This is the shortest day of the year with the least amount of light and the most darkness. You would think this would be a depressing day. However, the Celts had special festivals remembering that it has got as dark as possible and now the world gets lighter. The link between solstice, Christmas, and Yule feasting can be made. Not least was that often livestock wouldn't make it through the rest of the winter and needed to be slaughtered around this time, and so meat for feasting was available. It's a time of coming together and ensuring no one gets left behind in the darkness.

Winters can be cold, dark and bleak here in ways I had not experienced before. We first arrived in Birmingham in late November 2014, and it was quite a shock to the senses. We had previously only experienced the warmth of Bangkok and Melbourne at this time of year. Our eventual base at Newbigin House would not be available for another two years. Our Ninevah Road first home had been previously abandoned, with doors kicked in, the gas and the electricity not always working, but we quickly adapted it and made it ours. It was much bigger than any home we had lived in for 20 years and the adrenaline of new adventure carried us through. Our daughter Amy visited from Australia that first year and Aiden was settling into his own room in the attic level of our new home. That first Christmas was bleak in many ways, but I think we did experience God's newness too.

This time of year was normally hot for us, but also crowded. We were so used to constant streams of events, sharing life together with hundreds, sometimes even a thousand, at this time of year. Suddenly, that first year in Birmingham, that was gone.

We were in the UK together, but didn't know many people. It was a difficult shock, but there was also an enchantment to this season for us. It even snowed that winter! The sky grew deathly dark and then silently released its floating bounty on the earth. I remember that Anji and Amy came back from shopping one day and were soaking wet.

'What happened? There wasn't any rain today?' I asked.

'It snowed! We loved the snow, we were lying in it, but didn't realise we would get wet!'

Not every day is dark in winter here. In Bangkok, because of smog, we very rarely saw blue skies in our 12 years there. Crisp, blue sky mornings are a treat for me. My family quickly got sick of me saying 'my favourite days are these frosty cold ones with blue skies.'

Not all winters here are like that novel and strange first one either. We've come to expect dark seasons in our lives, but the Pandemic Winter of 2020-21 was something else. The number of new Covid cases and deaths in the UK rose and fell over us like ice-cold waves over the whole year, but as November 2020 emerged it felt like the tide was quietly sucking in, ready for a massive tidal wave of destruction. Even the most activist among us needed to pause and hold our breath in the face of a global pandemic that killed millions of people, stopped whole industries in their tracks, and wrecked economies.

By February 2021, however, a dark bleakness was released and crashed in full force all over us, especially for those of us living in Newbigin House. Like so many, we were exhausted by all the false starts and second guessing, but we also had a succession of break-ins at night while all nine of us were asleep upstairs. What made it worse was that we knew the young guys involved. They were bored and had started meeting in large groups in the bus stop in front of our house.

One night they broke in through a side door and stole my laptop, one of my few prized possessions, with decades of work inside it. Another time they took Louise's car keys and stole her car. Another time they just broke in and didn't take anything. I felt sorry for a poor police officer who came to investigate the next day. He went to look for them in the

17: Samhain - Winters Of Our Discontent And Discovery

community garden over our backyard, climbed up on the green metal fences and then the alpacas charged at him! He fell off the fence and on his arse in the mud! We laughed, but the jumpiness in the nights of half-sleep, listening for noises, began to drain the life out of us.

Then the Covid-19 virus itself hit us personally. I was pretty sure I'd had it in March 2020 (but testing wasn't available) and then in November 2020 Anji tested positive and was stopped in her tracks. When Anji had a strand of Dengue Fever in Bangkok it hardly impacted her, but here she was almost lifeless in her bed, hardly able to move. The whole house and ministry went into isolation for the required 14 days, but then on the 13th day as Anji started to recover, another housemate, John Carrol, tested positive and that started the isolation clock for another 14 days. All the time the various track and trace apps wouldn't work, then calls would come from the NHS days later and we would fumble along. Nothing seemed to work anymore.

Christmas 2020 was especially subdued. Waves of Covid infections and mortality hit the UK, but when four of us were able to get the vaccine in January, because of our foster-care responsibilities, we thought that the tide had turned. Little did we know that in early February five more of our housemates would test positive for Covid. This included John Harrison and Gwen Gardiner who were in their sixties with underlying health conditions, as well as the three younger housemates, including my son Aiden.

Cold and dark times like this remind me that I'm only as resilient as my support network. Whether it was friends who saw on Facebook that my laptop was stolen and gave money to replace it with an expensive one that could recover all my files; or relatives who found out that Louise's car was stolen and gave her one of theirs; or neighbours who brought over curries for us to eat or shared with the police their video footage of the young guys running down our driveway; or the extra financial support that helped us carry on when we shouldn't have been able to; or doctors, nurses, and researchers we'd never met, who helped us beat a deadly disease. Without these connections of light beyond ourselves, the darkness would have overcome us.

Winter's darkness can slowly wear you down. As the days get to their shortest the sun rises about 9:30am and is gone by 3:30pm. It is easy to go for weeks leaving and returning home in the dark and spend most of the days indoors. Our energy and motivations often dissipate as we kind of hibernate to survive. Even the smallest work seems to require enormous energy that is hard to find. This season can easily become depressing and disorientating.

There is a day the UK call's 'Blue Monday.' Typically, it's the third Monday of January, and said to be the most depressing day of the year. The fun and joy of Advent, Christmas, and New Year is a distant memory, and what is left is a relentless darkness and cold to face for months to come yet. To respond in Winson Green we have 'Blue Friday' parties at Lodge Road, a karaoke night where we wear blue, eat dyed blue food, and sing songs in defiance to how we feel. Things don't seem so blue when others are singing *Sweet Caroline* with us at the top of our lungs.

Change-making requires patient persistence in the dark. There are times when we just need to go through the motions and turn up. Blind duty to our call is okay sometimes. The old saying that '90 percent of life is just showing up' has stood the test of time because it rings true. If we are willing to keep showing up to what is important, even when there are hundreds of reasons not to, seasons will eventually change and so will we. Indeed, if we wait until we feel like turning up, we will keep being distracted and will miss what God is doing.

In lots of ways, small endings have been a common part of my calling. I've been privileged to be able to work on some amazing initiatives over the decades, but very few of them were 'full-time.' I have worked having lots of 'pots on the boil' rather than one big piece of work. Not often would all the pots come to boil at once. Mostly one pot needed some attention to get it going. Another pot just needed a glancing look. Another had been boiling for a while and needed to come off the flame for a bit. The point is to know what is important and needs attention at the right time. There are winter seasons when no momentum happens for anything we try, but this has been rare for me. Normally at least *something* is working. I'm at my best when I can work with some verve on an area and be patient with others, believing more light will come.

17: Samhain - Winters Of Our Discontent And Discovery

My problem has often been how to let go well. Letting go and the grief we feel is part of the winter season too. Over my three decades of ministry so far, I've been privileged to help instigate innovative organisations and to see other, more dynamic leaders go on to lead them further than I could. Some readers will know that I helped start Urban Neighbours of Hope,[152] Surrender Conferences,[153] as well as many campaigns, local churches, and social businesses. Since we moved to Winson Green, Birmingham in 2014 this dynamic seems to have sped up and to date has included Newbigin Community Trust, [154] Urban Shalom Society,[155] Soho Albion FC,[156] Red Letter Christians UK,[157] and the Greenhouse at Barnes Close.[158] At the time of writing, all these organisations are flourishing in different ways without me needing to lead them. I love all these initiatives and their leaders, and have often wished I didn't have to let go and could be the one to lead them further. I know now, however, there is a complexity after the design and start-up phases that needs a different kind of leadership.

Again, Lao Tzu's poem from 6th century BC is a good reminder to me.

> Go to the people.
> Live with them,
> Learn from them,
> Love them.
> Start with what they know,
> Build with what they have.
> But with the best leaders,
> The work done, the task accomplished,
> The people will say,
> 'We've done it ourselves.'[159]

This quote has shaped my approach to leadership from when we first relocated to Springvale, Melbourne in 1992. By empowering and equipping other leaders to 'do it themselves,' we were able to leave others to continue the work well, despite how painful it was for us.

Two of the most emotional events in my life have been endings. The first was in Springvale, Melbourne in 2002 as we launched to Bangkok. We had East Timorese, Aboriginals, Vietnamese, Cambodians, and Rainbow Church folks sharing what felt like our eulogies.

The second was also like that in Klong Toey, Bangkok in March 2014 when we left and set out for Birmingham. The community came together at the Klong Toey Community Centre for food, dancing, and a send-off we would never forget. Both farewells had the agony of leaving and lots of tears, but also a sense that we'd helped make a real difference in the lives of those we loved in those places and the reassurance they had the resources to go further without us. We'd left both places, and the people we served, better than we'd found them. That is real fruit to me.

Proper winter endings are rarely easy but are necessary. Whenever community programmes, jobs, relationships, or especially lives finish, grief emerges and pulses around our bodies.

There is a maxim I learned in the transition from leading UNOH for over 20 years to starting again in Birmingham: the longer and more we invest personally, the more difficult it can be to let go and pass on. Anji and I both love to start new initiatives with people and hand over responsibilities as quickly as we can. We've done this dozens of times with everything from football clubs to churches, conferences to networks. This happened leaving Melbourne for Bangkok, but leaving Urban Neighbours Of Hope to move to Birmingham was different. Anji has written about her deep grief leaving Bangkok in her book, *Missionary: Not Just A Position*,[160] but for me the grief was leaving UNOH. So much of me was personally invested.

I had begun and led UNOH with friends when I was 23 in 1993 and by the time of our farewell from UNOH in 2014 I was 44. Most of my adult life had been invested in growing UNOH workers and teams, but the winter had come for me. We'd been transitioning over the previous 18 months to be less dependent on my leadership, but it suddenly became clear I had led UNOH as far as I could. I needed to let go, get out of the way, and see the next generation of UNOH workers go in the direction they believed was right. It felt like I was now a roadblock to growth, and we started the transition that took another 18 months before we landed in Birmingham.

There was a kind of relief to this process. UNOH had become a very complex organisation for me to lead and I looked forward to the next season of life with fewer responsibilities, working more in my strengths. However, there was also deep loss, isolation and grief I had never experienced before. Suddenly, the central role I had in the life of UNOH colleagues, friends, and family for most of my adult life was now gone. We had been through so much together, but now we could hardly talk.

The 'hidden work' of pioneering leadership is rarely known. Certainly, few leaders can describe the kind of unseen, 'backroom' efforts required to found any not-for-profit start-up. Modelling and communicating what is needed can be seen, but growing a network of support, accessing resources and fundraising, governance, finances and budgets, organisational philosophy, conflict resolution, problem solving, not to mention how to recruit and grow diverse staff and volunteers is often far below the surface. If a start-up becomes a growing concern, few founders are willing to hand them over to others. It's hard, mostly relentless, thankless work with few guarantees, and few want the kind of responsibilities founders need to have.

I do wish I'd talked more about those kinds of pioneering efforts with teams and organisations I've started. In organisational literature there is a difference between 'pioneers' and 'settlers,' 'founders' and 'first generation' leaders. Understandably, some settlers want to make their own mark and not be in the pioneer's shadow. Some want to re-balance the perceived weaknesses of founders. Most commonly, however, settlers underestimated how fragile the ecosystem that started the organisation can be. It is true that we want leaders to know 'they did it themselves,' but there is also a role that pioneering leaders play in catalysing, inspiring, and releasing that is often unnoticed and undervalued. No one actually succeeds 'by themselves.' We all stand on the shoulders of others to reach where we need to reach.

My first winter season here in Birmingham was a wake-up call and a time of discovery. My personal identity needed to be separated from UNOH. I needed to grow beyond an organisation of my own making. As I look back now, I still feel sadness that UNOH didn't kick on the way I had hoped.

I can still feel my self-worth tied to UNOH's highs and lows all these years later. I guess I'll always be UNOH's founder. However, without this winter, this ending, this separation, I could not have been freed up to be and do what has happened since and all that is happening now.

For many reading this book the biggest barrier to pursuing God's Shalom with your local people and places will be time and space. 'I'm already too overstretched to even see my family, never mind my neighbourhood! I don't have the bandwidth!' Winters can help here. Letting go and simplifying our lives down to the essentials can create the time and space in our lives that we need to be available locally for what is needed from us. Sometimes winters happen for us, other times we must look out for them and catch the flow of this season ourselves. Either way, seeking Shalom with our lives can't be done in our spare time. A season of cutting down to the essentials gives us every chance of flourishing in a more sustainable and fruitful lifestyle in the long term.

Few people start with the expectation of death, but its shadow is always there. Change and grief go together, even if what is to come could be far more fruitful than before. Resistance to change then, can be part of the grief process for what is being lost. The winter brings us back to the bare essentials, to see what is really there.

We must therefore respect the winter seasons. For some these will be months, years, or even decades. We must face them honestly and boldly, but also find a deep hope that more is to come, that more light is on its way now. We need to look out for those bumps that become buds, for these will be where fruits come from.

Winter endings matter. Letting go of all the non-essentials needs to be part of our rhythm of life personally and in our churches, charities, communities, and organisations. Often winter seems forced on us, but if we take notice of the season we are in and go with that flow, we can find new beginnings that won't happen without proper endings.

17: Samhain - Winters Of Our Discontent And Discovery

Personal Reflections

1. When have you most experienced a dark, winter season in your life? What was it like? What was stripped away?

2. Why are endings just as important as beginnings for us?

3. If there was a spectrum of pioneer/founder to settler/staff, which end would you be closest too? Why? What unique joys and challenges does this give you in your endings and winter seasons?

4. What can you do to better prepare for your winter seasons and those of your community?

Chapter 18: The Celtic Season Of Imbolc - Spring's Gestations And Birthing.

There is no season like spring, when life's alive in everything
– Christina Rosetti

See! The winter is past;
*　　the rains are over and gone.*
Flowers appear on the earth;
*　　the season of singing has come,*
the cooing of doves
*　　is heard in our land.*
The fig tree forms its early fruit;
*　　the blossoming vines spread their fragrance.*
Arise, come, my darling;
*　　my beautiful one, come with me.*
Song of Songs 2:11-13

The Celtic season of Imbolc begins February 1. This is the festival of Brigid of Kildare (451-525), who is associated with the coming of spring. It is a time of new beginnings and the stirring of life after the long, dark winters here.

No Wastelands

St Brigid was a remarkable Christian leader, often hard to distinguish between an Irish goddess of the same name. She is credited with miracles, starting new monastic communities, leading a region of churches, and a school known for illuminated art. In Kildare, she and her nuns tended a perpetual fire, recorded as a perpetual 'ashless fire,' to keep the light burning physically and spiritually for generations. With her friend and colleague Patrick, she was a spark that God would use to light up the Dark Ages not only in her native Ireland, but from there to the ends of the earth. That springtime and Brigid go together is a wonderful reminder of what is possible.

St Brigid's day starts with liminality, in between times. Neither fully dark, nor fully light, there is a kind of 'threshold space' that is a recurrent theme with the character of Brigid.

> Born at a liminal time in a liminal place, she is said to have been born on the threshold of a door (neither within or without the house) and at the breaking of dawn (neither day or night). This liminality can also be seen in her association with a red-eared white cow, an animal always associated with the otherworld and the Daoine Sídhe (fairies).[161]

Although February is the start of Celtic spring, it rarely feels like it here. In fact, some of our biggest storms like the 'Beast from the East' happened from February 24, 2018 until March 4, 2018, as Anticyclone Hartmut hit the UK, bringing with it unusually low temperatures and heavy snow. We were supposed to go to Holy Island for a Change Makers weekend residential during this time, and despite our theme being 'resilience,' we had to cancel as there was no way onto the Island. It wasn't quite spring!

A common practice on St Brigid's Day is to clean out dark corners of our homes and sheds, physically and spiritually, ready for the spring season ahead. Taking time for a spiritual and physical spring clean is not a bad way to find our way out through the disorientation of winter.

Spring seasons are about gestation, seeding, and new birth. The birds and the bees are literally out and about, but there is also a new kind of perspective that grows too. What we start now can grow and bear fruit in time.

18: Imbolc - Spring's Gestations And Birthing

I have enjoyed pilgrimages as a kind of spring practice to clear away the cobwebs. My first pilgrimage was to set aside a week to walk the 100km St Cuthbert's Way with a few close friends in 2019. As we rambled through the borderlands between Scotland and England and finished to the welcome of seals shrieking on the Holy Island of Lindisfarne, my connections with God, as well as friends, felt renewed. As we walked those holy landscapes together, facing the physical challenges of hiking, my mind grew clearer, and my heart grew lighter, ready for a new season of life. Could this be a time of convergence for us? Could what we do and who we are be better sync together for more fruitful living?

A pilgrimage can help to gain that spring, renewed perspective. We have also explored 'timeline' exercises in previous chapters. The only way I know to experience a sense of future destiny is to take some time to look back, gain perspective and to re-focus. Out of that first St Cuthbert's Way pilgrimage I felt I needed to let go of some responsibilities to better focus my unique gifts with the right teams from the right bases. I'd been transitioning out of my leadership role with Red Letter Christians UK in favour of younger leaders.

I had a fresh sense of call to be planted in Winson Green to better discern and see God's dream for our neighbourhood come true. We belong here and are putting roots down. We relocated as a family to Winson Green in November 2014 and by 2019 it felt like we'd just begun to see our hopes starting to come true. I detected a desire to see this happen as a neighbour and a Christian Minister. David Bosch has an old saying about missionaries. They start off as Christian missionaries living overseas. The next term of service they are just Christians serving overseas. Then eventually they are just other expats enjoying life overseas. I didn't want to drift like that. More intentionality and letting go was needed.

My first pilgrimage to the Holy Land was the Jesus Trail in Spring 2019. I was turning 50 that year and the idea of a pilgrimage from Nazareth to Capernaum was timely. Walking where Jesus walked and swimming in the lake of Galilee was a mystical experience that also raised money for a local hospital in Nazareth.

I also went from Jerusalem to Jericho, following the path of the Good Samaritan parable. Even though I got lost in the outskirts of Jericho after dark and had to be picked up by my Airbnb hosts, these adventures made me ready for the next season of life.

My first Camino de Santiago, the renowned mediaeval pilgrimage, was also in spring; late February to early March 2023. The trek started at the cathedral in Porto and wound along the wild Atlantic coast before heading inland through the rolling hills and beautiful Spanish villages until I sat by the supposed grave of St James the apostle. Many hundreds of thousands do this pilgrimage each year now and the pilgrims' hostels and other infrastructure make this so accessible. This was a reboot at the end of my sabbatical, ready for the next seven years in Winson Green. I wrote earlier that five priorities emerged and that I needed to let go of other things to birth these. The internationalisation of Seedbeds and this book were a part of the fruit of that refocusing.

It is also no coincidence that Easter and springtime go together in the Celtic imagination. This was intentional. One of the ancient controversies was the method Celtic Christians used to calculate Easter's date. This method determined the date of Easter based on the full moon that falls on or after the spring equinox, typically around March 21. The Sunday following that full moon was celebrated as Easter Sunday. This method would typically result in Easter being celebrated on a different date than the one used by the Roman Catholic and Eastern Orthodox churches and was contested in the famous Synod of Whitby in 664 AD. Central to the spring season is that we remember Jesus's life overcoming death, light over darkness, as a reality that has begun. The Celts insisted that this was even tied to the changing of light in the spring equinox.

Easter blooms into new life. The point of the plum tree's flower, for example, is not the flower itself, rather the fruit and seeds that are to come. So too the Easter event and spring are a foretaste of what is to come in the world. Jesus' resurrection is the first fruit of new creation. What Jesus experienced in resurrection will be the newness experienced by us and the whole cosmos. Spring reminds us of this promise.

England feels like a different country when the sun comes out. All of

18: Imbolc - Spring's Gestations And Birthing

a sudden, the dark, damp days of winter give way to longer, lighter, brighter days of spring. There is even a kind of glowing optimism as people emerge out of their hibernations into active life. The darker the winter, the brighter the spring seems! Every dark corner seems to come alive with colour and growth. The dormant trees and plants start to burst open and new possibilities seem to emerge from out of the sloshing mud. While I've spent a lot of energy in this book focused on overcoming dark times, there are also seasons of life when even the most wonderful events can happen, far beyond our control and calculations.

I just met with our local Council about how new housing and our new high school opening will have the potential for generation change in Winson Green. We'd helped with the zoning of some derelict land near Newbigin House so it could be used by the community again, but now a state-of-the-art education facility was about to open that was far better than we could even imagine. Not just for nearly 1000 high school students who will go there, but because Windsor Academy Trust was willing to work with us on the design and even staffing roles, the facilities, like 4G football pitches, dance studios, and eco-park, will become an embedded part of local community life here.[162] What a crazy, wonderful gift this is!

Springtime generates germination. Those buzzing bees seem to be hyper-active in their movement from flower to flower and back to their hives. There does not appear to be any pattern, direction or purpose in their furious activity. While I'm sure they have fun doing this, they are also propagating the next generation of flowers and bees. Indeed, without these erratic journeys whole eco-systems would die with their generation. This is intentionally investing in the future, even though it looks frantic, risky, and unplanned.

Likewise, sharing our dreams with others is not a waste of time and resources. There are seasons when the next big idea of our lives happens in such encounters with others. Accessing new networks and passing on what we have picked up are activities that make-or-break visions and dreams. I know there are some leaders who seem to think it's spring all the time and never stop going to meetings and conferences. They are busy bees who are always busy, but they never get the flower's nectar back to their hive. Yet, I also know there are leaders whose idea's time has come, yet never get to see that potential fulfilled because of a lack of connection with the right networks of people. There are spring times when we need to let our ideas germinate with the right people.

Excitement ripples inside me when I meet people ready to start a new project or initiative whose time has come. What I often need, however, after these stimulating times, is a counting of the cost. What can I commit to this new idea? What do I need to let go of to do it? Jesus talks about counting the cost before we start to build (Luke 14:25-33).

The spring season sows and prepares for the harvest. Vegetable seeds like cabbages, pumpkins and carrots, for example, especially like to be planted in spring ready for an autumn harvest. The potential of those small vegetable seeds to feed and nourish people will not be reached unless it is first planted in the right soil.

We've already talked about Jesus' parable about the farmer who plants seeds. It's about what kind of lives help and hinder the receptivity and growth of God's good news and our willingness to be faithful. It's a warning that even good seeds won't grow everywhere at once, but also gives hope that where it does take root and grow strong, it multiplies its goodness exponentially.

I'm conscious too that in springtime I sometimes need to take the stones and rocks out of the soil first before I plant. The quiet, back-breaking preparation of soil is needed before I can plant the seeds and see them grow. This too is some of my most important work. There are no shortcuts or quick fixes if we want to see lasting fruit. These might be brighter days, but there is still tough work to do. There are seasons in life when we need to invest in preparation, even if we don't know exactly what seeds we are sowing. Even at a daily rhythm level, if we prepare as if it is spring, we may see goodness slowly grow during that same day. If we keep watering and nurturing, who knows what may happen?

Late spring, especially, brings nature's most flamboyant season here. When the bluebells start to pop up on the Waseley Hills, for example, it feels like God is just showing off.

18: Imbolc - Spring's Gestations And Birthing

Parker Palmer reminds us that:

> Late spring is potlatch time in the natural world, a great giveaway of blooming beyond all necessity and reason-done, it would appear, for no reason other than the sheer joy of it. The gift of life, which seemed to be withdrawn in winter, has been given once again, and nature, rather than hoarding it, gives it all away. There is another paradox here, known in all the wisdom traditions: if you receive a gift, you keep it alive not by clinging to it but by passing it along.[163]

There are seasons to launch out and to let people know who we are. To allow our natural colours full expression and to invite people to join us. Indeed, if we don't learn the art of explaining what we do and why, who do we think will do it for us? Who will join us if we don't feel inspired and can be infectious? This is about confidence and risking ourselves in the arenas that matter. In today's social-media-saturated world, we know there are some folks who seem to crave attention, needing to let us know what they had for breakfast. Yet, there are also those who fear shame and ridicule so much that they never get to express themselves and their ideas in public. Spring reminds us that there is a season to not lay dormant but to bloom in full colour.

Light and life are contagious. There are seasons when we can't hide in the shadows any longer. Certainly, our communities need our solidarity and fidelity in dark winter times, but they also need us blooming in the spring times. Sun's out, hope's out!

Personal Reflections

1. What do you do to 'blow away the cobwebs' after dark times? What has been helpful and unhelpful transitioning to such times?

2. Have you ever been on a pilgrimage? Why, why not? What could help you experience the benefits of sacred journeys for our body and soul?

3. Why would spring and resurrection naturally go together for the early Celtic Christians? What could our connections be?

4. The seeding and birthing of an idea can be an exciting phase of a project, enterprise or campaign. Is that season exciting for you? Why, why not?

5. How could you better connect with the spring seasons of life and initiatives?

Chapter 19:
The Celtic Season of Bealtaine - Summertime's Flourishings And Rests

Notice the fig tree, or any tree. When the leaves come out, you know without being told that summer is near.
— Jesus, Luke 21:30

Summers had a logic all their own and they always brought something out in me. Summer was supposed to be about freedom and youth and no school and possibilities and adventure and exploration. Summer was a book of hope. That's why I loved and hated summers. Because they made me want to believe.
— Benjamin Alire Sáenz

In contrast to the sensationalism of spring, summer is a steady state of plenty, a green and amber muchness that feeds us on more levels than we know.
— Parker Palmer

The Celtic season of Bealtaine begins May 1. This was a celebration of fertility and the coming of summer. Bealtaine literally means 'Mouth of Fire' and is a time of growth and abundance, but also rest.

No Wastelands

Bealtaine marked the beginning of the pastoral summer season when the herds of livestock were driven out to the summer pastures and mountain grazing lands. It is a cross-quarter day, marking the midpoint in the sun's progress between the spring equinox and summer solstice. Like the Festival of Samhain, opposite Bealtaine on October 31, this was also a time when the Otherworld was seen as particularly close at hand. That the veil between worlds, the Shield of Skathach, on this day was especially thin. This allowed the fae or fairies to cross over into our world. An enchanted worldview is easiest to imagine at this time of year when there are such long twilights. Even at 11pm in the summertime, there is still enough light to see.

Fires within the homes were extinguished and Bealtaine was celebrated by lighting hilltop fires. From these communal flames, household fires would be re-lit to celebrate summer coming. In the Celtic Christian imagination, summer shines potential into abundance and we savour life together. We don't just live to work but find a joy in living.

I despised the hot seasons in Bangkok. The walls on our slum home would be too hot to touch, my energy levels would evaporate and everything around me seemed to grind into a sweat-soaked halt. Even the locals dread the hot season and would often leave Klong Toey for family out of town or 'upcounty.' Summer in England isn't necessarily hot, but the blue-sky days we often get are some of my favourite days. Those clear, bright days, often sharing meals with friends in the back garden of Newbigin House, have created some of our fondest memories. Watching England play well in a World Cup and sipping a pint in a beer garden is a real joy for me, albeit a rare one. In summer we can enjoy the life we have and see clearly what is possible and yet still see more is to come.

One of my favourite times of the year happens when our Seedbed participants graduate. Change Makers, Change Incubator, Pioneers, and MAs all have graduated in summer months. I remember well the first Change Makers end-of-course Resource Panel, on May 12, 2017. The room in the community centre at Royal Docks, East London, seemed to burst with light and life. We had journeyed with this first cohort over the previous year.

19: Bealtaine - Summertime's Flourishings And Rests

All these Change Makers were identified by their local communities as young emerging leaders with massive potential who lived and served in urban priority areas. All seemed nervous as they got up to present their community building, organising, or enterprise ideas. Could their ideas help create change in their neighbourhoods?

Jess is a fifth-generation resident from East Ham in London. With passion and verve, she stood up and shared her idea for a charity shop on the High Street that could help generate income, create employment, and signpost opportunities that other residents could take up with her local church and charity. 'There's only one problem,' she said. 'The only shopfront we think will work is empty, but we can't find the owner. We've tried everything. I even thought about breaking in!'

Then it was over to the panel for feedback and potential resourcing ideas. There were seven on the panel, all with real experience in running, incubating, and investing in social businesses, charities, and church initiatives. Dr Tony Campolo, who had helped start 23 organisations himself, in between speaking all over the world, was the first panelist to respond. 'I think you *should* break in! Get the local media and police involved. Get arrested! Trust me. You won't have to try and find the owner anymore. *The owner will find you!*'

We all laughed, but then Tony shared some of the stories of people who had created change and what it takes, including the many times he had been arrested himself. Later that day Jess and others from her cohort were inducted as our first Urban Change Makers. The joy was tangible, as were the huge smiles and hugs in front of a whooping crowd, cheering them all on. Capacities for change, connections, and hope had grown before our eyes.

This was also the first day of our inaugural Change Makers UK tour with Tony Campolo and Shane Claiborne. As stories, insights, and opportunities were shared with potential local seedbeds for the next cohort of Change Makers in London, Luton, Manchester, and Birmingham, as well as in the media and churches, our dreams seemed to grow too. Something had germinated and started to grow and would bear fruit for years to come.

No Wastelands

Part of my response to the pandemic was to do what I could to better prepare for my days ahead. Since March 2020 I'd been up at 5am each morning to create intentional space to detect what this next season of life could look like. Some answers started to emerge for me and decisions that may have taken years to make, became easier.

Summer 2020 was a promise of what was to come. Two years earlier we were severely limited by what was possible with our only base at Newbigin House. At one point before the pandemic, we had over 500 people a week coming through our house for different community events and training. We were bursting at the seams and worried about the wear and tear on Newbigin House. At church one morning the story of Bartimaeus in Mark's gospel was read out. Jesus asked this man, 'What do you want?' Bartimaeus was blind so he said, 'I want to see.' Jesus healed the man, and he let go of his begging cloth and followed Jesus down the road as a disciple. In the same way I sensed Jesus asking me this same question. 'What do you want?' Quickly I said, 'Lord, we need more space.' I sensed Jesus was answering and that I needed to 'knock on every door and the right ones will open.'

We had no money, but I went to a retreat centre in the Waseley Hills the next day. We had visited with refugee families, and I knew from a friend that the charity, which had a long-term lease, was trying to sell it. The next day Ian Ring, the Community For Reconciliation's (CFR) coordinator welcomed me to Barnes Close and showed me around. This former Cadbury family mansion was now a run-down 30-bed retreat centre on five acres, backing onto over 200 acres of parkland at the foot of the Waseley Hills. I told him about our vision for growing leaders and communities into the fullness of life, how we needed more space. Ian was close to retirement after many years there and could see how we could be part of a legacy for what CFR had been doing there for decades. We could take over the CFR's 70-year lease for £100,000. This seemed a remarkable offer, but we had no money at all!

The next Sunday I was helping lead a chapel service in Winson Green prison. Before the service I was talking with Ronnie the Chaplain and John our volunteer guitarist. I shared the Barnes Close opportunity, and that we didn't have £100,000 to get started, never mind the significant costs in restoring the building.

19: Bealtaine - Summertime's Flourishings And Rests

John piped up. 'My family has a trust fund and it's my turn to distribute £50,000 to a charity project. Would you like it?' This was more than enough of a sniff to get us going!

It wasn't easy over the next two years to negotiate a way forward for this retreat centre, but we could see what was possible and continued on. Sensing a promise helped us persist. Having a deposit of £50,000 helped us negotiate too! In the end, the only way forward was for us to take responsibility for the whole Community for Reconciliation charity, including its 30-bed retreat centre. In February 2020 I became voluntary co-CEO of the charity, with Dave Mann from East London as chair, and we saw new CFR Trustees appointed with many older ones stepping down. Dave had been one of the great sources of inspiration here with a vision for the centre. I'd also be able to expand our special focus on leadership development for emerging community leaders and accredited programmes, which morphed from 'Newbigin School for Urban Leadership' to 'Seedbeds' at this time. We did look at whether we could partner with others and even merge Seedbeds, CFR, and Red Letter Christians UK together, but this proved too difficult in the end.

Barnes Close was close to derelict when we took up responsibility for the CFR charity in February 2020. That the global pandemic happened the next month made it even tougher. It seemed impossible at times! However, by Summer 2020 the Winson Green community, volunteers, and new board members had worked so hard to make the retreat centre safe and usable that we could host our Change Makers emerging leaders retreat, an MA intensive,[164] and Newbigin Community Trust youth and Forest school programmes, as well as offering Glamping in Yurts with Alpacas. What was known as 'Barnes Close' or 'The Big 'ouse' was soon renamed 'The Greenhouse at Barnes Close' and was abuzz with local people cleaning, washing and fixing, but also enjoying the summer sun. Over the next few years, the vision of the Greenhouse developed, and we were able to empower a new management team with Bishop Mike Royal as Chair and Helen Lawson as Director. Dave and I would step down; I concentrated on Seedbeds, and Dave could pick up Red Letter Christians as well. As I write, The Greenhouse is not yet out of the woods financially, but the joy of that first summer was tangible and showed its worth for the time and resources needed to renew life there.

No Wastelands

Many people experienced the lockdown over the summer of 2020 in similar ways. It forced us to stop and reconsider where to best invest the time we have left in life. Even the most activist among us needed to pause in the face of a global pandemic that killed millions of people, stopped whole industries in their tracks, and wrecked economies. We seemed to have more time to walk, reflect, and reconsider the kind of life we wanted to live. The birds even seemed to sing louder! Summer gives us more time to work in the light.

Summer can also be the season of abundance and renewal. It reminds me of family holidays at beaches. In Australia, where I grew up, the beaches can be breathtakingly beautiful, and our family had some great holidays on the beaches of the Sunshine Coast and Mornington Peninsula. Much of my early teenage years was spent scheming and pining to get to surf beaches an hour or so's drive away. I even got to spend one whole summer on the Gold Coast staying with my Uncle and Aunty, working part-time as a cleaner, and surfing every moment I could. In Thailand, my favourite family holidays were in huts on Goh Chang, which was a huge release from the pressures of slum life. Even today, just a walk on the sand, saltwater lapping at my feet, with a gentle breeze blowing in my hair, makes me glow inside like very few other experiences. As I write this first draft, I am desperately in need of recovery and renewal after an accumulated draining and difficult time. Where do I go? As I realised my need, I booked a cheap beach cottage on Airbnb for four nights by the beach in Barmouth, Wales. Just a few days of walking the beaches, praying, thinking, and reading, makes me feel like a different person. I've thawed out. This can feel like a luxury I don't deserve, and there is never a good time to do something like this, but if I don't have these moments of renewal, I will wear down and make mistakes. Finding small joys in life makes life worth living.

Sabbaticals for ministries like ours are supposed to happen every seven years. We've had only two three-month sabbaticals in 33 years of full-time urban mission, and in mid-2022 felt it was time to prepare to take up this practice again. I was shocked as I wrote up a contract, that after this next one, I will only have one sabbatical left before my retirement age!

19: Bealtaine - Summertime's Flourishings And Rests

Where have the decades gone? This brought urgency to the task of future planning. To invest well in the next seasons I had to identify what I needed. I met with Spiritual Directors, family, and team to test this list out. What I felt I needed was:

- Renewal (physically, spiritually, and mentally)
- Reconnections with family, friends, and churches in Australia
- Reboot to help prepare for the next season of ministry based in Winson Green
- Write my new book *No Wastelands: How to grow seedbeds of Shalom in your neighbourhood*

If you are reading this book, then at least one of these happened! The plan was to leave Birmingham on Saturday, December 3, 2022 and return on Saturday, March 4, 2023, and enjoy my first Australian summer in 20 years. I would spend most of my time hosted by family and friends in Victoria and Queensland and finish with a two-week Camino Portuguese pilgrimage. I am on the Gold Coast in Queensland as I first write this section, not far from where I spent that memorable summer as a teenager. The long walks along the stunning coastline over Burleigh Heads and body surfing in the warm Pacific Ocean have helped my writing and health. I'm certainly thawing out.

I loved my six weeks of Sabbatical in Victoria reconnecting with family, friends, and churches. Being a Victorian is a slightly different thing there than in the UK! I was born and bred in Melbourne and to go walking along the bay beaches, have an overnight hike in the Alpine region, and enjoy a three day and two night sailing trip in a yacht called 'Sabbatical' with some of my best mates Toby Baxter and Mark Watt, was pure grace. Reunions with old youth group friends were especially joyful as we reconnected and caught up on so many lost years together. Daily writing happened too as old stories flooded back into my imagination again. My Christmas Day in Melbourne was my first there with family in 20 years. It was a proper Aussie Chrissy too! Family together for pub seafood, roast, pavlova, and down at the beach for a swim! I was especially grateful to stay with my parents, with the Baxter family, at Paul and Lizzie Ellis's place, and at a Rosebud timeshare resort, as well as get into a hospital room for a sleep apnoea test!

I do feel healthier already, like I am rebooting for the next season to go even deeper in Winson Green and wider for community leadership development. I am grateful for Anji holding the fort in Winson Green with the teams there, enabling this sabbatical to be possible. The United Reformed Church even gave me a grant to cover my travel. This was all such a gift. It wasn't easy for Anji and the team and at times I felt guilty leaving them. What was summer for me in Australia was such a cold, dark winter for them. Hopefully, I will return renewed and with less snoring!

I've learnt a lot about Sabbatical seasons. Our needs differ at different life stages. There is never a good time to take one and they are worth the risk in planning before we fully need them. To experience goodness in life, away from day-to-day production, helps us remember our worth, gives us perspective on where we've been and builds our capacities for the future. They may seem like a luxury, but if they help us see more seasons through in better health and focus, they are not to be missed. Sabbaticals are underrated!

Joy in summer can be found in the UK too. Many in England experienced great joy in the summer of 2018. There is something about the England football team doing well that lifts the whole nation. An unexpected World Cup run even more so!

I'll never forget going into one of our local Primary Schools on behalf of our junior football club Soho Albion. The famous West Bromwich Albion (WBA) is less than a mile from our home and had helped us start the club. Over 1000 local primary school-aged kids came to our first trials at the WBA Academy ground, next to their Hawthorns stadium and quite a few of our boys had signed for the WBA Academy. Steve Hopcroft, then head of recruitment from WBA Academy was the brains behind this because he had grown up in the area and when we first met said that 'if Messi was here in Winson Green he wouldn't have a local club to start him out here anymore.' Steve was supposed to address the school assembly that day and invite all to the next trials. Unfortunately, at the last minute he had to cancel, and I needed to step in! Before I knew it hundreds of little eyes were looking up at me. In my best West Brom gear I tried to give a pep talk Steve had done hundreds of times

19: Bealtaine - Summertime's Flourishings And Rests

in schools. 'Give me a cheer if you support West Brom!' One lone boy at the back cheered. 'Ok… er.. tell me who is your favourite player?' A few hands go up this time. 'Ronaldo,' 'Messi,' 'Mo Salah.' Time for my pep talk…

> 'If you have the desire and if you have the talent, then it's amazing how far you could go. We all have different talents and gifts, but if you have that special talent for football then we have a pathway for you. All those superstar players you mentioned found their passion for football in a local club and honed their talents there. You can too. I mean someone's got to play for West Brom, why not you? Even if you don't go all the way to the Premier League, football is such a great way to make friends, be healthy, and connect with others in the community. West Brom are making this available for free. You just have to come up to the Hawthorns on Saturday with your parents or caregivers and see if this is for you. We've got these flyers… Any questions?'

I looked at the diverse faces from almost every racial mix and they looked back at me, waiting expectantly.

I'd run out of material… and still had 20 minutes left of School Assembly! What would Steve do here? England were to play Croatia in the Semi Final of the World Cup that week and so in desperation I pivoted there. 'Who's been watching England in the World Cup?' To my surprise almost every hand went up. Just then one of the teachers, who could see I was struggling, played a YouTube clip on the screen behind me with football anthem 'Three Lions on a Shirt.' Suddenly we all started singing the chorus 'football's coming home.' I'm running up and down like a crazy Panto character, yelling 'C'mon, footballs coming home! Let England hear you in Russia.' 'Football's coming home.'

There is real joy in football. A moment of collective hope like this can bond and uplift. Football has done that for me in every community I've lived in. It's worth noticing where we find joy and keep connecting with it when we can. Sometimes the summer season helps us to see that joy.

No Wastelands

Of course, I didn't go back to that Primary School when England lost that Semi-final to Croatia. How to grieve well is another lesson and one that England fans need in their emotional toolbox, but I think Steve Hopcroft would be needed for that one.

The summer experiences of joy, rest, renewal, abundance, and sabbaticals are so important. We need our days in the sun! Light helps us grow and gives energy. We are not machines or slaves. We are human beings created to live life to the full. Whether it's football or beaches or walking or sunrises or meals with loved ones, we are meant to take the time to be renewed. We can find life in meaningful work, but also in renewing play. All this helps us live lives of abundance. Indeed, Shalom living is not possible without taking time to enjoy these summer seasons when they come along. This is part of the great Shalom prophecy in Isaiah 65:2 (NRSV):

> They shall not build and another inhabit; they shall not plant and another eat; for like the days of a tree shall the days of my people be, and my chosen shall long enjoy the work of their hands.

This promise to enjoy life is part of what it means to share in God's abundance. Our work can and should be meaningful, but time to 'enjoy the work of our hands' is a crucial season too.

In summer we can often see further and for longer too. I love walking up to the top of mountains and hills in the summer. From the top of the Waseley Hills behind the Greenhouse at Barnes Close there is a kind of brass dial that points out the 360 degrees of places. In the winter gloom, it can be hard to see a few feet away, but in the summer you can see hundreds of miles to the mountains in Wales. Summer times are not just for rest, they are for taking stock and seeing new possibilities too. There is good fruit still to come too.

Personal Reflections

1. What are your fondest memories of summer holidays? What made it feel so good? What makes for a good summer 'life season' for you?

2. Have you ever had a sabbatical? Why, or why not? What could make a good sabbatical for you?

3. What role has joy and celebration had in your life and neighbourhood?

4. Light helps growth. Where do you get your spiritual light and life from? What helps and hinders this experience?

5. How could you better 'enjoy the work of your hands'? More satisfying and fruitful work? More renewing and restful enjoyment?

Chapter 20:
The Celtic Season of Fomhar - Autumn's Harvests And Endings (Again)

Autumn is the mellower season, and what we lose in flowers we more than gain in fruits.
— Samuel Butler

Only grief permits newness.
— Walter Brueggemann

The Celtic season of Fomhar means harvests. This season begins with the Festival of Lughnasadh on August 1. The first of three Celtic harvest festivals, Lughnasadh marks the end of summer, the beginning of Fomhar, and is about gathering the first fruits and grains as well as collecting the falling seeds. The second festival, Mabon, comes with the autumnal equinox on September 21 and is a time of thanksgiving for the harvest and acknowledges the balance between light and dark as days become shorter. The biggest Celtic festival of all, the Festival of Samhain, is on October 31 which is Celtic New Year's Eve. And, as we have said, the veil between the living and dead is understood to be thin. The Fomhar harvest season continues until the last sheep and cattle are brought in from their highland pastures and then it is winter again. Harvest festivals are times of fruition, abundance, and thanksgiving.

No Wastelands

We can't fast-track harvest seasons. Some church planting models seem to be in a hurry and miss out on real local fruit. They start first by relocating part of their large congregation to worship together in a new place. Once they establish a worship service, they hope that they can have an impact, one day, on the local community near where they meet and grow the congregation. We have found we should prioritise the opposite way around. Start with the community, then, maybe, one day start a worshipping congregation as the fruit of loving our place together. Sharing life as a resident in a local community first can eventually bear fruit in season as new projects, groups, and congregations emerge that begin life indigenous to the neighbourhood. However, this takes an unpredictable amount of time that few church planting funding models have an understanding of. Our Fresh Expression congregation only started to meet at Newbigin House every Sunday lunchtime five years after we first relocated to Winson Green. Those who participate and lead the congregation are often residents who have been part of Newbigin Community Trust events and programmes during the week, some for years, before they helped start and run the Fresh Expression congregation. After a few years we needed more space than could fit into Newbigin House. With help from friends, we bought a Mongolian Round Tent or 'Yurt' and planted it in our front garden. After a meal together with forty or so neighbours inside Newbigin House, the Yurt provided a sacred space to reflect on the week past, connect with God and prepare for the week ahead together.

This kind of backwards church planting and growth model was also how we came to be responsible for a large church building in Winson Green. Many church growth models focus first on finding the right paid clergy and pairing them with the right church building to be based in. Their own 'field of dreams' if they 'build it and they will come.' The belief is that the right paid leaders and church building will help attract the right people to church services. This has not been our experience. Starting with what we as residents had, and growing from there, is a much more sustainable and organic growth model for genuinely local churches. Interestingly, in January 2020, just before we took up CFR and Barnes Close and before the pandemic, we kept knocking on doors looking for local community space and a safe place for a growing number of new families to connect with.

20: Fomhar - Autumn's Harvests And Endings (Again)

We also needed a local base for Seedbeds training now that hundreds of people were filling Newbigin House each week. With the growth of our Fresh Expression congregation from mostly single men from HMO housing, we needed a safer space for families to worship too. We had been connected with these families as neighbours and with Newbigin Trust for many years by this point. I contacted the local Lodge Road United Reformed Church. I knew they only had a few elderly members left that met on a Sunday afternoon at 4pm. It was a barn of a building that would fit 1,000 people seated over two levels, but most of the building was unusable and unsafe, except for the chapel and the toilets. Would they be open to us starting a new 11am URC congregation and us taking up responsibility for the building, opening it back up for the community again? After all, I was an ordained Churches of Christ Minister, the URC had included Churches of Christ in its union, and I could do this as a volunteer ('Non-Stipendiary Minister of Word and Sacrament'). This building began as a local community asset, could it be back in the hands of the local community again?

We had an amazing day on Sunday September 27, 2020. After much prayer, discussion, agreements back and forward with the local community, URC Synod, and the members of Lodge Road URC, I was inducted as a United Reformed Church Minister with 32 new local members at what we would now call Lodge Road Community Church. A global pandemic is not the easiest time to start a new 11am Sunday family service to go with our 1pm Fresh Expressions Church in the Yurt. We would also support the existing traditional service at 4pm when it was safe for the mostly elderly folks to do so. Though they did eventually start again, they finished up meeting together at 4pm in mid-2021. The URC now has a thriving local congregation with the local church building full of local people again. This could not have been reverse-engineered. The typical approach of finding a suitable building and congregation for a suitable Minister was unlikely here. None of this could have been planned and orchestrated centrally. This fruitfulness could only come from the ground up and only then supported centrally from the denomination once it was clear what the local community needed and couldn't do themselves.

Our 11am family service has participatory involvement for all and finishes with a cooked lunch like the Fresh Expression, but has more structure to it. We have a band of local musicians who help us sing songs, bible teaching is often done in a series, we pray for needs, often lighting candles for situations and dropping stones into water for burdens we hold, and always share communion as an 'open table' to finish. We also have a large and creative children's programme. We share lunch together. Most of the congregation live locally and many have been through the Change Makers and some Pioneers programmes. Most help lead local projects with Newbigin Community Trust or are at least involved. Two original members of the traditional 4pm service continue to come, though one sometimes has difficulty getting public transport in. Somewhere between 30 and 40 people are involved most Sunday mornings at the time of writing.

With URC Lodge Road we inherited one of the few large community buildings in Winson Green. We've kept dreaming together what might be possible from here. It's become a base to release the unique God-given talents, dreams, and gifts of our neighbourhood. It is packed most days. This former near derelict church building has become a place of harvest and resurrection.

What does harvest look like in Winson Green? Imagine coming for a leisurely walk with me one morning.

If we started at Newbigin House we might see nine of us residents staggering into the kitchen to share our breakfasts and latest news together, before rushing off for broader community life. Our blacksmiths might already be at work with young people at the side of our backyard, heating up and beating confiscated knives into jewellery, ready to sell at the local market. On the front lawn is our Yurt, ready to host groups and the Fresh Expression. Jess might be preparing our dining and lounge room for kids clubs later that day. The three alpacas in our backyard need to be walked from Newbigin House to one of four local primary schools who claim the alpacas as their own.

Today we walk down the street with the alpacas to St Michael's Primary School, nearly a kilometre away. We see a mixture of smiles, surprise,

20: Fomhar - Autumn's Harvests And Endings (Again)

and occasionally have to watch out for guard dogs behind factories' wired fences! We see parents with children rushing off to school, many of who we meet later in the day at Lodge Road or one of the community hubs.

We walk past the Black Patch Park which was once overrun with old tires and construction debris, but is now home to Soho Albion FC, a walking track, wilderness area, and fresh grass for the alpacas to eat. The two brooks that meet have been boundary markers for centuries, but this park has become a place of bringing people together again too. Having saved the park, we also campaigned to re-zone a derelict piece of land opposite the park for a new high school. As I write this, a new £20 million high school is being built by Windsor Academy Trust ready for its first September 2023 intake. We see Sarah-Jane, the Principal, and talk with her about the latest updates and how a new community hub in the school might help the local community access these beautiful facilities after hours. Jon might be preparing his eco-park there as the school's eco-chaplain, ready to teach geography outside. Louise might be fussing over some children and talking with parents about support needs as the school's community hub leader. I might be impatient about when the 'walking football' can start on the school's new 3G football pitch.

We walk past a new housing development being built and see Ron there. Once a developer we campaigned against, he has become a close friend who is now ensuring at least 30 homes will be affordable among the 420, as well as providing a civic square, supermarket, coffee shop, and medical centre, none of which were on the original plans he had approved. We talk to Ron about how the Church of England now want to buy 100 of these apartments with their new Housing Association, and how we can take up a kind of place-making agenda to ensure all new residents feel welcome and at home.

We drop the alpacas off at Oasis Foundry Academy. This primary school, where Anji started out was once in special measures, ready to be closed, but now the signs on the front fences celebrate recent awards including 'school of the year for inclusions and diversity.' The disused paddock it owns opposite used to be a favoured spot for fly-tipping rubbish, but now hosts the alpacas and 'Warm Earth.' As we let the alpacas off their lead, we see Eric and Jon literally making Warm Earth from all the school food scraps. This composting and gas will help grow small seedlings to sell. This is also the site for festivals and includes a local market, jumping castles, games, and music.

There are still dark spots in Winson Green. We walk past the walls of a huge Victorian-era prison that is long past its use-by date and dominates the neighbourhood. We stop and pray for the men who are kept in cages. We pray that this site will one day be turned into a museum and a filmmaking studio. So much dark history is to be found there, like hangings, gouging, and other death-creating feats, but it also tells of the courage of suffragettes who sought the vote for women and were punished here. Even Ozzy Osbourne was once held there!

We walk down the hill from HMP Birmingham and turn down Benson Road to access the special gate to Benson Community School. There we meet Chrissy at the Newbigin Community Hub who introduces us to the sowing and knitting group in one of three portable classrooms that make up the hub. Most are mums from this primary school, and they come from diverse Muslim, Sikh, Hindu, and Irish backgrounds. The weekly programmes at Benson Hub engage hundreds of families each week with advocacy, groups, events, and support.

We walk the short distance from Benson Hub to Lodge Road Community Church. You smell the food cooking, with chicken curry, onions and potatoes on the menu today. Garmeet and the team are cooking up a storm with meals just £1.50 to be accessible to all. It might be 11 am by now, but the community cafe here is already packed. Some people are also waiting to see the advocacy services in the offices to the side. Some are here for the social enterprise, 'New Routes,' to get their bike repaired, preparing for the next group ride along the canals. Others are part of the Golden Ages and are shuffling into the chapel, ready for karaoke, dancing, and bingo. The musicians from our local band Mind Funk start to arrive and go upstairs to practice for a concert they will soon give here. Louse is quietly buzzing like a bee, helping organise the next beach outing and finding how many buses she needs this time.

20: Fomhar - Autumn's Harvests And Endings (Again)

I see Sharon, our Seedbeds operations manager, go upstairs into our office and we follow her up. On a whiteboard against the office wall, my scribbles outline what our upcoming community leadership programmes need next. My writing is pretty illegible, even to me, but somehow Sharon has found a way to translate them and make them accessible to all on her famous Excel sheets. We walk across the corridor to the training room and Matt is there getting the room ready for the Pioneer training session that night including folks zooming in from around the UK. I get distracted by our growing library there, noticing books I need to read next.

We must be careful as we walk across to access the upstairs community hall. The ceiling is literally falling down, and we can't go further. It's the last bit of the building we need to make safe and accessible. Anji wants roller skating here one day, but currently New Routes stores lots of their donated bikes there, ready to repair and give away. We can hear the music at the other end of the building as Mind Funk starts to play *Knocking on Heaven's Door*. That music room was full to the brim of old church keepsakes for many decades, just in case they came in handy. The local team of volunteers and tradesmen have transformed this into an art space, recording studio, kitchen, and hang-out space that no one wants to go home from!

Nearly every person we meet along this short morning walk has talents they are sharing. The more they share together, the closer they feel. The closer they feel, the more God's Shalom flows. For many, this includes participation in a genuinely local church, but even more, this harvest is about God, people, and place living in harmony together. This harvest is deeper and wider than just who comes to a weekly meeting. It's an eternal harvest, preparing this place and its people for when all things will be made new.

As I write today, I am conscious that we've only been in Winson Green eight years (nine years by the time this is published). This harvest so far has come at a cost, but I dream of the growth in Shalom over the next 14 years or so before my work-life retirement. What a place to grow old together!

Of course, autumn has another side. The trees around The Greenhouse at Barnes Close are spectacular in autumn, but their diverse colours and lights can be distracting. What the many deciduous trees here are doing is preparing for less sunlight. By shedding their leaves and digging their roots deeper into the earth they focus on finding different sources of life-giving energy. There is a letting go and a transition; a getting ready for a new season.

I've experienced such autumn seasons personally and for the organisations I've led. We often couldn't rely on previous sources of energy in the ways we once could and so we had to dig deeper in more diverse ways to prepare for what is to come. This is especially true when new places, teams, identities, and methods begin to emerge. There could be lots of new colours, changes, and transitions, but what we were really trying to do is dig the roots deeper into why we were planted here and to prepare that gift for a new generation.

We have known dark and lean times but are so grateful when God uses us to produce some fruit, especially if we can see it. It's worth the time to daydream about the fruit we want to see and then focus. Some of my best ideas have happened in those mornings and then during the day, I focus on a few actions to do.

Autumn can also be a season of thankfulness and acknowledgment of God's abundance. This helps grow us the trust and compassion we need. Harvest Sundays have traditionally helped us remember this as we bring our fruit, veggies, and other goods and place them at the front of the church, ready to be given away. This thankfulness ceremony begets generosity. To think about the fruit we can now see and be filled afresh with gratitude and trust for this.

Which of our many methods and efforts are actually working? The old 80/20 rule can be a helpful evaluation exercise here. Is there 20% of our work that is producing most of our fruit? If we gave that area more attention and resources and phased out others, could we see more fruit in new seasons? If we could focus more on what is producing fruit could we be more effective? I love the old Hudson Taylor quote: 'God's mission, done in God's way, never lacks God's resources.' I don't take this to mean we just wait passively for God's resources to float down from

20: Fomhar - Autumn's Harvests And Endings (Again)

heaven to us. Rather, we must take the time to discern God's mission and methods for us and have the courage to step out and follow this. Sometimes this requires picking up something new, often this requires letting go, always this requires the courage to focus. Resources follow vision, and not the other way around, but we need to be sure the fruit of this vision is worth the work and discipline.

After seasons of feeling buried, flooded, or burnt, we wonder if in this next season, we have actually been planted for a new time of fruitfulness. Discernment prayers are needed as new local leadership and global opportunities start to be taken. In the UK, this season often included new intakes of students in our Pioneers, MA, and Change Makers programmes, new expressions of church services, our first league football matches for Soho Albion of the season, and our first local discipleship events. Starts are always vulnerable, but these 'first fruits' could be significant moments of destiny for us.

Fruit should not simply be for tasting. The reason an apple tree produces apples is so that more apple trees will grow and multiply. Autumn harvests are as much about those new seeds that drop from the trees as the delicious fruit. For Seedbeds, I am conscious we want to multiply more compassionate, innovative, and resilient community leaders and see their local connections, ministries, and enterprises grow from within more local communities. I came back from sabbatical with a fresh desire to internationalise Seedbeds. All local communities can flourish, there are no wastelands, but not many local community leaders have access to key resources, self-awareness, approach frameworks, and connections to make their dreams for local change come true. Yet, these leaders are the very best people to see real change happen in communities from the inside out. We are piloting 'Train the Trainers,' 'Coach the Coaches,' and 'Prepare the Panelists' so this Seedbeds obsession can grow and multiply beyond us. How to detect what is essential to Seedbeds and what can be contextualised has become important research with our growing team. This book is part of this process. Please pray that God's impact would multiply even as we begin a new season. The autumn season can also be about endings as we prepare for winter again. When I look back at my life, what value will I have added to others? What harvest seeds will be passed onto the next generation?

I don't think people will remember my graft, work, and hard decisions. I think it will be the kind of person I made people feel. People and places can love you back in ways that the abstractions of organisations and work can't. Yet, in the modern world, organisational and infrastructure work creates the opportunity to break down barriers and overcome obstacles so that love between unlikely people can happen. It's hard to enjoy those fruits in season without the graft in the other seasons. The harvest can be plentiful, even in unlikely places some may consider wastelands, but only if we can see the potential and work with God to see multiple harvests happen. Yes, the harvest is plentiful, but the workers are still few.

Personal Reflections

1. When have you noticed the abundance of God, seeing fruit come from within our local community? What was it like? Was it easy to miss? Why, why not?

2. Can you identify fruit from your past labours? What (or who) are they? What of your labour helped or hindered this fruitfulness?

3. Can you identify seeds for the future? What (or who) are they? What of your labour can help or hinder the growth of these seeds?

4. What could you do next to grieve and let go of past harvests, to be ready to seed the next?

Part E. Practices to Try Eternal Seasons Labyrinth Walk

I first tried this practice on a Church Mission Society (CMS) retreat with other Pioneer trainers in the Lindisfarne Lounge Room at the Greenhouse at Barnes Close in May 2023. Jonny Sertin, part mad genius and part mystical missiologist, designed and set this up for about 20 of us weary souls. Most of us are, or had previously been, frontline, experienced pioneers and all are investing in the next generation of pioneers and community builders. There is a deep, tangible bond in the room here, but also a kind of simmering frustration. So many of our denominational systems, policies, and practices had worked against us and our students in their ministries, but here we all were, still standing. More than that, we were here and standing together. CMS often say that Pioneers are those who have 'a gift of not fitting in.' Here we were then, not fitting in together.

Jonny explained what he had designed and laid out before us. Many of us had walked the slow, meditative practice of a labyrinth before, but this was different. In a traditional labyrinth you start on the outside and slowly walk your way in through a kind of maze into a centre.

Often these are marked on the ground outside a church or retreat centre, sometimes they have even been designed with hedges. This ancient tradition, rooted in various cultures throughout history, can provide a unique and profound journey benefiting our mind, body, and spirit.

What was different about this labyrinth was the shape of the path (a kind of figure 8 on the floor) and the many words, objects, quotes, and artefacts along its path. Actually, it wasn't a figure 8 but the symbol of infinity, a figure 8 on its side. Jonny explained that this mystical symbol of infinity has no endings but continues to flow forever. Then there were two main areas at each of the ends of the infinity symbol. These represented the four seasons with different characteristic symbols of each season both personally and a pioneering life cycle. The idea was to walk slowly, silently, and meditatively along the infinity symbol path and stop at different points that we connected with. We could sit down on the outside of the Infinity symbol and notice what this season or one of its characteristics means to us. Others could walk by. We would then start walking again when we were ready and stop again when a new connection drew us. He checked in in with us and we broke our silence at about the 20-minute mark and then started again. We did this for over an hour and then reflected together. The themes we discovered about ourselves and our collective callings were profound. Above all it helped us discern what time and season it was for us personally and collectively and to start to prepare for it.

Could you try this exercise? Here are some ideas on how you can do this practice.

1. Find a large room or space outside (on a fine day!)

2. Mark a large infinity symbol (sideways 8) in chalk or with markers so it's easy to see and walk along.

3. Designate areas on the infinity path for each of the four seasons. This can simply be an area each with the words written large with winter, spring, summer, autumn in this order.

4. Populate each seasonal area with as many key words, symbols, nature, and quotes as you can to help represent and engage each of the four seasons. Some of these could include:

   a. <u>Samhain/Winter Season:</u> Words written on separate cards: 'Death,' 'Endings,' 'Discovery,' 'Discontent,' 'Cold,' 'Dark,' 'Shadows,' 'Evaluation,' 'Wet.' Symbols like ice, dirt, bare twigs, woolly hats and scarves. Quotes could include, Isa. 55:10, Job 37:6-10; "That's what winter is: an exercise in remembering how to still yourself then how to come pliantly back to life again" (Ali Smith); "There is a crack in everything, that's how the light gets in" (Leonard Cohen).

   b. <u>Imbolc/Spring Season:</u> Words written on separate cards, 'Gestation,' 'Seeding,' 'New Life,' 'Resurrection,' 'Birthing,' 'Start-ups,' 'Design,' 'Fertility,' 'Piloting.' Symbols like flowers, insects, seeds, easter eggs. Quotes could include, Song. 2:11-13, Deut. 32:2; "There is no season like spring, when life's alive in everything" (Christina Rosetti).

   c. <u>Beltaine/Summer Season:</u> Words written on separate cards could include, 'Fun,' 'Rest,' 'Abundance,' 'Enjoy,' 'Growth,' 'Sunshine,' 'Light,' 'Traction,' 'Good life,' 'Sabbath.' Symbols or photographs could include: sunglasses, beach towel, green plants, drinks with straws, a fun book to read. Quotes could include: Luke 21:30, James 1:17; "In contrast to the sensationalism of spring, summer is a steady state of plenty, a green and amber muchness that feeds us on more levels than we know" (Parker Palmer).

   d. <u>Fomhar/Autumn Season:</u> Words written on separate cards could include, 'Fruitfulness,' 'Harvests,' 'Abundance,' 'Destiny,' 'Shalom,' 'Finding New Seeds,' 'Grief.' Symbols could include pumpkins, fruit, autumn leaves, seeds. Quotes could include: Ps. 85:12, Gal.6:7-9; "Autumn is the mellower season, and what we lose in flowers we more than gain in fruits" (Samuel Butler); "Only grief permits newness" (Walter Brueggemann).

5. If with a group, brief the participants with something like: 'Before you is a labyrinth to walk meditatively and silently, like other labyrinths. This labyrinth is a bit different to most as it is in the figure of infinity (and never ends) and it has four seasons marked along it. Walk slowly starting in winter and move clockwise along the infinity path until you find something that catches your attention. Stop and connect with it and give it to God. What comes to mind? Why this? After a while, get up and walk again, stopping whenever something draws your attention. In about 20 minutes I'll check in and we can break the silence, reflect, and then go again. Let me pray for you now, have a few minutes of silence and when you are ready start walking.'

6. In about 20 minutes, break into the practice. 'How are you finding the practice? What are you drawn to? Why?'

7. To end the practice, debrief about seasons. 'Which seasons are you strongest and weakest? Why? What season do you find yourself and your local community in now? Why? What could it mean to grow with the flow of the season you are in now? What could you do next?'

There are many potential benefits to Labyrinths in general and this version of practice in particular:

1. **A Path to Mindful Meditation**: Labyrinths are a form of moving meditation and great for those of us who hate sitting still. As you walk the infinity path, you engage your senses, fostering mindfulness. Each step becomes a moment of focus, helping to quiet the constant chatter of the mind. This meditative quality can lead to reduced stress, improved mental clarity, and enhanced emotional wellbeing. It can help open us up to the world we cannot see.

2. **Physical Health**: Labyrinth walking also offers a gentle form of exercise and helps the blood flow in our body.

The act of walking, combined with the repetitive pattern of the infinite labyrinth, can promote physical relaxation, balance, and even improved circulation. It's a holistic approach to wellness that engages both body and mind.

3. **Problem Solving and Creativity**: This labyrinth can serve as a metaphor for life's seasons and movements. Walking its path can encourage gratefulness, creative thinking, and problem-solving skills. Many individuals find that they gain new insights and perspectives while walking this labyrinth, making it a valuable tool for personal and communal growth.

4. **Stress Reduction**: Stress is an ever-present companion in our busy lives. It's often in our bodies. This labyrinth walk provides a sacred space to detect, name, and then leave your concerns behind. As you follow the infinite path, you can gradually release tension and anxiety, leaving you feeling more centered and calm.

5. **Spiritual Connection**: Labyrinths have long been associated with spirituality and self-discovery. You don't have to be a Christian or person of faith, but it can help create awakenings. This practice can serve as a symbol of the faith journey, a quest for self-awareness, enlightenment, and faithfulness. Regardless of your religious or spiritual beliefs, an infinite labyrinth walk can help you connect with your inner, true self and find a sense of purpose and meaning in your local community at this time.

6. **Community and Ritual**: Labyrinths are often found in public spaces, inviting people from all walks of life to share in this ancient tradition. Participating in a labyrinth walk with others who connect with you and your place can foster a sense of community and shared experience, reinforcing the idea that we are all on this infinite journey of life together, through all the seasons.

An infinite labyrinth walk through the four seasons offers a simple yet powerful practice to detect what time it is for you and your community.

It can promote inner peace, reduce stress, create new insights, and enhance overall wellbeing. It is a timeless practice that invites individuals and communities to embark on a journey of self-discovery and mindfulness. Why not try this with your community or key local leaders?

Group questions:

1. Which seasons do you relate to most right now? Why?

2. Are your seasons in life different to the seasons your local community currently faces? What are similar, what are different and why?

3. Have you experienced an infinite labyrinth before? If so, what was helpful, unhelpful?

4. In what ways could you progress through this current season and onto the next?

Conclusions: Possibilities for Seedbeds of Shalom

I've come to give life and life in abundance.
– Jesus, John 10:10

They will rebuild the ancient ruins and restore the places long devastated; they will renew the ruined cities that have been devastated for generations.
Isaiah 61:4

And work for the peace and prosperity of the city where I sent you into exile. Pray to the LORD for it, for its welfare will determine your welfare.
Jeremiah 29:7

I've found myself in some very strange and unusual settings over the years. Maybe they found me? One friend said it's like I'm the anti-Forrest Gump. In the movie, Tom Hanks' character happened to be present in great moments of modern history, whereas whenever I am present there are disasters. I go to Bangkok and then riots and coups happen. I go to the UK and then Brexit and the Covid pandemic combine to kill over 250,000 people. I partner with friends in Kyiv for theological education and then Russia invades. I connect with old Burmese friends and then a civil war breaks out. Be warned and very careful if you invite me to your place!

As I have shared my stories and insights in this book, I am conscious of how blessed I have been. For most of my adult life I've had the opportunity to pursue what I have loved and been passionate about in meaningful ways. Obviously, we've not always been successful, but we've been persistent, nevertheless. These last nine years since we moved to the UK have been especially wild, even by our high standards of crazy.

I wonder, though, what crazy adventures are still to come. The following four scenarios are real situations I've been in recently, and I'm not yet sure what will happen in each. My intention in sharing them is that they can serve as case studies for you to try to apply some of the insights offered in this book. I hope these can help spark your imagination for what might be possible in your context. As you read them, consider the issues and challenges you see here. What are the capacities, approaches, and seasons you can see possible? Especially remember the Tree of Life C.I.R.C.L.E. that we have explored in this book. What could the 'root' qualities of local leadership such as Compassion, Innovation and Resilience, as well as the 'branches' approaches of Community Connecting, Liberative Learning, and Enterprise Development offer here? If you were in my position, what would, or could, you draw on to do next?

Scenario A: Winson Green, Birmingham, UK

November 2021 and I'm at home in Newbigin House. A local newspaper reporter rings me up about my thoughts on the Tower Blocks due to be approved by Council in a few days time. They are to be built right across the road from us and will mostly be one-bedroom 'giro drops' (addresses used for people to keep their name on rent books, solely to collect benefit cheques), with easy access to the city tramline. We'd been lobbying and working for secure and affordable family housing for years now and had been down dozens of dead ends. Nothing seemed to work, and we were getting desperate.

Conclusions: Possibilities For Seedbeds Of Shalom

Without affordable and secure housing, all our community building and connecting is undermined as local families are forced to move on and out of our neighbourhood. It's Monday and the Council decision for this development is due Thursday! We find out it's a done deal; a developer has bought the whole five acres of land and it needs a lot of work just to make the ground less hazardous. Covid has curtailed anyone from Council even coming out to see us. Apparently, there was a piece of paper stapled to a lamp post somewhere explaining what was happening, but no one could find it. The developer will not be required to put in any community facilities or create any affordable homes here. This development is also right across the road from where our new local secondary school will be built. We can see amazing potential and connections. These two new developments could be a catalyst for positive, generational change here, or else could create stigma and ghettos for generations to come. How can we quickly make this development so hot an issue it can't be pushed through without proper local consultation? How can we make those deciding what our community needs at least listen to us?

Scenario B: Mae Sot, Thai-Burma Border

July 2022 and I'm in a factory with undocumented Burmese workers on the Thai-Burma border. Busy manufacturing happens in the front, but we are in the back office supporting some remarkable Civil Disobedience Movement workers in our Seedbeds Incubator programme. We are here to help develop enterprises and income-generating ideas together with an asset-based approach. However, hearing story after story of desolation in Myanmar, as the military junta bombs, tortures, and destroys its own people, makes it hard for us to concentrate. There would be so many barriers to cross in normal times, like language, culture, and idea complexity, but the trauma everyone has experienced is palpable as we meet together.

I wake from my sleeping mat one morning to hear people crying, and I caught the name Ko Jimmy. I had met Ko Jimmy eight years ago in Melbourne. My friend Kyaw Soe Moe introduced me and immediately Ko Jimmy reminded me of a kind of Martin Luther King Junior figure for Burma. Both were passionate, articulate, and had dreams of a better life for their countries. Ko Jimmy was destined to be a voice for Myanmar. I was sure of it. I moved to the UK and Ko Jimmy went on to be that voice in numerous times of national crisis back in Myanmar.

That morning in Mae Sot was the next time I heard the name Ko Jimmy. News started to filter through that the junta had executed him, along with Ko Phyo Zeya Thaw, Ko Hal Myo Aung, and Ko Aung Thura Zaw. Mad flurries of calls and online searches eventually confirmed that the four were hung by the junta. We just sat around our table in that back office stunned and devastated. We wept and then after a while a few stood up, angry. We excused everyone from the session. Slowly students left with hands covering their faces, tears flowing. How could such evil happen to such good people? How could we look for what is strong to fix what is wrong here?

Scenario C: Kyiv, Ukraine

October 2022 and I'm in a classroom at the Ukrainian Evangelical Theological Seminary, Kyiv. It was a challenge just to be in the room here given the Russian attempts at occupation, including six Russian missiles hitting the campus in March, but now it was time to work with my class. At the last minute, I am asked to lead the morning devotion. I want to apply a key Jesus text into this unique context we found ourselves in, and to set up the rest of the week's teachings, taking an asset-based approach to holistic ministry. I think about the connections between the violence here and what is happening to our Burmese friends in the resistance movement where I had been only a few months earlier. The military junta terrorises its own people in Myanmar and the brutal Russian invasion is raining down death upon Ukrainians. These are evil moments in human history. What does Jesus ask of us in such times? What are the dreams, assets, and gifts that can hold back this tide of evil and usher in a new season of Shalom here?

Scenario D: Caravan park, Outback Queensland

January 2023 and I'm in a residential caravan park in outback Queensland Australia, with my friends Duncan and Trish Brown. We are shown around by one of the locals. It's steaming hot, isolated and dusty here, but 'Jenny,' one of the park residents and a member of the Brown's church, is keen to show us what is possible. We want to see the positives, take an asset-based approach, but are quickly struck by dozens of families and over 50 children living here. They all share one toilet block, as no caravans have toilets, showers, or cooking facilities. It's a long way from anywhere to here and since few residents have cars, most food and groceries need to be bought at the caravan park's expensive general store. Residents are also paying rents similar to regular housing costs, but it's one of the few flexible housing options available in this region. 'It's homelessness or this,' says Jenny's husband 'Brian,' 'this is better.'

We meet in the tin-roofed shed that has a sign out the front that says, 'House of God.' It's used as a kind of church and community centre that the owner of the park allows. We pray and share coffee and biscuits together. What assets are here? How can this place be anything but a dry and desolate wasteland?

Think about our Tree of Life C.I.R.C.L.E and the different roots and branches that are needed for growth. What can help or hinder seeds of Shalom growing here? What do you think you would have recommended doing next in these four case studies? How could we establish seedbeds of Shalom here? What is possible?

These scenarios were all not long before writing this conclusion and their stories are not yet completed. Here are some of the next steps I took and what possibilities I see for the future.

Possibilities A: Winson Green, Birmingham, UK

It would be a busy week.

Monday, we found out about the plan for these tower blocks via a journalist.

Tuesday, we alerted and networked 14 different local community groups. These included schools, football clubs, churches, and resident associations.

Wednesday, we all approved a letter to the Council, and a briefing statement to the press, that went public by the end of the day. A 'Fair Housing for Winson Green' campaign, complete with Facebook page, began! The journalist who alerted us from the local Birmingham Mail also picked up the story and photographed me and Ash Lewis standing with alpacas in the front yard of Newbigin House, the potential building site behind us.

Thursday was the Council decision day. We tried to listen online to proceedings as the public was not allowed to be present because of Covid restrictions. The development was approved by a vote of 9-4. The journalist asked for more comments. We said we would keep going, that we deserved better housing, and that we would like to talk directly with the developer.

Friday, the developer called me. I nearly shat myself. His name was Ron Whitehead and he wasn't very happy with us. Eventually, I got to put my case and remarkably Ron was willing to come down to Lodge Road to meet us. I also sent Ron a link to a YouTube presentation that a friend had put together illustrating what was possible for Winson Green's built environment.

That first meeting we were both a bit suspicious of each other. It turned out, however, that Ron's father used to live in Winson Green. He was really doing this in memory of him. I pleaded with Ron to reconsider, and for his Dad's memory to be celebrated in the local community. He promised to re-evaluate the situation.

Conclusions: Possibilities For Seedbeds Of Shalom

Within weeks the new plans included an increase in the number of two and three-bedroom family homes, with six lower-rise apartments. There was also space for a supermarket, medical clinic, civic square, and play area. How different these possibilities were from where we started!

Ron and I became good friends and now enjoy a pint together at the local Black Eagle pub. Ron and his architects took the time to not only listen to our needs as a local community, but also find creative ways that life could work better for the new residents in the proposed scheme too. Over the next two years, Ron met with residents from the Winson Green Residents Association, Lodge Park Residents Association, Newbigin Community Trust, Seedbeds Learning, Birmingham Diocese, YMCA, Bishop Latimer Parish Church, Soho Albion FC, and four local primary schools. All have been impressed with Ron and the new plans he has developed. We all want to be involved in connecting new residents into the life of our neighbourhood too.

As Lodge Road Community Church, and with the help of Newbigin Community Trust, we will support a scheme for affordable housing in the new development. We will also support Birmingham Diocese's exploration of buying one of the blocks for affordable housing too. This could be as many as 100 apartments. We want to be part of the place-making effort to foster real belonging, connections, and fullness of life here with all of the new residents.

My home is at 28 Handsworth New Road, Winson Green, so this new development will happen directly across the road from where I live. That we could have a nearby supermarket, coffee shop, public square, and medical centre is a real gift to us. Along with the new high school now being built near us on Handsworth New Road, we feel like this new housing development could be a catalyst for deep renewal in our neighbourhood.

The £20 million new Olympus High School has been opened and the first intake of students happened in September 2023. We played, and continue to play, a part in hosting and informing these plans. The School and Newbigin Community Trust are working together to develop a hub, so that the school facilities can be used by the local community after hours and on weekends. We love the new Principal, Sarah Jane, who often based herself at Lodge Road while the buildings were being completed.

Ron's new plans are developed, but at time of writing not yet been approved by Council. Ron and I keep having meetings with Council officers and while the expected October 2023 start date has come and gone, Ron will be on site any day now, ready to start building 420 new homes. We will have 30 apartments to help low-income earners access decent housing, plus the Church of England's 100 or so apartments. We have also met with investors who are looking to help Newbigin Trust buy Newbigin House and build some family homes near there too.

Design and the built environment matters. The opportunities for Shalom in Winson Green now feel endless. I want to grow old here with Anji and enjoy the benefits.

Possibilities B: Mae Sot, Thai-Burma Border

The next day the cohort was eager to return. They hadn't come this far to give up now. We tried to start the day taking it as easy as we could. My friend and colleague Chris Edwards ran some games to lighten the mood that had us all in fits of laughter. The participants eventually pitched their ideas for change to a resource panel.

These were all breathtaking efforts and inspired the resource panel who zoomed in from around the world. Some were simple projects like a sewing machine to sew clothes and teach others these skills. Some more were complex online platforms to help a variety of businesses including coffee and crafts. There were tears of joy as we gave out prizes and pledges of support on the final day. I also met with the National Unity Government's Ministers for Justice and Education who wanted more of these programmes including more vocational schools. It felt like, in those moments, Shalom was possible.

A month later I was asked to offer a Christian reflection for an online service of lament and prayers for Myanmar on August 21, 2022. It was also to honour the memory of Ko Jimmy along with Ko Phyo Zeya

Conclusions: Possibilities For Seedbeds Of Shalom

Thaw, Ko Hal Myo Aung, and Ko Aung Thura Zaw who had been executed just a month earlier. As I prepared for that day, a line from MLK's famous 'I have a dream' speech kept returning to me. I looked it up and wondered if it connects both MLK and Ko Jimmy:

> I am not unmindful that some of you have come here out of great trials and tribulations. Some of you have come fresh from narrow jail cells. Some of you have come from areas where your quest — quest for freedom left you battered by the storms of persecution and staggered by the winds of police brutality. You have been the veterans of creative suffering. Continue to work with the faith that unearned suffering is redemptive. Go back to Mississippi, go back to Alabama, go back to South Carolina, go back to Georgia, go back to Louisiana, go back to the slums and ghettos of our northern cities, knowing that somehow this situation can and will be changed.[165]

This idea of 'unearned suffering' as 'redemptive' is a core idea in the Christian faith. Indeed, Jesus said in John 15:12-14:

> This is my commandment, that you love one another as I have loved you. No one has greater love than this, to lay down one's life for one's friends. You are my friends if you do what I command you.

Like Jesus, Ko Jimmy and MLK made the ultimate sacrifice; this is not in vain. Ko Jimmy's love for his friends and country will be the seeds of the new life that Myanmar desperately needs.

What is unique in Jesus is the idea of resurrection. In the Christian imagination, death is not the end and Jesus' resurrection is the first fruit of a new creation. 1 Corinthians 15:2-23 tells us:

> But in fact Christ has been raised from the dead, the first-fruits of those who have died. For since death came through a human, the resurrection of the dead has also come through a human, for as all die in Adam, so all will be made alive in Christ. But each in its own order: Christ, the first-fruits, then at his coming those who belong to Christ.

Jesus defeated death and rose again so we all can. I look forward to the day when I see Ko Jimmy again. A day when all the earth, including Myanmar, is fully free from all evil, injustice, suffering, and death. A day when the Lord's Prayer is fully answered; heaven is on earth. Until that day let us keep loving one another with a sacrificial love that comes from God.

Let us pray the Lord's prayer together if we can:

> Our Father in heaven,
> hallowed be your name,
> your kingdom come,
> your will be done,
> on earth (including Myanmar) as in heaven.
> Give us today our daily bread.
> Forgive us our sins
> as we forgive those who sin against us.
> Lead us not into temptation
> but deliver us from evil.
> For the kingdom, the power,
> and the glory are yours
> now and forever.
> Amen.

I have continued to meet with my friend Kyaw Soe Moe, linked our participants and tutors online, as well as meeting with high-ranking National Unity Government leaders. We've been able to resource about ten projects so far. Many more have started with other resources too.

Meeting with the NUG Minister for Labour and the Minister for Justice convinced us to extend the pilot of the Change Incubator and we found ways we could improve it too. Not least was finding some more enterprise-minded leaders willing to help out. The second Incubator ran from April to June 2023 and we are due to start the third one in April 2024. There are over 350,000 Civil Disobedience Movement workers as I write this. All of these could be included in such an Incubator programme.

Conclusions: Possibilities For Seedbeds Of Shalom

We hope that the Military collapses and that democracy returns. The rebuilding of Myanmar will not be simple, but building with local people – especially with the 'root' qualities of local leadership such as Compassion, Innovation, and Resilience, as well as the 'branches' approaches of Community Connecting, Liberative Learning, and Enterprise Development outlined in this book – can be an integral part of this recovery. A recovering nation of citizens growing in these qualities and approaches will have a better chance of experiencing Shalom than if the vacuum is filled with more natural human responses of reprisals, retributions, and bitterness.

Possibilities C: Kyiv, Ukraine

I knew I couldn't answer for others in class, but I sensed a call to explore how the beatitudes of Jesus (Matt. 5:1-12 and Luke 6:20-26) could relate to the situation in Kyiv as we gathered that day. I was conscious that the word 'blessing,' as we use it in English, did not make much sense here. In his book *We Belong to the Land*, Elias Chacour (the Bishop of Galilee) picks up a more progressive, active meaning of *ashre* as 'blessed are.' He writes:

> How could I go to a persecuted young man in a Palestinian refugee camp, for instance, and say, "Blessed are those who mourn, for they shall be comforted," or "Blessed are those who are persecuted for the sake of justice, for theirs is the kingdom of heaven?" That man would revile me, saying neither I nor my God understood his plight and he would be right. When I understand Jesus' words in Aramaic, I translate like this: "Get up, go ahead, do something, move, you who are hungry and thirsty for justice, for you shall be satisfied. Get up, go ahead, do something, move, you peacemakers, for you shall be called children of God. To me this reflects Jesus' words and teachings much more accurately. I can hear him saying: "Get your hands dirty to build a human society for human beings; otherwise, others will torture and murder the poor, the voiceless, and the powerless." Christianity is not passive but active, energetic, alive, going beyond despair.[166]

No Wastelands

I could sense the connections here and wanted to create space for prayer and reflection. I explained Dave Andrew's reframing of the beatitudes to 'be' the change we want to see in the world.[167]

I asked them, which of the following BE-ATTITUDES best describes you now? Which of them least describes you? Why?

1. Blessed are the poor—or poor in spirit—who do not trust in status or riches.
2. Blessed are those who mourn—who grieve over the injustice in the world.
3. Blessed are the meek—who get angry but who never get aggressive.
4. Blessed are those who hunger and thirst for righteousness—who seek justice.
5. Blessed are the merciful—who are compassionate to everyone in need.
6. Blessed are the pure in heart—who are whole-hearted in desire to do right.
7. Blessed are the peacemakers—who work for peace in a world at war.
8. Blessed are those persecuted for righteousness—who suffer for just causes.

The responses were moving. Everyone had stories. Not least was how common mourning and grief were, and how difficult peace-making is right now.

For Jesus, peace (Shalom) was not just an absence of violence, but God, people, and the earth living in harmony together. How we see that vision happen locally and globally is often conflicting. Ukrainians taking up arms to resist and protect themselves from the military was understandable, but heart-breaking. Kyrylo even had a story of how a local Pentecostal minister here had become a sniper and was fundraising for better guns! I looked up at the ceiling in our classroom and saw the holes that missile shrapnel had left there. What would Jesus do?

I finished with prayer and encouragement to explore the theology of Dietrich Bonhoeffer. He was executed by the Nazis in a failed plot

Conclusions: Possibilities For Seedbeds Of Shalom

to assassinate Hitler and felt like he had to choose between two sins: neutrality or killing. He felt the least sinful response was the latter and paid for it with his life. Bonhoeffer's words were ringing in my ears:

> We have spent too much time in thinking, supposing that if we weigh in advance the possibilities of any action, it will happen automatically. We have learnt, rather too late, that action comes, not from thought, but from a readiness for responsibility. For you thought and action will enter on a new relationship; your thinking will be confined to your responsibilities in action. With us thought was often the luxury of the onlooker; with you it will be entirely subordinated to action.[168]

We continued classes that week and even took a field trip on the final Friday. We had to finish the morning session quickly and get into the bus waiting in the car park. We soon drove past a few blackened buildings as we set off via Bucha to Irpin. The seminary was hit six times with missiles, but it was considered a 'grey zone,' a contested area. After a few miles, we entered areas once held by the Russian army. Soon we passed row after row of apartment buildings blackened and broken, with jagged and smashed windows. When we had planned this MA unit last year we asked if we could take the class on a site visit to see local holistic ministry in action and reflect on good practice. We had no idea then what the local church in Kyiv was going to be asked of this year. Denys sat next to me in the bus. He interpreted for us all week in class and now he acted as my tour guide. 'This is where the Russian paratroopers landed. They were dropped in by helicopters just there.'

We drive west of the seminary where Russian forces performed some of their worst atrocities, including Bucha where Ivan, the Principal, lived. It's the random and indiscriminate nature of their destruction that hits me. Why are these apartments rubble but not those other ones next to them? Why is that shop untouched, but that cafe barely recognisable?

We drive down close to a river where a makeshift road is in place of the bridge that had been taken down to stop Russian advancement. It helped. Despite the Russian army circling the city, and Ukrainians massively under-gunned, the Russians were not able to take Kyiv and were eventually repelled. Ivan would later say, 'No one expected this. It's a miracle from God and the courage of our troops.' Later Denys points out a building that looks like a bomb landed right in the middle of it, but the other buildings are fine. 'That was our favourite cafe. We always met there. It was so good. I'm not sure they can rebuild now.'

When we get to Irpin Bible Church, about 30 minutes away, there is a long line of folks waiting for food supplies out the front of one building, and another long line for warm coats. There are also lots of groups of happy children running around. We meet the Pastor and then a volunteer, named Orest, who has stayed in Ukraine throughout. He explains what is happening now and what went on before. The sheer volume of intentional work was impressive: food, clothing, petrol, rebuilding homes, schools, and kindergarten all happening now. Orest elaborates:

> 'We give freely during the week and say we are Christians and do this because of God's love. We don't give anything out on Sunday so if people want to come, they can. The church has the same number of people coming as before the war now, but over 300 of our regulars have evacuated and not come back. Most are new.'

Orest explained that just before the Russian army arrived here, they were offered machine guns.

> 'I was eager to use it, actually, but we decided that we have so many elderly, women, and children hiding here that our guns will make it more dangerous. That turned out to be the right decision.'

While many members of the church evacuated, many like Orest stayed and served right through. They were the last functioning organisation and the first to get organised to support people. The credibility of the Christian church in the local community there is now palpable.

I continue to stand with the Ukrainian Evangelical Theological Seminary. My next MA teaching block is due in Kyiv, April 2024. I plan to be there in person again.

As well as developing more formal, accredited programmes, we would love to see incubator programmes established for enterprise and community building. The war has been brutal so far, but the rebuilding of Ukraine will be long and hard too. We will need to discover, connect, and mobilise every gift and talent possible in that task.

Possibilities D: Caravan Park, Outback Queensland

The Browns had visited us in Bangkok and Birmingham. It was no accident that we were in this caravan park together.

Duncan and Trish Brown also had me speak at their church and set up meetings with potential donors and other community leaders. I got to share some of our stories and learnings as well as our vision for Seedbeds as an organisation. It felt good and plans are afoot.

While the Brown's cattle farm seems miles from anywhere to me, they are in fact within a short drive to a few towns and caravan parks, including the one we visited together. Possibilities have sparked. Could emerging community leaders be nominated from these three or four local communities? Could we pilot a Change Makers programme that could incubate their ideas for change?

The Browns also own some properties in that region and have council permission to develop. Could this region become a food education and production precinct? Could they develop some innovative housing alternatives like a 'tiny home' village as an alternative to caravan parks? Could an old gym in a central town become a community hub and coffee shop?

I would love to see what we are learning internationally bear fruit in Australia. Despite not living in Australia for over 20 years, I am still an Aussie. This book is part of that attempt to share. Could a 'Seedbeds Australia' be another way to do that? If we had people on the ground in Australia, able to run the programmes themselves, then from the UK, we could connect, create, and help build their capacities to grow their own leaders and communities into the fullness of life too. We hope to formalise Seedbeds Australia in 2024. The interest in Myanmar too could mean a kind of twinning and collegial partnership both ways. Talents could be connected and shared.

As I write this, I am on my last day on North Stradbroke Island, Queensland, February 2023. The Parker family bungalow has been home for 10 days now and has done the trick. There have been long walks, reading, swims, and gawking at quintessential Australian wildlife such as kangaroos, kookaburras, dolphins, and sea turtles. I have survived the dangers of snakes, sharks, and goannas, though the blood-sucking March flies have taken chunks out of me!

I have a final ministry weekend in Melbourne starting tomorrow, but this is my last day to write here before I send this first full draft off to my editor, Stephen Parker. This full draft is ready. I don't know what he will make of all this. Will you, the reader, see the potential I see so often? Am I too optimistic that no local community needs to be a wasteland? Can seedbeds of Shalom really be grown in every local community, including yours? I feel refreshed, renewed and ready to try.

This writing project has brought back a lot of memories I had forgotten, painful ones too. I know no dream is pain-free, but I feel like my personal quest, destiny, and wellbeing is tied up in the pursuit of seedbeds of Shalom. I hope yours can be too. I hope this writing can support our unique journey into God's promised Shalom for you and the ones you love.

Endnotes

Introduction

1. Philip North, 'Hope for the Poor: Talk to the New Wine 'United' Conference,' The Diocese of Blackburn, July, 2017. https://www.blackburn.anglican.org/storage/general-files/shares/Resources/Talks%20articles%20and%20sermons/Hope_for_the_Poor_-__P_article__Word_document_.pdf.
2. Myanmar or Burma? It's complicated! National hero, Daw Aung San Sui Kyi, even encouraged people to use Burma and Myanmar interchangeably. Who am I to argue? It is controversial though as it was the military junta who renamed Myanmar, so many people still prefer Burma. Generally, at the international level we talk about the 'National Unity Government of Myanmar' which is the democratically elected government seeking international recognition in their fight against the military junta. Locally most people still say Burma!
3. Eugene Peterson, *Under the Unpredictable Plant* (Grand Rapids: Eerdmans, 1992), p.20.
4. Tearfund: https://www.tearfund.org.
5. Oasis: https://www.oasisuk.org.
6. Jonathan Walker, 'Birmingham has half the top ten constituency with the worst unemployment rates in the country,' *Birmingham Mail*, September 13, 2018. https://www.birminghammail.co.uk/news/midlands-news/birmingham-half-top-ten-constituencies-15147110.
7. Wilbert R. Shenk, 'Lesslie Newbigin's Contribution to the Theology of Mission,' *TransMission* Special Edition(1998): p. 3.
8. Geoffrey Wainwright, *Lesslie Newbigin: A Theological Life* (New York: Oxford University Press, 2000), p. V.
9. Richard Rohr, 'Lent with Richard Rohr: No Sign Will Be Given Except the Sign of Jonah,' *Franciscan Spirit Blog*, March 13, 2019. https://www.franciscanmedia.org/franciscan-spirit-blog/lent-with-richard-rohr-no-sign-will-be-given-except-the-sign-of-jonah/.
10. Joshua J Mark, 'Nineveh,' World History Encyclopedia, March 6, 2011. https://www.worldhistory.org/nineveh/.
11. Parker J Palmer, *Let Your Life Speak: Listening for the Voice of Vocation* (San Francisco: Jossey Bass, 2000), Kindle Loc. 530.
12. Vincent Harding, 'Life In The Asphalt Jungle,' Civil Rights Movement Archive. https://www.crmvet.org/poetry/harding-poem.pdf
13. Cormac Russell, 'From What's Wrong to What's Strong: A guide to community driven development,' Research Outreach, November 12, 2021. https://researchoutreach.org/articles/whats-wrong-whats-strong-guide-community-driven-development/.
14. Kerry Banks, 'Loneliness: The silent killer,' University Affairs, February 27, 2019. https://www.universityaffairs.ca/features/feature-article/loneliness-the-silent-killer/.
15. Wendell Berry, *The Art of the Commonplace: The Agrarian Essays* (Berkeley: Counterpoint, 2002), p. 186.

16 Lesslie Newbigin, *The Gospel in a Pluralist Society* (Grand Rapids: Eerdmans, 1989), p.119.
17 This verse is generally attributed to Lao Tzu (or Laozi), Taoist philosopher, author of the Tao Te Ching. Date approximate.
18 Paul Sparks, Tim Soerens, Dwight J Frieson, *The New Parish: How neighbourhood churches are transforming mission, discipleship and community* (Downers Grove: IVP, 2014), p.23.

Chapter 1: Weeds That Choke Potential

19 Social Mobility Commission, *Social Mobility Barometer: Public attitudes to social mobility in the UK, 2019-20,* January, 2020. https://assets.publishing.service.gov.uk/government/uploads/system/uploads/attachment_data/file/858908/Social_Mobility_Barometer_2019-2020.pdf (accessed July 19, 2021).
20 SMC, *Social Mobility Barometer: Public attitudes to social mobility in the UK, 2019-20.*
21 Social Mobility Commission, *Social Mobility Barometer: Public attitudes to social mobility in the UK, 2021,* March 11, 2021. https://www.gov.uk/government/publications/social-mobility-barometer-2021 (accessed July 19, 2021).
22 See also: Prov. 24:30-34; Isa. 5:3-6; Isa. 7:18-25; Isa. 32:11-15; Isa. 34:8-14; Isa. 55:13; Hosea 9:5-6
23 Dietrich Bonhoeffer, 'Thoughts on the Day of the Baptism of Dietrich Wilhelm Rüdiger Bethge May 1944,' *Letters and Papers from Prison* (New York: Macmillan, 1972), p. 298.

Chapter 2: Invasive Weeds That Choke The Harvest

24 Kleercut, 'Top 10 Most Dangerous Weeds,' July 18, 2018. https://www.kleerkut.co.uk/news/top-10-most-dangerous-weeds-uk/.
25 Plantician Guy (Mike), 'How and Why Do Weeds Grow So Fast Explained,' ask the Plantician. https://www.plantician.com/how-and-why-do-weeds-grow-so-fast-explained/.
26 Gabriela Bucher, 'Global inequality is a failure of imagination. Here's why,' World Economic Forum, January 16, 2023. https://www.weforum.org/agenda/2023/01/global-inequality-is-a-failure-of-imagination/.
27 United Nations Human Rights Office, 'Poverty inextricably linked to discrimination and racism – UN Special Rapporteur,' November 4, 2013. https://www.ohchr.org/en/press-releases/2013/11/poverty-inextricably-linked-discrimination-and-racism-un-special-rapporteur.
28 National Museum Australia, 'Defining Moments: Indigenous Australians' right to vote,' updated May 16, 2023. https://www.nma.gov.au/defining-moments/resources/indigenous-australians-right-to-vote.
29 BBC News Services, 'What is Windrush and who are the Windrush generation?,' July 27, 2023. https://www.bbc.co.uk/news/uk-43782241.
30 The Trevor Project, 'Unstable Housing and LGBTQ Youth Suicidality,' August 28, 2019. https://www.thetrevorproject.org/research-briefs/unstable-housing-and-lgbtq-youth-suicidality/.

31. *Fish out of water,* directed by Ky Dickens, (Yellow Wing Productions, 2009). View it online at https://www.youtube.com/watch?v=oSQuO8bMNfM.
32. See for example, Wyatt Houtz, 'The Clobber Verses,' PostBarthian, October 11, 2017. https://postbarthian.com/2017/10/11/clobber-verses-six-scriptures-cited-gays-lesbians-sex-relationships-lgbtq/.
33. Sally Mann, 'Red versus Black? Reflections on a Red Letter reading of the Bible,' Red Letter Christians UK, June 4, 2019. https://redletterchristians.org.uk/red-versus-black-reflections-on-a-red-letter-reading-of-the-bible/.
34. Zainab Ibrahim, Jayanthi Kuru-Utumpala, and Jay Goulden, 'Counting the Cost: The Price Society Pays for Violence Against Women,' CARE International Secretariat, 2018. https://www.care-international.org/files/files/Counting_the_costofViolence.pdf.
35. Jane Haynes, 'City Declares Housing Emergency,' *Birmingham Mail*, January 12, 2023. https://www.birminghammail.co.uk/news/midlands-news/city-declares-housing-emergency-thousands-25953423.
36. Oscar Lewis, 'The Culture of Poverty,' *Scientific American* 215, no. 4 (October 1966): p. 23. https://warwick.ac.uk/fac/arts/history/research/centres/ehrc/research/previous_research/poverty/lewis_culture_of_poverty.pdf.
37. CDC, 'Loneliness and Social Isolation Linked to Serious Health Conditions,' last reviewed April 29, 2021. https://www.cdc.gov/aging/publications/features/lonely-older-adults.html.
38. CDC, 'Loneliness and Social Isolation Linked to Serious Health Conditions.'
39. Amy Novotney, 'The risks of social isolation,' *Monitor on Psychology* 50, no. 5 (May 2019). https://www.apa.org/monitor/2019/05/ce-corner-isolation.
40. John Perkins, 'Revolution and Renewal,' Plough, July 26, 2016. https://www.plough.com/en/topics/faith/discipleship/revolution-and-renewal.
41. Christian Community Development Association, 'CCD Philosophy,' 2023. https://ccda.org/about/philosophy/.

Chapter 3: Weeds As Signs Of Life In Wastelands

42. Stuart Thompson, 'Chernobyl Has Been Reclaimed by Plants. Why Don't They Die From Cancer?,' Science Alert, June 25, 2019. https://www.sciencealert.com/chernobyl-has-been-reclaimed-by-plants-why-don-t-they-die-from-cancer.
43. Donna Boyle Schwartz, 'Keed, Don't Kill: 9 Weeds to Welcome,' BobVila, updated August 6, 2020. https://www.bobvila.com/slideshow/keep-don-t-kill-9-weeds-to-welcome-48926.
44. Eleanor Roosevelt, *You Learn by Living: Eleven Keys for a More Fulfilling Life* (Westminster: John Knox Press, 2009), Chapter 2.
45. Katherine Weber, 'Rick Warren: Why God Encourages Christians to 'Fear Not' 365 Times in the Bible,' Christian Post, April 30, 2016. https://www.christianpost.com/news/rick-warren-why-god-encourages-christians-to-fear-not-365-times-in-the-bible.html.
46. Martin Luther King Jnr, *Where Do We Go From Here: Chaos or Community?* (Boston: Beacon Press, 1968), p. 38.

47 Steve Chalke, 'Vision and frustration are two sides of the same coin,' Twitter, December 20, 2019, https://twitter.com/SteveChalke/status/1207927383149436930.

Chapter 4: Treating Weeds With Hope

48 Purple Property Shop, 'Japanese Knotweed,' September 17, 2019. https://purplepropertyshop.com/2019/09/17/japanese-knotweed-the-facts/.
49 Lesslie Newbigin, 'Evangelism in the City,' *Reformed Review* 41, 1987: p.4.
50 Cathy Ross, 'Hope is Tough: reflections in a time of COVID-19,' *Practical Theology* 14, no. 1-2: p. 91. DOI: 10.1080/1756073X.2020.1845932.
51 See Change Makers interviews on Seedbeds YouTube Channel, https://www.youtube.com/@seedbeds347.
52 Robert Clinton, *The Making of a Leader* (Chicago: NavPress, 2014), p. 32-33.
53 The StrengthsFinder tool has since been rebranded to CliftonStrengths: https://www.gallup.com/cliftonstrengths/en/254033/strengthsfinder.aspx.
54 Gallup, 'The 34 CliftonStrengths Themes Explain Your Talent DNA,' 2023. https://www.gallup.com/cliftonstrengths/en/253715/34-cliftonstrengths-themes.aspx.
55 Eeverse Clothing: https://www.eeverse.co.uk.
56 Seedbeds, 'Seedbeds Learning,' https://seedbeds.org/school-for-urban-leadership/.

Part A. Practices To Try

57 Palmer, *Let Your Life Speak*, Kindle Loc. 124.

Chapter 5: Place-making And The Seeds Of Shalom

58 You can see video footage of the park as it was here: https://www.birminghammail.co.uk/news/midlands-news/lorry-dumps-mountain-filth-black-12602420.
59 Josh Layton, 'Charlie Chaplin's son unveils memorial at Smethwick where his father is believed to have been born,' *Birmingham Mail*, July 26, 2015. https://www.birminghammail.co.uk/news/midlands-news/charlie-chaplins-son-unveils-memorial-9731467.
60 Jim Bear Jacobs as cited in Brian McLaren, *God Unbound: Theology in the Wild* (Norwich: Canterbury Press, 2019), p. XVIII.
61 Habitat III, 'The New Urban Agenda,' 2017. https://habitat3.org/the-new-urban-agenda/.
62 Barack Obama, *A Promised Land* (London: Penguin, 202), p.16.
63 Eugene Peterson in his foreword to Eric Jacobsen, *Sidewalks in the Kingdom: New urbanism and the Christian faith* (Grand Rapids: Brazos, 2003), Kindle Loc. 29-42.

Chapter 6: 'Fear Not!'- Seeds Of Shalom And Resisting Fear

64 UK Health Security Agency, 'Deaths in the UK,' accessed October 26, 2023. https://coronavirus.data.gov.uk/details/deaths.

Chapter 7: 'Great Joy' - Joy And The Seeds Of Shalom

65 Ross Langmead, 'Living for Shalom,' 1990. http://www.rosslangmead.com/songs.html.

66 Kenneth E. Bailey, *Jesus Through Middle Eastern Eyes: Cultural Studies in the Gospels* (Downers Grove: IVP, 2008), p. 35-36.

67 Jamie Oliver, 'Jamie cooks with Poo | Thai Massaman curry,' YouTube, May 25, 2014, video, https://www.youtube.com/watch?v=pBWKj9lezrc.

68 See an interview with Claire: Seedbeds, 'Meet Changemakers (Claire),' YouTube, video, June 29, 2021, https://www.youtube.com/watch?v=wiKzRxyAsac&t=21s.

69 John Mark Comer, *The Ruthless Elimination of Hurry: How to Stay Emotionally Healthy and Spiritually Alive in the Chaos of the Modern World* (London: Hodder and Stoughton, 2019), p. 25

Chapter 8: 'Shalom on Earth?'

70 Christopher Wright, *The Mission of God: Unlocking the Bible's Grand Narrative* (Downers Grove, IL: InterVarsity, 2006), p. 22-23.

71 Joel B. Green, *The Gospel of Luke* (Grand Rapids: Eerdmans, 1997), Kindle Loc. 2588.

72 Christian Community Development Association as cited by Hugh Whelchel, 'Understanding Shalom & the Grand Metanarrative of Scripture,' Institute for Faith, Work & Economics, August 16, 2021. https://tifwe.org/understanding-shalom-the-grand-metanarrative-of-scripture/.

73 Cornelius Plantinga Jr., *Not the Way It's Supposed to Be* (Grand Rapids: Eerdmans, 1995), p.10.

74 Eugene Peterson, *Run with the Horses: The Quest for Life at Its Best* (Downers Grove: IVP, 2018), p. 147.

75 Andre Van Eymeren leads the Centre for Building Better Communities. Read more about The Flourishing Framework® here: https://www.community.how/journal/the-flourishing-framework.

76 Seedbeds Change Incubator in Myanmar: https://seedbeds.org/change-incubator/.

Part B. Practices To Try

77 Victor Frankl, *Man's Search for Meaning* (New York: Random House, 1992), p. 19.

Chapter 9: Soils And Enchanted Worldviews

78 Robert Mountford, *The Mantle of Chad* (Stoke-on-Trent: Tentmaker Press, 2013), p.92-93.

79 Sparks, Soerens, Frieson, *The New Parish*, p.23.

80 See for example, Dietrich Bonhoeffer, *Voices in the Night; The Prison Poems of Dietrich Bonhoeffer* (Grand Rapids: Zondervan, 1999). Bonhoeffer uses the German word *stellvertretung*, 'most simply, is Bonhoeffer's description of how human beings are to be in the world. As Christ lived and died vicariously, his disciples are called to vicarious action and responsible love on behalf of the Other.' Stephen R. Haynes and Lori Brandt Hale, *Bonhoeffer for Armchair Theologians* (Kentucky: Westminster, 2009), p107.

81 See one of our *Songs of Praise* episodes here: https://www.youtube.com/watch?v=jeDwBTTH0I0&t=1140s.
82 You can see our *Songs of Praise* segment on Holy Island in the episode here: https://www.bbc.co.uk/programmes/p0c5rjyl.
83 Peter Neilson, 'Preparing the Soil' (unpublished).

Chapter 10: Hard Paths - Lacking Awareness

84 Anthony de Mello, *Awareness: A de Mello Spirituality Conference in His Own Words* (New York: Double Day, 1990), in 'On Waking Up.'
85 de Mello, *Awareness,* in 'Four Steps to Wisdom.'
86 de Mello, *Awareness,* in 'Sleepwalking.'
87 de Mello, *Awareness,* in 'Change as Greed.'

Chapter 11: Stony Fields - Lacking Grit

88 Brandan Fuller and Paul Romer, *Urbanization as Opportunity: Working Paper 1* (New York: Marron Institute, 2014), p. 1.
89 Angela Lee Duckwoorth, 'Grit: The power of passion and perseverance,' TED Talk, April 2013. https://www.ted.com/talks/angela_lee_duckworth_grit_the_power_of_passion_and_perseverance. See her book Angela Lee Duckworth, *Grit: The Power of Passion and Perseverance* (New York: Scribner Book Company, 2018).
90 Andy Flannagan, *Those Who Show Up* (Edinburgh: Muddy Pearl, 2015), p.IV.

Chapter 12: Thorny Ground - Lacking Trust

91 Robert Putnam, 'The Prosperous Community: Social capital and public life,' reprinted from *The American Prospect*. https://faculty.washington.edu/matsueda/courses/590/Readings/Putham%201993%20Am%20Prospect.pdf
92 Jonny Baker, *Pioneer Practice* (London: GETSidetracted, 2021), p.19.
93 Living Wage Foundation, https://www.livingwage.org.uk/what-real-living-wage.
94 See Stewardship, https://www.stewardship.org.uk.
95 McCrindle Research, 'A Demographic Snapshot of Christianity and Church Attenders in Australia.' https://mccrindle.com.au/article/a-demographic-snapshot-of-christianity-and-church-attenders-in-australia/.
96 Kathy Jacka and Ruth Powell, 'Number and size of local churches in Australia,' NCLS Research. https://www.ncls.org.au/articles/number-and-size-of-local-churches-in-australia/.
97 Ivan Illich, *Tools for Conviviality* (London: Marion Boyars, 2009), p.47. https://arl.human.cornell.edu/linked%20docs/Illich_Tools_for_Conviviality.pdf
98 Kaley Payne, 'A Wake-up Call: How Much Are We Really Giving Away?,' Eternity News, September 8, 2016. https://www.eternitynews.com.au/australia/a-wake-up-call-how-much-are-we-really-giving-away/.
99 Rev. Dr. David Millikan, 'God, power and money,' *The Sydney Morning Herald*, March 3, 2008. https://www.smh.com.au/world/god-power-and-money-20080303-gds3h4.html.

100 Palmer, *Let Your Life Speak*, Kindle Loc. 966-1030.

101 Walter Brueggemann, 'The Liturgy of Abundance - The Myth of Scarcity,' *The Christian Century* (March 24-31, 1999): p. 342.

102 Dave Andrews, 'The Special 'Fools-Rush-In-Where-Angels-Fear-To-Tread' Change Agent's First Aid Kit,' http://www.daveandrews.com.au/articles/WebSiteArticles10TheFirstAidKit.pdf.

Chapter 13: Good Soils - Praxis Understanding And Action

103 Warren Carter, *Matthew and the Margins: A Sociopolitical and Religious Reading: A Socio-Political and Religious Reading* (New York: Orbis, 2000), Kindle Loc. 8665.

Part C. Practices To Try

104 Robin Sharma, *The 5am Club* (London: Thorsons, 2018). Kindle.

105 מאד noun masculine muchness, force, abundance, exceedingly (compare Assyrian *mu'du, abundance*, Hom$^{ZMG\ 1878,\ 711}$('treasures *ana mu'di, in abundance*') DI$^{HWB\ 399}$)

106 Sabbath Manifesto, 'The Ten Principles,' 2010. http://www.sabbathmanifesto.org/

Chapter 14: Not All Roots And Branches Can Grow The Fruit We Need

107 Heidi Hirsch, 'South Africa needs a fresh approach to managing invasive trees like Eucalyptus,' The Conversation, December 6, 2019. https://theconversation.com/south-africa-needs-a-fresh-approach-to-managing-invasive-trees-like-eucalyptus-126777.

Chapter 15: Roots Systems For Sustainability

108 Walter Brueggemann, *Reverberations of Faith: A Theological Handbook of Old Testament Themes* (Louisville: Westminster John Knox Press, 2002), p. 126.

109 Walter Brueggemann, *Reverberations of Faith*, p. 126.

110 Marcus Borg, *Jesus: Uncovering the Life, Teaching and Relevance of a Religious Revolutionary* (New York: Harper Collins, 2006), p. 183.

111 Paulo Coelho, *The Pilgrimage* (London: Harper One, 1997), p.119.

112 Ash Barker, *Risky Compassion* (Birmingham: Urban Life Together, 2014).

113 Stephen R. Covey, *The 7 Habits of Highly Effective People* (London: Simon and Shulster, 2020), Kindle Loc. 1219.

114 Simon Sinek, 'Start with Why -- how great leaders inspire action,' TEDx, YouTube, September 29, 2009, video, https://www.youtube.com/watch?v=u4ZoJKF_VuA.

115 Ken Robinson, 'Do Schools Kill Creativity?,' TED, February 2006, video, https://www.ted.com/talks/sir_ken_robinson_do_schools_kill_creativity?language=en.

116 Edward de Bono, *Serious Creativity* (London: Vermilion, 2015). Find more about de Bono's ideas, including The Six Thinking Hats at https://www.debono.com.

117 Alistair Campbell, *But What Can I Do? Why Politics Has Gone So Wrong, and How You Can Help Fix It* (London: Penguin, 2023), Kindle Loc. 3277.

118 Wayne Cordeiro, *Leading On Empty: refilling your tank and renewing your passion* (Bloomington MN: Bethany House Publishers, 2009) p. 13. See book summary here: https://www.essentialleadershipapps.com/uploads/5/8/4/4/58449207/leading_on_empty_-_wayne_cordeiro.pdf.

119 Palmer, *Let Your Life Speak*, Kindle Loc. 528.

120 Brene Brown, *Daring Greatly* (New York: Penguin Random House, 2012) p. 74.

Chapter 16: Branches Prepared For Fruitfulness

121 Patrick Butler, "Skeletal' body of man who lay dead in Bolton flat for six years dsicovered,' The Guardian, May 12, 2023. https://www.theguardian.com/uk-news/2023/may/11/skeletal-body-of-man-who-lay-dead-in-flat-for-six-years-found-on-gas-check-visit.

122 Alex Haslam, Catherine Haslam and Tegan Cruwys, 'Loneliness. The silent killer as bad as cancer,' The Conversation, November 19, 2019. https://theconversation.com/loneliness-is-a-social-cancer-every-bit-as-alarming-as-cancer-itself-12764.

123 Cormac Russell and John McKnight, *The Connected Community* (Oakland: Berrett-Koeler, 2022).

124 Russell and McKnight, *The Connected Community*, p. 88-96.

125 SeedBeds, 'Meet the Change Makers - Helen,' YouTube, June 29, 2021, video, https://www.youtube.com/watch?v=0a_NjdnVS9c

126 Barack Obama, *A Promised Land*, (New York: Viking, 2020) p. 16.

127 Ann Hope and Sally Timmel, *Training for Transformation: A handbook for community workers Books 1-3* (ITDG Publishing, 1984).

128 Gustavo Gutiérrez, *A Theology of Liberation* (Maryknowel: Orbis, 1988), p. 6.

129 Virtual Plater: Catholic Social Teaching gateway, '6.2.2 Base ecclesial communities and Freire on 'conscientization',' https://virtualplater.org.uk/module-b/b-unit-6-contents-2/6-2-a-critique-from-the-left-liberation-theology/6-2-2-paulo-friere-and-conscientization/.

130 Fire with Fire Blog, 'An Introduction to 1 on 1 organising conversations,' April 19, 2020. https://firewithfire.blog/2020/04/19/an-introduction-to-1-on-1-organizing-conversations/.

131 Living Wage, 'Our History.' https://www.livingwage.org.uk/history#.

132 Living Wage, 'Our History.'

133 Martin Luther King Jr, *The Autobiography of Martin Luther King Jr* (New York: Warner Books, 2001), p. 325.

134 Seedbeds, 'Meet the Change Makers - Stacey,' YouTube, June 29, 2021, video, https://www.youtube.com/watch?v=EIidy_BBLf0.

135 Mark Russell, *The Missional Entrepreneur* (Birmingham: New Hope Publishers, 2010), p. 62.

136 Russell, *The Missional Entrepreneur*, p. 52.

137 Russell, *The Missional Entrepreneur*, p. 68.

138 Social Enterprise, 'All about Social Enterprise.' https://www.socialenterprise.org.uk/all-about-social-enterprise/.

139 Klong Toey Handicrafts is now called Roy Rak. https://www.royrak.org/.
140 Zlto: https://www.zlto.co.
141 NewLife Newham: https://newlifenewham.com.
142 Gear Up: https://www.gearupbirmingham.co.uk/.
143 New Routes: https://newroutesuk.wordpress.com/.
144 Seedbeds Change Incubator: https://seedbeds.org/change-incubator/
145 Dietrich Bonhoeffer, *Letters and Papers from Prison*, p. 298.
146 Brene Brown, *Dare to Lead* (New York: Random House, 2018), p. 4.
147 Lao Tzu (see note 17).
148 Newbigin Pioneering Hub: https://seedbeds.org/newbigin-pioneering-hub-2/.

Part D. Practices To Try

149 Generosity Dinners: https://www.commonchange.com/generosity-dinners/.

Chapter 17: Samhain - Winters Of Our Discontent And Discovery

150 Palmer, *Let Your Life Speak*, Kindle Loc. 875.
151 Walter Brueggemann, *Celebrating Abundance: Devotions for Advent* (United States: Presbyterian Publishing Corporation, 2017), Kindle Loc. 854.
152 Urban Neighbours Of Hope: https://unoh.org.
153 Surrender Conferences: https://www.surrender.org.au.
154 Newbigin Community Trust: https://newbigintrust.uk.
155 Urban Shalom Society: https://www.facebook.com/groups/UrbanShalomSociety/.
156 Soho Albion FC: https://sohoalbionfc.org.
157 Red Letter Christians UK: https://redletterchristians.org.uk.
158 The Greenhouse at Barnes Close: https://greenhouseatbarnesclose.org.uk.
159 Lao Tzu (see note 17).
160 Anji Barker, *Missionary Not Just A Position* (Birmingham: Seedbeds Communications, 2021). https://www.amazon.com.au/Missionary-Not-Just-Position-TBD/dp/0648472523.

Chapter 18: Imbolc - Spring's Gestations And Birthing

161 Ireland's Folklore and Traditions blog, 'Saint Brigid's Day Traditions,' January 28, 2017. https://irishfolklore.wordpress.com/2017/01/28/saint-brigids-day-traditions/.
162 Windsor Olympus Academy: https://www.olympusacademy.org.uk
163 Palmer, *Let Your Life Speak*, Kindle Loc. 950.

Chapter 19: Bealtaine - Summertime's Flourishings And Rests

164 Seedbeds Learning: https://seedbeds.org/school-for-urban-leadership/.

Conclusions

165 NPR, 'Read Martin Luther King Jnr's 'I Have a Dream Speech' in its entirety,' January 16, 2023. https://www.npr.org/2010/01/18/122701268/i-have-a-dream-speech-in-its-entirety.

166 Elias Chacour with Mary E. Jensen, *We Belong to the Land: The Story of a Palestinian Israeli Who Lives for Peace and Reconciliation* (San Francisco: Harper, 1990), p. 143,144.

167 Dave Andrews, *Plan Be: Be the Change You Want to See in the World* (United Kingdom: Authentic, 2020). Plan Be: https://wecan.be/

168 Bonhoeffer, *Letters and Papers from Prison*, p. 298.

URLs are accurate as of November 18, 2023.

www.ingramcontent.com/pod-product-compliance
Lightning Source LLC
Chambersburg PA
CBHW071952290426
44109CB00018B/1996